Spy and Mystery Stories

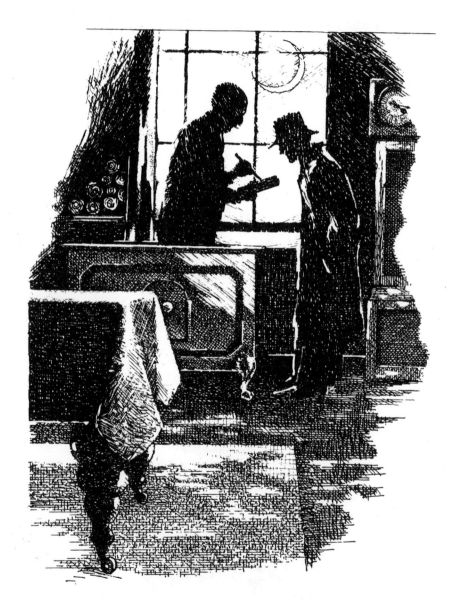

Spy and Mystery Stories

Edited by
Kenneth Allen

The editors acknowledge the contributions of the following artists:

Sam Dwyer 259, 263, 394
David Godfrey 44, 92, 97, 192, 284, 340, 379
Bob Harvey 87, 121, 140, 181, 250, 350, 370
Nigel Hewetson 340
André Leonard 14, 77, 110, 164, 220, 333
Lee Noel 24, 296, 358
David John Roe 238, 310
Geoff Taylor 53, 133, 153, 208, 214, 275
Mark Wilkinson 316
    (all the above represented by David Lewis)
Phil Stevenson 65

CONTENTS

First Published 1978 by
Octopus Books Limited
59 Grosvenor Street
London W1

ISBN 0 7064 0763 6

This arrangement © 1978 Octopus Books Limited

Edited and designed by Boondoggle Limited
600A Commercial Road
London E1

Produced by Mandarin Publishers Limited
22A Westlands Road, Quarry Bay, Hong Kong

Printed in Hong Kong

FROM SPY-CATCHER TO SPY

Geoffrey Palmer

On Sunday, 25 May 1913, a football match was played between two amateur teams belonging to a minor league in Prague, Czechoslovakia, which at that time was part of the Austrian Empire. The teams were Storm I and Union V, and the final score was 7–5 in favour of Union V. The following day a newspaper report on the match mentioned that Storm I's defences were weakened by the absence of two regular players, one of them named Wagner, the right-half. The writer of the report was Egon Kisch, a journalist who was also the captain of the losing team, so he was understandably annoyed at his team's defeat and the unexplained failure of Wagner to turn up. He decided to call on Wagner at his locksmith's shop and demand an explanation.

'I am sorry,' said Wagner, 'I was called away suddenly on an urgent job and there was no time to let you know.'

Kisch sniffed. 'A likely story. What was this job that was more important than the match?'

'I had to break open some locks in an officer's house.'

Kisch began to show a reluctant interest. 'Go on.'

Wagner leaned forward. 'I don't think I should be telling you really,

9

but now I've started I suppose I'd better continue, or you'll never believe me.'

'It's going to be hard,' Kisch said, 'but I'll try.'

Wagner drew a long breath. 'Well, it was a colonel's house, I think, that I was taken to, and I gathered that he had died that morning in Vienna. When I got there I saw several high-ranking army officers, and one I recognized was General Baron von Giesl, the Commander of the Prague Army Corps, who had come from Vienna. I had to force open the front door and then I was made to open all the drawers and desks in the colonel's office, and everything else in the house that was locked. It took me quite a while, I can tell you.'

'And what did you find?' Kisch was now definitely interested.

'Well, I didn't find anything, but the officers did—a great pile of papers, some of them in Russian, photographs and plans, and a large amount of money. And very amazed they seemed, and very angry too. "Who would have thought it?" I heard one of them say. Another said bitterly, "How can one trust anybody these days . . ." The general himself didn't say anything; he just looked sad, and kept shaking his head. I thought at first they had been looking for the colonel's will, but it was obviously something much more important. As soon as I had finished I was hustled out and told to say nothing to anybody. And now I have told you!' Wagner added ruefully. 'You won't split on me, will you?'

But Kisch was thinking hard, his newspaperman's nose twitching with excitement. Here was a story to follow up. What a scoop! Hardly hearing Wagner's promise that he would be at next Sunday's game, he bade him a brief farewell and hurried back to his office.

There he grabbed a copy of the morning newspaper and looked up a short paragraph tucked away in an obscure corner that he remembered having glanced at briefly. It was a message from Vienna announcing, with regret, the suicide of Colonel Albert Redl, Chief of Staff of the 8th Army Corps, 'a very gifted officer who would have risen to the highest rank'. He had shot himself in a moment of depression, brought on by weeks of insomnia.

Kisch paced up and down his office, his mind awhirl with facts and speculations. Wagner's story and Redl's suicide must be connected. Russian documents—photographs—plans—suicide—high-ranking officers searching the colonel's house—there was only one conclusion to come to: Redl must have been a spy! The soldier who might soon have been in command of the whole Austrian Army—a traitor! It was unbelievable, but Kisch believed it. It would be the most sensational scoop of all time!

Suddenly his excitement cooled. What a fool he was; of course he couldn't use the startling information. If he printed it in his paper the police would swoop down on him, suspend the paper, and he himself would land up in prison. Censorship was strict, and anyone who broke the law was treated harshly. But there must be a way out. He could not let the opportunity slip of telling his readers that something mysterious had happened.

After a few minutes he hit on a solution, and grinning broadly, took up a pen and drew a sheet of paper towards him.

The next morning the newspaper carried an item of news that could be safely printed, for it *denied* the rumour that Colonel Redl had betrayed military secrets to Russia, and stated that the search of his house concerned quite another matter. The fact that there had been no rumour in the first place did not matter. Kisch knew that his readers were used to reading between the lines. They would know that Colonel Redl *was* a traitor.

The next year the Great War broke out, and at the end of it the Austrian Empire broke up. It was only gradually that various documents came to light and interest in the Redl affair, which had quickly subsided in 1913, was revived. The many strands of the amazing story were gradually woven together and eventually the truth was known.

Alfred Redl had been a brilliant officer, full of energy and enthusiasm. In 1900, when still a major, he had been appointed as chief of the espionage and counter-espionage branch of the Austrian Secret Service, and he had made it the most efficient part of the whole organization. He was responsible for the capture of some clever spies, he discovered many secrets from foreign countries that were of the greatest use to Austria, and he thought up a number of practices that in their time were revolutionary.

The time came when he was promoted to colonel and posted to Prague as Chief of Staff to General von Giesl. His place in Vienna was taken by Captain Ronge, but his methods continued to be used, and

'Remember Redl' became the watchword of the organization.

Captain Ronge, inspired by Redl's reputation for alertness, set up a secret postal censorship. This was called the Black Bureau. Every letter coming from any place on the frontiers was examined minutely, and more than once unsuspected spies were caught. On 2 March 1913, two particular letters which reached the Black Bureau aroused great interest. According to the postmarks they came from Eydtkuhnen on the Russo-German border, and were addressed to 'Opera Ball 13' at the General Post Office in Vienna. Both contained a large sum of money but no letter or message. As Eydtkuhnen was known to harbour spies, Captain Ronge was determined to find out the identity of Opera Ball 13.

He set up a trap. A wire running between the post office and the police station next door was fixed up so that a postal clerk could press a button and a bell would alert the police. Two detectives were on duty day and night at the police station, with orders to arrest anybody who called for letters for Opera Ball 13 when the bell called them to action.

Two months went by, however, and no one called to collect the letters containing the money. It was not until 24 May, a Saturday afternoon, that the bell rang in the police station—and both detectives were out of the room at the time!

When they eventually heard the bell and rushed to the post office the man had gone. The clerk, shaking with excitement, stuttered, 'You—you've j–just missed him. He—he turned to the left.'

The detectives ran out to the street, and saw a taxi disappearing round a corner. It must have been carrying the man they wanted as there was no one else in sight. They looked around for another taxi, but it was twenty minutes before one came slowly towards them. They hailed it and jumped in, and one of the detectives recognized it as the one that had taken their quarry away. He pulled out his identification card and pushed it towards the driver. 'You have just dropped a fare. Where did you take him?'

'To the Café Kaiserhof,' the man replied.

'Then take us there too—and hurry.'

As they drove along the detectives fretted with impatience. Their chief was not going to be pleased with the way they had bungled things. One of them, shuffling his feet as though he could help the taxi to increase its speed, felt his boot touch something on the floor. He picked up the object. It was the sheath of a pocket knife, made of grey suede. Of course, it might have nothing to do with the man they were looking for, but it was better to take no chances, and the detective slipped it into his pocket.

The Café Kaiserhof was practically empty. Only two bearded old men were sitting at a table drinking beer. A waiter told them that a customer had been in half an hour before and had ordered a beer. He had not stayed long, and through the window the waiter had seen him go to the taxi stand on the other side of the square.

The detectives did not wait to hear more. There was only one taxi at the stand, the driver sitting at the wheel reading a newspaper. Yes, he said, in answer to an agitated question, a gentleman took a taxi about half an hour ago. Yes, he had heard where he wanted to go. It was the Hotel Klomser . . .

'Take us there immediately,' one of the detectives demanded.

At the Hotel Klomser they leaped out of the taxi and ran up the steps. The hotel porter was in the entrance. 'How many people have entered the hotel within the last half-hour?' he was asked.

'Let me see now.' The porter began to count on his fingers. 'One, two, three, oh, yes, four.'

'Do you know any of them?'

'Three of them have been staying here for some time, but the fourth gentleman only took a room yesterday. He looks like a soldier in civilian clothes . . .'

The detective took out the knife sheath. 'Take this,' he said, 'and I want you to show it to each of these men as he goes out. Ask him if he has lost it. Don't say that we gave it to you—you could have found it on the floor here. Act as casually and naturally as possible.'

'All right,' the porter said, indifferently.

The detectives retired to a corner of the lounge, their faces hidden by newspapers. There was a silence, broken only by the porter's yawns and the loud ticking of a clock.

At last there was the sound of footsteps coming down the stairs, and round the corner came a tall, military-looking man, iron-grey hair closely cropped, a monocle in one eye, wearing a fashionable overcoat. The porter stopped him at the entrance. 'Excuse me, sir,' he said, 'but did you by any chance drop the sheath of your pocket knife?'

'Why, yes, that is mine,' replied the military-looking man, taking the sheath. 'How careless of me. Where could I have dropped it?'

'Why, yes, that is mine,' the man replied, taking it. 'How careless of me. Where could I have dropped it——'

He stopped, remembering where he must have dropped it—in the taxi when he was opening the letters he had collected. His face went pale, and for a moment he seemed unable to move. Recovering quickly, he glanced round him. Two men, reading newspapers—they could not have overheard. How had the porter come by it? Better not inquire . . .

The porter had turned away. The man breathed once, quickly, and gained control of himself. He slipped the sheath into his pocket and walked slowly and firmly to the entrance. With straight-backed dignity he descended the steps and walked away from the hotel.

A detective hurried to the telephone at the reception desk and dialled a number. When a voice said 'hello' he blurted out, 'Opera Ball 13— it is Colonel Redl! He's staying at the Hotel Klomser—I've just seen him leave and we're going after him now.'

A few minutes later Captain Ronge was talking excitedly to the chief of the Black Bureau. 'The man on whom we have modelled our methods, the man we have looked up to and admired—a traitor receiving money from the Russians? It cannot be possible!'

Captain Ronge hurried to the post office and asked to see the form which every applicant for a letter held there had to fill in. He took it back to his office and compared the writing with that of a document written by Colonel Redl just before he had been promoted. There was no doubt about it: the two samples of writing were identical. Opera Ball 13 was his ex-chief, the receiver of suspicious letters containing large sums of money. There must be some innocent explanation . . .

At that moment there was a knock on the door, and one of the detectives entered. 'I have further proof, sir,' he said grimly, and placed on the desk a number of torn-up pieces of paper.

'What are these?' Ronge asked.

'We followed Colonel Redl from the hotel, sir,' the man replied. 'He walked down the Hersengasse as far as the Café Central. He looked round furtively several times, and I think he realized that he was being followed. He took some papers from his pocket, tore them into pieces and threw them down. I expect he thought that we would stop to pick them up and enable him to slip away, but we didn't. We continued the pursuit. He passed some taxis at a stand, but did not take one. My colleague took one, however, and went back to pick up the scraps of paper, leaving me to shadow the colonel, which I did relentlessly, and he couldn't shake me off. I was only a few yards away from him when he reached his hotel again, having gone a circular route in vain. I met up with my colleague, who handed over the papers, and here they are, sir.'

'You've done well. Leave them with me,' said Ronge.

It took Ronge a long time to piece all the scraps together, and when he had done so he sat back, appalled at what they revealed. There was a receipt for money sent to an officer in the Russian Secret Service, and three receipts for registered letters to enemy agents in Brussels, Warsaw and Lausanne—agents which Colonel Redl himself had placed on an Austrian black list! With a heavy heart Captain Ronge began a report on the affair to his chief.

That evening Colonel Redl had an appointment to dine with a friend, Dr Victor Pollock, one of the most prominent lawyers in Austria. They had arranged to meet at a restaurant called the Riedhof at eight o'clock. Before then, however, the detective who had followed him had got to know of the appointment and had arranged with the manager of the restaurant to take the place of the waiter who would be serving them.

Colonel Redl and Dr Pollock were given a private room. They had an excellent dinner, though the service was not as skilful as they might have expected. But they noticed nothing. The lawyer was in a cheerful mood, but Redl was very depressed and ate little.

'What is the matter with you, my friend?' said Pollock. 'You are acting as though this is your last dinner!'

Redl winced. If only his friend knew . . . But how could he tell him that he had been spying for Russia for ten years, had amassed a fortune from his activities, but now knew that the game was up and he had to face the consequences?

'Listen, Victor, I am in serious trouble. My doctors have told me that I am very sick mentally and not likely to get well if I continue my present mode of life. Recently I have not been responsible for many of my actions. In addition, I have been stupidly extravagant and my financial affairs are in a sorry state. I owe money to a great number of people and I am almost ruined.'

'Overwork, that's what it is!' the lawyer declared. 'You always did work too hard. What can I do to help you?'

'Can you help me to get back to Prague as quickly and quietly as possible? In Prague I believe I can get things sorted out and receive the medical help I need, and start to build my career again.'

'I can help you, and I will. I know the very man to contact.' The lawyer stood up from the table. 'I shall telephone him now. If anybody can arrange a quiet departure for you, he can.' There was a telephone in the room. The lawyer lifted the receiver and gave a number to the operator.

The waiter, who had just entered the room carrying a laden tray, heard what the lawyer had said, and froze to the spot. It was the number of Herr Gayer, the Chief of Police! What was the lawyer up to? Could he be working as a detective himself, or was it just a coincidence? As unobtrusively as possible he put down his tray and slipped out of the room.

Later that night, the dinner over, Colonel Redl said good-night to his friend and returned to the Hotel Klomser. He was very thoughtful. In spite of Dr Pollock's promise of help he could hardly believe that he would not have to face the consequences of his actions.

At midnight there was a knock on the door of his room. He put down the pen with which he had been writing and stood up. 'Come in,' he said quietly.

Four officers in full uniform stood on the threshold. None of them spoke. Redl made a formal bow. 'I know why you have come,' he said, 'and I am ready. I have just been writing letters of farewell to my friends. Will you give me a chance to do what I have to do alone? You have my word as an Austrian officer that I shall not flinch from my duty.'

'Have you any accomplices?' one of the officers said coldly.

'No, I have always worked on my own. You will find all the evidence you need in my house in Prague.'

'Have you a revolver, Colonel?'

'No, may I ask you to lend me one?'

Silently the officer produced his revolver and handed it to Redl. Then they all bowed stiffly and withdrew. The door closed and Redl was alone.

The officers took turns to wait outside the hotel. The hours dragged by slowly. No one entered or left. The hotel porter dozed in his cubicle.

Dawn broke and the watching men stirred. At five o'clock they gathered on the hotel steps and spoke sombrely to each other. Then one of them called the porter and gave him instructions. The man seemed reluctant to obey, but a sharp word of command sent him scurrying inside and up the staircase to the first floor.

He received no answer when he rapped on the door of Colonel Redl's room so he turned the handle slowly, opened the door a few inches and put his head through the narrow gap. The light was on and every object in the room stood out in the glare. Colonel Redl lay crumpled on the floor, a revolver by his side. Blood had oozed on to the carpet from a wound in his head.

The porter gulped and turned pale. Quickly he closed the door and ran down to the entrance hall where the four officers were waiting, hunched in their greatcoats, grim-faced and silent.

'Sirs,' the porter gasped. 'A dreadful thing has happened. Colonel Redl has killed himself . . .'

A doctor and the Chief of Police were soon on the scene, one to check that the colonel was indeed dead, the other to examine what he had left behind. There were two letters on the table—one to his brother, the other to General Baron von Giesl. On a half sheet of paper was another message: 'Pray for me—I pay for my sins with my life. I will die now. Pray for me . . .'

Only about twelve hours had passed between Colonel Redl's visit to the post office and the discovery of his body. Ten years of betrayal of his country had come to an end when he accidentally dropped a knife sheath. And the world would not have known the real reason for the death of a brilliant spy-catcher if a humble locksmith had not failed to turn up for a football match.

THE GOLD-BUG

Edgar Allan Poe

Many years ago I became friendly with a Mr William Legrand. He had once been wealthy but a series of misfortunes caused him to seek a new home. He chose Sullivan's Island, near Charleston in South Carolina.

It is a strange island, mainly of sand and about three miles long and never more than a quarter of a mile wide. Legrand built himself a small hut at the eastern end, or more remote part, of this island. He was living there when I first made his acquaintance. We soon became good friends. He was well educated and had many books. His chief amusements were shooting or fishing and collecting shells and bettles. He was usually accompanied by an old Negro called Jupiter who, although a freed slave, still felt it his duty to look after his young 'Massa Will', as he called Legrand.

I had not visited my friend for some time and decided to call on him about the middle of October. On reaching the hut I rapped on the door. There was no answer so I let myself in and waited for him to return. I sat by the fire, a most unusual sight in October on Sullivan's Island. He and Jupiter arrived soon after dark and made me very welcome. Whilst Jupiter bustled about preparing supper, Legrand sat opposite me. He seemed full of enthusiasm. He had found a new type of scarabaeus, or beetle, which he felt was entirely new.

I asked to see it but he told me he had lent it to a naval lieutenant, another enthusiast, for the night, and would send Jupiter down for it at sunrise. 'It is the loveliest thing in creation!' he said.

'What—sunrise?'

'Nonsense, no! The bug. It is of a brilliant gold colour—about the size of a large hickory-nut, with two jet-black spots at the top of its back and another, somewhat larger, at the base. The antennae are——'

'Dere ain't *no* tin in him, Massa Will,' Jupiter interrupted, in his strange manner of speaking. 'De bug is a gold-bug, every bit of him, inside and all, 'cept for his wing. Never felt half so heavy a bug in my life.'

Legrand suggested he made a drawing of the bug to give me some idea of its shape. He looked around for some paper, then said finally, 'Never mind, this will answer' and drew from his pocket a scrap of what I took to be very dirty foolscap. As he drew he told me of the brilliant and metallic lustre of the beetle's scales.

When he had done he handed the drawing to me, without rising. As I took it from him there came a loud growl and a scratching at the door. Jupiter opened it and a large Newfoundland dog bounded in and began to cover me with caresses. He knew me well for I had always made a fuss of him on previous visits. When his gambols were over I had my first chance to look at the drawing. I was rather puzzled.

'Well,' I said, after studying it for some minutes, 'this is a very strange scarabaeus. I've never seen anything like it before. It looks rather like a skull, or a death's head, than anything else.'

'A death's head!' he echoed. 'Oh—yes—well, it has something of that appearance on paper, no doubt. The two upper black spots look like eyes, eh? and the longer one at the bottom like a mouth—and then the shape of the whole is oval.'

We discussed it further and then I asked, 'But where are the antennae you spoke of?'

'The antennae?' queried Legrand, who seemed to be losing his temper. 'I am sure you must see them. I made them as distinct as they are in the original insect, and I presume that is sufficient.'

'Well, well,' I said, 'perhaps you have. Still, I don't see them,' and I handed back the paper. I was puzzled at the turn of affairs. His sudden ill-humour was odd, and as for the drawing of the beetle, there were positively no antennae to be seen. And the whole did bear a very close resemblance to a death's head.

He took the paper from me, very peevishly, and was about to crumple it, apparently to throw it in the fire, when a glance at it seemed suddenly to rivet his attention. The colour of his face appeared to change and he stared at the drawing very closely. Then he rose, seated himself on a sea-chest in the farthest corner of the room, and continued his close examination. Finally he took out a wallet, placed the paper carefully in it, then put both in a writing desk, which he locked.

He had lost his former ill-humour. Now he seemed absorbed in thought. This grew during the evening until, finally, I thought it best to leave. He did not press me to remain but, as I left, shook my hand with even more than his usual cordiality.

About a month later I received a visit at my home in Charleston from his man, Jupiter. He looked very upset and I feared that something had happened to my friend.

'Well, Jup,' I said. 'What is the matter now? How is your master?'

'Why, to speak de troof, him not so well as might be.'

'Not well! I am truly sorry to hear it. What does he complain of?'

'Dat's it! He never complains of nothin'—but him sick for all that.'

'Jupiter! Why didn't you say so at once?' and I listened while the good Negro began to tell me of his fears for his master. He then went on, 'Todder day he gib me de slip 'fore sun up and was gone for de whole of de blessed day.'

'Has anything unpleasant happened since I saw you?' I asked.

'No massa. There ain't been nothin' onpleasant *since* den—'twas *before* den I'm feared. 'Twas the berry day you was dare.'

'The what?'

'De bug. I'm berry certain dat Massa Will bin bit somewhere 'bout de head by dat gold-bug.'

'You think then that your master was really bitten by the beetle, and that the bite made him sick?'

'I don't think—I knows it. What makes him dream about gold so much if 'tain't because he was bit by the gold-bug?'

'How do you know he dreams about gold?'

''Cause he talks about it in his sleep—dat's how I knows.'

He then handed me a letter from Legrand. Although most of it chided me for not visiting the island sooner, it ended on an air of urgency. '*Do* come,' it said. 'I wish to see you *tonight*, on business of importance. I assure you that it is of the *highest* importance.'

How could I refuse such a summons? I went down to the wharf with Jupiter and saw, in the bottom of the boat, a new scythe and three spades. In answer to my question Jupiter replied, 'Massa Will insisted on my buying 'em for him in de town,' and that was all he knew.

When we reached the hut, Legrand was waiting for us. His face was pale and his deep-set eyes glared with unnatural lustre. We talked for a time and then he handed me the beetle, now in a glass case. It was an entirely new species. There were two round black spots near one extremity of the back, and a long one near the other. The scales were exceedingly hard and glossy, with all the appearance of burnished gold. Its weight was remarkable and I could well understand Jupiter's idea that it was of solid gold.

Legrand looked at it. 'That bug is to make my fortune, to reinstate me in my family possessions. I have only to use it properly, and I shall arrive at the gold of which it is the index.'

He assured me that he was not ill, adding, 'I am as well as I can expect to be under the excitement which I suffer. If you really wish me well, you will relieve this excitement.'

'And how is this to be done?'

'Very easily. Jupiter and myself are going on an expedition into the hills, on the mainland, and we shall need the aid of some person in whom we can confide. You are the only one we can trust. Whether we succeed or fail, the excitement which you now perceive in me will be equally allayed.'

We argued about this for a while and then, with a heavy heart, I agreed. We started about four o'clock—Legrand, Jupiter, the dog, and myself. Jupiter had with him the scythe and spades. I had charge of a couple of lanterns while Legrand contented himself with the scarabaeus, which he carried attached to the end of a bit of whipcord, and twirling it to and fro, with the air of a conjuror, as he went.

We crossed the creek at the head of the island by means of a skiff and, after about two hours, entered a region more infinitely dreary than any

yet seen. It was a sort of tableland, near the summit of an almost in-
accessible hill, densely wooded and interspersed with huge crags. Deep
ravines, in various directions, gave an air of still sterner solemnity to the
scene. We finally reached the foot of an enormously tall tulip-tree,
which stood with some eight or ten oaks, on the level, and far surpassed
them all, and all other trees which I had then ever seen, in the beauty of
its foliage and form, in the wide spread of its branches, and in the
general majesty of its appearance.

When we reached this tree, Legrand turned to Jupiter and asked him
if he thought he could climb it.

'Yes, massa. Jup climb any tree he ebber see in his life.'

He was ready to prove this, but hesitated when Legrand told him to
take the gold-bug with him. Eventually he agreed, however, and began
the ascent of the huge tree. When he was about some sixty or seventy
feet from the ground Legrand shouted up to him to count the limbs
below him. When the Negro shouted down the number he ordered
him to go one limb higher, to the seventh. When this was done, Legrand
shouted out again, 'Now Jup, I want you to work your way out on that
limb as far as you can. If you see anything strange, let me know.'

Going very carefully, Jupiter edged his way along the seemingly
rotten branch and then we heard his terrified shriek.

'Lor-gol-a-marcy! What is dis here pon de tree?'

'Well!' cried Legrand, highly delighted, 'what is it?'

'Why, 'tain't noffin but a skull. Somebody bin left him head up de
tree, and de crows done gobble every bit of de meat off.'

'A skull, you say. Very well. How is it fastened to the limb?'

'Why dis berry curious sarcumstance. Dere's a great big nail in de
skull what fastens it on to de tree.'

Even more delighted now, Legrand shouted up to Jupiter to find the
left eye of the skull. This caused some argument for the Negro was
left-handed, but the problem, finally, seemed resolved. Legrand
shouted up, 'Let the beetle drop through it as far as the string will reach
—but be careful not to let go of the string.'

He did as he was told and the scarabaeus, glistening like a globe of
burnished gold in the last rays of the setting sun, hung clear of the
branches and, if allowed to fall, would have dropped at our feet. Legrand took the scythe and cleared a circular space some ten or twelve

23

The beetle hung clear of the branches, glistening like a globe of burnished gold in the last rays of the setting sun.

feet in diameter, just beneath the hanging insect. He then ordered Jupiter to let go the string and come down from the tree.

With great exactness Legrand drove a peg into the ground at the precise spot where the beetle had fallen and then, with Jupiter having used the scythe to clear away the brambles, set all three of us digging. We dug steadily for two hours, reaching a depth of five feet. Yet there was no sign of any treasure. We continued digging. Still nothing. Then suddenly Legrand strode up to Jupiter and hissed, 'You scoundrel. You infernal black villain. Speak, I tell you! Answer me this instant! Which—which is your left eye?'

The terrified Jupiter replied, hastily, 'Ain't dis here my lef' eye for sartain?'—and placed his hand on his *right* eye!

'I thought so. I knew it. Hurrah!' cried Legrand and led the way back to the base of the tree. He asked Jupiter, 'Was it this eye or that through which you dropped the beetle?' and he touched each of the other's eyes in turn.

''Twas this eye, massa—de lef' eye—just as you tell me'; and here it was his right eye that he indicated.

'That will do. We must try again.'

Legrand removed the peg which marked the spot where the beetle fell to a spot about three inches to the west of its former position. He took out a tape measure, which he had used before, and marked out a fresh spot several yards from where we had been digging.

Once again we all set to with the spades. After we had been at work for perhaps an hour and a half, we were interrupted by the violent howlings of the dog. He leapt into the hole, tore up the mould frantically with his claws and in a few seconds had uncovered a mass of human bones, forming two complete skeletons, intermingled with several buttons of metal, and what appeared to be the dust of decayed woollens. One or two strokes of a spade upturned the blade of a large Spanish knife and, as we dug farther, three or four loose pieces of gold and silver coin came to light. Legrand urged us to continue digging and the words were hardly uttered when I stumbled and fell forward, having caught the toe of my boot in a large ring of iron that lay half buried.

In ten minutes we had unearthed an oblong chest of wood, some three and a half feet long, three feet broad and two and a half feet deep. At first we found it difficult to open until we saw that the fastenings of the lid were two sliding bolts. These we drew back—trembling and panting with anxiety. In an instant, a treasure of incalculable value lay gleaming before us. As the rays of the lantern fell within the pit, there flashed upward a glow and a glare from a confused heap of gold and of jewels that absolutely dazzled our eyes.

A later examination showed that, within the chest, there was not a particle of silver. All was gold of antique date and of great variety. There were diamonds—some of them exceedingly large and fine—a hundred and ten in all, and not one of them small; eighteen rubies of remarkable brilliancy; three hundred and ten emeralds, all very beautiful; and twenty-one sapphires, with an opal. Besides all this there was a vast quantity of solid gold ornaments, crucifixes, censers, sword-handles and nearly two hundred superb gold watches.

When the intense excitement of the time had, in some measure, subsided, Legrand entered into full details of all the circumstances connected with it.

'You remember,' he said, 'the night when I handed you the rough sketch I had made of the scarabaeus. You recollect that I became quite vexed at you for insisting that my drawing resembled a death's head. I was about to crumple it up and throw it angrily into the fire.'

'The scrap of paper, you mean,' I said.

'No. It had much the appearance of paper, but when I came to draw on it I discovered it at once to be a piece of very thin parchment. My glance fell upon the sketch at which you had been looking when I perceived the figure of a death's head just where, it seemed to me, I had made the drawing of a beetle. I took a candle and, seating myself at the other end of the room, proceeded to scrutinize the parchment more closely. On turning it over I saw my own sketch on the reverse, just as I had made it. Yet I remembered, positively, that there had been *no* drawing on the parchment when I made my own sketch.

'I then thought back about the finding of the beetle. When I first picked it up it gave me a sharp bite which caused me to let it drop. Jupiter, with his usual caution, looked about for a leaf, or something of that nature, by which to take hold of it. It was then we saw the scrap of parchment, which I then supposed to be paper. It was lying half buried in the sand, a corner sticking up. Nearby was the remnants of the hull of what appeared to have been a ship's longboat. The wreck seemed to have been there for a very great while.

'Later, I established a kind of connection. There was a boat lying on a sea-coast, and not far from the boat was a parchment—*not paper*—with a skull depicted on it. The skull, or death's head, is the well-known emblem of the pirate.'

'But,' I interposed, 'you say that the skull was not on the parchment when you made the drawing of the beetle.'

'Ah, hereupon turns the whole mystery, although the secret, at this point, I had comparatively little difficulty in solving. You may remember you were seated near the fire as I handed you the parchment. Then Wolf, the Newfoundland entered, and leaped on your shoulders. With your left hand you carressed him and kept him off, while your right, holding the parchment, was in close proximity to the fire. It was the *heat* which had been the agent in bringing to light, on the parchment, the skull which I saw designed on it.

'I saw more. As I examined the parchment even more closely I saw, at the corner, the figure of a goat or kid. But why? Pirates have nothing to do with goats; that is for farmers. Then I realized. It was of the pirate chief, *Captain* Kidd. It was his stamp or seal.

'When you had gone, I held the vellum to the fire, but with no success. I then thought it possible that the coating of dirt might have something to do with the failure. So I carefully rinsed the parchment by pouring warm water over it, placed it in a tin pan, with the skull downward, and put the pan on a furnace of lighted charcoal. In a few minutes, the pan having become thoroughly heated, I removed the slips. To my inexpressible joy, I found it spotted in several places, with what appeared to be figures arranged in lines. Again I placed it in the pan and suffered it to remain another minute. On taking it off, the whole was just as you see it now.'

Here Legrand, having reheated the parchment, submitted it to my inspection. A whole collection of characters were rudely traced, in a red tint, between the death's head and the goat. The whole was obviously a cipher, but one far beyond my powers. The list of symbols read:

'53‡‡†305))6*;4826)4‡.)4‡);806*;48†8¶60))85;1‡(;:‡*8†83(88)5*†; 46(;88*96*?;8)*‡(;485);5*†2:*‡(;4956*2(5*—4)8¶8*;4069285);)6†8) 4‡‡;1(‡9;48081;8:8‡1;48†85;4)485†528806*81(‡9;48;(88;4(‡?34;48)4 ‡;161;:188;‡?'

27

Consequently, Legrand began to carefully explain how he had solved the riddle. He first counted up the various characters, to see how many times each appeared.

'Now in English,' he said, 'the letter which most frequently occurs is *e*. As the predominant character in the code is 8, we will commence by assuming it to be the *e* of the natural alphabet. To verify the supposition, let us observe if the 8 be seen often in couples—for *e* is doubled with great frequency in English, in such words as "meet", "fleet", "speed", "seen", "been", "agree", etc. In the present instance we see it doubled no less than five times, although the cryptograph is brief.

'Let us assume eight, then, as *e*. Now, of all the *words* in the language, "the" is the most usual. On inspection we find no less than *seven* such arrangements, the characters being ;48. We may, therefore, assume that ; represents *t*, 4 represents *h*, and 8 represents *e*—the last now being well confirmed. Thus a great step has been taken.'

And so, step by step, Legrand explained how he had finally solved what he considered to be 'the very simplest series of cryptographs'. The final message said: *'A good glass in the bishop's hostel in the devil's seat forty-one degrees and thirteen minutes northeast and by north main branch seventh limb east side shoot from the left eye of the death's-head a bee-line from the tree through the shot fifty feet out.'*

Legrand then explained how he divided this sentence so that it at least made some sense. But only to him, for I said, 'Even this division leaves me still in the dark.'

'It left me also in the dark for a few days, during which I made diligent inquiry in the neighbourhood of Sullivan's Island for any building which went by the name of the "Bishop's Hotel"—for, of course, I dropped the obsolete word, "hostel". My search led me to the plantation, where I asked among the older Negroes of the place. At length, one of the most aged of the women said that she had heard of such a place as *Beesop's Castle*. But it was neither a castle nor a tavern, but a high rock. She showed me the place and I climbed up the side of the "castle". Then my eyes fell upon a narrow ledge in the eastern face of the rock. I had no doubt that here was the "devil's seat" alluded to in the message, and now I seemed to grasp the full secret of the riddle.

'The "good glass", I knew, referred to a telescope and the following phrases were intended for the levelling of the glass. After a great deal of trial and error I finally fixed my newly-bought telescope on a large tree that over-topped its fellows in the distance. It had a circular rift or opening in its foliage. In the centre of this rift I perceived a white spot. Adjusting the focus of the telescope I now made it out to be a human skull.

He smiled. 'Most of the rest you know,' he said.

'I suppose you missed the spot in the first attempt at digging, through Jupiter's stupidity in letting the bug fall through the right instead of through the left eye of the skull?'

'Precisely. This mistake made a difference of about two and a half inches in the "shot"—that is to say, in the position of the peg nearest the tree. Had the treasure been *beneath* the "shot", the error would have been of little moment; but the "shot", together with the nearest point of the tree, were merely two points for the establishment of a line of direction. Of course the error, however trivial in the beginning, increased as we proceeded with the line, and by the time we had gone fifty feet, threw us quite off the scent. But for my deep-seated impression that the treasure was here somewhere actually buried, we might have had all our labour in vain.'

'Now there is only one point which puzzles me,' I said. 'What are we to make of the skeletons found in the hole?'

'That is a question I am no more able to answer than yourself. There seems, however, only one plausible way of accounting for them. It is clear that Kidd—if Kidd indeed secreted this treasure, which I doubt not—it is clear that he must have had assistance in the labour. But his labour concluded, he may have thought it expedient to remove all participants in his secret. Perhaps a couple of blows with a mattock were sufficient, while his assistants were busy in the pit.

'Perhaps it required a dozen—who shall tell?'

GEORGE BLAKE — DOUBLE AGENT

Alastair Scott

It was Wednesday, 31 May 1961. The No. 1 Court of the Central Criminal Court was hushed as all eyes turned towards the prisoner in the dock. Pale and tired, dressed in a dark, grey suit, he listened as the Clerk of the Court read out the charges against him—five serious charges, any one of which would have marked him down as a master spy. There was a pause and then the prisoner, George Blake, answered the question 'How do you plead? Guilt or not guilty?' in almost a whisper: 'Guilty, sir.'

Before that single word had been spoken, the Lord Chief Justice of England, Lord Parker, had ordered the court to be cleared for a while so that part of the case should be heard *in camera*. This meant that almost everyone had to leave the court, which was then locked and guarded by the police.

It was almost an hour before the press and public were allowed back into the court.

There was a strange tension as the judge looked at the comparatively young man facing him. Then, breaking the silence at last, Lord Parker began to address him in slow, measured phrases.

'Your full written confession reveals that for some years you have been working continuously as an agent and spy for a foreign power. Moreover the information communicated, though not of a scientific nature, was clearly of the utmost importance to that power and has rendered much of this country's efforts completely useless. Indeed, you yourself have said in your confession that there was not an official document of any importance to which you had access which was not passed to your Soviet contact.

'When one realizes that you are a British subject, albeit not by birth, and that throughout this period you were employed by this country— your country—in responsible positions of trust, it is clear that your case is akin to treason. Indeed, it is one of the worst that can be envisaged other than in time of war . . .

'You are not yet thirty-nine years of age. You must know and appreciate the gravity of the offences to which you have pleaded guilty. Your conduct in many other countries would undoubtedly carry the death penalty. In our law, however, I have no option but to sentence you to imprisonment and for your traitorous conduct extending over so many years there must be a very heavy sentence.'

There was absolute silence in the court as Lord Parker continued. 'For a single offence of this kind the highest penalty laid down is fourteen years' imprisonment and the court cannot, therefore, even if so minded, give you a sentence of life imprisonment.

'There are, however, five counts to which you have pleaded guilty, each dealing with separate periods in your life during which you were betraying this country.

'The court will impose upon you a sentence of fourteen years' imprisonment on each of the five counts. Those in respect of counts one, two and three will be consecutive, and those in respect of counts four and five will be concurrent, making a total of forty-two years' imprisonment.'

At this there was an audible gasp in the courtroom. Only Blake himself appeared unmoved. This was the longest sentence ever imposed on a prisoner in modern times. The warder touched his arm, and the prisoner turned and disappeared from sight to the cells below.

How had George Blake come to be in this position? How was it that a man in a position of trust had proved such a traitor to his country? To

31

determine this, it is necessary to go back to Blake's earlier days, and to one of the most extraordinary lives ever experienced by a young man.

Blake's father's name was Albert Behar, a man of Spanish–Turkish origin who had been born in Cairo. He came to Britain during the First World War and fought bravely with the British Army. He was wounded and gassed, and finished the war as one of the Intelligence staff of Field–Marshal Earl Haig. For his courage and devotion Behar gained several awards, including the Order of the British Empire. He was also granted British citizenship. He married a beautiful Dutch girl in London, and they set up home together in Rotterdam.

Their son George, named after George V, was born on 11 November 1922. Albert Behar was to die in 1935, and the young lad was sent to Egypt for two and a half years. He returned home just before Christmas in 1938.

Nine months later the Second World War began and the boy, then only sixteen, saw his home town of Rotterdam cruelly bombed by German planes. Within two hours over one hundred and fifty thousand people were made homeless. By nightfall, Rotterdam was one huge sea of flames, and the event aroused in the boy a hatred of the Germans that he was never to lose.

Soon the German Army was marching into Holland and the Gestapo, following, began to arrest all suspicious persons. Because of his father's British nationality, young George was arrested and thrown into an SS prison. It was not long before he showed how expert he was at slipping out of such places. He escaped and went 'underground'. Taking on the name of Max van Vries, he became a member of a resistance group. It was well organized, its leaders working closely with the exiled Dutch Government in London, the British Secret Service and the SOE (Special Operations Executive). One of the tasks young George enjoyed doing most was helping to sabotage trains taking food away from a starving Holland to feed the population in Germany.

In time, however, due to Dutch carelessness in London, the German Secret Service was able to break the code of the SOE and George decided to leave Holland, especially when he learned that the Gestapo were close on his trail. He had the impudent idea of cycling all the way to Belgium, wearing the clothes of a Trappist monk. As he cycled past them he received a number of rude comments from German soldiers, but such strange sights were familiar on the roads at that time and no one stopped him for questioning. He finally reached Brussels.

He then went on to the French frontier and hoped to cross France into Spain. But this was more difficult as Spain, although officially neutral, was very pro-German. Consequently, their border guards were on the watch for anyone who seemed even slightly suspicious. He was caught on the frontier and taken to a prison where there were already more than four thousand others. After a while he managed to get a letter to the British Embassy, claiming that he was British, as indeed he was. An official came and took him away from the camp by car, first to Madrid and then to Gibraltar.

Once on the Rock, MI5 arranged for his passage to England.

At first he had to undergo a number of tests and examinations, for a lot of bogus 'exiles' were coming into England and the officials had become very wary. He was finally cleared and hoped for a job in Intelligence. When this did not materialize, he joined the Royal Navy.

He found himself on board ship with the lowest of all ranks—that of ordinary seaman—but when it was discovered that he could speak fluent English, Dutch and French and also had a good working knoledge of German, he was recommended for a commission. He became a sub-lieutenant, posted to Naval Intelligence and finally to the Dutch section of the SOE.

By then he had changed his name from Behar to 'Blake'.

He became a full-time British Intelligence Officer and after the war worked for a while in Holland, where he spent much of his time questioning high-ranking German officers who had been caught there at the time of the cease-fire.

Blake then returned to Britain and, on 1 September 1948, was attached to the Far Eastern Department with the rank of Vice-Consul in Seoul, the capital of Korea. But already this city, like so much of the country, was subject to Communist pressure. North Korea was invaded during June 1950, and Seoul occupied four days later. A number of British and French diplomats and journalists were captured, Blake among them.

After being kept in various prisoner-of-war camps, Blake was moved from what was literally a death camp at Jadjang to far more comfortable quarters in a farmhouse. Here he and a few others were 'brainwashed' by Russian and Chinese diplomats. This began during the autumn of 1951; the ordeal was over by March 1953, and Blake arrived back in England the following month.

Almost immediately he was appointed a Foreign Office official and soon important and highly confidential papers were passing through his hands. But unknown to those about him, the agents in Korea had done their work well. In his case, the brainwashing had been completely successful. He now regarded Communism as the only real way of life, regarding it as 'a more just society' than that in Britain.

He approached the Russian Embassy and offered to work for them. His offer was accepted and, as was said at the subsequent trial, 'he agreed to make available to the Soviet Intelligence Service such information as came his way in the course of his duties in order to promote the course of Communism.'

For nine and a half years, during which he was employed in a responsible position within the government service and drew his salary from the state, he worked as a secret agent for the Russians.

So, despite the fact that a sentence of forty-two years, if served to the full, would mean that he would be an old man of eighty before his release, it was generally felt that the sentence was justified.

Had it been wartime he would have been shot.

But George Blake was not prepared to wait that long. After serving little more than five years of his sentence, he escaped from Wormwood Scrubs Prison on 22 October 1966.

His escape had taken place on a Saturday—a carefully chosen day, for this was the one day of the week on which those in the long-term wing of the prison were allowed to mix freely and watch television. This was at 5.30 p.m. Blake was not due to be locked up until 7 p.m., and by then he had gone. After the television show the prisoners were rounded up and taken back to their respective cells. Blake's absence was not discovered until 7.30, at almost exactly the same time as a patrolling prison officer found a dangling rope ladder.

The alarm went out immediately, with ports and airfields especially being watched. Foreign cargo ships lying in the London and Tilbury docks, which included three Russian and two Rumanian vessels, had a special guard placed on them.

But it was to no avail. Blake had got clean away.

Investigations at the prison revealed that a window bar had been sawn through, the cut having been disguised by a piece of adhesive tape blackened with shoe polish. Obviously Blake—or an accomplice—had sawn through this bar ready for the day of escape.

Another clue was that of the rope ladder, some fifteen feet of nylon, its rungs strengthened with steel knitting needles. It was found on the outside wall of the prison together with yet another clue, a pot of pink chrysanthemums. The police held the theory that the pot had been a marker to show exactly where the ladder should be thrown over the wall.

The police retraced Blake's path. They concluded that he had slipped between the remaining bars of the window, dropped down on to the roof of a covered way, and then on to the wooden lid of a bin which was placed immediately beneath. Thus, by selecting the right window, Blake had saved himself a drop to the ground of some twenty feet.

He must then have dashed across the yard to reach the wall within seconds, found the ladder, shinned up it, thrown it over the top and dropped down the other side, where his rescuers were waiting for him.

Later, of course, many solutions were put forward for his escape. One, published in a German magazine by a gentleman calling himself 'Michael Rand', was later found to be so full of holes that it was finally rejected as a work of pure fiction, despite the great amount of detail employed by the author.

And so, for some years, the name of George Blake disappeared from the press. He was no longer 'news'. Some believed that he was no longer alive. He had, perhaps, been 'liquidated' by his former colleagues of the Soviet Secret Service.

Then came a surprise announcement. On 16 February 1970, the official Russian newspaper *Izvestia* carried a startling story. George Blake had been awarded the Order of Lenin and the Soviet Military Order of the Red Banner. The newspaper went on to describe Blake's career, how he had worked as a double agent since his release from internment in Korea. It stated that he gave accounts of various operations by members of the British Secret Service and also the American Central Intelligence Agency, and said that they not only spied on Communist countries but also on France, Sweden, West Germany and Japan as well as each other.

Quoting Blake, the article said that it was common for British agents to bug rooms and eavesdrop on conversations of Russian and East Berlin diplomats, while they also opened the 'diplomatic bags' of other nations. Blake took credit for having exposed the secret tunnel beneath Berlin which Western Intelligence services used to listen in to Communist communications.

In an amusing confession he stated that he had set himself out to subvert a 'Russian' woman, who turned out to be an American agent!

He accused the BBC and British journalists of organizing anti-Soviet campaigns and further declared that most of the members of British and Commonwealth trade conventions, together with seemingly innocent tourists, were in fact all spies. The list of these agents, he said, was known as 'the order book'.

When asked how he had borne his five years in gaol he said that he knew the risks he was taking before he was caught and felt that, 'in the end, I was convinced of the justness of my choice.'

And so, the man who had caused the death of many of his colleagues and had betrayed his country had a brief moment of glory and, thankfully, has since disappeared from history.

THE VEILED LADY

Agatha Christie

I had noticed that for some time Hercule Poirot had been growing increasingly dissatisfied and restless. We had had no interesting cases of late, nothing on which my little friend could exercise his keen wits and remarkable powers of deduction. This July morning he flung down the newspaper with an impatient '*Tchah!*'—a favourite exclamation of his which sounded exactly like a cat sneezing.

'They fear me, Hastings—the criminals of your England they fear me! When the cat is there, the little mice they come no more to the cheese!'

'I don't suppose the greater part of them even know of your existence,' I said, laughing.

Poirot looked at me reproachfully. He always imagines that the whole world is thinking and talking of Hercule Poirot. He had certainly made a name for himself in London, but I could hardly believe that his existence struck terror into the criminal world.

'What about that daylight robbery of jewels in Bond Street the other day?' I asked.

'A neat *coup*,' said Poirot approvingly, 'though not in my line. *Pas de finesse, seulement de l'audace!* A man with a loaded cane smashes the plate-glass window of a jeweller's shop and grabs a number of precious stones. Worthy citizens immediately seize him; a policeman arrives. He is caught red-handed with the jewels on him. He is marched off to the police station, and then it is discovered that the stones are paste. He has passed the real ones to a confederate—one of the aforementioned worthy citizens. He will go to prison—true; but when he comes out, there will be a nice little fortune awaiting him. Yes, not badly imagined. But I could do better than that. Sometimes, Hastings, I regret that I am of such a moral disposition. To work against the law, it would be pleasing, for a change.'

'Cheer up, Poirot. You know you are unique in your own line.'

'But what is there on hand in my own line?'

I picked up the paper. 'Here's an Englishman mysteriously done to death in Holland,' I said.

'They always say that—and later they find that he ate the tinned fish and that his death is perfectly natural.'

'Well, if you're determined to grouse!'

'*Tiens!*' said Poirot, who had strolled across to the window. 'Here in the street is what they call in novels a "heavily veiled lady". She mounts the steps; she rings the bell—she comes to consult us. Here is a possibility of something interesting. When one is as young and pretty as that one, one does not veil the face except for a big affair.'

A minute later our visitor was ushered in. As Poirot had said, she was indeed heavily veiled. It was impossible to distinguish her features until she raised her veil of black Spanish lace. Then I saw that Poirot's intuition had been right; the lady was extremely pretty, with fair hair and large blue eyes. From the costly simplicity of her attire, I deduced at once that she belonged to an upper stratum of society.

'Monsieur Poirot,' said the lady in a soft, musical voice, 'I am in great trouble. I can hardly believe that you can help me, but I have heard such wonderful things of you that I come literally as a last hope to beg you to do the impossible.'

'The impossible, it pleases me always,' said Poirot. 'Continue, I beg of you, Mademoiselle.'

Our fair guest hesitated.

'But you must be frank,' added Poirot. 'You must not leave me in the dark on any point.'

'I will trust you,' said the girl suddenly. 'You have heard of Lady Millicent Castle Vaughan?'

I looked up with keen interest. The announcement of Lady Millicent's engagement to the young Duke of Southshire had appeared a few days previously. She was, I knew, the fifth daughter of an impecunious Irish peer, and the Duke of Southshire was one of the best matches in England.

'I am Lady Millicent,' continued the girl. 'You may have read of my engagement. I should be one of the happiest girls alive, but oh, M. Poirot, I am in terrible trouble! There is a man, a horrible man—his name is Lavington; and he—I hardly know how to tell you. There was a letter I wrote—I was only sixteen at the time; and he—he——'

'A letter that you wrote to this Mr Lavington?'

'Oh *no*—not to him! To a young soldier—I was very fond of him— he was killed in the war.'

'I understand,' said Poirot kindly.

'It was a foolish letter, an indiscreet letter, but indeed, M. Poirot, nothing more. But there are phrases in it which—which might bear a different interpretation.'

'I see,' said Poirot. 'And this letter has come into the possession of Mr Lavington?'

'Yes, and he threatens, unless I pay him an enormous sum of money, a sum that it is quite impossible for me to raise, to send it to the Duke.'

'The dirty swine!' I exclaimed. 'I beg your pardon, Lady Millicent.'

'Would it not be wiser to confess all to your future husband?'

'I dare not, M. Poirot. The Duke is a very jealous man, suspicious and prone to believe the worst. I might as well break off my engagement at once.'

'Dear, dear,' said Poirot with an expressive grimace. 'And what do you want me to do, Milady?'

'I thought perhaps that I might ask Mr Lavington to call upon you. I would tell him that you were empowered by me to discuss the matter. Perhaps you could reduce his demands.'

'What sum does he mention?'

'Twenty thousand pounds—an impossibility. I doubt if I could raise even a thousand.'

'You might perhaps borrow the money on the prospect of your approaching marriage—but *eh bien*, it is repugnant to me that you should pay! No, the ingenuity of Hercule Poirot shall defeat your enemies! Send me this Mr Lavington. Is he likely to bring the letter with him?'

The girl shook her head.

'I do not think so. He is very cautious.'

'I suppose there is no doubt that he really has it?'

'He showed it to me when I went to his house.'

'You went to his house? That was very imprudent, Milady.'

'Was it? I was so desperate. I hoped my entreaties might move him.'

'Oh, *lá lá!* The Lavingtons of this world are not moved by entreaties! He would welcome them as showing how much importance you attached to the document. Where does he live, this fine gentleman?'

'At Buona Vista, Wimbledon. I went there after dark——' Poirot groaned. 'I declared that I would inform the police in the end, but he only laughed in a horrid, sneering manner. "By all means, my dear Lady Millicent, do so if you wish," he said.'

'Yes, it is hardly an affair for the police,' murmured Poirot.

'"But I think you will be wiser than that," he said. "See, here is your letter—in this little Chinese puzzle box!" He held it so that I could see. I tried to snatch at it, but he was too quick for me. With a horrid smile he folded it up and replaced it in the little wooden box. "It will be quite safe here, I assure you," he said, "and I keep the box itself in such a clever place that you would never find it." My eyes turned to the small wall safe, and he shook his head and laughed. "I have a better safe than that," he said. Oh, he was odious! Do you think you can help me?'

'Have faith in Papa Poirot. I will find a way.'

These reassurances were all very well, I thought, as Poirot gallantly ushered his fair client down the stairs, but it seemed to me that we had a tough nut to crack. I said as much to Poirot when he returned. He nodded ruefully.

'Yes—the solution does not leap to the eye. He has the whip hand, this M. Lavington. For the moment I do not see how we are to circumvent him.'

Mr Lavington duly called on us that afternoon. Lady Millicent had spoken truly when she described him as an odious man. I felt a positive tingling in the end of my boot, so keen was I to kick him down the stairs.

He was blustering and overbearing in manner, laughed Poirot's gentle suggestions to scorn, and generally showed himself as master of the situation. I could not help feeling that Poirot was hardly appearing at his best. He looked discouraged and crestfallen.

'Well, gentlemen,' said Lavington, as he took up his hat, 'we don't seem to be getting much farther. The case stands like this: I'll let the Lady Millicent off cheap, as she is such a charming young lady. We'll say eighteen thousand. I'm off to Paris today—a little piece of business to attend to over there. I shall be back on Tuesday. Unless the money is paid by Tuesday evening, the letter goes to the Duke. Don't tell me Lady Millicent can't raise the money. Some of her gentlemen friends would be only too willing to oblige such a pretty woman with a loan— if she goes about it the right way.'

I took a step forward, but Lavington had wheeled out of the room as he finished his sentence.

'My God!' I cried. 'Something has got to be done. You seem to be taking this lying down, Poirot.'

'You have an excellent heart, my friend—but your grey cells are in a deplorable condition. I have no wish to impress Mr Lavington with my capabilities. The more pusillanimous he thinks me, the better.'

'Why?'

'It is curious,' murmured Poirot reminiscently, 'that I should have uttered a wish to work against the law just before Lady Millicent arrived!'

'You are going to burgle his house while he is away?' I gasped.

'Sometimes, Hastings, your mental processes are amazingly quick.'

'Suppose he takes the letter with him?'

Poirot shook his head. 'That is very unlikely. He has evidently a hiding-place in his house that he fancies to be impregnable.'

'When do we—er—do the deed?'

'Tomorrow night. We will start from here about eleven o'clock.'

At the time appointed I was ready to set off. I had donned a dark suit and a soft dark hat. Poirot beamed kindly on me.

'You have dressed the part, I see,' he observed. 'Come, let us take

41

the underground to Wimbledon.'

'Aren't we going to take anything with us? Tools to break in with?'

'My dear Hastings, Hercule Poirot does not adopt such crude methods.'

It was midnight when we entered the small suburban garden of Buona Vista. The house was dark and silent. Poirot went straight to a window at the back of the house, raised the sash noiselessly and bade me enter.

'How did you know this window would be open?' I whispered, for really it seemed uncanny.

'Because I sawed through the catch this morning.'

'What?'

'But yes, it was most simple. I called, presented a fictitious card and one of Inspector Japp's official ones. I said I had been sent, recommended by Scotland Yard, to attend to some burglar-proof fastenings that Mr Lavington wanted fixed while he was away. The housekeeper welcomed me with enthusiasm. It seems they have had two attempted burglaries here lately—evidently our little idea has occurred to other clients of Mr Lavington's—with nothing of value taken. I examined all the windows, made my little arrangement, forbade the servants to touch the windows until tomorrow, as they were electrically connected up, and withdrew gracefully.'

'Really, Poirot, you are wonderful.'

'*Mon ami*, it was of the simplest. Now, to work! The servants sleep at the top of the house, so we will run little risk of disturbing them.'

'I presume the safe is built into the wall somewhere?'

'Safe? Fiddlesticks! There is no safe. Mr Lavington is an intelligent man. You will see, he will have devised a hiding-place much more intelligent than a safe. A safe is the first thing everyone looks for.'

Whereupon we began a systematic search. But after several hours' ransacking of the house, our search had been unavailing. I saw symptoms of anger gathering on Poirot's face.

'*Ah, sapristi*, is Hercule Poirot to be beaten? Never! Let us be calm. Let us reflect. Let us reason. Let us—*enfin!*—employ our little grey cells!'

He paused for some moments, bending his brows in concentration; then the green light I knew so well stole into his eyes.

'I have been an imbecile! The kitchen!'

'The kitchen,' I cried. 'But that's impossible. The servants!'

'Exactly. Just what ninety-nine people out of a hundred would say! And for that very reason the kitchen is the ideal place to choose. It is full of various homely objects. *En avant*, to the kitchen!'

I followed him, completely sceptical, and watched while he dived into bread bins, tapped saucepans and put his head into the gas oven. In the end, tired of watching him, I strolled back to the study. I was convinced that there, and there only, would we find the *cache*. I made a further minute search, noted that it was now a quarter past four and that therefore it would soon be growing light, and then went back to the kitchen regions.

To my utter amazement, Poirot was now standing right inside the coal bin, to the utter ruin of his neat light suit. He made a grimace.

'But yes, my friend, it is against all my instincts so to ruin my appearance, but what will you?'

'Lavington can't have buried it under the coal!'

'If you would use your eyes, you would see that it is not the coal that I examine.'

I then saw that on a shelf behind the coal bunker some logs of wood were piled. Poirot was dextrously taking them down one by one. Suddenly he uttered a low exclamation.

'Your knife, Hastings!'

I handed it to him. He appeared to insert it in the wood, and suddenly the log split in two. It had been neatly sawed in half and a cavity hollowed out in the centre. From this cavity Poirot took a little wooden box of Chinese make.

'Well done!' I cried.

'Gently, Hastings! Do not raise your voice too much. Come, let us be off before the daylight is upon us.'

Slipping the box into his pocket, he leaped lightly out of the coal bunker, and brushed himself down as well as he could. After leaving the house by the same way as we had entered, we walked rapidly in the direction of London.

'But what an extraordinary place!' I expostulated. 'Anyone might have used the log.'

'In *July*, Hastings? And it was at the bottom of the pile—a very ingenious hiding-place. Ah, here is a taxi! Now for home, a wash and a refreshing sleep.'

'I handed my knife to Poirot. He appeared to insert it in the wood, and suddenly
the log split in two. It had been neatly sawed in half . . .'

After the excitement of the night, I slept late. When I finally strolled into our sitting-room just before twelve o'clock, I was surprised to see Poirot, leaning back in an armchair, the Chinese box open beside him, calmly reading the letter he had taken from it.

He smiled at me affectionately, and tapped the sheet he held.

'She was right, the Lady Millicent—never would the Duke have pardoned this letter! It contains some of the most extravagant terms of affection I have ever come across.'

'Really, Poirot,' I said, 'I don't think you should have read the letter. That sort of thing isn't done.'

'It is done by Hercule Poirot,' replied my friend imperturbably.

'And another thing,' I said. 'I don't think using Japp's official card yesterday was quite playing the game.'

'But I was not playing a game, Hastings. I was conducting a case.'

I shrugged—one can't argue with a point of view.

'A step on the stairs,' said Poirot. 'That will be Lady Millicent.'

Our fair client came in with an anxious expression on her face which changed to one of delight on seeing the letter and box which Poirot held up.

'Oh, M. Poirot, how wonderful of you! How did you do it?'

'By rather reprehensible methods, Milady. But Mr Lavington will not prosecute. This is your letter, is it not?'

She glanced through it.

'Yes. Oh, how can I ever thank you! You are a wonderful, wonderful man. Where was it hidden?'

Poirot told her.

'How very clever of you!' She took up the small box from the table. 'I shall keep this as a souvenir.'

'I had hoped, Milady, that you would permit me to keep it—also as a souvenir.'

'I hope to send you a better souvenir than that—on my wedding day. You shall not find me ungrateful, M. Poirot.'

'The pleasure of doing you a service will be more to me than a cheque —so you permit that I retain the box.'

'Oh no, M. Poirot, I simply must have that,' she cried laughingly.

She stretched out her hand, but Poirot's closed over it. 'I think not.' His voice had changed.

'What do you mean?' Her voice seemed to have grown sharper.

'At any rate, permit me to abstract its further contents. You observe that the original cavity has been reduced by half. In the top half, the compromising letter; in the bottom——'

He made a nimble gesture, then held out his hand. On the palm were four large glittering stones, and two big milky-white pearls.

'The jewels stolen in Bond Street the other day, I rather fancy,' murmured Poirot. 'Japp will tell us.'

To my utter amazement Japp himself stepped out of Poirot's bed-room.

'An old friend of yours, I believe,' said Poirot politely to Lady Millicent.

'Nabbed, by the Lord!' said Lady Millicent, with a complete change of manner. 'You nippy old devil!' She looked at Poirot with almost affectionate awe.

'Well, Gertie, my dear,' said Japp, 'the game's up this time—fancy seeing you again so soon! We've got your pal, too, the gentleman who called here the other day *calling himself* Lavington. As for Lavington himself, alias Croker, alias Reed, I wonder which of the gang it was who stuck a knife into him the other day in Holland? Thought he'd got the goods with him, didn't you? And he hadn't. He double-crossed you properly—hid 'em in his own house. You had two fellows looking for them, and then you tackled M. Poirot here, and by a piece of amazing luck he found them.'

'You do like talking, don't you?' said the late Lady Millicent. 'Easy there, now. I'll go quietly. You can't say that I'm not the perfect lady. *Ta-ta*, all!'

'The shoes were wrong,' said Poirot dreamily, while I was still too stupefied to speak. 'I have made my little observations of your English nation, and a lady, a born lady, is always particular about her shoes. She may have shabby clothes, but she will be well shod. Now, this Lady Millicent had smart, expensive clothes, and cheap shoes. It was not likely that either you or I should have seen the real Lady Millicent; she has been very little in London, and this girl had a certain superficial resemblance which would pass well enough. As I say, the shoes first awakened my suspicions, and then her story—and her veil—were a little melodramatic, eh? The Chinese box with a bogus compromising letter in the top must have been known to all the gang, but the log of wood was the late Mr Lavington's own idea. *Eh, par exemple*, Hastings, I hope you will not again wound my feelings as you did yesterday by saying that I am unknown to the criminal classes. *Ma foi*, they even employ me when they themselves fail!'

THE QUEEN'S SUPER-SPY

Avis Murton Carter

A young-looking man in his mid-thirties was pacing up and down an elaborately furnished room. His face showed his anxiety. The concern was understandable, for he had been summoned by England's greatest statesmen, William Cecil, Lord Burghley. This famous minister's care for his beloved Queen Elizabeth, helped by the many spies he employed, had saved her from assassination—and his country from war—on several occasions.

The assassin's dagger had even been directed against Burghley in several instances, too, but each time he had been forewarned by one of his spies and had escaped harm.

And now this great man—the most powerful in England—had sent for the youngster. It was obviously on a matter of national importance, for Burghley was not one for idle gossip. When his visitor was beginning to wonder whether he had been forgotten, a door opened and an attendant stood in the opening.

'Sir Francis Walsingham,' he said with a bow. 'My Lord Burghley will see you now.'

Walsingham entered. Before him stood a tall, elegant, long-bearded

man, his back to a large fireplace. 'Good day to you, Sir Francis. John'—
this to the attendant—'bring the wine to this table and then leave us.
Stand on duty outside to see that no one interrupts us until we have concluded our discussion.'

When both men were seated, it did not take Burghley long to give
the reason for this summons. Looking down at a piece of parchment in
his hand, he said, 'In the first place, Sir Francis, I must tell you that her
majesty and I were delighted with your activities abroad on our behalf.
It was I, you may recall, who sent you to the Court of France as our
ambassador and I never had cause to regret that appointment. May I also
add, in her majesty's own words, that you showed "great fidelity, dili-
gence and caution". Many of the reports you sent back to use have
proved of great use in thwarting the many plots against her majesty's
life.'

He paused for a moment, sipped his wine and looked down at his
notes. 'Now then, let me see. You were born in Chislehurst in Kent in
1536 and have been in the royal service since her majesty's accession in
1558. That means that you have served us loyally for fifteen years and
have now reached, er, thirty-seven years of age. But enough of that.
Let me come to the real reason for summoning you here.'

He stopped again and then said, slowly, 'I am going to suggest, Sir
Francis, that you undertake special duties—duties, I might add, that are
essential to the well-being of this realm.

'As you know, for many years past I have controlled a system of
espionage, by means of my organization known as the "Defence of the
State". It is a system that I have built up during the whole of her
majesty's reign. Thanks to a number of men, both base-born and in
high places, I have been kept informed of threats against the Queen's
life and, God be praised, have thwarted them.'

He took another sip of wine and looked hard at the man before him,
who was following every word with the greatest interest.

'Now then. From what I have read into your reports from abroad
when you were our ambassador, and from many things I have noticed
since, you also seem to have a liking for such counter-spy work. Indeed,
like myself, you consider it a duty and a privilege to root out these
cursed traitors that constantly threaten the peace of our realm. seize
them and, if necessary, see that they do no more harm. Indeed, I recall

49

how you employed several agents of your own.

'My suggestion is this. Busy as I am with constant affairs of state I would like you, Sir Francis, to take over complete control of all our agents, at home and abroad. You need only consult me when you feel it necessary to do so. If you agree to this, I am empowered to tell you that within a few days you will attend upon her majesty to be sworn in as a member of her Privy Council. Well then, what do you say?'

The other did not hesitate. He rose, then knelt at the feet of Lord Burghley. 'Sir, I thank you,' he said. 'This is something which I have always desired. You have my solemn word that, day and night, I will not cease in my endeavours to preserve her majesty and to thwart all wrong-doers who would threaten her sacred life, and the security and safety of this realm.'

Walsingham was made Principal Secretary to the Council and both the Queen and Burghley allowed him a free hand to work as he wished. It was not long before he had redesigned the somewhat rough and ready system that had served Burghley so well. He fully realized—as indeed he had realized for some time—the tremendous importance of a system that would stop any attempt on the Queen's life before it was fully matured. It was to that work that he was to devote the rest of his life. Had Elizabeth been assassinated, civil war between Protestant and Catholic might well have broken out, foreign powers would have added their support and the whole of the country would not only have become a battlefield but even, perhaps, a vassal of another and more powerful European country.

Before Walsingham's preferment, there had been a serious plot to assassinate Queen Elizabeth, place Mary, Queen of Scots on the throne and restore the Catholic religion in England. This was in 1571. The chief agent was Robert Ridolfi, a Florentine banker living in London. His plan, once Elizabeth was dead and Mary established on the throne, was to have her marry the Catholic Duke of Norfolk. In this he was backed by the Bishop of Ross and by many of England's leading Catholics.

During April 1571 Charles Bailly, a servant of the Queen of Scots acting as a messenger for Ridolfi, was arrested at Dover on Burghley's orders. A packet of letters was discovered on him which, being in cipher, created suspicion. The Bishop of Ross managed to obtain them from Lord Cobham, in whose hands they were, saying he wished to study them before they were sent to the Council. He then cleverly substituted others in a similar cipher, but quite innocent in context.

But Bailly was sent to the Tower and confessed on the rack that he had received the letters from Ridolfi. Although the Bishop of Ross was arrested and Mary—who had then been in captivity for three years—was cross-examined, nothing definite was discovered.

By September the whole plot was revealed. Several of the leading conspirators, including the bishop and the Earls of Arundel and Southampton, were arrested. The bishop made a full confession and Norfolk, as the centre of the plot, was sent to the Tower. Attempts to rescue him caused a bill to be passed in parliament. It declared:

'That if any person should go about to deliver any man imprisoned upon the Queen's writ for treason, or suspicion of treason, before his arraignment, the said person should forfeit his life and state, and be imprisoned during the Queen's pleasure. If arraigned, he should incur the penalty of death; if condemned, the penalty of high treason.'

To underline the sincerity of parliament, Norfolk was beheaded on Forest Hill in June 1572.

That plot had begun only a year before Walsingham took office. It had been thwarted, but much luck had been involved. Walsingham now set out to create a better organized system of espionage, and soon had spies working on his behalf nearly everywhere. What he developed then became, in effect, the basis of the British Secret Service of today.

Yet there was nothing new about the use of spies. The first recorded use of spies was by Moses and Joshua in the fifteenth century BC, whilst many of the great nations of those days used them to advantage, including the Medes, the Persians and the Syrians.

The first recorded use of spies in Britain was during the time of Julius Caesar. He briefly invaded England in 55 BC and, when he left, some of the Belgae tribe stayed on to keep him informed of what was happening. The following year, on their advice, he returned, and although he again left soon afterwards, Roman merchants remained behind to help create a new type of civilization in England.

The story of King Alfred who, during the ninth century, passed himself off as a minstrel in the enemy camp, is well known. He sang Danish ballads and listened carefully as he did so to what was being said by the invaders.

Another monarch who used espionage to his advantage was William of Normandy. He had planted agents in England and they told him the exact time to invade—when King Harold and his warriors were tramping north to repel Harald Hardrada at Stamford Bridge. William was able to land his own armies, unopposed, and finally overcame the tired and depleted Saxon army that had hastened south again at the news of his arrival. Had he not been so advised, it is possible that the warriors led by Harold would have had little difficulty in throwing back the Norman invaders. What a change of direction English history would have taken had this happened! Had it not been for his spies, William might probably have never been able to call himself 'the Conqueror'.

Spying, in various forms, was used by almost all the monarchs of England from that time on, ambassadors in particular being valuable sources of information to the king or queen of the time. But it was Walsingham who was mainly responsible for reorganizing and coordinating the whole system so that future monarchs had an espionage system on which they could depend. Indeed, at the outbreak of both world wars, it was soon realized that the British agents were far superior to their German counterparts and it is intriguing to think that this success was due to an almost unknown man—Sir Francis Walsingham—who had lived four centuries earlier.

Much of Walsingham's work was connected with the captive Mary, Queen of Scots. She was to spend nineteen years in captivity in various castles throughout Britain, and hardly a month passed without some attempt to rescue her. Many were inspired by Philip II of Spain, whose marriage to Mary Tudor, and a divine sense of purpose, gave him an interest in restoring a Catholic to the English throne.

One of these conspiracies was headed by Thomas Throckmorton. The year was 1583 and in the ten years since he had taken over command of the Secret Service, Walsingham had greatly extended the scope of the service. Now there was scarcely a noble household in England, Scotland, Spain or France that did not have one of his agents working within it in some capacity. He even had his spies amongst the Jesuits, the

The fourth time he was racked Throckmorton made a full confession.

most active Catholic agents acting on behalf of Philip and Mary.

He intercepted a letter written to the Scottish Queen by a Catholic agent named Morgan, stating that the Duke of Guise was ready to invade in the south of England. Throckmorton, mentioned in the letter, was immediately arrested and racked three times without effect. On the fourth occasion, however, he made a full confession, stating that the Spanish ambassador Mendoza was in the plot. When Throckmorton's rooms were searched, two trunks were found in which were two catalogues, one of the chief ports and the other of the principal Romanists in the kingdom. They were due to be passed on to Mendoza. Although Mendoza denied all the charges, he was ordered to withdraw from England and his accomplice, Throckmorton, was hanged.

Another important plot followed three years later, and it became known as the Babington Conspiracy. It began with Anthony Babington, 'a young man of family and fortune', and a Jesuit priest named John Ballard. Several conspirators joined them and all were sworn to remove Elizabeth, either by shooting or stabbing her when she was alone or only in the company of her ladies-in-waiting.

Babington, who was fascinated by the charms of the Queen of Scots, led the conspirators. Mainly gentlemen of position, they chose six of their number to commit the crime and were very confident of success, not realizing that Walsingham's agents were already in on the secret.

Unfortunately for Queen Mary, Babington revealed the whole plot to her in a letter which, like all the rest, passed through Walsingham's hands. The way he did this was unusual. At the time, Mary was kept close prisoner at Chartley and each week a brewer from Burton would bring a barrel of beer for her household. And each week the brewer hid a waterproof packet in the beer and the Queen's reply would come out of Chartley in the empty barrel. Neither she nor Babington, of course, knew that the brewer was acting under Walsingham's orders and that a copy of every letter to and from the Queen was read by the master-spy.

In one letter Mary urged Babington to act without delay. This ultimately sealed her fate. Ballard was arrested on 4 August 1586 and Babington, with four others, was taken ten days later in a barn at Harrow. Meanwhile, Mary had been invited to join a hunting party and while she was out of her room it was searched. Many incriminating papers and letters were found, and from then on she was a doomed woman. Some even claimed that the whole affair had been staged by Walsingham.

Mary was sent to Fotheringay Castle in Nottinghamshire, tried, and found guilty of treason. On 8 February 1587, she was beheaded.

Her death stirred Philip of Spain to action. For some time he had been building a vast fleet of ships with which to invade England, a fact well known to Walsingham. Indeed, many of his spies were actually helping to build the ships, posing as carpenters, rope-makers and so on.

He took on even more agents. One of them was recruited in an unusual way. He was Sir Edward Stafford, the English ambassador in Paris. But he was a Catholic, and a great supporter of the Queen of Scots, and one of Walsingham's agents discovered that he was not only in touch with other Catholics in England but was also in the pay of Philip. Instead of having him brought back to England and executed as a traitor, Walsingham persuaded Stafford to become a 'double agent'— the first important one in history. From then on Stafford not only sent reports to Philip that were originally the work of Walsingham, but he and his staff also collected information from both France and Spain and sent it back to London for Walsingham to digest.

The effort to launch his Armada, the greatest collection of ships the world had ever seen, used up all Philip's resources—a fact his spies were quick to report to Walsingham. They also reported that the very size of the galleons was against them for their guns were perched so high that they would fire above the lower-lying English ships. They were unwieldy too; while the English craft were generally smaller, they were much faster. Indeed, when the fighting began on 31 July 1588, this soon became obvious. At one stage the *Ark*, when surrounded by a number of galleons, slipped between them so fast that one Spaniard said, 'Though the swiftest ships in the whole Armada pursued her, they seemed at comparison to be at anchor.'

The Armada consisted of 129 vessels carrying 8,000 sailors, 20,000 soldiers, 600 priests and a large number of slaves of various nations, who rowed the galleys. The fleet carried enough provisions to feed the would-be invaders for a year.

By comparison the English ships had ammunition for only two days' fighting and provisions for less than a week. When Drake's fire-ships had dislodged the Spanish fleet from their anchorage at Calais, the English were forced to borrow shot and powder from each other. It was then that huge waves and shrieking winds completed the destruction of what had been called the 'Invincible Armada'. Yet while the fighting was still in progress, wild rumours were sweeping across Europe. Rome and Madrid were thrilled to hear of a great Spanish victory off Newcastle, in which forty English ships had been sunk; Drake had been captured and it was reliably stated that 8,000 Spaniards had landed near Plymouth.

The truth, when it came out, must have been even more distressing. Only a few galleons, shattered by wind and weather, finally limped home into Spanish harbours. The words 'He blew with His winds and they were scattered' was engraved on medals and on the hearts of the English people. Praise was showered on the great Tudor sea captains—Howard, Drake, Hawkins and the rest. Yet few knew how much was due to Walsingham; he had known exactly when the Armada was to sail, how the ships would be built and provisioned, and the strengths and weaknesses of each one.

By then he was a sick man, however, and two years later he died. His character was such that with every opportunity of amassing a fortune for himself, he died so poor that there was barely enough money to pay for his burial. At the time the Queen herself owed him well over £5,000!

A seventeenth-century biographer said of him: 'His head was so strong that he could look into the depths of men and business, and dive into the whirlpools of state. Dextrous he was in finding a secret; close in keeping it. His conversation was insinuating and reserved; he saw every man, and none saw him.'

THE SIGNALMAN

Charles Dickens

'Halloa! Below there!'

When he heard a voice thus calling to him, he was standing at the door of his box, with a flag in his hand, furled round its short pole. One would have thought, considering the nature of the ground, that he could not have doubted from what quarter the voice came; but instead of looking up to where I stood on the top of the steep cutting nearly over his head, he turned himself about, and looked down the line. There was something remarkable in his manner of doing so, though I could not have said for my life what. But I know it was remarkable enough to attract my notice, even though his figure was foreshortened and shadowed, down in the deep trench, and mine was high above him, so steeped in the glow of an angry sunset that I had shaded my eyes with my hand before I saw him at all.

'Halloa! Below!'

From looking down the line, he turned himself about again, and, raising his eyes, saw my figure high above him.

'Is there any path by which I can come down and speak to you?'

He looked up at me without replying, and I looked down at him without pressing him too soon with a repetition of my idle question. Just then there came a vague vibration in the earth and air, quickly changing into a violent pulsation, and an oncoming rush that caused me to start back, as though it had force to draw me down. When such vapour as rose to my height from this rapid train had passed me, and was skimming away over the landscape, I looked down again, and saw him refurling the flag he had shown while the train went by.

I repeated my inquiry. After a pause, during which he seemed to regard me with fixed attention, he motioned with his rolled-up flag towards a point on my level, some two or three hundred yards distant. I called down to him, 'All right!' and made for that point. There, by dint of looking closely about me, I found a rough zigzag descending path notched out, which I followed.

The cutting was extremely deep and unusually precipitate. It was made through a clammy stone that became oozier and wetter as I went down. For these reasons, I found the way long enough to give me time to recall a singular air of reluctance or compulsion with which he had pointed out the path.

When I came down low enough upon the zigzag descent to see him again, I saw that he was standing between the rails on the way by which the train had lately passed, in an attitude as if he were waiting for me to appear. He had his left hand at his chin, and that left elbow rested on his right hand, crossed over his breast. His attitude was one of such expectation and watchfulness that I stopped a moment, wondering at it.

I resumed my downward way, and stepping out upon the level of the railroad, and drawing nearer to him, saw that he was a dark sallow man, with a dark beard and rather heavy eyebrows. His post was in as solitary and dismal a place as ever I saw. On either side, a dripping-wet wall of jagged stone, excluding all view but a strip of sky; the perspective one way only a crooked prolongation of this great dungeon; the shorter perspective in the other direction terminating in a gloomy red light, and the gloomier entrance to a black tunnel, in whose massive architecture there was a barbarous, depressing and forbidding air. So little sunlight ever found its way to this spot that it had an earthy, deadly smell; and so much cold wind rushed through it that it struck chill to me, as if I had left the natural world.

Before he stirred, I was near enough to him to have touched him.

Not even then removing his eyes from mine, he stepped back one step, and lifted his hand.

This was a lonesome post to occupy (I said), and it had riveted my attention when I looked down from up yonder. A visitor was a rarity, I should suppose; not an unwelcome rarity, I hoped? In me, he merely saw a man who had been shut up within narrow limits all his life, and who, being at last set free, had a newly-awakened interest in these great works. To such purpose I spoke to him; but I am far from sure of the terms I used; for, besides that I am not happy in opening any conversation, there was something in the man that daunted me.

He directed a most curious look towards the red light near the tunnel's mouth, and looked all about it, as if something were missing from it, and then looked at me.

That light was part of his charge? Was it not?

He answered in a low voice, 'Don't you know it is?'

The monstrous thought came into my mind, as I perused the fixed eyes and the saturnine face, that this was a spirit, not a man. I have speculated since, whether there may have been infection in his mind.

In my turn I stepped back. But in making the action, I detected in his eyes some latent fear of me. This put the monstrous thought to flight.

'You look at me,' I said, forcing a smile, 'as if you had a dread of me.'

'I was doubtful,' he returned, 'whether I had seen you before.'

'Where?'

He pointed to the red light he had looked at.

'There?' I said.

Intently watchful of me, he replied (but without sound), 'Yes.'

'My good fellow, what should I do there? However, be that as it may, I never was there, you may swear.'

'I think I may,' he rejoined. 'Yes; I am sure I may.'

His manner cleared, like my own. He replied to my remarks with readiness, and in well-chosen words. Had he much to do there? Yes; that was to say, he had enough responsibility to bear; but exactness and watchfulness were what was required of him, and of actual work—manual labour—he had next to none. To change that signal, to trim those lights, and to turn this iron handle now and then, was all he had to under that head.

Regarding those many long and lonely hours of which I seemed to make so much, he could only say that the routine of his life had shaped itself into that form, and he had grown used to it. He had taught himself a language down here—if only to know it by sight, and to have formed his own crude ideas of its pronunciation, could be called learning it. He had also worked at fractions and decimals, and tried a little algebra; but he was, and had been as a boy, a poor hand at figures. Was it necessary for him when on duty always to remain in that channel of damp air, and could he never rise into the sunshine from between those high stone walls? Why, that depended upon times and circumstances. Under some conditions there would be less upon the line than under others, and the same held good as to certain hours of the day and night. In bright weather, he did choose occasions for getting a little above those lower shadows; but, being at all times liable to be called by his electric bell, and at such times listening for it with redoubled anxiety, the relief was less than I would suppose.

He took me into his box, where there was a fire, a desk for an official book in which he had to make certain entries, a telegraphic instrument with its dial, face, and needles, and the little bell of which he had spoken. On my trusting that he would excuse the remark that he had been well educated, and (I hoped I might say without offence) perhaps educated above that station, he observed that instances of slight incongruity in such wise would rarely be found wanting among large bodies of men; that he had heard it was so in workhouses, in the police force, even in that last desperate resource, the army; and that he knew it was so, more or less, in any great railway staff. He had been, when young (if I could believe it, sitting in that hut—he scarcely could), a student of natural philosophy, and had attended lectures; but he had run wild, misused his opportunities, gone down, and never risen again. He had no complaint to offer about that. He had made his bed, and he lay upon it. It was far too late to make another.

All that I have here condensed he said in a quiet manner, with his grave dark regards divided between me and the fire. He threw in the word 'sir' from time to time, and especially when he referred to his youth—as though to request me to understand that he claimed to be nothing but what I found him. He was several times interrupted by the little bell, and had to read off messages and send replies. Once he had to stand without the door, and display a flag as a train passed, and make some verbal communication to the driver. In the discharge of his duties, I observed him to be remarkably exact and vigilant, breaking off his discourse at a syllable, and remaining silent until what he had to do was done.

In a word, I should have set this man down as one of the safest of men to be employed in that capacity, but for the circumstance that while he was speaking to me he twice broke off with a fallen colour, turned his face towards the little bell when it did *not* ring, opened the door of the hut (which was kept shut to exclude the unhealthy damp), and looked out towards the red light near the mouth of the tunnel. On both of those occasions he came back to the fire with the inexplicable air upon him which I had remarked, without being able to define, when we were so far asunder.

Said I, when I rose to leave him, 'You almost make me think that I have met with a contented man.'

(I am afraid I must acknowledge that I said it to lead him on.)

'I believe I used to be so,' he rejoined, in the low voice in which he had first spoken; 'but I am troubled, sir, I am troubled.'

He would have recalled the words if he could. He had said them, however, and I took them up quickly.

'With what? What is your trouble?'

'It is very difficult to impart, sir. It is very, very difficult to speak of. If ever you make me another visit, I will try to tell you.'

'But I expressly intend to make you another visit. Say, when shall it be?'

'I go off early in the morning, and I shall be on again at ten tomorrow night, sir.'

'I will come at eleven.'

He thanked me, and went out at the door with me. 'I'll show my white light, sir,' he said in his peculiar low voice, 'till you have found the way up. When you have found it, don't call out! And when you are at the top, don't call out!'

His manner seemed to make the place strike colder to me, but I said no more than 'Very well.'

'And when you come down tomorrow night, don't call out! Let me ask you a parting question. What made you cry, "Halloa! Below there!" tonight?'

'Heaven knows,' said I, 'I cried something to that effect——'

'Not to that effect, sir. Those were the very words. I know them well.'

'Admit those were the very words. I said them, no doubt, because I saw you below.'

'For no other reason?'

'What other reason could I possibly have?'

'You have no feeling that they were conveyed to you in any supernatural way?'

'No.'

He wished me good-night, and held up his light. I walked by the side of the down line of rails (with a very disagreeable sensation of a train coming behind me) until I found the path. It was easier to mount than to descend, and I got back to my inn without any adventure.

Punctual to my appointment, I placed my foot on the first notch of the zigzag next night as the distant clocks were striking eleven. He was waiting for me at the bottom, with his white light on. 'I have not called out,' I said, when we came close together; 'may I speak now?' 'By all means, sir.' 'Good-night, then, and here's my hand.' 'Good-night, sir, and here's mine.' With that we walked side by side to his box, entered it, closed the door, and sat down by the fire.

'I have made up my mind, sir,' he began bending forward as soon as we were seated, and speaking in a tone but a little above a whisper, 'that you shall not have to ask me twice what troubles me. I took you for someone else yesterday evening. That troubles me.'

'That mistake?'

'No. That someone else.'

'Who is it?'

'I don't know.'

'Like me?'

'I don't know. I never saw the face. The left arm is across the face, and the right arm is waved—violently waved. This way.'

I followed his action with my eyes, and it was the action of an arm gesticulating, with the utmost passion and vehemence, 'For God's sake, clear the way!'

'One moonlit night,' said the man, 'I was sitting here, when I heard a voice cry, "Halloa! Below there!" I started up, looked from that door, and saw this someone else standing by the red light near the tunnel, waving as I just now showed you. The voice seemed hoarse with shouting, and it cried, "Look out! Look out!" And then again, "Halloa! Below there! Look out!" I caught up my lamp, turned it on red, and ran towards the figure, calling, "What's wrong? What has happened? Where?" It stood just outside the blackness of the tunnel. I advanced so close upon it that I wondered at its keeping the sleeve across its eyes. I ran right up at it, and had my hand stretched out to pull the sleeve away, when it was gone.'

'Into the tunnel?' said I.

'No. I ran on into the tunnel, five hundred yards. I stopped, and held my lamp above my head, and saw the figures of the measured distance, and saw the wet stains stealing down the walls and trickling through the arch. I ran out again faster than I had run in (for I had a mortal abhorrence of the place upon me), and I looked all round the red light with my own red light, and I went up the iron ladder to the gallery atop of it, and I came down again, and ran back here. I telegraphed both ways, "An alarm has been given. Is anything wrong?" The answer came back, both ways, "All well".'

Resisting the slow touch of a frozen finger tracing out my spine, I showed him how that this figure must be a deception of his sense of sight; and how that figures, originating in disease of the delicate nerves that minister to the functions of the eye, were known to have often troubled patients, some of whom had become conscious of the nature of their affliction, and had even proved it by experiments upon themselves. 'As to an imaginary cry,' said I, 'do but listen for a moment to the wind in this unnatural valley while we speak so low, and to the wild harp it makes of the telegraph wires.'

That was all very well, he returned, after we had sat listening for a while, and he ought to know something of the wind and the wires—he who so often passed long winter nights there, alone and watching. But he would beg to remark that he had not finished.

I asked his pardon, and he slowly added these words, touching my arm: 'Within six hours after the appearance, the memorable accident on this line happened, and within ten hours the dead and wounded were brought along the tunnel over the spot where the figure had stood.'

A disagreeable shudder crept over me, but I did my best against it. It was not to be denied, I rejoined, that this was a remarkable coincidence, calculated deeply to impress his mind. But it was unquestionable that remarkable coincidences did continually occur, and they must be taken into account in dealing with such a subject. Though to be sure I must admit, I added (for I thought I saw that he was going to bring the objection to bear upon me), men of common sense did not allow much for coincidences in making the ordinary calculations of life.

He again begged to remark that he had not finished.

I again begged his pardon for being betrayed into interruptions.

'This,' he said, again laying his hand upon my arm, and glancing over his shoulder with hollow eyes, 'was just a year ago. Six or seven months passed, and I had recovered from the surprise and shock, when one morning, as the day was breaking, I, standing at the door, looked towards the red light, and saw the spectre again.' He stopped, with a fixed look at me.

'Did it cry out?'

'No. It was silent.'

'Did it wave its arm?'

'No. It leaned against the shaft of the light with both hands before the face. Like this.'

Once more I followed his action with my eyes. It was an action of mourning. I have seen such an attitude on stone figures on tombs.

'Did you go up to it?'

'I came in and sat down, partly to collect my thoughts, partly because it had turned me faint. When I went to the door again, daylight was above me, and the ghost was gone.'

'But nothing followed? Nothing came of this?'

He touched me on the arm with his forefinger twice or thrice, giving a ghastly nod each time.

'That very day, as a train came out of the tunnel, I noticed, at a carriage window on my side, what looked like a confusion of hands and heads, and something waved. I saw it just in time to signal the driver "Stop!" He shut off, and put his brake on, but the train drifted past here a hundred and fifty yards or more. I ran after it, and, as I went along, heard terrible screams and cries. A beautiful young lady had died instantaneously in one of the compartments, and was brought in here, and

'He touched me on the arm twice or thrice, giving a ghastly nod each time.'

65

laid down on this floor between us.'

Involuntarily I pushed my chair back, as I looked from the boards at which he pointed to himself.

'True, sir. True. Precisely as it happened, so I tell it you.'

I could think of nothing to say, to any purpose, and my mouth was very dry. The wind and the wires took up the story with a long lamenting wail.

He resumed, 'Now, sir, mark this, and judge how my mind is troubled. The spectre came back a week ago. Ever since, it has been there, now and again, by fits and starts.'

'At the light?'

'At the danger-light.'

'What does it seem to do?'

He repeated, if possible with increased passion and vehemence, that former gesticulation of 'For God's sake, clear the way!'

Then he went on. 'I have no peace or rest for it. It calls to me, for many minutes together, in an agonized manner, "Below there! Look out! Look out!" It stands waving to me. It rings my little bell——'

I caught at that. 'Did it ring your bell yesterday evening when I was here, and you went to the door?'

'Twice.'

'Why, see,' said I, 'how your imagination misleads you. My eyes were on the bell, and my ears were open to the bell, and if I am a living man, it did *not* ring at those times. No, nor at any other time, except when it was rung in the natural course of physical things by the station communicating with you.'

He shook his head. 'I have never made a mistake as to that yet, sir. I have never confused the spectre's ring with the man's. The ghost's ring is a strange vibration in the bell that it derives from nothing else, and I have not asserted that the bell stirs to the eye. I don't wonder that you failed to hear it. But *I* heard it.'

'And did the spectre seem to be there when you looked out?'

'It *was* there.'

'Both times?'

He repeated firmly: 'Both times.'

'Will you come to the door with me, and look for it now?'

He bit his lower lip as though he were somewhat unwilling, but arose. I opened the door, and stood on the step, while he stood in the doorway. There was the danger-light. There was the dismal mouth of the tunnel. There were the high, wet stone walls of the cutting. There were the stars above them.

'Do you see it?' I asked him, taking particular note of his face. His eyes were prominent and strained, but not very much more so, perhaps, than my own had been when I had directed them earnestly towards the same spot.

'No,' he answered. 'It is not there.'

'Agreed,' said I.

We went in again, shut the door, and resumed our seats. I was thinking how best to improve this advantage, if it might be called one, when he took up the conversation in such a matter-of-course way, so assuming that there could be no serious question of fact between us, that I felt myself placed in the weakest of positions.

'By this time you will fully understand, sir,' he said, 'that what troubles me so dreadfully is the question: what does the spectre mean?'

I was not sure, I told him, that I did not fully understand.

'What is its warning against?' he said, ruminating, with his eyes on the fire, and only by times turning them on me. 'What is the danger? Where is the danger? There is danger overhanging somewhere on the line. Some dreadful calamity will happen. It is not to be doubted this third time, after what has gone before. But surely this is a cruel haunting of *me*. What can I do?'

He pulled out his handkerchief, and wiped the drops from his heated forehead.

'If I telegraph danger on either side of me, or on both, I can give no reason for it,' he went on, wiping the palms of his hands. 'I should get into trouble and do no good. They would think I was mad. This is the way it would work: Message: "Danger! Take care!" Answer: "What Danger? Where?" Message: "Don't know. But for God's sake, take care!" They would displace me. What else could they do?'

His pain of mind was most pitiable to see. It was the mental torture of a conscientious man, oppressed beyond endurance by an unintelligible responsibility involving life.

'When it first stood under the danger-light,' he went on, putting his dark hair back from his head, and drawing his hands outward across

67

and across his temples in an extremity of feverish distress, 'why not tell me where that accident was to happen—if it must happen? Why not tell me how it could be averted—if it could have been averted? When on its second coming it hid its face, why not tell me, instead, "She is going to die. Let them keep her at home"? If it came, on those two occasions, only to show me that its warnings were true, and so to prepare me for the third, why not warn me plainly now? And I, Lord help me! A mere poor signalman on this solitary station! Why not go to somebody with credit to be believed, and power to act?'

When I saw him in this state, I saw that for the poor man's sake, as well as for the public safety, what I had to do for the time was to compose his mind. Therefore, setting aside all question of reality or unreality between us, I represented to him that whoever thoroughly discharged his duty must do well, and that at least it was his comfort that he understood his duty, though he did not understand these confounding appearances. In this effort I succeeded far better than in the attempt to reason him out of his conviction. He became calm; the occupations incidental to his post as the night advanced began to make larger demands on his attention: and I left him at two in the morning. I had offered to stay through the night, but he would not hear of it.

That I more than once looked back at the red light as I ascended the pathway, that I did not like the red light, and that I should have slept but poorly if my bed had been under it, I see no reason to conceal. Nor did I like the two sequences of the accident and the dead girl. I see no reason to conceal that either.

But what ran most in my thoughts was the consideration how ought I to act, having become the recipient of this disclosure? I had proved the man to be intelligent, vigilant, painstaking, and exact; but how long might he remain so, in his state of mind? Though in a subordinate position, still he held a most important trust, and would I (for instance) like to stake my own life on the chances of his continuing to execute it with precision?

Unable to overcome a feeling that there would be something treacherous in my communicating what he had told me to his superiors in the company, without first being plain with himself and proposing a middle course to him, I ultimately resolved to offer to accompany him (otherwise keeping his secret for the present) to the wisest medical practitioner we could hear of in those parts, and to take his opinion. A change in his time of duty would come round next night, he had apprised me, and he would be off an hour or two after sunrise, and on again soon after sunset. I had appointed to return accordingly.

Next evening was a lovely evening, and I walked out early to enjoy it. The sun was not yet quite down when I traversed the field-path near the top of the deep cutting. I would extend my walk for an hour, I said to myself, half an hour on and half an hour back, and it would then be time to go to my signalman's box.

Before pursuing my stroll, I stepped to the brink, and mechanically looked down, from the point from which I had first seen him. I cannot describe the thrill that seized upon me, when, close at the mouth of the tunnel, I saw the appearance of a man, with his left sleeve across his eyes, passionately waving his right arm.

The nameless horror that oppressed me passed in a moment, for in a moment I saw that this appearance of a man was a man indeed, and that there was a little group of other men standing at a short distance, to whom he seemed to be rehearsing the gesture he made. The danger-light was not yet lit. Against its shaft a little low hut entirely new to me had been made of some wooden supports and tarpaulin. It looked no bigger than a bed.

With an irresistible sense that something was wrong—with a flashing self-reproachful fear that fatal mischief had come of my leaving the man there, and causing no one to be sent to overlook or correct what he did—I descended the notched path with all the speed I could make.

'What is the matter?' I asked the men.

'Signalman killed this morning, sir.'

'Not the man belonging to that box?'

'Yes, sir.'

'Not the man I know?'

'You will recognize him, sir, if you knew him,' said the man who spoke for the others, solemnly uncovering his own head, and raising an end of the tarpaulin, 'for his face is quite composed.'

'Oh, how did this happen, how did this happen?' I asked, turning from one to another as the hut closed in again.

'He was cut down by an engine, sir. No man in England knew his work better. But somehow he was not clear of the outer rail. It was just at broad day. He had struck the light, and had the lamp in his hand. As the engine came out of the tunnel, his back was towards her, and she cut him down. That man drove her, and was showing how it happened. Show the gentleman, Tom.'

The man, who wore a rough dark dress, stepped back to his former place at the mouth of the tunnel.

'Coming round the curve in the tunnel, sir,' he said, 'I saw him at the end, like as if I saw him down a perspective-glass. There was no time to check speed, and I knew him to be very careful. As he didn't seem to take heed of the whistle, I shut if off when we were running down upon him, and called to him as loud as I could call.'

'What did you say?'

'I said, "Below there! Look out! Look out! For God's sake, clear the way!"'

I started.

'Ah! it was a dreadful time, sir. I never left off calling to him. I put this arm before my eyes not to see, and I waved this arm to the last; but it was no use.'

Without prolonging the narrative to dwell on any one of its curious circumstances more than on any other, I may, in closing it, point out the coincidence that the warning of the engine-driver included, not only the words which the unfortunate signalman had repeated to me as haunting him, but also the words which I myself—not he—had attached, and that only in my own mind, to the gesticulation he had imitated.

THE GERMAN WHO SUCCEEDED

John Bulloch

Jules Crawford Silber is the one German spy known to have been completely successful throughout the First World War. There were a few others who made quick trips to Britain and managed to return with scraps of information, but Silber alone lived and worked in enemy territory for years, constantly sending reports of the utmost importance to Germany. He was probably one of the most consistently effective spies of all time.

Silber did not merely live in Britain for the duration of the war. For the whole of the four years he worked in one of the major branches of counter-espionage. He was highly intelligent and resourceful, and by his choice of employment devised a method of sending material safe against all fears of detection. He took great risks to find out what he needed to know, but never aroused the suspicion of those he questioned; at the same time that he was working so diligently for the Germans, he managed to impress his English superiors with his ability and rose to a position of trust and responsibility. And he was an amateur, who had volunteered his services without being sought out by the German Intelligence organizations.

Silber was born in Silesia, and as a youth was sent to South Africa to a job in the offices of a German firm there. He quickly learnt English, and also acquired a lasting respect for the British, which was to colour his attitude when he came to spy against the people he admired so much. It was largely because he never made the fundamental German error of underrating his opponents that Silber was able to work so well for so long.

When the Boer War started in 1899, Silber saw a chance to widen his experience and to escape from his somewhat humdrum routine. He offered his services as an interpreter, and was appointed to several prisoner of war and internment camps before being sent to India with 15,000 Boer prisoners who were to be kept there. He was briefly at camps in Ceylon and Bombay, then spent one-and-a-half years in the Punjab, at a station which was then garrisoned by the 2nd Battalion of the King's Own Royal Rifles. Silber soon made friends with a number of the junior officers there, and joined them in hunting expeditions and many of the sports which filled so much of the time—another factor which enabled him to operate so successfully years later. To an Englishman, mutual acquaintanceships are as good an introduction and passport as anything else.

In 1902, when the war ended, Silber returned with the Boer prisoners to South Africa, but decided that the postwar conditions there did not give him enough scope. He migrated to America, where he worked until 1914.

All this time Silber had thought little of his German nationality. He was one of those apparently rootless people, more common now than then, who integrated themselves completely in whatever country they happened to find themselves. Only the most major events can bring back to them the basic patriotism which is supposed to be natural to all men.

The declaration of war had this effect on Silber. As he said later: 'The catastrophe which had befallen Germany had aroused me from the indifference with which I had hitherto regarded its political affairs and fortunes. I felt myself suddenly bound to the country, which, though I scarcely knew it, was my native land, and I was carried away by a passionate, irresistible urge to serve it now that it was in need.'

Silber would have preferred to return to Germany and join one of the fighting services, but he could see that this would be almost impossible. He realized too that his knowledge of English and the English way of life would make him more useful in another field, and he resolved to become an Intelligence agent in Britain.

It was a decision he reached alone, without any prompting or approach by his compatriots, who were quite unaware of his existence. Once he had made up his mind, he applied himself methodically to the task of fitting himself for the role he had chosen. First he got in touch with the German Embassy in America, and from the undercover Intelligence officers there learned what to look out for when, and if, he got to England, and was also given a number of cover addresses both in America and on the Continent to which he could send his reports. That was the full extent of the help he was given. The rest was up to him.

In his lodgings in New York he read every book he could find in the public libraries on the British Army and Navy. He studied technical works so that he would be able to assess the value of anything he heard. And he laid his plans for getting to England.

The biggest snag was that he had no passport. In the halcyon days before the war, many people of all nationalities were never issued with these now-essential documents, for travel then was far freer than it is now. Silber had moved quite easily between South Africa, India and America because he was part of a British-directed contingent, but he found that his lack of credentials presented him with a most serious handicap. On the other hand, possession of German identity papers, the only ones to which he was properly entitled, would have made his scheme more difficult still.

Silber realized it would be impossible to go direct from New York to Britain, as passengers on all vessels from America were carefully screened before being allowed to land. Many reputable citizens who had left without passports in the early days of the war were summarily shipped back to the United States, so that the shipping companies soon insisted on inspecting travel documents before they would issue tickets. Silber decided his only way was via Canada—a sound decision which was to be endorsed fifty years later by such spies as Colonel Rudolph Abel and Gordon Lonsdale. He spoke French, and knew something of the patois used in Quebec province, and therefore chose to adopt this as his home.

Silber went to Montreal, but found that there the shipping companies were almost as strict as in New York. After much touring of offices, he eventually managed to get one of three berths in a freighter bound for Manchester, and on 19 September 1914 he sailed from Canada. Eleven days later his ship steamed slowly up the canal from the Mersey, and he began his life in enemy territory.

As he had no passport, Silber had to undergo a rigorous questioning by the immigration officers. His appearance, short and Gallic, with a neat, pointed beard, and the care he had taken to prepare himself for the ordeal, carried him through successfully. But then, as later, it was letters and testimonials which had been given him during his service with the British in South Africa and India that finally convinced his interrogators.

That hurdle taken, Silber travelled to London. It was his first visit there, but through luck or his innate shrewdness he did not put a foot wrong. He found himself a small flat in Charing Cross Road, over-looking Cambridge Circus, then set about getting a job in the department he had chosen as the most likely to serve his purpose.

Silber's choice of work was brilliant. From what he had been told in the German Embassy in America, he had fixed on the postal censorship as the one organization where he had every prospect of being accepted, where he would have access to information, and where there was a very good chance that he would be able to pass on to Germany the material he gathered.

His reasoning was sound. By October, when he arrived, recruits were being taken on daily to enlarge the important work being done. His application was accepted and in the years that followed he found that he was in the ideal position to carry out his self-imposed task.

The department which stemmed from a decision of the Committee of Imperial Defence taken years earlier, was at first intended merely to stop information passing to Germany, or her allies, or to the neutral countries bordering on Germany, which could easily be used as 'post boxes'. But in a very short while the work was expanded, until letters from Britain to every part of the world were being examined before being sent on. The censors originally had to deal only with naval or military communications but special sections were soon set up to study commercial matters. News extracted from business letters and cables, and collated and analysed by experienced officials seconded from the

Board of Trade, had a real bearing on Britain's wartime economic policy, and enabled the blockade of Germany to be made completely effective.

The department also played an important part in the work of counter-espionage. Many German spies had been trapped before through the messages they sent or received, and in the majority of cases, when suspicion had once been aroused, it was evidence found in letters which made it possible for the Special Branch to satisfy the courts of a suspect's guilt. Now that war had come, the general censorship enabled MI5 to identify German agents as soon as they attempted to communicate with their headquarters. On several occasions, it was galling for Silber to see one of his countrymen getting further and further into the meshes of the counter-espionage net, and to be powerless to give any warning.

The value of Kell's work in the five years before the war was proved over and over again. Each address in Holland, Belgium, Germany or any of the Scandinavian countries used by Ernst or the other spies who had been watched so carefully, had been filed in that quiet office in the Strand. The result was that when the censorship department was established within days of the declaration of war, the officials there were quickly provided with a 'black list' of addresses. Any mail going to one of these was automatically stopped and sent to Captain Kell, who arranged for the writer to be investigated. On occasion, as in the case of Hahn, the letters were sent on suitably amended. But always the writer was watched, and in ninety-nine cases out of one hundred, he was found to be a German agent.

The censorship department was yet one more responsibility of the Director of Military Operations, and at first was in charge of Colonel Pearson. It was originally housed at Mount Pleasant, the London Post Office headquarters, but as the volume of work grew, moved successively to Salisbury House, then to two buildings in Kingsway, and finally to a large block in Carey Street, behind the Law Courts. Branches were opened in Liverpool and Folkestone, in addition to the special army units on duty in France and at the base camps all over England. By the end of the war, 3,700 people were employed in London alone, and another 1,500 in Liverpool.

With the demand for staff that existed in 1914, Silber had little difficulty in being accepted, but because of the nature of the work, prospective employees were carefully interviewed, and preference was given to people of British nationality, particularly those with connections with the services—a very large number of retired officers found useful wartime employment there. Silber, with his command of languages, and the convincing Canadian background he had invented for himself, had little trouble in satisfying the officers who dealt with his application. His record of service in South Africa and India, and his genuine friendships with officers of the Rifles, again seemed to his interrogators to support conclusively the story he told.

On 12 October 1914, Silber reported for duty, armed with an official letter of appointment and pass number 216, which carried him safely past the doorkeepers. It was the start of four years of strain and subterfuge for him, four years in which he did the most valuable espionage work possible.

As soon as he started work, Silber found methods of sending out the information he pieced together from the mass of letters he read each day. He discovered that often innocent correspondence to neutral countries included requests for purely personal messages to be passed on to friends or relatives in Germany. This seemed to him to show that the people to whom the letters were posted had German sympathies, so he frequently slipped messages of his own into such envelopes, asking that they should be forwarded to his own contact. It was found later that without exception this was done.

The first piece of information sent in this way was a copy of the list of suspect addresses, a move which caused MI5 a lot of trouble until they had built up a new 'black list'. Even after this, however, MI5 found the original list of use, as due to some slip-up or lack of liaison between the German Intelligence departments, many of the spies who came to England continued to use the old ones.

In his early days in the censorship department Silber found means of communicating with Germany presented to him regularly. He was for a time dealing with the letters of prisoners of war, which went direct to Germany. With these too, he put his own messages, and had no doubt they would be forwarded.

Silber, as he was transferred to different sections, found more and more material was coming his way—so much that it was impossible

Silber was able to photograph documents he 'borrowed', reduce them in size, and include one or two small negatives in letters sent to Germany.

for him to rely on his memory, and he could not, of course, take notes under the eyes of his colleagues. To overcome this difficulty, and to avoid having to include bulky letters of his own with those he had censored, he took a second set of rooms in the Haymarket, and there this versatile man set up a photographic studio, carefully buying the things he needed at shops all over London so that he would not arouse suspicion by large purchases in one place.

With this second hide-out, Silber was able to photograph documents he 'borrowed' overnight, reduce them in size, and then include one or two small negatives in letters sent to Germany. But by the beginning of 1915 that avenue was closed to him, as the censorship became more stringent, and an order was issued that any letters to neutral countries containing requests for messages to be forwarded to Germany were to be stopped. As Silber had been moved from the section dealing with prisoners' mail, he had to devise some entirely new method of getting his reports out.

It took him only a few days to find a way. Letters went to the censors already stamped and franked, so that when they were returned to the Post Office the only addition was the tag over the envelope flap showing they had been opened and examined. This gave Silber his opportunity. Those from the London area were normally sent back to the Post Office on the evening of the day after they had originally been posted. So each day Silber posted letters to himself in time to arrive first thing in the morning, before he went to work. He used 'window' envelopes, in which a cellophane piece in the centre allows the address written inside to be seen.

As soon as he received the letters, he threw away the contents, a sheet of paper blank but for his own address showing through. He was then armed with an envelope properly stamped and franked and showing the correct postal time for onward delivery that day. At his office, he put in the report he wished to send, and wrapped around it a piece of paper with an address taken from the suspect list in the country whose mail he was dealing with that day. Then he sealed the envelope with his own 'opened by censor' tag, and the letter was in all respects, apart from its contents, similar to all the other genuine ones sent to the sorting office.

In December 1915 Silber was transferred to Liverpool, where a new branch of the department had been opened to deal with mail for America. At the same time he was promoted, so that he was in a position to call for any letters which he thought might contain useful information. Against this there was the disadvantage that only North and South America was dealt with, so that all his reports had to go by this long and roundabout route.

To overcome this, whenever he had something he considered of special importance to send, Silber travelled to London, and called on his old colleagues there, slipping the message he had already prepared into the file for the appropriate country, stacked up on one of the long tables used by the censors. This was a risky proceeding which could not be used too often. Frequently Silber came near to disaster, but he always managed to avoid it. In Liverpool there were no suspicions about his trips away, as by his smiling silence he encouraged the generally held belief that it was to meet a woman friend that he made the journeys.

When information of value was scarce, Silber did not rest on his laurels. He thought up several other ways of embarrassing the Allied cause, falling just short of direct sabotage.

At this time, for instance, England was buying large numbers of shells in America. Often the British required them made to some particular specification, and sent drawings and details to the English ordnance officers in America. These men went there ostensibly as civilian members of purchasing commissions, but this was merely to respect the letter of the American neutrality laws. No one was taken in by the deception, though everyone pretended to be.

Silber planned to add to the difficulties of these officers. He did not have the technical knowledge to alter the blueprints in such a way that production would go on, but the finished result would be unusable, so he made up his mind that to delay manufacture of the arms so desperately needed on the Western Front would serve just as good a purpose. His method was simple, but effective. Even to the eye of the layman, it was always apparent which part of any drawing would ruin the whole if it were not there. That decided, it was a simple matter to spill burning ash from a pipe, or 'accidentally' drop a blob of ink from a pen. At times, he even contrived to 'lose' the drawings altogether. Eventually, there was so much trouble and delay that letters addressed to the British officers in the States dealing with munitions were put on the 'white' list, which contained the names and addresses of all those people—diplomats, statesmen, or British agents—whose mail was never opened by the censors. Even then, Silber managed to lose one or two.

Another way in which he caused frustration and hindrance was by over-zealousness. Ships arriving with cargoes of munitions in Liverpool had to have all their papers, as well as any mail they were carrying, cleared by the censor before unloading could begin. Silber saw to it that these papers were examined meticulously by two or three people before being returned to the ship's master, who was only then able to discharge his cargo. The delays thus caused, sometimes only a matter of hours, sometimes days, had a very real effect on the flow of supplies. After the war, Silber estimated that in this way he had arranged for hold-ups equal to the loss of 400,000 tons of freight space in a year.

But to a man as dedicated and resourceful as Silber these were only petty actions, to be indulged when there was no more important work to do. He was never afraid to taks risks, and he was always quick to see the importance of scraps of information contained in letters. In the summer of 1916 he saw a reference to the British tanks which were to cause such a sensation when first used. In a letter he examined a woman wrote to her sister saying that her husband, serving with the Royal Engineers, was testing 'tanks'. Silber had no idea what was meant, but doing his duty as a British censor, he refused to send the letter on. Then, in his role as a German spy, he visited the woman who had written it, ostensibly to warn her against any such mention in future, in fact to discover as much as possible. He learnt that caterpillar tracks were also involved, and from this built up a very fair idea of what was afoot. He sent his report off to Germany, but if it was ever received, little notice seems to have been taken.

In the same way, Silber heard of the use of Q-ships to tempt submarines to the surface and then destroy them with previously concealed guns. A young girl wrote to her sister in Canada saying that their brother had been decorated for gallantry in action while serving in a new type of ship 'which would soon end the U-boat campaign'. The girl even gave the name of the port in which the new ship was lying.

Silber very properly returned the letter, then went himself to the port to see what he could discover. Again, he interviewed the girl on the pretext of emphasizing the official warning given when her letter was sent back, and found out all he could from her. He studied the Q-ship of which she had written, which was still at anchor in the port, and in the next two months he travelled on several occasions to the small harbours used as bases for these vessels to try and work out their secrets. He succeeded very well and, satisfied he could do no more, sent off two reports to Germany, one by the pro-German mate of a Swedish ship, and one to an address in Holland through his regular method via the London censorship department.

One of the reports got through, and German U-boat commanders rapidly became more cautious in their attacks on apparently helpless merchant ships.

As the end of the war drew near, Silber's difficulties increased. Conscription had been introduced in 1916, and although he had been given a certificate saying he was doing essential work, this was no longer any use when the volunteer principle was dropped. To get around this, he constantly dosed himself with drugs, and made himself into a semi-permanent invalid. As it was, he had to have regular medical examinations for service, and only the end of the war saved him from the final one, at which he was certain he would have been passed fit for some form of duty.

Silber remained in the censorship department in Liverpool until it was disbanded on 27 June 1919. After he left, a certificate of service was sent on to him, in which he was described as 'a very able man, a good linguist, thorough and competent'. His conduct was said to be 'exemplary'.

At the end of the war, Silber's health, which had been giving him genuine trouble for some time, broke down completely. The strain of his double life, plus the effort he had made to simulate illness to avoid conscription, finally took its toll. He worked occasionally for film companies in England, but in general did little more than await the time when he would be able to return to his own country. That time did not come until the spring of 1925, because of the restrictions on travel which remained in force after the war. Silber left Britain after eleven years, having managed to spy successfully throughout the war, as well as winning promotion in his job as censor.

Silber did not go entirely unsuspected during that period. Quite early on in London, MI5 became suspicious that information was passing through the censorship, and Silber, among others, was investigated. In Liverpool, a man who saw him buying photographic equipment followed him, but was persuaded that there was nothing wrong. In both these instances, and in others, Silber's care to cover his tracks, and the routine precautions he always took, saved him from discovery.

He was a brilliant man, motivated entirely by patriotism. He volunteered for the hard task of espionage, and he succeeded where so many chosen by the Germans failed.

THE SPY WHO NEVER WAS

Noel Lloyd

At Huelva in southern Spain there is a tombstone marking the grave of a British subject named William Martin—Major Martin of the Royal Marines who, according to the inscription, died on 24 April 1943, a month or so after his thirty-seventh birthday. Nothing special about that, one might think—except that in 1943 a world war was raging, Spain was supposedly a neutral country, and one would have thought that Britain had more urgent things to do than arrange for the building of a monument to a dead soldier.

But there is a strange story behind the burial of the unknown Major Martin, and it would never have been uncovered if it had not been for the curiosity of a journalist who had once been a spy and was used to extraordinary happenings in ordinary circumstances. Major Martin was a sort of spy himself—or he would have been if he had ever existed . . .

In the autumn of 1942 the war was not going well for the Allies. All Europe was in German hands, and the Germans were even making inroads into Russia. The time was not yet ripe for a full-scale Allied invasion of Europe, so North Africa was chosen as the object of a massive offensive. The Secret Service had the difficult task of keeping this information from the enemy at all costs. Intelligence work consists not only of finding out military secrets but, often equally important, also of giving out false and misleading facts to the enemy. The problem facing Intelligence was how to convince the Germans that the planned invasion was to be of Greece and not North Africa. For the invasion to be successful it was necessary that German troops should be sent to Greece and that Africa should be only lightly defended.

All the well-tried ways of deceiving the enemy had already been used. Some agents had pretended to defect to the Nazis and had given away British 'secrets'; others had let similar 'secrets' drop into eager ears in neutral countries, knowing that they would soon reach the enemy. Rumours were started, the movements of troops were 'accidentally' talked about. But on this occasion none of the usual methods was appropriate. Something more spectacular was needed to convince the Germans that Greece was the target—something that was entirely believable. Many ideas were discussed by Intelligence chiefs, but none of them seemed quite right.

The solution to the problem came from Spain, a country whose 'neutrality' consisted of passing on as much information as it could get hold of to the Germans and of withholding information from the Allies. British Intelligence knew of, and accepted, Spain's one-sided neutrality, hoping that one day it could at least be put to good use.

That day came when one of the men planning the invasion deception came across an Intelligence report from an agent in Cadiz. A body from a wreck had been washed up on a Spanish shore after a British plane had crashed into the sea. There were a number of papers on the body, papers which turned out to have no military significance, as it happened, and these were handed over to the British Ambassador by the Spanish police. The agent went on to report, however, that he believed the police had first shown the papers to the German Embassy before handing them over. In this case, the fact that they had been examined by the enemy was unimportant. But what would have happened if the dead airman's possessions had contained vital secrets, perhaps about the movements of important people, or information that would help the Germans? The results might have been disastrous for the Allies. It was from this frightening thought that an idea was born—the idea of planting information that had been deliberately placed on a dead body.

It was a gruesome thought, but this was war, and the task of the Intelligence service was to help to bring the war to a successful end. At first the idea was regarded with suspicion by the planners. How, they asked, could a body be produced out of thin air? Britain was a democratic country. Bodies, dead or alive, could not just disappear. How, even assuming that a body could be found, could it be made to be washed up at a specific place? And how could the body be made to prove to German doctors who would examine it that it had really been drowned?

There were so many questions to be answered before the plan could begin to take shape, and none of the answers seemed to be forthcoming. The idea was not thrown out completely, however, because it was a good one if it could be made to work. A committee was formed. It consisted of members of the Armed Forces Intelligence, the Secret Service, and those connected with 'double agents'. They agreed to go ahead with the plan, and the job of working out the details was given to two men—Lieutenant-Commander Ewen Montagu of Naval Intelligence and Flight-Lieutenant Cholmondeley.

Montagu and Cholmondeley began by giving a name to the fictitious spy and concocting a story about his background, even before the actual body had been found. He was to be William Martin, a major in the Royal Marines, the son of John Glyndwyr and Antonia Martin of Cardiff. He was to have a girlfriend who wrote to him regularly; and letters from her, and a photograph of her, were to be found in his wallet. A real girl was found to fulfil this role—it was necessary to have a real person in case the Germans, with their usual thoroughness, should make investigations. A bank account was opened for Major Martin so that a bank statement would also be found—a statement which showed that the major's account was overdrawn!

Having created Major Martin on paper, the next and much more difficult task was to find a body to fit the mythical soldier. Ewen Montagu was a friend of the coroner for the St Pancras district of London, and went to him for help. The coroner made it clear how difficult it would be to find a body that would match the major's in age, height and build, and one that had not been mutilated in an air raid or had suffered a violent death. Moreover, whoever it was that was chosen must appear to have been drowned. However, he held many inquests, and perhaps one day they would be lucky . . .

And lucky they were, sooner than they had expected. A corpse taken to a mortuary fitted the major's description in every detail. It was as though there really had been a Major Martin whose life had been ended by drowning. It was uncanny. The man's relatives were found, and they were asked to give their permission for his body to be used as a decoy. After agreeing, they were sworn to secrecy. Then the distinguished pathologist, Sir Bernard Spilsbury, was consulted on the best way of making sure that death would appear to have been by drowning. The body was then put in a deep freeze until the time for action.

Preparations for the deception continued. Official documents, all cleverly faked, were put into a government briefcase. The most vital document was a letter to General Alexander from the Vice-Chief of the General Staff which gave details of the plan to invade Greece. The briefcase was locked, ready to be chained to Major Martin's body. A final, brilliant touch was to place two stubs of tickets for a London theatre in his pocket. They were dated 22 April, thus serving the double purpose of underlining how important the letter to General Alexander was for Martin to have flown with it rather than going by sea, and showing that the information was absolutely up to date.

Soon all was ready. The corpse was taken out of refrigeration and dressed in uniform. The all-important briefcase was chained to him and the body was then placed in a large container marked: HANDLE WITH CARE: OPTICAL INSTRUMENTS, and taken aboard the submarine *Seraph*.

The *Seraph* began to make for the coast of Spain. The chosen spot was Huelva in Andalucia, for it was there that British agents had discovered a large concentration of German spies with a very strong organization; they would be grateful for any information about what the Allies were up to. Just when and where the body of Major Martin should be released into the sea had been carefully worked out with the aid of tide tables and current charts provided by the Admiralty.

A mile out from Huelva beach the spy was slipped into the water, and his body drifted slowly but surely towards land.

The body was found by some fishermen and handed over to the Spanish authorities. The briefcase was passed on to the Germans and was duly examined. The letter to General Alexander caused great excitement. So Greece was to be the invasion target . . .

A mile out from Huelva beach the spy was slipped into the water.

The Germans swallowed the bait—hook, line and sinker. They were still expecting the attack on Greece as the Allies were building up their shipping in Gibraltar. Troops, ammunition and supplies arrived on the island, and little attention was paid. The eyes of the Germans were focused on the other end of the Mediterranean. The British trick had been a complete success!

But the organizers did not believe in leaving anything to chance. Major Martin's name appeared in a casualty list as 'missing, presumed dead', and when the British Ambassador was informed by his Spanish authorities that the body of a British officer had been washed up at Huelva, he arranged for a funeral to be held and a tombstone to be erected to the memory of the dead man. Only personal documents—letters, a photograph, tickets—had been found on the body. No briefcase came to light, and no one on the British side was in the least surprised. It was enough that the letter had achieved what was intended.

The identity of the real 'Major Martin' was never revealed; his family kept the secret zealously. They could be proud that the spy who never was had done such a sterling job for his country at so critical a time.

FRANKENSTEIN

Mary W. Shelley

*Frankenstein . . . a name that strikes a sudden chill. Frankenstein . . .
probably thought of as the most famous and terrifying 'monster' in all
literature. Yet this was not the name of the monster, but that of the
fictional scientist who created him. And the creator of both was a
young, delicate girl.*

*She was Mary, wife of Percy Bysshe Shelley, one of Britain's
great poets. She and her husband were spending the summer of 1816
in Switzerland, where one of their friends and neighbours was the
equally famous Lord Byron. It proved to be a wet and miserable
summer and the friends were constantly kept indoors. Finally, almost
as a piece of fun, Byron suggested that each of them write a ghost story.*

*This was not to prove difficult for Shelley and Byron, both accom-
plished writers, but for the young Mary it was far from easy. One
evening, however, she sat quietly, listening while her husband and
Lord Byron discussed the writings of a scientist who had suggested
that a corpse could be given back life. As she later wrote: 'Night
waned upon this talk; and even the witching hour had gone by before
we retired to rest. When I placed my head on my pillow, I did not
sleep. I saw—with shut eyes, but acute mental vision—I saw the pale
student of unhallowed arts kneeling beside the thing he had put together. I saw the hideous phantasm of a man stretched out, and then,
on the working of some powerful engine, show signs of life, and stir
with an uneasy, half vital motion.'*

*And so, almost as if in a dream, the fantastic and mysterious story
of Frankenstein was born . . .*

The story begins with letters from Captain Walton to his sister in
England. His ship lay becalmed, nearly enclosed in ice, when he and
his men saw a strange sight. 'We perceived a low carriage, fixed on a

sledge and drawn by dogs, pass on towards the north, at the distance of half a mile. A being which had the shape of a man, but apparently of gigantic stature, sat in the sledge and guided the dogs. We watched the rapid progress of the traveller with our telescopes, until he was lost among the distant inequalities of the ice.'

The following morning the captain went on deck and found some of his men talking to someone. By the side of the ship was a sledge which had drifted towards the vessel during the night on a large piece of ice. Only one dog remained alive, but there was a human being within it, whom the sailors were persuading to come aboard the ship. The man was not, as the other traveller had seemed to be, a savage inhabitant of some undiscovered island, but a European. When Captain Walton looked over the side of his ship the stranger addressed him in English, although with a foreign accent. 'Before I come on board your vessel, will you have the kindness to inform me whither you are bound?'

The captain was amazed at such a question. The stranger's limbs were nearly frozen and his body thin from fatigue and suffering. He had never seen a man in so wretched a condition. When told that the ship was on a voyage of discovery to the North Pole, the stranger seemed satisfied and allowed himself to be carried on board.

The stranger spoke little but once, when the ship's lieutenant asked him why he had come so far upon the ice in so strange a vehicle, and he replied, gloomily, 'To seek one who fled from me.'

'And did the man whom you pursued travel in the same fashion?'
'Yes.'
'Then I fancy we have seen him; for the day before we picked you up, we saw some dogs drawing a sledge, with a man in it, across the ice.'

This news seemed to rouse the stranger and, with rest and good food, his health steadily improved. He and the captain became friends and finally he decided to tell him the whole, terrible story . . .

His name was Frankenstein and had been born in Geneva. For a while he had been an only child and then his parents, who had always wanted a daughter, adopted Elizabeth—'my more than sister, the beautiful and adored companion of all my occupations and pleasures.'

After a while the young Frankenstein had to go to college. Here he was greatly influenced by a Professor Waldman, who quickly saw in his young pupil a student of genius. After a while he took him into his laboratory and explained to him the uses of various machines. He told his pupil what he should procure, promising him the use of his own equipment when he had advanced enough not to spoil the mechanism of his machines. He then gave him a list of books to read and, grateful for the professor's interest, young Frankenstein left the laboratory.

But that visit had decided his future destiny.

He worked hard at the university for two years and made some discoveries in the improvement of some chemical instruments, which procured him both esteem and admiration among those around him. One of the phenomena which had particularly attracted his attention was the structure of the human frame and, indeed, any animal endowed with life. He decided that to examine the causes of life, one must first understand death. He studied anatomy but it was not sufficient; he also had to observe the natural decay and corruption of the human body. He began to spend days and nights in vaults and charnel-houses.

He paused, examining and analysing all the facts that occurred during the change from life to death, and from death to life, until from the midst of darkness a sudden light broke in on him—a light so brilliant and wondrous, yet so simple, that he became dizzy with the immensity of his findings. At the same time he was surprised that among so many men of genius who had directed their inquiries towards the same science, he alone should be the one to discover so astonishing a secret.

Frankenstein's ideals were of the highest, and he had long decided to use his new-found secret for the good of mankind. He had discovered himself capable of giving life to lifeless matter, but the effort of preparing a frame for the reception of this life, with all its intricacies of fibres, muscles and veins, was obviously to be one of incredible difficulty and labour. But after much thought he decided to go ahead with the task—to create a human being. As the minuteness of its parts would slow his work, he resolved to make a being of gigantic stature. He would create a human being of some eight feet in height and proportionately large.

That decided, he began to collect the necessary materials.

He collected bones from charnel-houses and disturbed the tremendous secrets of the human frame. In a solitary chamber, or rather cell, at the top of his house, and separated from all other rooms by a gallery and staircase, he kept his experiment to himself. The dissecting room and the slaughter-house furnished many of his materials, yet his own nature often turned with loathing from his occupation. Still, urged on by an eagerness which increased as the work went on, he found himself nearing completion.

After a year and more it was finished at last. It was a dreary night in November when, with an anxiety that almost amounted to agony, he collected the instruments of life about him that he might infuse a spark of being into the lifeless thing that lay before him. It was already one o'clock in the morning, the rain pattered dismally against the panes, and his candle was almost burnt out when, by the glimmer of the half-extinguished light, he saw the dull yellow eye of the creature open. It breathed hard, and a convulsive motion began to move its limbs.

As he told Captain Walton: 'How can I describe my emotions at this catastrophe, or how delineate the wretch whom with such infinite pains and care I had endeavoured to form? His limbs were in proportion and I had selected his features as beautiful. Beautiful! Great God! His yellow skin scarcely covered the work of muscles and arteries beneath; his hair was of a lustrous black, and flowing; his teeth of a pearly whiteness; but these luxuriances only formed a more horrid contrast with his watery eyes that seemed almost of the same colour as the dun-white sockets in which they were set, his shrivelled complexion and straight black lips.

'I had worked hard for nearly two years, for the sole purpose of infusing life into an inanimate body. For this I had deprived myself of rest and health. I had desired it with an ardour that far exceeded moderation. But now that I had finished, the beauty of the dream vanished and breathless horror and disgust filled my heart. Unable to endure the aspect of the being I had created, I rushed out of the room and continued a long time traversing my bedchamber, unable to compose my mind to sleep.

'I threw myself on the bed in my clothes, endeavouring to seek a few moments of forgetfulness. But it was in vain. I slept, indeed, but I was disturbed by the wildest dreams. I thought I saw Elizabeth, in the bloom of health, walking in the streets of Ingolstadt. Delighted and surprised, I embraced her, but as I imprinted the first kiss on her lips they became livid with the hue of death, her features appeared to change,

91

He saw the dull yellow eye of the creature open . . .

and I thought that I held the corpse of my dead mother in my arms; a shroud enveloped her form and I saw the grave-worms crawling in the folds of the flannel. I started from my sleep with horror; a cold dew covered my forehead, my teeth chattered, and every limb became convulsed, when, by the dim and yellow light of the moon, as it forced its way through the window shutters, I beheld the wretch—the miserable monster whom I had created.

'He held up the curtain of the bed and his eyes, if eyes they may be called, were fixed on me. His jaws opened, and he muttered some inarticulate sounds, while a grin wrinkled his cheeks. He might have spoken, but I did not hear. One hand was stretched out, seemingly to detain me, but I escaped and rushed downstairs. I took refuge in the courtyard belonging to the house which I inhabited; there I remained during the rest of the night, catching and fearing every sound as if it were to announce the approach of the demoniacal corpse to which I had so miserably given life.

'Oh! no mortal could support the horror of that countenance. A mummy again endowed with animation could not be so hideous as that wretch. I had gazed on him while unfinished; he was ugly then, but when those muscles and joints were rendered capable of motion, it became a thing such as even Dante could not have conceived.'

When morning came at last, Frankenstein did not dare return to his apartment, but hurried into the street, although drenched by rain which poured from a black and comfortless sky. At last he came to an inn, where he was greeted by an old friend, Henry Clerval. They chatted for a while and then Frankenstein asked, 'Tell me how you left my father, brothers and Elizabeth?'

'Very well and very happy, only a little uneasy that they hear from you so seldom. But my dear Frankenstein,' the friend went on, gazing full in the other's face, 'I did not before remark how very ill you appear; so thin and pale. You look as if you had been watching for several nights.'

'You have guessed right. I have lately been so deeply engaged in one occupation that I have not allowed myself sufficient rest, as you see. But I hope that all these employments are now at an end, and that I am at length free.'

Accompanied by his friend, Frankenstein made his way back to his apartment. He dreaded to look at his monster, but feared even more that Clerval should see him. He asked him to remain at the bottom of the stairs for a few minutes and then paused at the door of the room, his hand on the handle. He then forcibly threw the door open, expecting to see the monster on the other side. But there was no one there; his room was freed from its hideous guest.

He invited Clerval to breakfast but behaved in such a strange manner that his friend was finally glad to go. He felt ill and began a nervous fever that confined him to his room for several months. Had it not been for the unremitting attentions of his friend he would surely have died. The form of the monster he had created was always before his eyes, and he raved incessantly about him.

It was spring when he finally recovered and soon became something of his old, cheerful self. He wrote to his beloved Elizabeth, telling her of his return to complete health, and then went back to the university and to his studies.

He went on holiday in May with Henry Clerval and returned feeling perfectly restored. But a letter that awaited him quickly dashed his spirits. It was from his father, telling him that his younger brother William had been murdered! When it was learned that the young boy was missing, a search was made and Elizabeth insisted on looking at the corpse when it was found and carried home. She entered the room where it lay, hastily examined the neck of the victim and then exclaimed, 'O God! I have murdered my darling child!'

She explained that she had been teased by the boy, who asked her for permission to wear a very valuable miniature that had belonged to his mother. Elizabeth finally allowed him to do so the previous evening, and when the body was found the miniature was missing. The girl was convinced that he had been murdered for this jewel.

Frankenstein hurried home to Geneva to try and console his father and Elizabeth. When he arrived in the environs of the city the gates were shut and he had to spend the night in a village nearby. Heavy with his sadness he went for a walk, and decided to visit the spot where William had been murdered. A sudden storm broke over the countryside, yet he walked on, ignoring the rain that beat about him. He stood for a while to watch the tempest and, clasping his hands and exclaimed aloud, 'William, dear angel! This is thy funeral, this is thy dirge!'

As he spoke he saw in the gloom a figure which stole from a clump of trees nearby. He stood, gazing intently. He could not be mistaken. A flash of lightning revealed its shape—its gigantic stature; and the deformity of its aspect, more hideous than belongs to humanity, told him at once that it was the filthy demon to whom he had given life. What was the monster doing there? Could he be, and Frankenstein shuddered at the thought, the murderer of his brother? At once he was convinced of the truth of the thought and he was forced to lean against a tree for support. Nothing in human shape could have destroyed that fair child. *He*, the monster, was the murderer! There could be no doubt about it.

Almost two years had passed since the night on which he had given him life. Was this his first crime? Wet, cold and miserable, Frankenstein spent the rest of the night in the open, realizing that he had turned loose into the world a wretch who delighted in carnage and misery.

He returned to a confused house. To his surprise, a young girl called Justine had confessed to the crime. This seemed impossible, yet on the morning on which the murder of the boy had been discovered, Justine had been taken ill and confined to her bed. One of the servants had happened to examine the clothes she had been wearing on the night of the murder and had discovered the miniature in one of her pockets. On being charged with the fact, the poor girl confirmed suspicion by her extreme confusion of manner.

Both Frankenstein and Elizabeth spoke up on behalf of the girl, but to no avail. She was put to death for murder and Frankenstein, who was sure he was guilty of the death of both, sat sorrowfully by their graves. They were, he was sure, the first hapless victims to his unhallowed arts.

Hoping to forget, for a while at least, something of his terrible feelings of guilt, Frankenstein went off on his own, wandering through the countryside in the neighbourhood of Mont Blanc. Then, once again, he saw the horrific figure of the monster he had created. He tried to escape but finally was forced to listen to the other's story. He learned how the monster he had created had slowly discovered the elementary things of life—of the warmth of fire, the pleasures of natural food, the protection given against snow and rain by the simplest cottage. But he learned, too, that his monster, which had started out with good feelings towards everyone, slowly became despondent, then angry, when all who saw him ran away as if they had seen the devil himself.

He turned on Frankenstein. 'Hateful day when I received life! Accursed creator! Why did you form a monster so hideous that even *you* turned from me in disgust. God, in pity, made man beautiful and alluring, after his own image, but my form is a filthy type of yours, more horrid even from the very resemblance. Satan has his companions, fellow-devils, to admire and encourage him; but I am solitary and abhorred.'

He continued his sad story until he came to the part which caused Frankenstein to hang on his every word. He said that he had just awakened from sleep when he was disturbed by the approach of a beautiful child, who came running towards his resting place. As he passed he seized the boy and tried to assure him that he meant him no harm.

But the boy struggled violently. 'Let me go. Monster! Ugly wretch! You want to eat me and tear me to pieces. Let me go, or I will tell my papa!'

'Boy, you will never see your father again; you must come with me.'

'Hideous monster, let me go! My papa is Monsieur Frankenstein. He will punish you. You will not keep me.'

'Frankenstein! You belong to my enemy—to him towards whom I have sworn eternal revenge. You shall be my first victim,' and the other listened with horror as the monster described how he had grasped the boy's neck and so killed him.

But he went on. 'As I fixed my eyes on the child I saw something glittering on his breast. I took it. It was a portrait of a most lovely woman.'

He then went on to explain to the horrified Frankenstein how he had left the dead boy and entered a barn nearby, where he saw a young girl asleep. Delighted with her beauty, he bent over her and placed the portrait in a fold of her dress. Then, as she moved in her sleep, he fled.

Finally, he said, 'You must create a female for me. This you alone can do; and I demand it of you as a right which you must not refuse.'

Although Frankenstein at first refused to do this, he finally agreed when the monster promised to take his new mate and fly far from the habitations of man, dwelling where only the beasts of the field would be their companions.

It was a long time before Frankenstein could bring himself to begin this new task. He found that he could not compose a female without again devoting several months to profound study. He learned of an English philosopher who had much knowledge on this subject, and decided to visit England. It was also agreed that he would marry Elizabeth on his return. His travelling companion was his old friend Henry Clerval. Together they visited London and many other cities in England, then arrived in Scotland, for Frankenstein had decided to complete his labours in some obscure nook of the northern highlands. Leaving Clerval in Perth, he found a small hut on one of the most remote of the Orkneys, and began work, at every moment expecting to look up and see the terrible face of his monster staring at him.

This was to happen. He had almost completed a female counterpart when, on looking up, he saw by the light of the moon the demon at the window, a ghastly grin wrinkling his lips as he watched the other at work. He had followed him on his travels, hiding in caves or taking refuge on wide and deserted heaths. Now he had come to mark the other's progress. It was too much! With a sense of madness at the thought of creating another such monster, Frankenstein tore to pieces the creature on which he had been working. The monster saw him, and with a howl of devilish despair and revenge, moved away from the hut.

Later that night, Frankenstein heard the creaking of his door. Next he heard a voice say, from the darkness, 'You have destroyed the work which you began; what is it that you intend? Do you dare to break your promise? I have endured toil and misery. I left Switzerland with you; I have followed you everywhere. I have endured incalculable fatigue and cold and hunger. Do you dare destroy my hopes?'

'Begone! I *do* break my promise. Never will I create another like yourself, equal in deformity and wickedness.'

They argued bitterly for a while then the monster, seeing that the other's mind was firmly fixed, left at last. Before he went, however, he uttered a chilling threat: '*I will be with you on your wedding night!*'

Frankenstein left the island, after hiding the remains of his half-finished creature, and went on board a little skiff. A storm blew up and when he was able to reach land, he was immediately arrested. A handsome young man had been found on the beach; he had apparently been strangled, for there was no sign of any violence, except the mark of

The monster seemed to jeer as he pointed to the corpse of the girl.

fingers on his neck. A woman came forward who swore that she had seen a boat, with a single man in it, an hour before the discovery of the body; and her evidence was supported by another.

Frankenstein entered the room where the corpse lay. As he looked at it he was parched with horror for there, before him, lay the lifeless body of his friend, Henry Clerval. The human frame could no longer support the agonies that he endured and he was carried out of the room in strong convulsions. A fever succeeded this. He lay for two months on the point of death and his ravings were terrible to hear, as he often felt he, too, was being strangled, and cried out aloud with agony and terror. He stayed in prison for a while but it was finally proved that he was on Orkney at the hour the body of his friend had been discovered, and he was released.

He travelled home with his father, looking forward to being re-united with Elizabeth, whom he was soon to marry. Their meeting was a joyful one and soon afterwards the pair were united in marriage. Their plan was to spend their honeymoon at a villa she owned on the shores of Lake Como and, saying goodbye to the guests, they set sail for

Evian, where they were to stay the night. As Frankenstein stepped ashore he suddenly felt those cares and fears revive which were soon to cling to him forever.

They reached a small inn, and whilst Elizabeth went to their room, he walked up and down the passages of the house, carefully looking into every corner that might afford a hiding place for his enemy. But there was no trace of him and he began to feel more at ease. Then, suddenly, there came a shrill and dreadful scream. It came from the room into which Elizabeth had retired. For a moment he seemed paralysed then, as the scream was repeated, he rushed into the room. There, before him, thrown across the bed, her head hanging down, her pale and distorted features half covered by her hair, lay the lifeless body of his new wife.

For a moment he stared at the terrible sight; the next he fell senseless to the ground. When he recovered he found himself surrounded by the people of the inn, but their horror seemed to him a mockery. He ran back to the room and saw Elizabeth, who had been moved to a new posture, her head on her arm, as if she but slept. But as he bent forward to take her cold body in his arms, he saw the murderous mark of the fiend's grasp was on her neck.

While he still held her in the agony of despair, he happened to look up. The window shutters had been thrown back and he saw at the open window the hideous and abhorred figure. A grin was on the face of the monster, he seemed to jeer as with his finger he pointed towards the corpse of the young girl. Frankenstein rushed to the window, drew a pistol from his breast, and fired. But the other eluded him, leaped from his place and, running with the swiftness of lightning, plunged into the lake.

A search was begun immediately, but without success. The monster had scored again. The death of William, the execution of Justine, the murder of Clerval and, now, the death of his beloved wife. Then, as the horror slowly sunk in, Frankenstein had a further terrible thought. Even at that moment his father might be writhing in the monster's grasp or his other brother, Ernest, might be dead at his feet. There was no time to lose.

He raced home to find that his father and Ernest were still alive—although the former sank under the terrible tidings he bore.

After a period of utter misery, Frankenstein formed in his heart a resolution to pursue his creature to its death. And so his wanderings began. Revenge and guilt kept him alive; he dared not die and leave his enemy in being. The chase followed the windings of the Rhône, went along the shores of the blue Mediterranean; he followed him by ship from the Black Sea to the wilds of Russia.

As he pursued his journey to the north, the snows thickened and the cold increased in a degree almost too severe to support. Yet still Frankenstein hunted the monster he had created. He procured a sledge and dogs, and covered the snows with tremendous speed. He now found that he was gaining on his quarry. Reaching a small hamlet by the sea he learned from the terrified inhabitants that a gigantic monster had arrived the night before. He had carried off their store of winter food and, placing it on a sledge, had harnessed some dogs and then continued his journey across the sea in a direction that led nowhere.

Exchanging his land-sledge for one better fashioned for the frozen ocean, and purchasing a large stock of provisions, Frankenstein went after him. It was during this chase that the monster, and then the scientist himself, had been sighted by the men of Captain Walton's ship.

Almost as soon as Frankenstein had finished his long and terrible story, the ice had become such that it was necessary that the ship was to give up her mission and return to England. Hearing this, Frankenstein said, 'Do so if you will, but I will not go with you. You may give up your purpose, but mine is assigned to me by heaven, and I dare not.'

Yet for a time the scientist was obviously too weak to leave the ship. The captain, who had become his close friend, spent many hours talking to him and doing his best to cheer him, whilst the ship's cook and surgeon brought him nourishing broths. Yet he gradually weakened until the sad moment when Captain Walton saw that the scientist was dead. Grieving in his cabin, he suddenly heard strange sounds coming from the dead man's cabin. He entered it and saw a form, gigantic in stature, yet uncouth and distorted in its proportions. When he heard the captain enter he stopped uttering his sounds of grief and sprang towards the window. The captain had never seen a vision as horrible as the creature's face, one of such loathsome and appalling hideousness. Yet without realizing what he did, Captain Walton called on him to stay.

The monster paused, looking on the other with wonder. Then, turning back towards the lifeless form of his creator he seemed to forget the other's presence, and every feature and gesture seemed moved by the wildest rage of some uncontrollable passion.

'That is also my victim!' he shouted. 'In his murder my crimes are consummated. Oh, Frankenstein! Generous and self-devoted being! What does it avail that I now ask thee to pardon me? I, who destroyed thee by destroying all thou lovest. Alas! He is cold; he cannot answer me.

'It is true that I am a wretch. I have murdered the lovely and the helpless. I have strangled the innocent as they slept, and grasped to death by the throat one who never injured me or any other living thing. I have devoted my creator, the finest of all that is worthy of love and admiration among men, to misery. I have pursued him to ruin. There he lies, white and cold in death. You hate me, but your abhorrence cannot equal that with which I regard myself. I look on these hands which executed the deed. I think on the heart in which the imagination of it was conceived, and long for the moment when these hands will meet my eyes, when that imagination will haunt my thoughts no more.'

He turned to stare at the captain. 'I shall quit your vessel on the ice-raft which brought me hither, and shall seek the most northern extremity of the globe. I shall die. He is dead who called me into being; and when I shall be no more, the very remembrance of us both will speedily vanish. Then my spirit will sleep in peace. Farewell!'

He sprung from the cabin window as he ended, landing on the ice-raft which lay close to the ship. As the captain and crew watched, the monster was soon borne away by the waves to be lost in darkness and distance, never to be seen again.

ANNEMARIE —
THE 'LADY DOCTOR'

K. Alan Macdonald

A big, thick-set man smiled grimly across at another, facing him. As he did so, he casually swung a heavy-knobbed stick. Both men had been posted at the barrier to the small station of Charleville in France. Their task was to capture, by force if necessary, a young man and woman suspected of being spies. At this time France was very sensitive to all such rumours, since this was 1913, the year before the outbreak of the First World War.

For the two suspects there could be no escape. Already a small group of men were searching the station buildings while the two on the barrier would make sure that no one passed *them*. For a while everything was quiet. Then suddenly a young girl ran forward and panted, urgently, 'Come quickly! Some men are fighting a man and a woman at the other end of the platform . . . and I think the man has a revolver!'

With muttered thanks, the two barrier guards ran off in the direction of her pointing finger. Almost immediately, another man slipped from where he had been hiding, took the girl by the hand, and hurried her out to a waiting landau—the taxi of the time. Telling the driver they wished to go for a short drive, they quickly settled in and were soon out of sight of the station. By changing carriages, by hiring a motor-car which took them into Belgium, and thence by train from Charleroi to Cologne, they were safe. The two Germans—for such they were—were in their own country again. And, as on several previous occasions, the girl's quick thinking had helped in their escape.

As time was to show, she was to prove one of the greatest woman spies of both world wars, with a record of successful espionage that was far ahead of any other. Yet how had she become a spy? And at such an early age, too, for she was barely out of her teens?

She had fallen in love with a handsome man who, formerly an army captain, had been recruited into the small but efficient German Secret Service. She could not understand, however, why he had to leave her for weeks at a time and he would not tell her the reason. Finally, despite his protests, she insisted on going with him. It was then that she found out his real occupation . . . a spy. Although shocked at first, she soon began to enjoy working at his side and was prepared for any danger as long as she could be with him.

The head of the spy ring—a quiet, very ordinary-looking man called Matthesius—was delighted with the work of his new recruits. The ex-captain, Carl von Wynanky, was good; and the girl, the young Annemarie Lesser, already showed tremendous possibilities. Although German she spoke perfect French and, moreover, she was a skilled artist, and the sketches of fortifications she began to send in were proving of tremendous help.

The lovers, Carl and Annemarie, were delighted at the success of their mission, because they had managed to obtain important details of new French fortifications. Annemarie had drawn them, Carl had added technical notes, and the whole were then stitched into the lining of his waistcoat. During the train journey home, however, the young officer began to feel ill. He grew steadily worse and by the time the train reached Cologne he was in such agony that he collapsed as he stepped from the train.

He was rushed to hospital and, as Annemarie sat at his bedside, died of appendicitis during the night.

She was now all alone, except for the one man she had never met—the strange Herr Matthesius, whose tiny office was in Berlin and who sat at his desk like a spider in the centre of a web. She sent a telegram telling him the sad news, then went back to her hotel room to weep in solitude. Carl's family had always despised her, and she was not even invited to attend her dead lover's funeral. But as she sat in her hotel room, her heart breaking from her loss, there came a knock on the door. It was an officer from the local garrison. He had received orders from Berlin to call on Annemarie and ask for the plans. She faced him with a sense of shock: they were still sewn inside Carl's waistcoat!

Things then happened quickly. Carl's family were seated quietly in the chapel of the hospital in which he had died and in minutes the coffin containing the body was due to be taken away for burial. Suddenly the chapel door opened and the officer walked in. He stepped up to the side of the surprised priest, turned, and said, 'By order of the general commanding, this body is to be taken away for a short while!'

The stunned family sat in the chapel in absolute silence until, shortly afterwards, the coffin was returned and the service continued. None of the relatives noticed that the corpse no longer had a waistcoat!

When Matthesius received the plans and notes, he immediately recognized their great value, although he could not fully understand them. So the officer again returned to Annemarie's room and handed her a letter from Matthesius, requesting her to come to Berlin and meet him.

'I know that you are suffering a great deal at the moment,' the letter continued, 'but I need your help. You and Carl went through much danger to obtain these facts for the Fatherland—do not let your joint work be wasted. Think of it this way; you are doing it for him, as he would have wished, and not for yourself.'

That was enough. She realized the truth in his statement and, although still shattered by the suddenness of her lover's death, boarded a train and arrived in Berlin. She was soon seated in a small office with the man who was to be her new boss and for a time she forgot her grief as she explained the notes and pointed out facts about trenches, gun emplacements and fortifications that she had sketched herself. They worked through the night. When they had finished, dawn had broken and Matthesius had long appreciated what a brilliant girl he had before him. He told her to leave for a while and get some sleep whilst he spoke to his own superior officer.

Within two days everything had been arranged. Realizing the plans the spy-master had put forward for her future was what Carl would have wished, the girl agreed to do everything he suggested. She was now a spy in her own right.

A few weeks later a 'schoolgirl', with two long pigtails, boarded a train that was to take her to France . . . and adventure. It was not long before she reached a village in the French Vosges and settled into a boarding-house with her trunks and hat-boxes. Also, most important, she had her easel and artist's materials, for her passport showed that she was but sixteen years old, an art student from Switzerland, and one who had come to paint the surrounding area in all its autumn beauty.

Every day she went out to paint; and every day she found time to chat to the local people, who soon made a pet of this charming little 'Swiss' girl. From then, quite casually, she learned of the new roads that were shortly to be built, of an extension to the railway that would carry supplies to forts that were to be constructed in the Vosges, and similar little items that could, really, hardly interest such a sweet young girl as Annemarie.

Then, once again, everything changed. A division of the French Army marched in and were billeted at various houses in the village. Some of the officers were staying at her boarding-house and she asked a tough, middle-aged captain what was happening. Charmed by his pretty young companion, he replied, 'We're on manoeuvres, my dear. It's going to be one of the largest in our peace-time history. We've brought almost a whole army corps into this area, with artillery and the rest. It will go on for several days.'

'How thrilling. Do you think I could watch it?'

'M'm. I'm not sure. We cover a lot of ground, you know, and our men can march for hours. How will you keep up with us?'

'The owner of this boarding-house has a chaise and the most beautiful little horse you've ever seen. I know he would allow me to hire it for a few days—if I may be allowed to come with you, that is?'

Who could refuse such a sweet, innocent girl? The next day, when the soldiers marched out of the village, Annemarie followed the manoeuvres, her agile brain noting every detail of the men—the way they fought, the way they marched, and how their officers deployed the various divisions. Whenever he could spare the time, her friend the

105

captain was at her side, happy to be seen with such an attractive girl. He was very proud too, despite the grins of his fellow officers, to pose while she took photographs of him for her 'album'. He never noticed that she always chose the background with great care. Sometimes it was a trench system, sometimes a new type of gun, but always something interesting for her employers.

Finally, after some hesitation—for there was quite a difference in their ages—he asked her to marry him.

'I find you charming and gallant,' she told him, 'and I think that, in a very short while, I could easily learn to love you. But I must ask you this: what does an officer's wife do with herself when her husband is away? Please tell me your duties, and perhaps then I shall be able to understand.'

Excited at the thought of marrying this beautiful creature, the captain told her everything. How things had changed since he had first joined the army, how much easier it was to kill the enemy now that the guns were more powerful; how the area of fire had changed; how much faster they could travel in a day; how the construction of both fortifications and trenches had improved. As he spoke he was delighted to see how she hung on his every word. Although a young girl, and obviously one who understood little of what he was saying, there was no doubt that she was greatly interested. There was no doubt, either, that she would make an excellent officer's wife—and he went out to have some more photographs taken.

'I shall need these,' she told him, 'to show Mama in Geneva.'

'In Geneva?' he asked, anxiously.

'Yes. I have to return home for a while to tell Mama of all the exciting things that have been happening here, and how I have become engaged to such a fine and brave captain.'

Realizing that the sooner she saw her mother the sooner they might be married, the captain arranged a fast car for her while a sergeant was ordered to accompany her to the train. To do so they had to cross the border. Their car was stopped by customs men, but the sergeant immediately smoothed out that difficulty.

'This is the captain's fiancée and he has told me that she is not to be put to any trouble. She has been on a sketching holiday in the Vosges. Surely there is nothing wrong in that? I must particularly ask you not to bother with a search of her luggage. You may spoil some of her paintings with your clumsy hands!'

'But what about these photographs?'

The sergeant smirked. 'They are all of my captain. She is taking them back to show her mother what a good-looking officer she is going to marry.'

The customs officer grinned in reply and waved the car on. Annemarie settled back with a sigh. She had her ticket for Geneva, but long before reaching that city she changed trains and was soon in Berlin. The next day she took her sketches and photographs to Matthesius. As he glanced through them he became very excited, especially when the photographs revealed details of French artillery that made many of the guns used by the German Army appear obsolete.

When Annemarie finally left his small office she was relaxed for the first time since her lover's death. She was actually happy. She had done her work well. Carl would have been proud of her.

Less than a week later, however, reaction set in, causing her to speak to Matthesius on the telephone. 'I must work. I can't go on without something to keep me busy. What do you want me to do next?'

The other did not hesitate. 'I quite understand how you feel,' he replied gently. 'Come and see me tomorrow and we will discuss things.'

The outcome of the meeting was that she was confirmed as one of his few full-time agents. She was paid a regular salary and was given a code number used in an emergency by all secret agents. In her case it was 'One and Four, G and W'. Day after day she worked with Matthesius, learning from him details of enemy armament, fortifications and other military installations. She also spent hours studying details of uniforms, cap badges and vehicle markings in order to recognize at a glance what regiments were in her vicinity.

The whole winter was spent in study of this nature and then, in the spring of 1914, she was ready to start. Her first task was to go to Beverloo in Belgium, a huge expanse of ground near the Dutch frontier, which could be used for large-scale troop manoeuvres. Nearby were the huge Belgian fortresses of Liège and she was asked to find out the number of guns they contained, their calibre and range, and where exactly they were positioned.

She arrived first in Brussels, checking in at the Hôtel Anglais, as a French girl from Paris. Later in the day she strolled into the dining-room and it was not long before she was in conversation with a hand-some young Belgian lieutenant named René Austin. He was very much attracted by the beautiful and poised young woman. Had he seen a photograph of her as she was the previous year—a sixteen-year-old schoolgirl with long pigtails—he would never have believed it to be one and the same person.

'What brings you to Brussels?' he asked her.

'I am an art student and have loved Belgian artists since I first began to paint. You know, people like Peter Paul Rubens, the van Eycks, Frans Floris, and the rest. The best of their work seems to be here, in Brussels, so I have come to study at the feet of the masters, as it were. I shall spend most of my time working in this city's marvellous art galleries.'

She paused for a moment then added, with a smile, 'I can see that you are an officer, so I had better be careful what I say!'

'What do you mean?'

'Well, I am French and my father was an officer in my country's army. I have inherited a great love of the army and army life from my dear father, now dead, alas,' and she heaved a great sigh.

After he had done his best to comfort her he asked, 'But what did you mean by the remark that you had better be careful what you say?'

She smiled again. 'Well, my father always declared that his army—the French Army—was the finest in the world. He never had any time for those of other countries, especially the Belgian Army.' She suddenly threw her hand over her mouth. 'You see, I've said the wrong thing already.'

He smiled in return. 'How long ago did your father die?'

'Oh, it must be ten years ago at least.'

'Well, we've changed a lot in those ten years,' he retorted, and began to tell her of the many improvements: of the Belgian Army's new guns, the revisions that had been made throughout with new chains of command, and so on. He was flattered by the attention this charming new companion was paying to his words. In order to impress her to the full, he told her of items still very much on the secret list, knowing that as a young woman, even with a father who had once been an officer but was now long dead, she would understand very little of what he was telling her . . .

That evening was the first of several such meetings, and he soon found himself falling in love with her. He did not appreciate how much he cared until she disappeared for a week without a word of farewell. Then to his great joy she was back again. She had been on a sketching trip, she told him, and to prove it opened a portfolio of charming drawings. They were all in pen and ink or water-colour. There were some oil paintings too, but these she did not bother to show him. Instead she had them packed up and sent to an address in Berlin.

Matthesius stood by as these oil paintings were unpacked and only briefly admired the subjects—landscapes, barges on a canal, a thickly wooded landscape, and so on. Then, taking up a knife, he began to gently scrape away the paint from the first painting. Beneath he found another, of a military subject, which he found far more interesting!

Soon afterwards Annemarie told Austin that she was about to leave on another such expedition. Indeed, she had bought a new two-seater car to carry her around the countryside. He could not bear to let her go off again, leaving him alone, so he hastily arranged to take a week's leave so that they could go together. Quite by 'chance', Beverloo was a district covered in their excursion. Still acting the part of an officer's daughter, she continually asked her companion questions about the district, the fortresses and the number of guns contained in each.

During one brief halt, when Austin had got out of the car to look at the engine, she began to write some notes on a piece of paper. A sudden gust of wind, however, caused it to flutter away. Austin ran after it, to recover it, although she told him not to bother. Finally he returned and said in a strained voice, 'I'm sorry. I couldn't catch it. The wind carried it away!'

They started off again and when the girl cast a quick look at her companion she saw at once what had happened. He *had* found the paper— and read what was written on it. Her fears were soon confirmed, for as they drew into the next village a gendarme was seen standing nearby. Austin stopped the car, leapt out and shouted, 'Officer, come here! At once!'

That was enough for Annemarie. She started the car and took it

Annemarie started the car and took it racing through the village.

racing through the village. As she turned the corner at the far end, however, there came disaster. Unfamiliar with her new car, she skidded right across the road and struck a tree. She scrambled out and was only a few paces from the car when it suddenly burst into flames. She did not stop to watch but started running. She reached a nearby wood and finally came out on the banks of a canal. To her joy she saw a large barge moving past. She dived into the water and, swimming alongside the barge, clambered on board.

The old Dutch bargee who was at the helm stared at her in utter surprise. She did not hesitate. She thrust a bundle of wet notes at him. 'Here you are. Money. I am being chased by some men who have accused me of smuggling. But I am innocent I tell you, innocent. Just get me over the Dutch border and this money—three thousand francs—is yours!'

This conversation was overheard by the bargee's wife, and she did not hesitate for a second. To her, such money meant a fortune and she was not going to lose it. She hid Annemarie in a small cupboard until the innocent-looking barge crossed the frontier into Holland. Annemarie was safe.

She waited in Amsterdam for Matthesius to join her and then handed over all her notes with the exception, of course, of the page that had been 'lost'. Austin had seen this page and quickly realized that the notes with which both sides were covered related to the number of guns, and their calibres, in the two fortresses he had been able to show her.

After she had concluded her work with Matthesius she went to the Hook of Holland, intending to visit England. Once again her whole appearance had changed. This time she wore glasses and her hair was pulled back in a most unflattering manner.

She landed at Dover and was soon making boat trips along the coast, always with her sketch book and pencil—the typical woman artist. But she soon found that security in England was better than she had found in France or Belgium. With her sixth sense she felt that she was being watched. One evening she slipped into the bar of the small inn where she was staying and heard some men talking about her. She was right. They were about to arrest her as a spy.

That same night she crept from the inn, made her way to Dover and travelled to Calais by a French steamer. Using a Swiss passport, she had no trouble in reaching Berlin, although a great search was going on for her back in England. From this visit, Matthesius gained valuable information—that the British and Belgian secret services were exchanging information and had decided that the woman who had travelled with René Austin, and the lady artist in England, were one and the same. Typically the English, because of her glasses and severe expression, had nicknamed her the 'Lady Doctor'. This was also adopted by the French as 'Mademoiselle Docteur', a name she was to bear for the rest of her life.

Matthesius saw that it was time for her to take a rest. This lasted until July 1914, when she was sent to Milan to help a German agent stationed there. His task had been to find out whether new earthworks were being built and, if so, their importance and extent. He had already reported that such a task would take him several months. Annemarie's brilliant mind solved the problem. She obtained copies of every small newspaper in Italy, looking for advertisements which invited local firms to put in tenders for work which required both excavation and the use of reinforced concrete. Within a few days—and with the help of a good map—she was able to estimate the areas in which the earthworks were to be erected, and the extent of their fortifications.

It was not long before it was obvious that war was imminent. Annemarie was in Italy at the time and, realizing the seriousness of the situation, she slipped into Paris in the guise of a nursing sister. She hastened to the office of the principal German agent in France, a Monsieur Pissard, and introduced herself with her secret code number. With a look of relief he warmly greeted the now famous 'lady doctor'.

'So you have come,' he said. 'Even to Paris. And with war only a few days, or even hours away . . . so it seems.'

He handed over to her all the information he had obtained by speaking to mobilized French soldiers, listening to conversations in cafés and at railway stations and similar places. When he had finished she hid the thin sheets of paper, on which she had written notes, on her person.

She now changed her identity yet again. Now she became a Belgian nurse with a Belgian passport, and one about to visit a Belgian field hospital. Using all her considerable charm, she managed to obtain a seat in a train carrying high-ranking officers and she looked and mentally noted all the strengths—and weaknesses—of the French defence system as they travelled along. She also talked to French staff officers and found out one vital item—something that not even Matthesius had been able to learn. This was the fact that should war break out, Belgium would fight on the side of the French.

Further talks that she overheard revealed another important fact. If war broke out, Britain would immediately land six divisions of infantry and eight brigades of cavalry—something like 160,000 men—at Antwerp. She now realized that this information must be got back to Berlin without delay—and also saw that her life was in danger should anyone check her references. But she still stayed on.

That evening she dined with some of the French staff officers and learned one more crucial fact—that if French troops marched into Belgium, this would not be regarded as a violation of neutrality.

It was now time for her to do the best she could. By means of her passport and forged papers she left Brussels and actually obtained a seat in the train taking Belgian staff officers to the fortress of Liège.

Some days later, on the night of 3 August 1914, Annemarie crossed the frontier between Belgium and Germany and, after some argument at the command post, managed to get a message to Matthesius. The next day, acting on his favourite agent's instructions, he passed on her report to the High Command. The German Army marched into Belgium and the fortress of Liège fell two days later.

The First World War had begun with Austria's attack on Serbia in July 1914 following the murder of the Archduke Ferdinand at Sarajevo. Russia came to the aid of Serbia and Germany to that of Austria. War was then declared on France as Russia's ally, and the invasion of Belgium brought Britain into the struggle—as Annemarie had already warned her country. Then, at that critical time, Monsieur Pissard, Germany's chief agent in Paris, disappeared.

Annemarie went to see what had happened to him, travelling from Holland to England, then to Bordeaux and finally to Paris. She found that the agent, an apparently good Frenchman, had been called up but had shot himself. Now Germany was without its most valuable French agent at a time when he was most needed. After a search, Annemarie had him replaced with a Greek named Coudoyanis.

She then met a young officer attached to the counter-espionage

113

department of the French Army. It was not long before he, like the others before, was in love with her. And, as before, she was able to gain from him a number of secrets that should never have been revealed. Then one day he casually told her, 'We are informed that there is a German spy, a woman, working in France. We do not know her real name, but she is known as the "lady doctor". A man named Coudoyanis had promised to tell us who she is, but first he wants a hundred thousand francs. Once he has the money he will lead us to her and she will end up in front of a firing squad!'

Annemarie had to act quickly. That evening she met Coudoyanis, the traitor, and gave him a letter, telling him to take it to a certain inn just outside Paris, where an agent would be waiting for him at seven o'clock the following morning. If he handed over the letter he would be given fifty thousand francs. This was a bait the greedy agent could not refuse and he promised to do it.

That same night the counter-espionage bureau in Paris also had a letter. It denounced the Greek as a German spy. More, if the French caught him at the inn at seven o'clock the next morning, they would find the necessary evidence. Her plan worked. The first letter was found on Coudoyanis, proving he was a spy, and he was later shot by a firing squad. Before he died he revealed that his death was due to a woman, but refused to give her name, merely saying, "She is a wonderfully beautiful woman. She is extremely clever and amazingly energetic. She has such an influence over me that I could not resist her. She masters everyone who comes into contact with her, even officers of the highest rank . . .'

His death put the French counter-espionage on their guard, especially as they had found a list of German spies. Once again, something had to be done, and quickly. Once again it was Annemarie who did it. She disguised herself completely, this time as a slovenly-looking and ignorant peasant girl, and went back to Paris. Employment was no problem, for serving girls were hard to find in wartime. She chose her position with care, because she had come with a specific purpose. The house where she was to work and live was actually the central office for French counter-espionage!

After warning the rest of the German agents who were on the captured list to leave France immediately, Annemarie settled down to a life of hard work and little food. She managed to change her shift so that she spent most of her time on duty at night and during the long, dark hours she would talk to the French sergeant on duty. Then, one night, she slipped behind him and pushed a chloroform-drenched cloth over his face. An hour later, her appearance altered once again, she slipped from the house. With her went the lists of every French agent, not only in Germany but also in neutral countries. It was a great haul for the master spy.

For a while she then worked in Berlin, but her health was now beginning to show the strain of the long years of anxiety, and she had to resort to drugs to keep her going.

Her last great exploit was towards the end of the war. Germany was about to make one final, drastic effort and it was necessary to find out the morale of the French troops. To do so Annemarie, once again, changed her whole appearance. She turned up in Barcelona, stating that she had just arrived from South America to visit the field hospitals of the French Army, and talked seven lady members of the Spanish Red Cross into going with her. Their path took them along the Western Front and frequently the ladies would don nursing uniforms and help tend the wounded.

Then, as Annemarie bent over one wounded Belgian officer, he opened his eyes wide, struggled up in bed and shouted, "Quick! Arrest her! This woman is a German spy!'

The wounded officer was René Austin. With several officers standing nearby, Austin shouted again, 'I know her! I know her! She is the spy they call the "lady doctor".'

At the sound of these two words a French captain moved forward to arrest her. But she acted faster. She seized his cloak, to which his revolver holster was strapped, and ran out of the hospital tent. Once again she was saved by a nearby wood although, as she ran, bullets crashed into the trees all about her. After a while, however, she had to stop to regain her breath, sheltering behind a tree. As she did so she saw two French soldiers coming towards her, their rifles ready. She waited calmly until they were a little nearer then raised the officer's revolver and fired . . . twice.

Some minutes later, what seemed to be one of the soldiers was running through the dark night. But it was Annemarie, who had dressed herself in one of the dead men's uniforms. Led by the sound of the guns on the Western Front, she made her way towards them, dodging the French outposts. As dawn was breaking she was spotted by a group of German soldiers on early patrol.

'Halt!' shouted the officer leading them. 'Hands up or we fire!'

One of the Frenchman's hands flew skywards, the other jerked off a cap and a woman's long hair came tumbling over the shoulders. As the officer stared, amazed, she said urgently, 'Quick. I am a German spy. I have important news. Take me to your commanding officer at once!'

Her report, given a few hours later, was astounding. Looking round at the officers about her she said, 'All I can say, gentlemen, is that we have lost this war. Fresh troops are already pouring into the area. They include thousands of American soldiers, well equipped and eager to fight.'

The General Staff officer who had been sent for watched as she quickly sketched in the positions of the vast army massing before them. He then studied the tired, drawn face of the woman before him. Like so many, he had heard of the 'lady doctor' and knew she was always reliable. He rushed her to a plane and very soon she was at Imperial Headquarters in Berlin. Once again she gave her report and the faces of the officers of the General Staff grew sombre as they listened . . .

Soon afterwards, on 11 November 1918, the armistice was signed. The war was over. And so was the work of the 'lady doctor'. Exhausted from years of nervous strain and ill from the drugs she had taken to keep herself going, she finally entered a mental hospital in Switzerland.

Her duty done, the greatest woman spy of the First World War was never seen outside the hospital walls again.

THE THIRTEENTH MAN

Lt. Col. Oreste Pinto

Lt. Col. Oreste Pinto, famed for his counter-espionage activities in two world wars, joined MI5 at the start of the Second World War. On many occasions he must have needed every ounce of resourcefulness at his command, but in this thrilling story the enemy is outwitted by a quirk of character.

It was the first week of September 1940. Four months earlier the last remnants of the British Expeditionary Force had been evacuated from Dunkirk, leaving the German Wehrmacht on the edge of the Channel. On a clear day their soldiers, lustily singing their favourite song, *Marching against England*, could see the misty outlines of the coveted prize across that narrow strip of water, narrow enough for a good swimmer to cross. Only one gigantic stride was required, it seemed, for the all-conquering Wehrmacht with its crack Panzer troops, self-propelled guns and Stuka dive-bombers to snatch the one plum that remained beyond its grasp. Hitler himself had supervised the drawing up of his favourite plan—the invasion of England—under the code name of 'Operation Sealion'.

Air reconnaissance and information from our secret agents on the Continent confirmed the possibilities. Flotillas of barges and small ships were moving into position along the coast between Ostend and Le Havre. One hundred and sixty bomber aircraft were transferred from Norway to the Channel area. Short-range dive-bombers were spotted on the forward airfields in the Pas de Calais. As Mr Winston

Churchill later wrote in Volume II of his great memoirs: 'Moon and tide conditions between the 8th and the 10th [of September] were favourable for invasion on the south-east coast . . . The Chiefs of Staff concluded that the possibility of invasion had become imminent.'

I had spent the night on duty in my office. Dawn was breaking as I rose, stretched myself and yawned, then went off to shave. I had just returned when a young Intelligence officer rushed into the room. He was obviously excited.

'A message for you, sir,' he blurted out.

I took the message and held it up to the pale light from the window. The code signature showed that it came from one of our most trusted and resolute agents, who had been left on the Continent to spy for us. The message read: 'U-boat departs Zeebrugge tonight 2130 hours carrying 4 spies instructed land England before daylight south coast map reference 432925 these men carefully selected and trained for special mission regarding German Operation Sealion.'

I looked up at the excited young man and smiled. 'This means business,' I said. 'Come one, let's get to work.'

We consulted a large-scale map of the south coast. There was the spot indicated by the map reference and it had obviously been chosen with care. It was a small secluded cove, and behind it the steep cliffs stood almost sheer, providing cover from inquisitive eyes. But if they would serve to keep the casual observer out they might as easily serve to keep the silent invader in. Manned by resolute watchers, these cliffs could be a death-trap for the four spies. The cove was crescent-shaped and far from any village, or even house, if the map were correct. It was wide open to the sea, but there was only one exit on the land side.

I smoked a cigarette while I ran over the simple plan that was forming in my mind. Then I conferred with the Field Security Officer, a captain, who had already been detailed to work with me.

'This is how I see it,' I said. 'The plan is simple, but on a dark night the more simple it is the less likelihood of things going wrong. All we need do is to place men at short intervals along the foot of the cliffs—you see on the map how the beach is funnel-shaped—and you and I will post ourselves at the neck of the funnel—here. This little path—or track—is the only exit from the beach, short of scaling the cliffs. To go right ashore these four spies have got to get past us.'

'How many men will you require, sir?' he asked.

'Let us say a dozen. And have them change into civilian clothes, less conspicuous.'

'Armed, of course, sir?'

'Yes, of course. But on no account are they to open fire without my orders. That must be strictly understood. We want to get these men alive.'

'Yes, sir.'

'They must all carry flashlights. We can work out a series of signals before we leave. Any more questions?'

'No, sir.'

'Right. We must be in position by midnight. Have your men ready to leave by seven o'clock. That should give us ample time to drive there in comfort.'

It was growing dusk as we drove along the Great West Road and gradually darkness blotted out the countryside. The black-out on all sides and the feeble beams from our shuttered headlamps gave us the eerie sensation of moving through a strange fourth dimension. The moon had not risen and we felt like ants in a bottle of ink with the cap screwed on. I was chain-smoking. Being a heavy smoker, I knew the coming torment of perhaps six hours without being able to light up in case the glow of the cigarette-end betrayed our position. I was trying to build up a reserve of the nicotine content in my bloodstream and in the darkness smiled at this fantasy. From time to time I glanced at the luminous dial of my watch. We were making good progress and at this rate would easily be in position by the appointed hour.

As I peered out into the blackness of the passing countryside, a strange fancy seized me. In my mind's eye I could see the outlines of the map fifty miles on either side of the English coast. Two lines were converging, one from the land and one from the sea, on that lonely funnel-shaped cove. But the lines of the cliff-edge which I had memorized were no longer funnel-shaped in my imagination. They had become the jaws of a trap. Once we were in position the trap would be ready for springing. I thought for a while of the four spies at this moment huddled in the U-boat that was nosing its way towards the English coast. What kind of men were they? Fanatic patriots taking the supreme risk for their country? Or trained men carrying out orders instinctively? And then I thought of our Field Security fellows who would man the trap. It suddenly occurred to me that the captain and his men were thirteen in number. Was this to be an unlucky omen?

We reached the cliffs at the back of the cove on the stroke of midnight. I quickly ran through the orders with the twelve men and their captain huddled round me, dark, unrecognizable shapes against the dark countryside. Man the foot of the cliffs at equal distances apart, no talking, no smoking, above all, no shooting except in absolute self-defence. The signal if any spy came within tackling distance—three short flashes from the nearest flashlight. There were no questions and, one by one, we threaded our way down the narrow cliff-path in silence save the occasional muttered curse as someone tripped over an obstruction. At the foot of the cliff the captain and I watched the men disappear into the darkness on either side of the cliff-path. We stood together at the junction of the beach with the path, the neck of the 'funnel'. We could hear the quiet crunching of the men's footsteps on the sand as they crept into position, and then silence.

Silence—except for the monotonous ripple of the tide on the beach and the sucking noise it made on the ebb. Ripple and suck, ripple and suck, as it had done from time immemorial. Tonight the time seemed immemorial and the minutes crawled away. After what felt like a whole night of waiting I was surprised to hear a distant clock in a village church chime the hour of one. Only one o'clock! I turned up my greatcoat collar, plunged my hands deeper in my pockets, and hunched up my shoulders against the damp cold of the beach. I ached with all my being for a cigarette. Once, when my hand brushed against the packet, I was sorely tempted. But no! The flicker of a match and the red glow of the cigarette-end would have been seen miles out to sea, especially if, as I suspected, keen eyes were already scanning the shore through binoculars.

Two o'clock crept towards us, arrived, and then receded as slowly. Then three o'clock. I checked my watch with the village church chimes at three o'clock and, what might have been half an hour later, glanced at it again. Only five past three. I held it to my ear but it ticked away steadily. I was too fast in my impatience, not the watch too slow.

'I counted them—one, two, three. The fourth spy was missing.'

It was nearly four o'clock. I turned to the captain and whispered, 'I wish to God the blighters would . . .'

Suddenly I saw flashes—one, two, three short jabs of light against the black cliff-side. A prowling figure was silhouetted against the shifting beams. As two other flashlights cut beams into the darkness, a second and a third figure could be observed, immobilized by surprise. A light went out suddenly and I could hear the sound of a scuffle. The ring of torchlight closed in and there was a moment of confusion, of shouting and boots plunging in the soft sand. The captain and I rushed to the centre of the confusion and as we arrived, order returned. There were our twelve men triumphant with their dumb-founded and dejected captives. As I had the prisoners lined up, I thought to myself, 'It is almost too easy.' I counted them—one, two, three. It had been too easy. The fourth man was missing.

I was certain in my own mind that the message had been correct in mentioning four men. A spy who risks his life in getting a vitally important radio message out of enemy-held territory makes sure that his details are right. Four men, the message had said, and four men there were going to be. But now that the element of surprise was lost, finding the fourth man would be almost impossible before daylight. He could be lying up somewhere between the sea and the cliffs and only the luckiest beam from a torch or the accident of actually stumbling over him would betray his hiding place. So far we had made a satisfactory haul but our night's work would be ruined if we allowed one man to slip through our fingers. The fact that we had not caught him at the first opportunity probably meant that he was the most dangerous and cool-headed of the bunch. He could do incalculable damage, perhaps ruin our chances of defeating the invasion that seemed imminent. There was one reassuring factor. He must still be on the beach. The cliff-path had been guarded throughout and that was the only exit.

I turned to the Field Security captain. 'Well, there's only one thing for it. We'll have to stick here until daylight and pick him up then. In the meantime, let's see what we have hooked.'

The three men were searched. My admiration for German thoroughness rose by a few degrees. Each of the prisoners was well-dressed in an English suit obviously cut by an English tailor and carrying a well-known London tailor's label. They had plenty of English money in notes of small denomination. They even had the proper identity cards, coloured grey for aliens and duly filled in and stamped. Each one carried a compact but powerful radio transmitter.

I ordered the three to be moved sufficiently far apart to be out of ear-shot of each other and then began to question them. The first two I interrogated were Germans, named Waldberg and Meyer. Like many Germans, although resolute under fire, they offered little resistance when they knew the game was up. They answered all my questions sullenly but in detail.

Before I had spoken to the third man, he broke out in English with, 'Could I have a word with you, please, sir?' In surprise I flashed a light in his face. He stood there blinking. I studied him. His accent was marked but it was not a German accent. He was obviously frightened.

'Well?' I said.

And then the story came tumbling out. He was not a German but a Dutchman. He was not really a spy; in fact he was glad to be caught so soon. It saved him the trouble of giving himself up at the nearest police station he could find. He had been too smart for the Germans. He had fooled them into thinking he wanted to be a spy in England, when all the time his one aim was to get over to England and enlist on the side of the Allies. He gave an ingratiating grin as he ended.

It was not the first time I had heard this kind of story but my disgust did not grow less. I can admire an honest spy who risks his life and accepts the consequence of capture with courage. But this glib cowardice was only contemptible. To save his own skin the man would cheerfully betray his comrades. He might, nevertheless, be useful to us.

'All right, you say you are on our side. How many of you came ashore tonight?'

'Four, sir.'

'You are absolutely certain there were four of you?'

'Yes, sir. Myself, Waldberg, Meyer and Van der Kieboom, sir. That makes four.'

'Van der Kieboom. That's not a German name.'

'No, sir. He is Dutch—like me.'

So that was established. There really had been four and the message was correct. But where was Van der Kieboom? Perhaps daylight would tell.

And so our vigil continued. Five o'clock and then six o'clock came and went. At last, when the night seemed never ending, a streak of pale light showed on the horizon and crept across the still sea towards us. Soon it was possible to distinguish rocks from men and a quarter of an hour later there was enough light to begin the last search.

Our men fanned out in a line and, starting from one end of the beach, slowly paced towards the other. There was gorse and undergrowth, thorny bushes and sand hollows, but every inch of the ground was searched in the half light before the dawn. The Field Security captain and I stood back and watched them gradually making their way forward, bending down under every bush, moving all objects that might afford cover. They were a third of the way along the beach, then halfway, then three-quarters. And then they converged at the far end empty-handed. There was no trace of Van der Kieboom.

I swore out loud, then shouted to them to retrace their steps. The line fanned out again as they returned towards us, searching the ground as meticulously as before. This was fantastic. Van der Kieboom *had* to be on the beach. Wild thoughts flashed through my mind. Could he have swum back to the U-boat when he heard his comrades captured? But no, there had been no sound of splashing from the sea except the ripple and suck of the monotonous tide. Could he have scaled the cliffs? A glance upward assured me that not even a mountain goat could have ascended in the dark without at least dislodging stones and boulders to give its position away. So Van der Kieboom must still be on the beach. But where?

I clenched my fists in my exasperation and watched the approaching line of searchers. It was light enough to see the white blur of each face but not to recognize the owner. I looked along the line from right to left and then back again. Suddenly the solution hit me and I laughed aloud. 'Clever devil,' I said.

The captain looked startled. 'What's the matter, sir?'

'What a clever devil,' I repeated and then raised my voice. 'All right, you men, halt where you are.' They halted. I turned to the captain. 'Will you come with me? I'm going to introduce you to our friend.'

The captain and I strolled along the line of searchers, pausing long enough to recognize each one. Eight, nine, ten. We were nearing the end of the line. Eleven, twelve and—we halted and I put a hand on the last man's shoulder. 'Good morning, Van der Kieboom,' I said. He was the thirteenth man.

In the half light and the confusion he might have got away with it, if we had decided to call the search off. He could have brought up the rear of the party climbing the cliff-path and then lain low until the cars departed. He was a clever, resolute man.

If it had not been for the fact that exactly twelve men were chosen for the job and my superstitiousness had caused me to remember this, I should not have counted them mentally as they approached in line through the grey dawn light. On such slender threads does a man's life hang.

Van der Kieboom, Meyer and Waldberg were tried, sentenced to death and executed. It was the only case in the Second World War where trial and execution of three spies simultaneously were carried out. The fourth man, who had turned King's evidence, was kept in an English prison until the end of the war and was then transferred to a

Dutch prison. I have never heard what happened to him after that.

Van der Kieboom fought hard at his trial to save his life. He made the passionate plea that he was a misguided youth, led astray against his better judgment. He asked for one more chance—to enlist in the service of the Allies and be sent to the front line, where a soldier's death might retrieve his honour in the eyes of the world, of his country and of his mother. But his plea was in vain.

He was a convinced and fanatical Nazi. In his last letter written to his mother on the eve of his execution, he begged her forgiveness for the pain and sorrow his death would cause her. 'If only you hadn't known, Mother,' he wrote, 'then I would be the happiest and proudest of men in dying for the great cause and my Führer.' In the will he drew up at the same time he directed his mother to sell his property, his camera and binoculars and all his prized possessions, and forward the proceeds to the German Red Cross if it were possible.

Yes, he was a fanatical Nazi and paid the supreme penalty. But he was also a cool and resourceful man who was captured only because one of the search party happened to be superstitious.

CAPTAIN ROBERTON'S SECRET

Michael & Mollie Hardwick

The dark man was sitting on a rock, watching two half-naked youths skinning a seal. It was not a pretty sight, nor was the butchery of other seals that was still going on, farther along the shore. But it did not seem to put the dark man out in the least or spoil the flavour of the long cigar he was smoking. Captain William Smith, who was used to seeing all sorts of human riff-raff in these islands of the Bass Strait, between Tasmania and the south-eastern tip of Australia, was struck by the unusual appearance of this nonchalant character. Tall, dark to swarthiness, elegantly slim with a look of the swordsman about him, he was dressed in a dark blue jacket and breeches, gilt-buttoned and of good quality. The high stock that almost engulfed his chin was clean, and clean linen on Cape Barren Island was a rarity in the year 1826. On second thoughts, the man might be a naval officer. Smith decided to find out.

The dark man acknowledged his greeting unsmilingly, and accepted the offer of a swig from Smith's pocket-bottle of rum. Smith noted that his accent was curious—predominantly Scottish, but with a flavour of something else as well, suggestive of warmer countries—while his eyes were at the same time dark and cold, an unusual combination except in reptiles. Their gaze rested thoughtfully on the schooner *Caledonia*, rocking gently at anchor.

'Yours?' the man inquired.

'That's right.' Smith was also a man of few words. 'Been with her a good few years.'

'She looks a tight enough craft.'

'You're a good judge. Thought she was breaking up on me last year, though. Found myself in Westernport—over there.' He nodded toward the Australian mainland. 'Nearest thing to the end of the earth. Not a drop of tar and pitch to be had for her seams.'

'How did you get her seaworthy, then?'

'Melted down the gum of the grass-trees. Worked like a charm.'

The stranger said nothing, but his appraising look registered approval of Smith's resourcefulness.

'What's your trade?' he asked.

'Anything I can get. Sealskins from here. Wallaby skins over yonder. Wattle bark. Tusks. Stuff the black boys carve.'

The dark man smiled coldly. 'A species of sea pedlar.'

'Call it that. I've not much choice of goods.'

His companion appeared to be about to say something, but changed his mind. His long, Scottish mouth shut in a thin line. Smith's curiosity was now thoroughly aroused. He was a sharp-witted, enterprising man with a nose for a bargain and he scented in this apparently casual conversation the possibility of something good coming his way. He sniffed the air exaggeratedly.

'Devil of a stink round here, with them skins. Care to step aboard and take a glass with me?'

The stranger contemplated his cigar which was almost smoked through. This appeared to make his mind up for him and he rose to his feet. He was even taller than Smith had judged at first and, glancing sideways at the impassive, satanic face as they walked towards the *Caledonia*, Smith thought involuntarily of the legendary Flying Dutchman. If the dreaded Vanderdecken ever existed, Smith thought, he might have looked very like this.

'Welcome aboard the *Caledonia*, Mr—I didn't get the name.'

'I didn't give it. Captain Roberton.'

'Smith. William Smith.' They shook hands formally and sat down at the table in Smith's cabin. A bottle of rough red wine was followed by another, and under their influence Roberton's dour aspect began to soften a little. Drink, shrewdly noted Smith, who himself had a head like teak, was the key to Roberton and to any useful information he might have.

Gradually details began to emerge. It was not clear where Roberton had earned his title of captain, but he had certainly been at sea. During the last few years he had served under the British admiral Lord Cochrane, first in the Chilean Navy, fighting Spain, then in the fleet which in the previous year, 1825, had won the independence of Brazil. From fighting he had turned to whaling and had landed on Cape Barren Island a few days before from a whaler that had come down from the North Pacific. Smith sensed that these autobiographical details omitted a good deal. There was a strong Spanish flavour about Roberton's conversation, particularly in the oaths he dropped as the wine flowed more and more freely. Smith felt there might be a whiff of piracy about his new acquaintance, but he was not one to quarrel with that or with the offer that was forthcoming.

'Sick of peddling, aren't you, Smith? Stinking hides and bits of gim-crackery—that's a poor cargo for a good vessel.'

'I told you, captain, it's all I can get. Unless—unless you know of something better.'

Roberton's face was inscrutable. 'I might. You're a canny man, I take it?'

'I can keep my own counsel.'

'Aye, but can you keep mine?'

'If it's worth my while, captain.'

Roberton leaned forward, elbows on the table. "Here you are, then. Will you let me charter the *Caledonia* for a private voyage?'

'Depends where, captain.'

'To the Ladrone Islands—north of New Guinea, south of Japan. Some call them the Marianas. Will you take me?'

'Depends how much, Captain.'

'Fourteen thousand Mexican dollars.'

Smith concealed his excitement. 'It's a long way.'

'It's a lot of money.'

Smith appeared to deliberate. 'Cash down?'

'I'd be a fool to carry that much cash in these parts, wouldn't I? But my word's my bond—you can rely on that.'

Smith looked dubious. 'I'd have to know what was at the end of it, captain. An honest trading vessel can't afford to get mixed up in anything, you know.'

'*Madre di Dios!* You've a lot of scruples for a poor man.' Roberton pushed back his chair and rose. 'There are plenty will take me if you won't.'

Smith casually reached into the cupboard behind him and produced a brandy bottle, from which he poured two liberal measures.

'Sit down, captain. You can trust me. Stands to reason, before I hire out my ship, I've got to know why—now don't it stand to reason?'

Roberton drained his glass of brandy. His face was no longer sallow, but had a purplish flush. He stared at Smith with a kind of triumphant defiance.

'All right, *mi amigo*, since you're so particular. I'm after treasure—gold, silver, jewels—lovely treasure, lying about in Tom Tiddler's Land for the right man to pick up. Now are you interested?'

Smith was interested. He was no more immune to the beckoning sparkle of treasure than the next man, and in any case fourteen thousand dollars was a heap of money. Even without cash in hand, he agreed to Roberton's proposition. Roberton, who knew the North Pacific waters better than he did, should pilot the *Caledonia* while Smith was retained as master. The bargain was concluded over the rest of the brandy, after which Roberton collapsed sideways on to the cabin floor, unconscious and snoring.

But Smith was still perfectly sober.

Before they could embark, the *Caledonia* had to be fitted out for the long voyage. Smith went for this purpose to Launceston, in northern Tasmania, the nearest place of any size where he could get the supplies he needed. Roberton remained behind on Cape Barren Island, lazily smoking and saying little to anybody. There the *Caledonia* picked him up and set off on her long and pleasant voyage. Around the New Hebrides she wove, in and out of the Solomon Islands, in the languorous airs of those tropic seas. And first all was well aboard. There was plenty to drink, the vision of treasure glittered before Smith's eyes, Roberton was relaxed and good-tempered. He said things under the influence of rum, wine and brandy which suggested that they were after a splendid prize indeed. But what it was, and exactly where, even the most potent cup could not induce him to reveal, and Smith's prodding questions usually provoked a flare-up of black rage and a volley of polyglot oaths.

Smith's own temper did not improve either. After all, he had not yet seen a whisker of his fourteen thousand dollars—which was not all that good pay for such an expensive voyage, when he came to think of it. He had had to take on extra crew, more provisions: where did Roberton think the money was coming from? They began to quarrel openly.

Then Smith saw Roberton in what looked like a conspiratorial conversation with one of the crew. The few words he could overhear confirmed his suspicions. He had the man in and questioned him fiercely. Yes, Roberton had been talking—about treasure; about how he would lead them to it if they would agree to ditch Smith. Closely pressed, the man admitted that this was to be done by the old-time method of knocking Smith out and throwing him over the side.

Smith's face was thunderous. Shoving the man violently to one side, he strode past him out of the cabin and up on to the deck where Roberton was lounging in the sun. Smith marched up to him.

'So you'd plot against me with my own men, would you? Steal my ship and grab the loot yourself?'

Roberton smiled contemptuously.

'Don't believe everything you hear, skipper.'

'I've heard enough! Why, you slimy scum, I'll knock you from here to——'

As he approached Roberton, flailing his fists, the other man jumped nimbly to his feet and closed with him. The noise brought the crew up on deck. They were wise enough to stand back and let the fighting cocks alone. It was a short battle, for Roberton was younger and tougher. A cracking blow to Smith's jaw from his iron knuckles sent the captain reeling backwards. His clawing hands could not catch at solidity. Over the rail he went, and into the sea with a tremendous splash.

Roberton advanced triumphantly towards the watching men.

'Well? Now he's out of the way, you'll find you've a better captain, lads. Let's have a drink all round to celebrate!'

But the crew were not, as he had thought, unanimously anti-Smith, and they did not trust Roberton's ability as a pilot. A boat was lowered and the floundering Smith retrieved. The evening was not a cordial one, but, much as he would have liked, Smith cared too much about the treasure to have Roberton ditched. Over a bottle, the two agreed hypocritically to forgive and forget.

'But you'd be well advised to tell me where we're making for,' Smith said. 'Suppose you were to be taken with one of them tropic fevers? Why, you'd be dead in a matter of hours, and we'd have made the voyage for sweet Fanny Adams.'

'You'd be inconsolable, I'm sure,' smiled Roberton. 'All the same, I'll keep my own counsel till we get there.'

No amount of sly prodding, outright questioning or alcohol would change his mind. *Caledonia* sailed smoothly on. She was very near her objective now. The island of Guam, southernmost of the Ladrones, was little more than a day's sailing away. Captain Smith's spirits rose—only to be severely dashed one morning when he awoke to find his best boat gone, together with Roberton and the pick of the crew.

What he said is best left to the imagination. Then, without wasting time, he steered straight for Guam. The Ladrones were under Spanish rule, and from what Roberton had let slip in his cups about his activities when fighting the Spaniards under Cochrane, Smith guessed that they might be more than willing to catch and punish him.

Landing in Guam, he reported to the Governor, Don Francisco Villalobos. Don Francisco was charming. Of course he sympathized with Smith. He had no personal knowledge of Roberton's part in the Chilean naval war, but obviously the man was a villain. He, Don Francisco, would organize his pursuit and capture. A Spanish brig would give chase, under the able command of Don Francisco Miranda.

'I'd like to go with him,' hastily interrupted Smith. 'I want to see justice done.'

'Of course, of course. There is just a small difficulty . . ."

Don Francisco's interpreter then explained that Señor Smith had, quite innocently, broken the law. No foreign vessel was allowed to put into Guam without a licence from the King of Spain. Señor Smith did not have such a licence? No? Then, regrettably, *Caledonia* and her

131

skipper would have to remain in Guam until official permission had been obtained.

'But the treasure—if Roberton gets his hands on it . . .'' Smith spluttered.

'I think you may leave that to us, señor.' Don Francisco handed the frustrated Englishman a particularly fine cigar.

So Smith did not have the satisfaction of seeing Roberton taken—and taken by an old enemy. For in the war years Roberton and Miranda had met when Roberton was a sailor of fortune and had thrown in his lot with Chilean independence, and Miranda was a much-respected Spanish naval officer. Roberton had captured him in a skirmish between their two vessels, had taken him aboard and had him mercilessly flogged. It had been a peculiarly embittering experience for the proud Spaniard. Now the hour of his revenge had come. Captured at sea before he could reach his goal, Roberton had been brought before Miranda for judgment.

They faced each other on the deck of the brig. Both dark faces were impassive.

Miranda spoke first.

'This treasure. You will tell us where it is.'

Roberton sneered. 'Find it.'

'You British talk much about fair play. I will give you another chance. Tell us the location and your punishment will be lighter.'

Roberton's reply, in Spanish, was unprintable. Miranda turned to the men beside him.

'Tie him up.'

They lashed Roberton to the mast. Two large, strong Negroes, each armed with a cat-o'-nine-tails, took up positions on each side of him while another stripped him of jacket and shirt.

'Is the treasure on Guam?' asked Miranda. Roberton stared back at him defiantly, lips set. The cat fell—once.

'Is it on Agana?' Another terrible stroke. The man with his face to the mast did not cry out. Only an involuntary quiver showed that he had felt anything.

'Is it on Rota? On Tinian? On Saipan? On Anatahan? Pagan? Asunçion? Uruacas?'

When Miranda had run out of islands, the strokes continued relent-

The cat fell. The man with his face to the mast did not cry out.

lessly. Altogether three hundred fell, until Roberton's back was an angry mass of raw meat. Then they rubbed salt into it and threw him into the hold.

Next morning the questioning went on.

'Were you, perhaps, misleading *el Capitan* Smith? It is not on the Ladrones at all, but in Japanese territory. On Marcus Island, perhaps?'

Roberton's sufferings were dreadful, but he neither spoke nor cried out for the first twenty-nine strokes of the cat. At the thirtieth he broke.

'I'll tell! Let me go and I'll tell—blast your eyes, you . . .' He was sobbing and cursing incoherently as they cut him free. A cup of wine was offered him, but he jerked his head aside.

'Very well. You will take us to the treasure personally.'

Roberton nodded.

'Is it far from here? Near enough to reach by boat?'

He nodded again, and Miranda gave orders for a boat to be lowered. Roberton seemed too enfeebled to get into it unaided. A man at each side, they lifted him in. But with one spring he slipped out of their hands like a flash and leapt over the side into the sea.

Consternation followed. Miranda shouted orders from the brig: a Manilan diver who was in the boat must go after the escaping man. This was easy enough, for Roberton was too badly injured to swim powerfully and the lithe native soon brought him to the boat's side. They had him alive! Then, with one desperate twist, he was free. He plunged downward into the green depths and all the diver's skill could not find him again. Captain Roberton, mystery man, was gone, and his secret with him.

But perhaps luck was with Spain. For when his belongings were searched a map was found—yellowed, dog-eared, but undoubtedly a map indicating treasure. Here was the shape of an island—here a palm tree, a rough drawing of a chest, a cross and some figures. This was the clue they wanted; they had only to find the island.

Northward they sailed, towards Japan, pausing at and scouring every island. Miranda was a thorough man, and had an excellent working knowledge of the Ladrones. But not a trace did he find of anything resembling the island represented on Roberton's map, nor a single dollar of treasure. Defeated, he returned to Guam and confessed failure.

Now it was Smith's turn for interrogation. Because Don Francisco

Villalobos in his wisdom sensed that the Englishman was too stupid not to reveal any knowledge he might have, only verbal questioning was used, and it was clear that Smith knew nothing. Courteously waiving regulations, Don Francisco allowed him to reclaim the *Caledonia* and bade him a polite farewell.

Back to Australia went Smith, the poorer for the cost of his long voyage, back to run-of-the-mill trading, a sadder and a wiser man. Roberton's story of treasure had been a pack of lies, he decided, and it would be a long time before he listened to any more such tales from the riff-raff of the islands.

In the Governor's residence on Guam, Villalobos considered evidence to the contrary. Close inquiries had revealed that years ago Roberton's varied career had placed him on a Manila-bound vessel laden with treasure—among it ninety thousand dollars in gold. She had left Callao, but had never made the port of Manila. Just another ship lost at sea, it was thought at the time. But there were strong indications that Roberton, at some point in the voyage, had taken charge, gained the support of some of the crew and disposed of the others. Then, after sinking the ship, he had buried the treasure.

But where? Even the guile of Spain could not extract that information. Perhaps the map left behind by Roberton was deliberately misleading—it was the sort of joke that would have appealed to him. And to this day the Callao treasure may still lie buried beneath golden sand on one of the Ladrones, or somewhere else. Only Roberton knew—and they could not make him tell.

THE EYE OF THE DAWN

Alan Stuart

In the year 1905, all Paris was talking excitedly of a new sensation. At one of the music halls, the Musée Guimet, a young and beautiful girl had proved so astonishing that the people in the audience rose to their feet and shouted for more. To the rhythmic, stirring music of the Far East, she had performed a series of exotic oriental dances.

The name on the posters outside the theatre was Mata Hari. Those who knew a little of the Malay language were quick to tell others what this name meant. Mata means 'the eye', Hari 'the dawn'. And so she was called . . . Mata Hari, the Indian dancer, 'The Eye of the Dawn'. She told the pressmen who clustered around her after her first show that she had revealed age-old, secret dances that were performed by the temple-dancers of the Orient, and which had now been seen by a Western audience for the first time.

'How do you come to know them so well, mams'elle?' asked one reporter.

For a moment she looked sad. 'My mother was a temple-dancer who died when I was born. The priests of Siva took care of me and trained me to dance in her place. But I felt that what I had learned was so strange, yet so beautiful, that I wished to share this beauty with the rest of the world. That is why I am here.'

This, and much more like it, was printed in all the leading French newspapers and soon thousands were thronging to the theatre to watch this new sensation. It was not long before the great theatres of Paris were bidding for her services—the Folies Bergères, the Scala, and the rest. She soon became the most famous dancer of her day . . . almost a legend, although still quite young.

Curiously, no one bothered to find out about her earlier life. Her tale of being a temple-dancer, almost from birth, was enough. Her dancing spoke for itself, satisfying everyone.

Yet her whole story was one big lie.

She had been born in Leeuwarden, a town in Holland. Her maiden name was Margheretha Zelle. When still a young girl she married a captain in the Dutch Army with, for a Dutchman, the unusual name of MacLeod. Soon after the marriage he was posted to Borneo and Sumatra, then to Java. His new wife, of course, went with him. But her young life seemed ruined by his ill-treatment of her. He drank far too much, frequently lost his temper and shouted at her, and at times beat her. She gave birth to two children, a boy and a girl, but the young lad died. It was whispered that he had been poisoned by one of the servants whom MacLeod had cruelly whipped. It had been his revenge.

To get away from the sad surroundings of her home, Margheretha began to spend long hours in quiet temples, watching the dancing of the girls; then, at home and in secret, would copy what she had seen. This form of release was to prove very useful in the years ahead.

Finally, the behaviour of Captain MacLeod forced his superior officers to send him back to Amsterdam in 1901. But the Dutch capital soon proved too much for his expensive tastes yet small pay. Owing money everywhere, he suddenly left home, taking his daughter, Jean Louise, with him. For the first time in her life she fought back; she went to court and was allowed to have her daughter with her. But life was still very difficult with no money, and finally, leaving Jean Louise with her parents, she left home.

Still young, and with a love of life that even her unfortunate marriage had not dimmed, she went to Paris, hoping that in Europe's most exciting capital she would be able to find work. Her beauty attracted many admirers and she was soon receiving gifts of money, jewels and expensive clothes in exchange for her favours. Then she disappeared for a while. When she was next seen it was on the stage of the Musée Guimet. Margheretha MacLeod had gone for ever; in her place was Mata Hari, without question the most exciting woman in Paris—and one destined to become the best-known spy of all time.

Yet she came into espionage almost by accident. Her fame as a dancer, together with her elegance and beauty, attracted many men. Among them were some of the most noble in Europe. From Paris she travelled on—to Rome, Vienna, Berlin—always finding herself surrounded by admiring groups which included princes, ministers and generals.

On one of her visits to dance in Berlin in the summer of 1914 she was approached by a high official in the German Secret Service.

'Fraulein,' he said, 'I know you are a very busy woman so I will not take up much of your time. But what I have to ask of you may well be to your advantage.'

'Out with it then. As you say, I *am* a busy woman and I have to appear at the theatre in less than two hours. What is it you want of me?'

'We, my colleagues and I, have noticed that you spend much time with several important gentlemen, especially with some who are of interest to us.'

'Of interest to you?' she asked, puzzled.

'Yes, Fraulein. Generals, admirals and the like. You see, Fraulein Hari, we are anxious to learn what other nations are thinking and planning. There is every reason to believe that Germany may be forced into war very soon. So, when you are being your own charming self to these gentlemen, er, if you could make them say a little more than they should, well . . . we would be grateful, most grateful indeed.'

By this time, because of her success both on and off the stage, Mata Hari would do nothing unless money or an expensive gift was given to her for her time and trouble. So, almost before the other had finished speaking, she asked, 'How grateful?'

'If what you can tell us, Fraulein, is what we expect, you will find us very grateful indeed,' and he mentioned a figure that startled even Mata Hari.

She was still in Berlin during the early days of August 1914 when the First World War began. Almost immediately she left for neutral

Amsterdam where she stayed for a while. On two occasions she actually braved the dangers of a cross-Channel journey and visited London. She then returned to the scene of her first great triumph—Paris. Being by then such a well-known person, constantly on the move, she had attracted the attention of the British and French Intelligence Services; but they could not prove anything against her.

Both services had been alerted by a telegram received in Paris towards the end of 1915. It read: 'While examining the passenger list of a Japanese vessel at Naples we have recognized the name of a theatrical celebrity from Marseilles, named Mata Hari, the famous Hindu dancer. She has, it seems, renounced her claim to Indian birth and become Berlinoise. She speaks German with a slight Eastern accent.'

From that moment on, wherever she went, secret service men were watching and waiting—waiting for her to make a fatal slip.

Yet her return to Paris was a triumph. Crowds flocked to see her and, once again, she was surrounded by a constant stream of admirers. And then, when at the height of her fame, she surprised everyone by saying that she was going to give up her dancing in order to spend the rest of the war looking after the wounded. When she asked to be sent to Vittel the French counter-espionage department became particularly interested; Vittel was an important French aerodrome.

By day she nursed the wounded. The evenings she spent in the officers' mess where, understandably, she was a popular visitor. She drank and flirted with the dashing young airmen, while carefully listening to what they had to say. Everything of interest that she overheard went back to Berlin. Then the French authorities decided it was time to act. When she returned to Paris on a visit she was asked by two detectives to go with them to meet their chief. Wondering what this was all about, she found herself sitting opposite Captain le Doux, head of France's counter-espionage service.

He glared at her. 'Mams'elle, I have heard unsettling reports of your recent behaviour. It has become necessary for me to ask you to leave this country without delay. Both France and Britain are gravely suspicious of your actions and we, of France, can have you within our borders no longer!'

'But monsieur. Why are you asking me to leave? To leave Paris, the city I love so much?'

'Both France and Britain are gravely suspicious of your actions, mams'elle,' *explained the captain, 'and we can have you within our borders no longer!'*

The other paused, tapping the desk with his pen. 'Well, mams'elle. Let us be frank. We have grave suspicions that you are acting as a spy. You will return to Holland, to your native country, which for reasons best known to itself is content to remain neutral in this great struggle.'

She protested. 'But Monsieur le Doux. However did you get such an idea? To think that I, Mata Hari, who have nothing but the warmest affection for France, should seek to harm her in any way.'

And so the talk went on, Mata Hari protesting that she had never done anything to harm her beloved France, Captain le Doux flatly stating that she had to leave Paris—and without delay. Finally her persuasion even overcame the tough chief of the French bureau, and she left, smiling to herself. She had been given permission to stay in France —but now she was expected to act as a spy for that country.

Despite her promises, however, she continued to send reports to Germany until a friend told her that le Doux, now more suspicious than ever, was about to have her arrested. Desperate, she went to his office to give him some important information to show her good faith. Acting on what she told him, le Doux gave orders that sent French destroyers and submarines racing to the coast of Morocco. As she had promised, there, at anchor, lay two German submarines. The French flotilla surprised and sank both.

The reason she gave le Doux this important piece of information was that she desperately wished to stay in France. Whilst nursing at Vittel she had met Captain Maroff, a Russian who had been blinded in action. For the first time in her life she was in love and she was determined to stay near him. After all, she reasoned, she was Dutch, a native of a neutral country and owed nothing to France or to Germany.

But Captain le Doux was still not satisfied. He learned that Mata Hari had several diplomats of neutral countries amongst her circle of admirers and that they were sending her letters abroad without fear of censorship. He decided to test her loyalty, and sent for her yet again. 'Mams'elle, I am prepared to believe you when you declare that it is your wish to help our great country. So, here is what we wish you to do. You are to journey to Brussels—at the moment, alas, under the control of the Boche—and make a rendezvous with General von Bissing. As I am sure you know, he is the German Governor-General of Belgium. Also, or so I am given to understand, he was once your lover. Find out what secrets you may from him and let me have them on your return.'

He paused and then, opening a drawer, took out five envelopes.

'These are letters to our agents in Brussels. Each one, as you see, has the address of the person clearly shown. Deliver these before you leave Brussels. Do you understand, mans'elle?'

'Certainly monsieur,' and she took the envelopes, thrusting them into her handbag. What she did not know was that they were part of le Doux's plan. Four of the five French agents to whom they were addressed had already been arrested by the Germans. The fifth had only just arrived in Brussels and so far had done nothing. There was, as yet, no reason for the German counter-intelligence service to suspect him. Yet soon after Mata Hari's arrival in Brussels the unfortunate agent was arrested and shot.

Now, in le Doux's mind, there was no doubt. She *must* be a spy.

From Belgium she went to neutral Holland then to neutral Spain. Here she made contact with the German naval attaché for further instructions. The official was charming and helpful so that she was not to know that even as he spoke to her he was already planning her destruction. He told her to return to Paris and that she would hear further from him. In due time, as he had promised, she received her new instructions. But the Germans, now anxious to be rid of her, used a code which they knew the French had already broken.

She was arrested at her hotel and taken before a court-martial on 24 July 1917. Being sure that she would come to no harm, she faced the twelve-man court with great confidence. But she began to wilt under the barrage of questions that were fired at her until, in desperation, she cried, 'Messieurs, you must understand that what little I have done has always been for our beloved France!'

But all her charm, wit, beauty and intelligence were useless. Even before the court had met it had been decided to find her guilty, and by now there was a mountain of evidence to prove her guilt. Towards evening on the second day of the trial the court retired briefly to confer. They filed back again and the president said, 'Mata Hari. You will stand!' Then, turning to the twelve officers of the court, he ordered 'Attention!'

They clicked to attention, and the clerk of the court read out in a flat, emotionless voice: 'In the name of the French nation this military court declares that Mata Hari is guilty of espionage and sentences her to death!'

There was a long silence as all eyes turned to the figure in the box. She seemed to sway for a moment. Then, drawing herself up, her face pale but proud, she walked firmly from the court between her two guards, back to her cell. Her lawyers and many of her former lovers—some of them in high, political positions—fought for her pardon, or at least a commuting of her sentence to life imprisonment. But it was not to be. All who visited her in her cell during the next three months or so remarked on her pride, courage and even her cheerfulness.

At last, however, after what must have been an agony of waiting, she was taken to the place of execution. An officer came forward with a bandage for her eyes. She waved him away. Then, standing proud and erect, before a bullet-scarred wall, she faced the twelve men of the firing squad. Her composure amazed all who were there. At that moment she was at her best.

The officer stepped forward, raised his sword, then lowered it. As he did so a scattered volley of shots rang out and she fell immediately.

Perhaps her braveness had affected those French soldiers who formed the firing squad, for only one of the twelve bullets actually pierced her beautiful body.

But that one was enough. It had found her heart.

A DREADFUL BELL

Leopold Lewis

It was one of those large and important hotels that seem to swoop down and take possession of little villages. The first object that caught the eye of the traveller as he approached the hamlet over the neighbouring hill was the new grand hotel, with its white staring walls and numberless windows, and the letters of its name in black paint running across it. It had scattered the little houses to the right and left of it. It had fixed itself in the best possible situation in front of the sea, and had swallowed up in its erection all the most time-honoured and distinguished characteristics of the locality. In short, instead of the hotel being considered as belonging to the village, the village was now looked upon as an accessory to the hotel. The cause of this change was that the little fishing hamlet being prettily situated on the sea-coast in North Wales, 'the Faculty' had passed its opinion in favour of the place, and the hotel had in consequence sprung up like magic—'The Montmorency Hotel', with plate-glass windows and a grand portico, hundreds of bedrooms and sitting-rooms, bathing-machines, hot and vapour baths, invalid chairs, and various other conveniences.

How I came to be stopping at The Montmorency was in this way:

my old college chum, Tom Marlowe, had just got married to his Julia, and having spent their honeymoon abroad, they took it into their heads that a little repose and a little peaceful enjoyment of each other's society would not be an inappropriate change. Accordingly they had taken apartments in one of the houses in Montmorency Terrace. Tom had heard that I was going to Ireland for my vacation, and had written to ask me to stop and see him on my way.

I accepted the invitation, and put up at the hotel, as there was no vacant room in Tom's house, and I intended to make only a flying visit.

On an evening when the village was undergoing one of its very heartiest squalls, and the wind and the rain and the sea were all roaring together, I had enjoyed a pleasant dinner with Tom and his Julia. The storm without had made the windows rattle rather noisily in their frames: and the street door would persist in flying open suddenly, and when once open, banging itself; the chimneys, too, were altogether uncomfortable, and grumbled incessantly, and the whole establishment had exhibited decided symptoms of a general shakiness of constitution peculiar to mansions that are rapidly 'run up' in rising localities. But we were so merry, and had so much to talk about—Tom was in such good spirits, and his Julia was emphatically what he had so often described her to me to be, 'a born angel'—that I believe if the house itself had been carried away bodily out to sea, it would have been a matter of indifference to them, provided they had gone with it, in each other's society. The time had passed so pleasantly and quickly that I was quite startled when a clock struck eleven; and, as I knew they were early people at The Montmorency, I rose to take my leave.

'By Jove! What a night!' said Tom, as he opened the street door to let me out. 'Will you have a rug to put round you, or my top-coat?'

'No, thank you.'

'Well, get home as fast as you can. How it does come down, and as dark as pitch. Come round in the morning, there's a good fellow.'

'All right. Good-night, old boy.'

The Montmorency was only about five hundred yards distant. I ran as fast as I could, and soon reached the portico, but the whole of the hotel was in darkness. Everybody had evidently gone to bed.

'They are early people with a vengeance,' I muttered, as I seized the bell and rang vigorously.

'They will think that rather a strong pull, but one can't wait out long in such a night as this.'

And it was a night! The portico afforded no protection. The wind howled round its columns, and the rain dashed through it. There was not a soul about. The sky and the sea were both as black as ink.

'Confound it,' I said, after I had waited some considerable time. 'I wonder when they're going to open the door. I'll wait two minutes more and then I'll ring again.'

The two minutes seemed to be twenty, and no one came.

Surely it was not intentional to keep me out in the rain, to give me the street for shelter, because I was not in before the door was shut. It certainly was a hotel where such an arrangement might have been adopted as a rule, but the mere thought of such an absurdity gave me new vigour, and I rang the bell violently for several minutes, and only desisted from sheer exhaustion. I had just commenced to consider whether in the circumstances I should not be justified in throwing a few stones and smashing one or two of the upstairs windows, when, through the pane of glass at the side of the door, I saw to my great relief a faint glimmer of light thrown into the hall. This gradually became brighter and brighter, as if some one were slowly coming down the principal staircase, which was at right angles with the door, bearing a light. It proved to be so, for the next moment I saw, standing on the last step of the stairs, an old gentleman of about sixty, with perfectly white hair, habited in a dressing-gown, and carrying high above his head a lighted bedroom candle.

'Someone I have awakened at last by my ringing,' thought I. 'One of the visitors, no doubt. I shall apologize to him when he has opened the door, and the early hour at which I commenced to ring, and the state of the night will surely be a sufficient excuse.'

I steadily fixed my eyes on the old gentleman, and got nearer to the door ready for the chain to be dropped and the bolts to be drawn, for I was becoming more bitterly cold every minute. The old gentleman advanced cautiously into the hall and crossed it, without however once looking towards the door. When he had reached the side of the hall farthest from the stairs he looked up, as if contemplating something fearfully high upon the wall, and as he did so I saw that his arm which held the candle trembled violently.

146

'You shall hear me at any rate,' thought I, and I rang again.

To my utter astonishment immediately I had done this, the old gentleman, still without looking towards the door, gave a start, and appeared to shake from head to foot. By his profile, which was towards me, I could see that the expression of his face was one of intense alarm. I heard him utter a shout of horror, and then with a bound he turned on his heel, dashed up the stairs he had so lately descended, and the hall was once more plunged in darkness.

I had scarcely time to question myself as to what could possibly be the meaning of these strange proceedings, before my attention was attracted by a great noise in the upper part of the hotel. It sounded to me as if a number of people were running about. Then doors banged violently. Then there was a succession of crashes. Then shouts of men and screams of women. Nobody, however, appeared in the hall. I rushed into the road and looked up at the hotel. Gracious heavens! What was the matter? Nearly all the windows, before so black, were now illuminated with a bright light. Dark outlines of the human form passed hurriedly backwards and forwards upon the blinds looking like struggling and excited phantoms. Still not a window opened. The noise continued with unabated fury; then, as gradually as it had commenced, the shouting ceased and became murmurs, the doors banged off one by one, until there seemed no more to bang, the lights went out like specks of fire upon a burnt paper, and then all was again in darkness and silence.

What could it mean? In vain I asked myself the question, and no one came to the door to enlighten me upon the subject, or to give me admittance. 'I'll try once more,' I exclaimed, 'and this shall be the last time.' I rang feebly and despairingly. Instantly bells seemed to ring all over the house and passages. Big bells and little bells, near bells and distant bells, upstairs bells and downstairs bells, burst out together in one long continuous angry jangle. The last little bell was still tinkling away somewhere up in the garrets, when a light once again appeared, and this time as if it were coming up a trap in the floor of the hall. I saw it was borne by the head-waiter. He was only partly dressed, and he wore a nightcap made out of a red handkerchief. He looked for an instant towards where I stood, and then shambled in his slippers to the door, let down the chain, half opened the door, put his nose through the opening, and breathed out a ghostly, inflamed, husky whisper, 'Who is it?'

'It's me,' I said somewhat petulantly, 'open the door.'

He rubbed his eyes, held up the light, looked intensely hard at the wick of the candle, said 'Oh!' and opened the door.

'Well, you have kept me a pretty time outside,' I said as I entered. 'I have been ringing the bell since eleven, and by George, there goes one o'clock. I'm wet to the skin and nearly dead with cold.'

The head-waiter was putting the chain up in a fumbling uncertain sort of gaoler fashion. He didn't seem to be altogether quite awake yet, and from the fumes of rum and the smell of tobacco smoke that pervaded him, and the very fishy and winking condition of his eyes, I concluded that Bacchus had assisted Morpheus in the task of lulling him to sleep. In reply to my observation he simply breathed out another rum-and-water 'Oh!' and hoisted his apparel about his waist in a dreamy way.

'Has anything been the matter?' I continued, as I lighted a bedroom candle. 'What a terrible row there was in the house at about half-past twelve.'

'Was there, though?' he said, with a yawn, a hiccup, and a lurch. 'Now was there, though? Well, you knows best, I've no doubt.'

And without another word he shuffled away, with his two long braces dragging behind him and bumping their buckles on the floor, looking like a drunken old bashaw, whilst I went off to bed.

I never slept so sound in my life as I did that night. It was nearly eleven o'clock before I came downstairs and entered the coffee-room to order breakfast. There was only one gentleman in the room, and he was seated at a table at the extreme end having breakfast, with a newspaper balancing against the coffee biggin, and simultaneously devouring the news and the buttered toast in the heartiest manner possible. He was a small, middle-aged gentleman, and was evidently suffering from severe nervousness, for he made a great clatter with the cups and spoons, knocking them together loudly; and I noticed that his hands and head shook so continuously that he had the greatest difficulty in carrying anything in a direct line to his mouth. His hair, which was short and black, stood up very straight and stiff, and he wore a large pair of gold eye-glasses. As I entered and took my seat at a table near the window, he fixed his glasses with greater steadiness upon his nose, and directed at me a long and anxious gaze. Apparently, however, finding that I was a stranger, he turned the newspaper with much gesticulation, and went on with his breakfast.

It was not a rude look. It was only the stare of a short-sighted man; but still it made me think of three trifling incidents that had occurred to me on my passage downstairs from my bedroom to the coffee-room. On the first landing I had met the chambermaid. Immediately she had seen me she had backed into a corner, and had stared at me with mingled curiosity and terror until I had passed. On a lower floor I had encountered the boots. On seeing me, he had instantly dropped a bootjack, two chamber-candlesticks, three pairs of slippers, and a warming-pan, with a terrible clatter, and then wagged his head reprovingly at me as if I had done it. Finally, in crossing the hall, the second waiter—a limp wretch in a perpetual perspiration—on meeting me, turned on his heel, and, with a half-smothered cry, fled up a passage. The head-waiter here entered the room. He had resumed his usual dignified appearance; his white cravat was stiff and spotless, and his black wig was curled and oiled into quite a lustrous condition. He made a complete circuit of the room, walking in a solemn manner, and looking at me gravely the while; and, having done this, he approached my table, leant over it on the knuckles of his hands, and contemplated me sternly and inquiringly.

'Breakfast, waiter, if you please.'

'Oh! breakfast?' he repeated, without altering his position. 'Well now, sir, did you order breakfast?'

'Yes,' I answered; 'and I should like it as quickly as possible.'

'Ah!' said the waiter, heaving a deep sigh, and still in a contemplative condition. 'Should you? Mind, I don't say you shouldn't. Only it may be difficult—and then, again, it's rather unnatural—that's all.' And then, before I could express my surprise at this extraordinary conduct on his part, he bent his head near to mine, and whispered in my ear: 'You've done it.'

'Done it! Done what? What do you mean?' I said, instinctively adopting a whispered tone.

'Horful!' gasped the waiter in the same horrid whisper, and throwing his head and eyes up. 'No one could have believed it. I am not a bad sort, sir; but I am a family man, sir; I have a wife and three small children, one of 'em, sir, now in arms and cutting its teeth, sir; and when a family man has been examined in the way I have been; when it's been extricated out of me by threats—threats of the most horrid nature—when a hunder waiter has been threatened to be put over my head—a hunder waiter so ignorant of 'rithmetic that he don't know plated spoons from silver ones—how could I help it?'

'Help what?' I said. 'What are you talking about? I don't understand a word of what you are saying. Am I to have any breakfast or not?'

At this last question the head-waiter drew himself up to his full height, and in a perfectly serious—indeed, solemn—manner, said: "Well, sir, if you ask me as a matter of opinion, I should say that you are *not* to have any breakfast. Mind, it is a matter of opinion on my part. However, no one have ever accused me of possessing the feelings of a wolf, and so I will go and make the inquiry.'

Either the waiter was mad, or he had not entirely recovered from his last night's drinking. I ordered him again to bring the breakfast, and threatened to speak to the proprietor of the hotel if he any longer delayed doing so.

'Well!' he said, looking at me curiously. 'Well, I always said philosophy were a wonderful invention, but if ever I see such a go as this—skewer me! You knows what I mean, and what you've done—you knows you did!' And then, with a look full of meaning and reproach, he whispered 'F.D!' and slid gravely out of the room.

I was still lost in astonishment at the waiter's conduct, when, happening to look round, I perceived that the little gentleman at the other end of the room, having by this time clattered through his breakfast and finished with the newspaper, was now steadily observing me. He had certainly not been able to overhear my whispered conversation with the waiter, but he had evidently noticed that what had taken place had been the cause of exciting my anger, for he now said: 'Stupid fellow, that!' I experienced quite a feeling of gratitude towards the stranger for his sympathy.

'I cannot think what is the matter with him,' I said, as I passed down the room to a table nearer to the little gentleman. 'He don't seem in condition to take an order for breakfast.'

'Oh!' said the stranger, fidgeting in his chair, and nervously endeavouring to fix the cruets in their stand. 'Ah, it's very extraordinary! I can't make him out either. He has been bringing me wrong things all the morning. I ordered fish, and he brought me cutlets. I don't like cutlets. Then he brought me a fish-slice to cut the butter with. Ridiculous! And, look at these cruets, not one of them will go into the stand. As an excuse, he says he has been greatly agitated. So have I been agitated! So has every one been agitated after the disgraceful proceedings of last night.'

'Indeed?' said I. 'I heard something, but I was unable to distinguish what it was.' The little gentleman stared hard at me.

'You must be a sound sleeper, young man—a very sound sleeper; but perhaps it did not happen to you. Did it?'

Not having the remotest idea as to what the question referred, I answered in the negative.

'Perhaps,' said the little gentleman, 'you do not even know what did happen—eh?'

'No.'

'Very extraordinary,' said the little gentleman, and then he went on nervously: 'I never went through such a night—never. A man of my weak nerves, too. My doctor sent me down here for quiet and repose. "Go down, Bamby," he said, "no railway station within three miles, no organs, no yelling black men, no Punches and Judies, in fact, a paradise of peace and comfort." So I came. I arrived yesterday in the midst of the most terrible storm I ever saw. I went to bed about half-past ten, and, contrary to my usual custom, soon dropped off to sleep.

'I am a bad sleeper, young man. About half-past twelve o'clock I was woken by someone knocking violently at my door. I had bolted it before getting into bed. Judge of my alarm at such a proceeding at such an hour. The knocking continued in violence, then a heavy body seemed to be thrown against the door, which, after repeated shocks, burst open, and a man fell head foremost into my room—a tall, powerful man, in a coloured gown and Wellington boots, with a pair of trousers tied round his throat. Before I had time to utter a word, he had started to his feet and assumed a threatening attitude. "Help! Murder! Fire! Thieves!" I shouted out at the top of my voice. "I'll help you," he cried, dancing wildly round me, "come out of this!" And in a moment he had seized the bed-clothes and had dragged off the counterpane and blankets. "Come out of this!" he again cried, and again pounced upon me, this time clutching me by the ankle of my left leg and commencing to drag me—a man of my weak nerves—bodily off the bed.

'Maddened with terror, I clung to the head of the bedstead, and shouted still louder for assistance. The more I shouted the more the villain tugged at my leg. The struggle was fearful. Chairs, table, drawers, looking-glasses and fire-irons all seemed to be tumbling and crashing about the room indiscriminately. The very bedstead, with myself still madly clinging to it, seemed to be whirled round and round in the fury of the conflict. At length my assailant appeared to weaken in his efforts, and summoning all my remaining strength with my disengaged leg, I gave him one terrible kick full in the chest that sent him staggering back on to the wash-stand, in his fall knocking it down, smashing the jugs and basins into atoms, and deluging the room with water. Just fancy the situation to a man of my weak nerves!'

'Did you capture him?'

'No. Before I could recover myself he was on his legs again—had rushed out of the room and was gone. Winding the remains of the bed-clothes round me, I dashed out after him, shouting, "Stop thief!" To my astonishment I found the whole house in an uproar. Ladies and gentlemen, in the most extraordinary state of deshabille I ever saw, were running about with lights, asking each other what it was, and where it was, and who had done it, and what it meant? Everybody seemed to have been served in the way I had been. The mistress of the hotel appeased us by saying that the matter should have full inquiry in the morning, and eventually we retired to rest again. You must admit, young man, you were a very sound sleeper not to have been awakened by these proceedings.'

I was considerably astonished at this recital. This, then, accounted for the excitement in the hotel whilst I was ringing at the door.

'And what was the explanation of this extraordinary affair?' I inquired.

'The explanation,' continued Mr Bamby, 'as far as I have heard it, is more mysterious to me than the affair itself. The landlady, in answer to my inquiries this morning, informed me it was the F.D., and everybody I have asked has answered me in the same way; but who the F.D. is, or

'*I gave him one terrible kick full in the chest that sent him staggering back into the wash-stand.*'

153

what the F.D. is, or why the deuce the F.D. pulled everybody out of bed last night, by the leg, is a problem I mean to have unravelled before I leave this place.'

I gave quite a start of astonishment. The head-waiter had whispered these mysterious letters into my ear. For a moment a thought flashed through my mind that I might be suspected of being the perpetrator of the outrages described by Mr Bamby; but then I was not in the hotel at the time they occurred, and no one knew this better than the head-waiter, who had opened the door to me. "Do you think you would know your aggressor again,' I said, 'if you saw him?'

'I don't know,' said Mr Bamby. 'It was so dark at the time, and I was so bewildered; but dear me, how very late it is. What a thing it is to have one's rest disturbed. It loses one's whole day. I should like to catch my friend the F.D. or the Funny Devil, or whatever he is, I'd show him some fun, although I am a man of weak nerves. Good-morning.'

And Mr Bamby took up his hat and umbrella, and trotted out of the room. As he went out the head-waiter came in. I looked hungrily towards him, but he only carried an empty plate in one hand, and advanced with great solemnity, bearing it before him like a churchwarden going round after a charity sermon. He presented it to me. I looked at him and then at the plate.

'What's this? Where is the breakfast, fellow? What in the name of heaven is the meaning of all this? What's that plate for?'

Without a movement of his face he still advanced the plate before me. I really think I was about to take it out of his hand and hurl it through the window, when I caught sight of a paper lying upon it. I took it up and looked at it. It was my bill!

'What's this?' I demanded fiercely.

'What is that, sir?' said the head-waiter. 'That is the bill, sir. We have *not* charged for breakfast. We have *not*, I believe, charged for a bed tonight; but the attendance is included.'

'I will see the proprietor at once,' I cried, 'and have this affair explained. A pretty hotel this seems to be. I am kept waiting half the night ringing at the bell. Breakfast is refused me, and my bill is thrust upon me without my asking for it. What do you take me for? Eh?'

I advanced upon the head-waiter; he retreated in terror.

'Don't, sir, don't. I am a family man, and not a bad sort: but hotels is hotels, sir, and can't afford to be ruined. Whole families turning out—families from the Philippine Islands—two Nabobs, and one a General—ain't they nothing? Then, to see the deluges—the breakages—the spoiled linen—oh! to see it—'

It was clear I was taken for the author of the last night's proceedings—the mysterious F.D. referred to by Mr Bamby. I heard no more. I rushed out of the room, intending at once to have an interview with the proprietor of the hotel and explain matters. In the hall there were groups of servants, all talking anxiously. As I made my appearance there was a general movement of excitement amongst them; all eyes were directed towards me, and I again heard the mention of the mysterious letters in an undertone, clearly, in reference to myself.

'Can I see the proprietor?' I addressed a young woman in the bar of the hotel.

'Walk this way,' she answered, in a sharp, snappish tone.

I passed through the bar and into a back room. Here was seated the landlady, with a large book before her. As I entered, and she saw who it was, she started up, took off her spectacles, and confronted me with a glare of terrible indignation.

'So, number twenty-four,' she said, before I could open my mouth, 'I hope you are satisfied with the mischief of which you have been the cause. The affair of last night may be my ruin, and I have to thank you for it.' She pointed to the book. 'I am now making out the bill of number four, a gentleman suffering from the gout. How can he be expected to remain in a hotel where he is pulled out of bed in the middle of the night, and dragged about his room by the leg? Here is the family in number eighteen, who have been in hysterics ever since, and who threaten me with an action for the loss of wigs and teeth and all sorts of valuable property. And here is the Indian General in number eighty-two, who declares he will have your life, and there will be murder on the premises in the height of the season. It's shameful, disgraceful.'

'Madam,' I interrupted, 'I assure you I am perfectly innocent of the outrages which I have heard were committed last night in this hotel.'

'How dare you, number twenty-four,' cried the landlady, 'utter such wilful falsehoods? Is it not enough what you have done? I have perfect confidence in the statement made to me by Mr Loverock, our head-waiter.'

155

'If Mr Loverock,' I urged, 'has made a charge against me of being the author of this affair, he is a villain, since he knows that such a charge is false.'

'He is no villain,' said the landlady, now in a towering passion. 'He is no villain; and he is not false. He was not at first willing to divulge you; and it was only when I threatened to remove him from his situation that he made the statement he did. He is no villain, number twenty-four. It is you, and you alone, who are the villain. You, who have been the cause of all this misery and ruin.'

The matter was becoming to me momentarily more inexplicable. I was about to make further reply to the landlady, when I was startled by a loud noise outside the bar, and I heard a man's voice explaining: 'Where is he? Where is he? Where is the ruffian? Let me reach him. Let me grasp his throat. Let me revenge my wife. Let me revenge my three daughters. Out of the way!'

'It is the General!' shrieked the landlady; and at the same moment a gentleman in a furious rage bounded into the room. He carried a boot-jack in one hand, which he waved wildly over his head, and he was advancing to seize me, when another gentleman jumped into the room after him, threw his arms round his waist, and held him as if he were in a vice.

'Let me go,' shouted the first gentleman, struggling to get free.

'I shan't,' shouted the second gentleman. 'What do you want to do?'

I knew the voice. It was Tom Marlowe.

'Tom,' I cried, 'what is all this about? I am charged with the most extraordinary conduct. Speak for me, old fellow.'

'Why—what——' exclaimed Tom, putting his head round the General's body without relaxing his hold. 'Good gracious! Is it you? If this gentleman would only have the kindness to leave off struggling, and abandon his bloodthirsty intentions, I could discuss the matter with him. There is some mistake.'

'There's not!' roared the General.

'There is!' I shouted.

'You had better retire, sir,' interposed the landlady, addressing me. 'Your presence only serves to excite the General's frenzy. I am willing to explain matters to Mr Marlowe.'

'Go into the next room, will you,' said Tom, again putting his head round the General's body, 'and lock the door on him, ma'am. I won't let go of this gentleman unless you do.'

'Go, sir!' exclaimed the landlady to me, and pointing to an inner room in a Lady Macbeth attitude.

I entered. The door was immediately closed and locked upon me. It was quite an hour before Tom made his appearance. Directly he came in he fell into a chair, and burst into a fit of laughter. When he had partially recovered himself, he said: 'Excuse me, my dear fellow, laughing in this wild manner; but for the last hour I have been dying with suppressed emotion. I have been wanting to laugh, and have not dared.'

'What is it all about?'

'Well, my dear boy,' said Tom, 'it seems it was you who did it after all.'

'Impossible! I wasn't in the hotel.'

'Just listen for one moment. I have been making inquiries all over the house, and have had interviews with the parties concerned. I think I have found it all out, and if I know anything of the laws of cause and effect, it was you who did it. However, don't make yourself uneasy. I have cleared up the matter now, and appeased the landlady, and they have determined to forgive you.'

'Forgive me—but what for? What have I done?'

'It seems,' said Tom, 'that there is an elderly gentleman from America stopping in the house with his family. He is of very nervous temperament, and from having some short time ago severely suffered from the effects of a fire on his premises, exists in a perpetual state of alarm as to one breaking out wherever he may be. In fact, he is almost a monomaniac upon the subject. Now, it appears that it was you who rang the bell last night. Loverock, the waiter, who sleeps downstairs, says he opened the street door to you at one o'clock. You left me at eleven, so that you were at it about two hours.'

'That's true,' I said. 'They wouldn't open the door. What was I to do?'

'Precisely,' continued Tom. 'At about half-past twelve o'clock it further appears that the fire-fearing gentleman, having listened to a violent and almost continuous ringing of a bell for an hour and a half, at length took it into his head to travel out of his bedroom to discover the cause. On reaching the hall——'

157

'Yes, I saw him through the door-window.'

'On reaching the hall, he examined all the bells upon the wall, and seeing a particularly large one madly ringing came to the conclusion it was the fire-bell. The alarm of fire always drives him out of his senses, and the instinct of preserving his fellow-creatures at such a time is so strong upon him that it becomes a madness. It was this feeling that drove him through the house shouting for help, bursting open doors, pulling the furniture out of the rooms and the people out of their beds—in fact, acting as if a fire were actually raging in the hotel.'

'But why should he have thought it was the fire-bell?'

'Come and see,' said Tom.

We passed into the hall. In the midst of a cluster of bells hanging upon the wall, each of which had its number, was one bell of an unusually large size, and underneath this, painted in red, were the mysterious letters, 'F.D.'

'That's the bell you rang,' said Tom. 'The American gentleman, in his excitement, not unnaturally concluded it gave the alarm of fire. You see, in the United States, where this gentleman came from, the letters "F.D." represent the "Fire Department".'

'And what, in the name of heaven, do those initials really stand for?'

'Front door!'

THE YOUNG SABOTEURS OF THE CHURCHILL CLUB

Samuel Epstein & Beryl Williams

On the afternoon of 8 April 1940, the boys of the Cathedral School in Aalborg, Denmark, raced for their bicycles the moment classes were over. Everything seemed just as usual. One group paused to discuss the model aeroplanes they were building. Another stopped to compare notes on a quiz they had done that day.

They were all in high spirits. Spring was in the air. Even in the modern city of Aalborg, with its tall buildings and its traffic-crowded streets, they could feel a hint of the first warm breezes from the south.

When the boys finally separated to ride off to their homes that afternoon, they were still calling to one another, planning games and sports for the next day.

But that night something happened that shattered all their plans. That night the Germans marched into Denmark. At six o'clock the next morning Denmark's government was in German hands, and the Danish King Christian was a prisoner. Denmark, smallest of the Scandinavian countries, had become a 'protectorate' of Nazi Germany.

After that nothing was the same in Aalborg. There were German soldiers in the streets and German officers riding round in fine cars. All

Danes had to carry identity cards and be ready to show them at any time.

And yet, after the first shock was over, the people in Aalborg went to work every day as they always had. The trams ran on time. The boys of the Cathedral School were told to report to their classes as if nothing had occurred.

The younger boys were puzzled.

'Why don't we fight the Germans?' they asked. 'Why don't we make them go away?'

The older boys looked grim. 'Because Denmark is a small country,' they explained, 'and Germany is a big, powerful country. We have to do whatever the Germans want us to.'

'Will they make us go to prison?' the little boys asked. 'Will they throw us in a dungeon and make us live on bread and water?'

The older boys shook their heads. They had been talking with their parents and listening to the radio, and they understood what was going on.

'No,' one of them said. 'They won't put us in prison. They just want us to go on making machinery and growing food, the way we have always done, so that they can take it all for Germany.'

'That's right,' another of the older boys agreed. 'And they're being very polite to us. They think that will make us happy, so that Denmark will be what they call a "model protectorate"—an example of how fine it is to be conquered by the Germans. Then they can say to other countries, "Don't fight against us. Just let us take you over, the way we did Denmark".'

'Some day,' one of the little boys announced, 'I shall go up to a German soldier and hit him.'

'No, you won't,' his big brother commanded. 'Didn't you hear what Father said? He told us not to make any trouble—to obey all the new German laws and do just what the Germans want us to. Then, Father says, they won't hurt us.'

But sometimes, when the older boys were alone, they admitted that they, too, would like to hit out at the German soldiers in their shiny boots. They felt this more and more strongly as the months went by, and Nazi Germany won victory after victory. She conquered Norway, little Luxembourg, Belgium and the Netherlands.

'She tells them all to be good—the way Denmark is—and then they'll be all right,' one of the boys said angrily. 'We ought to be ashamed to do everything the Germans tell us. We *ought* to strike back.'

'Yes—but how?' his friend asked.

And none of the boys could answer that question.

Then one day two new boys moved to Aalborg from the Danish town of Odense. Their names were Knud and Jens Pedersen, and they, too, became students at the Cathedral School.

'In Odense,' Knud told his new friends, 'we had a club to fight the Germans. We called it the Royal Air Force Club.'

The Aalborg boys all began to talk at once.

'Tell us about it!'

'What did the club do?'

'That's what we want!'

They planned a club of their own that very day. They called it the Churchill Club, in honour of the British Prime Minister.

All the members of the Churchill Club were students at the school. Some were only ten years old. The eldest were fifteen and sixteen. Knud and Jens Pedersen were two of the club's leaders. Another pair of brothers, Alf and Kaj Houlberg, and another Knud—Knud Andersen, his name was—were also leaders of the group.

The first rule of the organization was absolute secrecy.

'No one must know that our club even exists,' Knud Pedersen said. 'Not the Germans, and not any of the Danes who like the Nazi ideas. Even our parents mustn't know. They wouldn't let us work against the Germans. They'd be afraid we'd be caught and punished.'

'And besides,' Jens Pedersen added, 'if we are caught they can tell the Germans truthfully that they didn't know anything about our club— and perhaps then the Germans won't punish them along with us.'

'What is our club going to do?' one member asked.

It was a difficult problem. They were all young. They had no experience. They had read in their history books about children who had served as spies—who had gathered information about the enemy or who, as couriers, had carried messages across enemy lines.

But there was no courier work for them in Aalborg, for there were no vital messages to be carried. And there was little point in trying to spy on the Germans. The Germans in Denmark were not fighting or planning to fight. They were just standing guard to make sure the Danes behaved themselves and continued to produce food and machinery for their conquerors.

'We'll have to concentrate on sabotage work,' Knud Pedersen said. 'We'll try to do everything we can that might make trouble for the Germans.'

The first step was to divide the club into four sections. Each one would take charge of a certain part of their programme.

One section had only one member—the boy whose job it was to collect the subscriptions each month. They knew they would need money for supplies and equipment. The other sections were the propaganda section, the technical section and the sabotage section.

The boys had to have many long, secret meetings before those three groups were ready to go to work. And even then they started out very slowly.

The propaganda section finally got hold of a duplicating machine, with which they could make many copies of a single letter or poster. They used it to print a picture of the German swastika surrounded by arrows. Underneath was a message to their German conquerors.

'This is the warning of a revolutionary flame!' it said. 'It will spread like lightning through all the countries the Germans have occupied, and it will bring death to those four German criminals—Hitler, Himmler, Goering and Goebbels!'

All over Aalborg those messages mysteriously appeared. They were tucked under doors and poked into letter-boxes.

The propaganda section also painted that same picture and message on every blank wall they could find and sometimes on the hood or the door of a German car.

The grown-ups of Aalborg began to whisper among themselves. 'Where do those handbills come from? Who paints those signs?' they asked each other. But no one knew.

The Germans became angry. They told the Danish police to find the people who had distributed the handbills and painted the signs and to punish them. But the Danish police said they were just as puzzled as everybody else.

The boys were being very careful not to be caught. They went out after dark, on their bicycles, only one or two at a time. They were all good cyclists. Their neighbours had always called them 'the cowboys of the asphalt'. They could speed away so fast, once their job was done, that no one ever saw them at work.

In the meantime the technical section was busy, too. The boys in that group were trying to make bombs, in the hope of being able to blow up German property. But they found it was very hard work. They did not know much about chemistry and which things should be mixed together to make a substance that would blow up. All their first efforts ended in failure.

But finally they made a report to the sabotage section—the group which would use the bombs when they were ready.

'We think we have a real bomb this time,' the leader of the technical section announced. 'Now it's up to you.'

A special committee of the sabotage section took the bomb out one dark night. They carried it carefully until they found a German car parked in a quiet street. Quickly they slipped the bomb under the car, lit the fuse and then ran off to hide nearby. They held their mouths wide open. They had heard that this was a protection against injury during an explosion.

They waited and waited. The fuse sputtered. And then it died out. Nothing happened. The bomb did not go off.

'You'll have to try again,' they told the technical section. 'Your bomb didn't work. Can't you make one that will really explode?'

But while they were waiting for a successful bomb, the members of the sabotage section found other jobs to do. They started with small tasks, such as removing the road signs the Germans had put up.

'It won't cause them very much trouble,' the leader said, 'but it will be good experience for us. It will teach us how to work right under the eyes of the police, how to get on with our jobs even when we can hardly breathe for fear of being caught.'

When they were used to working, no matter how afraid they were, they went on to bigger jobs. They set fire to German cars by pouring paraffin over the engines and lighting it. They stole small things that they could carry away quickly on their bicycles—hub caps, petrol-tank covers, German soldiers' knapsacks and hats.

Finally they became so daring that they stole German weapons. They slipped into a restaurant during a busy dinner-hour and snatched a rifle that a German officer had left hanging in the cloakroom. One boy even crept inside the German barracks and took a soldier's rifle from its hook over the bed, while the soldier to whom the weapon belonged was busy doing something in the same room.

None of the boys knew anything about guns, but they were all eager to learn. They all hoped that some day an Allied army would march into Denmark to free them from the Germans, and they wanted to join that army as soon as it arrived. So they all took turns aiming their first gun and learning how to press its trigger.

Suddenly, to the boys' great excitement, British planes began to fly over Denmark and drop boxes of guns and ammunition for the Danes' use. All the members of the Churchill Club were on the alert for the packages that came drifting down out of the sky, attached to floating parachutes. They wanted to find them before the Germans did. The technical-section boys gave up trying to make bombs, although by then they had actually made a few that worked, and devoted themselves to collecting the English gifts.

They made a fine new secret hiding place for those they found. In the

Every day the boys grew more daring . . .

garden of one of the members they dug a hole in the ground and covered it with a wooden trap-door. Then they put a layer of earth on top of the door and planted parsley on it. Even the boy's mother never suspected that her son's garden was really an arsenal of weapons.

Every day the boys grew more daring. They burned the blueprints for the new barracks the Germans were about to build. They destroyed an expensive instrument belonging to a team of German surveyors. They stole a typewriter for the use of their propaganda section. They burned German railway cars standing in the goods yard, including one wagon that held aeroplane parts and another loaded with tyres for aeroplane-landing gear.

Every time they performed one of their acts of sabotage they left behind a few scrawled words—a message daring the Germans to put a stop to the thefts and fires and explosions that by then were happening all over Aalborg. The Germans grew more and more angry. Every day they ordered the Danish police to catch the culprits.

'If you don't put a stop to this sabotage,' the Germans said, 'we'll have to step in and do your work for you.'

The police had not really been trying very hard to capture the sabo- teurs. Like the rest of the people of Aalborg, they thought the attempts at sabotage were dangerous and foolhardy; but they also were glad to know that there were some Danes daring enough to strike back at the conquerors. They did not want those daring people to be caught.

But one day a restaurant cloakroom attendant told a policeman that she had seen a young boy grab a German rifle from her cloakroom and make off with it.

'I could identify him if I saw him again,' she said.

'A young boy?' The policeman was surprised. He was sorry, too. But he knew he had to do his duty. 'Very well,' he said. 'Come with me. We'll walk the streets of Aalborg until you see the boy again and point him out to me.'

The Churchill Club was very busy just then, planning one of its greatest feats. The members had stolen some hand grenades from a box they found at the railway goods yard, awaiting delivery. They were going to set of a huge explosion at a German anti-aircraft post.

But the very day of their planned explosion—it was a lovely spring day, about two years after the Germans had seized Denmark—the woman from the restaurant said, 'There—that's the boy I saw stealing the rifle!'

A minute later the police captured one of the leaders of the club. Other members were rounded up before the day was over. By night the ten chief members were in gaol.

The parents of the boys could not believe their eyes when their sons were arrested. They were sure the police had made a mistake.

'It's not a mistake,' one of them told his mother. 'We just wanted to prove to the whole world that Denmark will never be a "model pro- tectorate", that we'll fight against our German conquerors as long as they stay here. We're proud of what we did—except for having to lie to you. That was the hardest part of our whole job.'

The Danish police made the boys as comfortable as possible in the city gaol. Two and a half months later the trial took place. The Danish judge wanted to let the club members off easily, but the boys admitted their guilt. He had to send them all to the big prison in King Hans Street.

The club members felt pretty sad and discouraged at first, even though they knew they had become famous in Aalborg.

'Why did we have to get caught just when we were learning how to make real trouble for the Germans?' one asked grimly. 'Why couldn't we have stayed out of gaol a little while longer?'

'I guess we were careless,' another said. 'They began to suspect us.'

'Wait a minute!' The third of the three boys in that cell jumped to his feet. Then he sat down again and lowered his voice so that the guard in the corridor could not hear. 'If we could manage to sneak out of gaol at night,' he whispered, 'and do some sabotage work and then sneak back in again—wouldn't that be a wonderful trick to play on the Germans? They certainly wouldn't suspect us then. They'd think we were safe behind bars.'

His two friends stared at him. 'But how could we possibly sneak out of here?' one demanded.

The third boy jumped up and stood at the small window of their cell. 'Look,' he said. 'There's a ledge outside this window. We could walk along it to that wire netting over the exercise yard. We could cross that by lying flat on our stomachs and inching along. When we got to the wall on the far side we could climb over it and drop down into the warden's orchard. Then we'd only have to squeeze through a hedge and we'd be free!'

'But first we'd have to get through the window,' his cautious friend pointed out. 'And—in case you haven't noticed—we *are* behind bars here, just as the Germans think.'

'I know. But if we had a hacksaw, we could cut through one of the bars, so that it could be removed. Then we'd have room enough to crawl through. We could put the bar back in place from the other side.'

'I think your idea is nonsense,' the cautious boy said.

But the other was already excited. 'We could do it!' he said. 'Just the way he says. And the next time my brother comes to visit me, I'll tell him what we need.'

One day not long afterwards the brother came. When the guard had his back turned for a moment, one of the prisoners whispered quickly, 'Bring us a hacksaw!'

The brother looked blank. The prisoners did not know whether he understood or not.

The next time the brother arrived at the gaol he was carrying a folded newspaper.

167

'Here,' he said. 'I thought you might like to read this.' He winked as he handed it to his prisoner brother.

The Churchill Club member slipped the paper quickly into his pocket. He could feel something long and hard between the pages.

'What's that you've got there?' the guard asked suddenly. 'What did your brother give you?'

'Just a Danish family newspaper. Do you want to see it?' The prisoner pulled the paper carefully out of his pocket. He shook it as he did so, just enough so that the long, hard thing inside fell back into the pocket as the paper came out.

The guard studied the paper a moment and then returned it. 'All right,' he said. 'I think you can have that.'

When their visitor was gone and the guard was out of sight, the boys huddled in a corner to inspect their smuggled gift. It was a hacksaw blade—just what they wanted!

'Let's get to work at once!' one whispered.

'No—we'd make too much noise. The only times we'll be able to use it is when there's a plane flying overhead. Then the guard won't be able to hear us.'

'But we'll never cut through a heavy iron bar if we can work only a few minutes a day!'

'It can't be helped. We mustn't risk it any other time.'

From that moment on life in the Aalborg gaol had a new excitement. The three boys took turns sitting close beside the window, the hacksaw blade carefully hidden. The moment a plane zoomed overhead, the blade appeared and went to work. Sawing through iron is a slow process. Sometimes they thought they would never finish the job.

But one day they realized that noticeable notches were beginning to show at the top and bottom of the bar.

'We're making progress,' one of them said. 'We're almost halfway through at each end. But our work is beginning to show. Suppose the guard notices these notches?'

'Don't worry,' his friend said. 'I've got an idea.'

The next day, while they were having their exercise period in the yard, he was playing ball when there was a crash and a tinkle of glass.

'Oh!' The young prisoner sounded very surprised. 'My ball slipped! I broke a window!'

'It's all right,' a kindly guard assured him. 'You couldn't help it. It can easily be fixed.'

Soon afterwards, when the window was replaced, the ball player showed the others something hidden in his pocket.

'It's a piece of putty,' he explained. 'I broke the window on purpose, so that workmen would come to put a new one in. And I squeezed off some of the new putty while it was still soft. We'll mix it with ink until it's the same colour as the iron bar.'

They felt safer from then on. Every day the notches at the top and bottom of the bar grew a little deeper, but the putty hid them entirely. And finally the bar was free, sawn clean through at both ends.

They could hardly wait to see if they could squeeze through the narrow space that the removal of the bar would leave. At last the day guards went off duty, the night guards arrived and the lights went out. The gaol grew very quiet.

But it was not until two o'clock in the morning that one of the boys whispered quietly, 'All right. Now!'

He pulled the putty away and slipped the bar out of place. Then he put his head through the hole and very slowly and carefully began to squeeze the rest of his body through. When he was on the ledge outside the window he said, 'All right. You next.'

But the second boy was bigger. He got his head through—and then he stuck.

For a long moment he could move neither forward nor back. He looked so funny, half in and half out of the window, that all three boys began to giggle. They stuffed their firsts in their mouths so that they would not be heard.

'It's no use,' the big boy said finally. 'You'll have to pull me back in.'

The third boy, still inside the cell, tugged at his friend's heels and at last jerked him back into the cell.

The big boy was bitterly disappointed, but he said, 'It's all right. You two go on, anyhow.'

The second boy slipped through the opening, and then both crawled along the ledge until they reached the netting, and cautiously inched themselves across it on their stomachs. Once a guard stepped into the exercise yard below them, and they held themselves desperately still, not daring to breathe, until he turned and went back inside the gaol.

At the far side of the netting was the wall. The barbed wire on top of it tore at their hands, and they almost cried out at the pain. But they managed somehow to keep silent. And at long last they jumped down into the warden's orchard and ran across it. There they lay flat and peered through a thick hedge to the quiet, empty street beyond, lit by a single lamp shaded for the black-out.

It was their first sight of freedom for many bleak days.

They took a deep breath before they slipped through the hedge. They knew the risk they were taking. According to German law no Dane was allowed to be out on the streets after the curfew bell rang in the early evening—and anyone caught out of doors after the curfew sounded had to show a special permit and also his identity card. Of course the boys had neither. Even if no one recognized them as escaped prisoners, they would be in trouble just because they were on the streets so late at night.

But for several hours that evening they prowled the streets of Aalborg —and returned safely to their cell before morning.

'We can do it!' one of them whispered to the friend anxiously awaiting their return. 'We keep in the shadows and hide in doorways if we think we see anything moving—anything that might turn out to be a policeman or a German. It's easy! Now we can start the Churchill Club's sabotage programme again!'

The next morning the biggest boy bravely offered to change cell places with a smaller friend, a boy who could squeeze through the opening. They managed the exchange just in time, because that same day all the Churchill Club members, except the three boys in that one cell, were moved to a prison in another city.

'It's all up to us now,' one of the three said. 'We have to uphold the honour of the Churchill Club alone.'

After that, night after night, strange things happened in Aalborg again.

A German car on Sankelmarke Street, right opposite a German guard post, burst into flames and burned to a pile of twisted metal.

A huge German truck mysteriously caught fire, and it, too, was destroyed.

German motors which were left in perfect condition at the end of a day's work often refused to start the next morning. Inspection showed

170

that vital parts were missing, or that ignition wires were broken and tangled.

Sometimes two boys left the cell at once. Sometimes all three went out together. And with each successful trip they grew more daring. They even went to their own homes, woke up their startled families and enjoyed a fine meal in the middle of the night.

Once more, all over Aalborg, people were wondering who was daring enough to injure German property.

'It looks like the work of the Churchill Club,' people said, 'but it can't be. The members are all in gaol—poor, brave boys!'

Once more the Germans grew angry. Again they ordered the Danish police to find the culprits and punish them.

And still the strange events kept happening, almost every night.

Another German car was burned and battered until, as one boy said, 'It looks like a poor, beaten dog.'

Somehow one German car found its way down to a pier and kept going until it crashed over the end and fell into the sea with a great splash.

On a certain evening the boys were getting ready to leave the cell.

'This will be our nineteenth trip,' one of them said. And he put a tiny dot beside the date on his calendar, as he had done to mark each of their other excursions.

That night they destroyed still another German car, and then made their way to the home of one of the boys for a good meal and a visit with their friends.

At four o'clock in the morning they got up from the table. 'That tasted fine, Mother. Now we've got to be going back home.'

They always made a joke of having to 'go home' after a night's outing from the gaol.

They turned out all the lights in the house before they dared to open the door and slip into the street. It was quiet and deserted as usual. They hurried along in the shadows.

Suddenly a long wail tore the silence. They stopped dead in their tracks. They knew the sound. It was an air-raid warning siren. Allied planes were overhead, preparing to attack German installations. The siren was warning all civilians to go immediately to the air-raid shelters.

The boys were terrified.

'What shall we do?' one whispered.

Air-raid wardens would soon be tramping the streets. Police would appear to guide people to the shelters.

'We can't get back to my house. We can't get back to the gaol. We'd surely be caught if we tried to get through the streets,' the other said.

Even as he spoke they saw two policemen approaching. Quickly the boys stepped inside a darkened shop doorway, but it was not big enough to shelter them both. The police came closer—and stopped right in front of them.

'Who's there?' one policeman demanded. 'What are you doing hanging about on the streets? Don't you know you should be in an air-raid shelter? Let me see your identity card.'

'I—I—I'm afraid I forgot it.'

'And you?' The policeman looked at the second boy.

'I—forgot mine, too.'

'H'm. Strange. Two young men out at this hour—both without identity cards.' The policeman thought for a moment. 'You'd better come along with me to the police station.'

The moment the boys stepped inside the police station they were recognized.

'But it's impossible!' an officer said. 'They can't be Churchill Club members. Those boys are in gaol.'

But when the police went to the gaol and found only one boy in the cell, and found the loosened bar and the calendar with its tiny dots marking all the dates on which sabotage had occurred—then the fate of the three boys was sealed.

Once more they were tried and sentenced, this time to longer terms and in another gaol. Their career of sabotage was over.

But the boys of the Churchill Club had given courage to all the people of Denmark. Even with the boys safe in prison, the Germans went on having trouble. Other people were carrying on the programme the boys had begun. No longer could the Germans pretend to the world that Denmark was a 'model protectorate'.

Finally, in the year 1945, the war in Europe was over. The Germans, who had conquered so many countries, were themselves conquered in the end by the Allies.

And the boys of the Churchill Club were all released from gaol and hailed as heroes—foolhardy heroes, perhaps, but heroes nevertheless.

One day they received an invitation to visit a British General who had helped defeat the Germans.

'I've heard about you,' the General said. 'I'd like you to tell me everything you did—from the very beginning.'

So they told him about the signs, the weapons hidden in the parsley bed, the burned goods wagons, the explosions, the German cars that had gone up in flames.

'That's a good story,' the General said when they had finished. 'I'm going to tell it to Winston Churchill himself.'

WHO KILLED
SIR HARRY OAKES?

Elizabeth Bennett

Lying some one hundred and twenty miles off the south coast of America—the plane journey from Miami is about an hour—lies Nassau, the playground of the rich. It has fabulous houses, acres of lawns and magnificent shops. Men looking for fields of investment took over Freeport, building sumptuous hotels, and the economy supported an army of bankers and property companies. Nassau was a tax haven for Englishmen and many well-known people 'retired' to Nassau to build fine houses, each complete with its swimming pool.

There was plenty of 'hired help', although many of the residents preferred to do their own shopping for the local supermarkets were filled with American produce, while Bay Street had more exclusive shops with a wealth of English bone china, French perfumes and alcohol at reduced prices.

The temperature never falls below warm and frosts are unknown. Only the risk of hurricanes means that everyone with a good property has to install hurricane shutters . . . just in case!

This, then, was the 'paradise island' I went to live on in March 1969. My home was on the Eastern Road, some six miles from the town centre and, typically, I soon found I had collected a host of friends. I was soon being invited to coffee mornings and ladies' lunches and, of course, the popular American 'plate lunches'—where every invited lady takes along her favourite dish. We were a cosmopolitan lot and the dishes reflected this fact; the lady from Greece took along stuffed vine leaves, a Scottish friend turned up with a dish of shortbread and I had a great triumph with a bread and butter pudding—just one of thirty or more different types of dishes, but one that proved very popular.

It was while driving home from one of these parties that a fellow passenger casually said, 'That is Sir Harry Oakes' house.'

'Was that the man who was murdered?' I asked.

Immediately a strange silence fell and I realized then that I had said something no one else wished to hear.

Nevertheless, I tried again. 'Did anyone find out who did it?' One of my friends turned to me and said, 'No, we didn't, although there are many ideas. In any case, Elizabeth, it is better not to talk about it while you are here in Nassau.'

Later, a friend told me, very confidentially, that there had been a girl on the island who had been Sir Harry Oakes' secretary. She was in a bar and the subject cropped up. She hinted that she had an idea of the people who had been involved and that was all. She left the bar about ten o'clock that evening and went home. The next morning when she did not arrive at her office someone went to call on her, thinking she might be ill.

She was more than ill . . . she was dead, with her throat cut!

No wonder that my friends, and all residents of Nassau warned me, 'Don't talk about it; everyone is afraid.'

The Oakes murder had taken place on 8 July 1943, and here it was, 1969, and I was still warned not to talk about the murder! Yet this silence made me very intrigued. I wasn't allowed to talk—but I could still read, and I went to the local library to look up the facts.

The murder of Sir Harry Oakes was news in papers all over the globe, despite the fact that world war was raging at the time. He was said to be the richest man in the world, a resident of Nassau with his wife, Eunice, and a respected member of a large social circle. As property owners, they were involved in the business life of the island and, with so much wealth, he owned a great deal of property.

Sir Harry was born in Maine, USA, his father being a land surveyor who also taught school. Harry was sent to a fine school in Brunswick, Maine, and later studied law. As a boy he loved the beautiful woods of his home state and was considered something of a 'loner'. He was a quiet boy, but whenever he was asked what he was going to do when he grew up (adults always ask that!) he would reply 'I'm going to make a fortune.'

He studied medicine for two years and then, realizing there was not much money in that career, turned his attention to a gold mining camp called Dawson City. Such camps were generally the haunts of hobos and drop-outs, men used to roughing it and who could sleep anywhere and live on a very sparse diet. But Harry Oakes was able to get some money from home; he was not dependent on handouts and could afford to move from place to place, following the rumours of new strikes and claims. He soon built up a useful knowledge of the precious ore everyone was seeking. Unlike most of the other men, he preferred to work alone, shouldering his eighty-pound pack and moving from place to place.

His obsession with dreams of wealth gave him the impetus he needed to survive very long working hours and to overcome the physical hardships he had to endure. He found one claim in the Yukon, but it proved useless; it was played out. News of another find took him to Nome in Alaska, but again he was unlucky. But he was not dismayed—following the scent of gold strikes became an obsession with him. He went to the Philippines and then to Australia; there he worked in the desert wastes, where the temperatures were almost unbearable and where the fight to stay alive was even harder than the icy temperatures of the Yukon or Alaska!

His great helper was his sister, Gertrude. She was working as a government secretary in Washington D.C. and every month she sent him some of her wages. He could, probably, have done without the money, but she gave him moral support as well, encouraging him in his search for gold. She had great belief that her brother would, eventually, be successful in his quest.

Her beliefs were to be justified. At the Kirkland Lake in northern Ontario, some two years after his arrival, what would become the second largest gold mine in the world was discovered.

There are many stories about how Harry Oakes became the owner of the claim, but the most popular was that he bought the rights for five dollars from a starving Chinese cook. He himself insisted that the Kirkland Lake strikes were the result of his hard work and experience in assessing where other strikes had been found and that his theories had paid off. In any case, fourteen years of work and frustration were over.

He had bought the claim; the rich, untapped source of gold was now his. But he did not have enough capital to work it, and was forced to take other men into partnership so that the mining could continue. This was frustrating for him—he still preferred to work alone—and he decided that, as soon as possible, he would pay off his partners. He called them the 'Tough Boys'—they were four brothers—and they helped him with money to register the mine which was called the Tough Oakes Mine. When it was seen that the strike was a very rich one he organized the capital for the mine, raising two million dollars. He kept one million for himself and repaid those who had helped him along the road, especially his devoted sister.

He then started to think how he could get rid of his partners. He could not get money from the government, and he needed special equipment to sink shafts down to the levels where the rich deposits lay. No bank would help and even the newspapers refused to accept his advertisements asking for money to promote his mine. It was to take a number of bitterly fought lawsuits between himself and the Tough Boys before he could gain sole control of the mine.

Grim, dogged determination had made him what he was—a rich and successful man, but a hard man, one who had lived rough but who had a good education behind him and a legal knowledge which stood him in good stead. By 1921, twenty-three years after leaving medical school, he had achieved his ambition—he had made his fortune. But the struggle had changed him. He had become somewhat crude in his manners; the years of living rough had made his forget how to behave in polite society, and the language he had acquired among the hard-working, hard-swearing miners was far from fit for ladies' ears.

Yet he met and married a girl who was his opposite in every way. She was half his age, gentle, always smiling and the daughter of a government official in Sydney, Australia. At first they lived in a chalet near the mine but his wife, Eunice, did not like the solitary area and

177

persuaded him to move into a sprawling rebuilt castle near Niagara Falls. It was said that King Edward VII had once spent a night there!

Now, living in a castle, the richest man in Canada yet a man without taste or graciousness, Oakes came to a great decision. He would renounce his American nationality and become a Canadian citizen. Yet the Canadian elections of 1930 made him unhappy, especially when he realized that at eighty-five per cent he was the most heavily taxed payer in Canada. So he decided to build another home, this time in Palm Beach, Florida, where all the rich Americans were buying houses. But he was now threatened with even higher tax.

At Palm Beach he met a real estate man from Nassau who had ideas which he 'sold' to the attentive Harry Oakes. 'Invest your money in the Bahamas,' he told him. 'There is no income tax, no wealth tax, no inheritance tax and even no death duties. That's the place for you!'

It did not take Oakes long to see the strength of this argument. He was sixty years old and if he died as a Canadian the rate of tax on his money would be something like ninety-five per cent. He moved with his wife and five children into a house in Nassau called 'Westwood'— a mansion with twenty rooms and within easy reach of the Bahamas Country Club. This was the house that had been pointed out to me from the car.

Once installed, he began to change the life-style of the whole island. He built a golf club, bought a Moorish-styled, pink-painted hotel known as the British Colonial and even started his own bus line. This, however, was not a success. Daily servants were supposed to work from nine till five, but most arrived late and left early because the bus line, which the locals called a 'Jitney', had a most irregular service. White people rarely used the 'Jitney'. I was told by my own servants that the other users would smell and that you would probably catch fleas!

Having established themselves in the British colony on Nassau, Harry and Eunice Oakes went to London. They bought a house in Sussex and became interested in British and colonial affairs. They also became involved in local charities and, perhaps remembering his earlier medical training, Harry Oakes gave half a million dollars to help St George's Hospital, London. Because of this, and other generous gestures, his name appeared in the honours list for King George VI's birthday in 1939. Sir Harry and Lady Oakes than decided they would like to be of more consequence in the land they had made their home, and the former gold miner was asked to become a member of the Bahamas House of Assembly.

He was now a 'made' man. He was well in with Bahamas society and was entertained by, and entertained in return, the new Governor of the Bahamas, The Duke of Windsor and his wife, 'The Duchess'.

Then came disaster. Harry Oakes' friend was an estate agent named Harold Christie, who arranged a meeting between Sir Harry and some men who wished to open some gambling clubs and casinos on the island. Lady Oakes was in America at the time and Sir Harry agreed to meet the representatives of the proposed syndicate on a power-cruiser in the harbour.

What Christie probably did not know was that the men were leaders of a gang headed by a man named Meyer Lansky. He was a powerful force in America, where he controlled many gambling clubs and was connected with the Mafia; and he was ruthless when he met any opposition to his plans. He had successfully run ships between America and the Bahamas when the former country was living under strict prohibition laws and where the sale of alcoholic spirits was illegal. Lansky was one of those who had made a fortune smuggling illicit drink into the USA and many lives had been lost in the foolhardy ways they adopted to land the contraband.

It was necessary for Lansky to obtain three of the most influential men on Nassau to sign a contract which would allow him to start work on his gambling clubs and, it is said, Sir Harry had promised his help. He had done this because Harold Christie, his friend, would benefit from the sale of land and the subsequent building. Both men's friendship with the Governor made it almost a certainty that the Duke of Windsor would raise no objection to the proposals, and the whole venture was obviously poised to succeed.

So Sir Harry met Lansky's men on the cruiser, as arranged. But something must have come up during the discussion that caused him to have second thoughts and to speak his mind. His lifetime spent with the tough men of the mining camps had not taught him diplomacy and by now he had become a spoilt, arrogant man, used to having his own way. But in Lansky he had met his match. The gangster was ruthless and determined, a man used to disposing of people if they crossed him. His

179

reputation was well known and it is certain that Harold Christie, aware of the confrontation between the two men, tried to warn his friend. But Sir Harry was determined to go ahead with the scheme.

The two men went to the cruiser, were received by one of Lansky's lieutenants backed by some sinister-looking men, and were shown down to the main cabin. What lines the discussion took is not known, but it was enough to make Sir Harry lose his temper completely. He finally told Lansky's man what he could tell his boss, and as far as he was concerned he wished to have nothing further to do with the project.

Lansky's lieutenant soon realized that the other was adamant; he would not help. He turned slightly, looked at one of his men, and gave a slight nod. The next moment the henchman moved forward, brought back his arm, and struck Sir Harry on the head with a winch lever. He collapsed with a groan while Christie looked on, paralysed and helpless.

When he began to protest, the men assured him that Sir Harry had only been knocked unconscious—to teach him a lesson. It did not pay to trifle with Meyer Lansky! They then half carried, half dragged the unconscious Sir Harry on to the quayside and laid him, none too gently, in his station wagon. Then one of them ordered Christie to sit in a car and direct him to the mansion called 'Westwood', the station wagon following.

When they reached the house, Lansky's men ordered Christie to help move his unconscious friend up to his bedroom, dragging the body up the hall stairway. By the time they had managed to get him into his bedroom, both men realized that Sir Harry was no longer unconscious . . . he was dead! Lansky's man saw that Christie was still in a state of shock and he made him help undress Sir Harry, put him into his pyjamas, and into his bed. He then left, leaving the shattered Christie to sit in a chair in the bedroom, almost unaware of what was going on.

The drama was not finished. The gangster later returned with a home-made torch. Whilst Christie watched, hypnotized, the other set fire to the mattress top and bottom and, when the blaze was quite considerable, ordered Christie to lay the body on the fire. Realizing that he might well suffer a similar fate to his friend if he argued, Christie did as he was told.

The two men watched for a moment or two then the gangster swung

Sir Harry collapsed with a groan while Christie looked on, paralysed . . .

on the frightened Christie. 'Stay away from the telephone,' he snarled, 'and don't try and make contact with anyone until after seven tomorrow morning! D'ya hear me?' he repeated, his voice sounding loud above the crackling of the flames. 'No one!' He turned and raced from the room.

His warning about the time was to allow the cruiser to get well away from Nassau and hide among the hundreds of other boats in and around the island.

That is the story as it was told, but what surprised me—and the other residents of Nassau—was the subsequent lack of urgency. When the Governor was told of the death of Sir Harry, quite obviously one of murder, he delayed nearly a whole day before taking any action to track down the murderers. He then alerted the Miami police, who sent two of their men to look into the facts. As it happened, on that particular day, Sir Ettiene Depuch, the owner-editor of the local newspaper, had an appointment with Harold Christie. He soon learned from him the story of the murder and within hours the world's newspapers were carrying that same story. Yet no one knew why—or who did it!

Later that same day Christie made contact with the Royal Governor and told the Duke of Sir Harry's death, together with the grim details. He was a very frightened man and communicated his fears of *their* safety. I was told several times that the life of the Duchess of Windsor was also threatened and that, perhaps, might have been the reason for the delay in seeking to establish the identity of the murderers.

No action was taken until the arrival of the two senior detectives from Miami. They seemed to ignore all the known facts and immediately summoned everyone near to Sir Harry to explain their whereabouts at the time of the killing. Despite Christie's eye-witness story, the detectives chose their own major suspect—Alfred de Marigny, Sir Harry's son-in-law, who had married his eldest daughter Nancy. De Marigny lived in a house nearby and had given a dinner party on the evening of the murder. He had taken two ladies who had been at the party back to their respectives homes, and had asked another guest, a gentleman, to accompany him.

The detectives were not satisfied with his story. De Marigny, they decided, was the murderer. He was arrested and, on Monday, 18 October 1943, he was brought to trial, some thirteen weeks after the murder.

It was to prove by far the most sensational in the islands' history. The court was hushed as the prisoner was brought in and the indictment was read:

'Marie Alfred Fouquereaux de Marigny, you are charged with murder under Section 335 of the Penal Code (Chapter 60); particularly of the offense being that during the night of the 7th and 8th July, 1943, at New Providence, you did murder Sir Harry Oakes, Baronet. Are you guilty or not guilty?'

The prisoner replied in a firm, confident voice, 'Not guilty!'

And so the trial began. As it happened, Godfrey Higgs, my friend and neighbour, was engaged as the attorney to defend de Marigny. He had to fight hard for his client, for many things were said at the trial to discredit the defendant. He had married Nancy Oakes in America when she was but eighteen, and without asking her parents' permission. Much time was taken up by the prosecuting attorney in trying to prove that he had married her for her money. This line of questioning collapsed, however, when it was proved that the Oakes had sent their daughter a very substantial cheque as a wedding present, but she had returned it. She was sorry to do so, she had said, but she and her husband hoped to make their own way in life without outside help.

Godfrey Higgs proved himself a clever and subtle attorney and, as the trial continued, he slowly but brilliantly exposed the evidence for the Crown as a tissue of lies and half-truths dreamed up by the two detectives, Captain Melchen and Barker, who had been brought over from Miami to handle the case by the Royal Governor.

The trial lasted for eight days, and at the end of it de Marigny was declared 'not guilty'. Yet he had been made a scapegoat by the American police, and will obviously bear the scars of his ordeal for the rest of his life.

Why the case was handled in the way it was will always remain a mystery. The fact that a perfectly innocent man should be forced to fight for his life on a charge of which he was so obviously innocent amazed everyone on the island. So many aspects of the case are still puzzling. When the Governor asked for help from the Miami police—he told them it was a case of suicide—he knew the detective he asked for help, having met him when previously he had been assigned as a royal guard. The Americans may have thought that Harold Christie's story was too far-fetched and concocted in order to protect the son-in-law.

On the other hand, however, there may have been a more sinister motive. It was said later that the American police were already involved with the Lansky gang. It is well known that policemen are often bribed to 'look the other way', while they sometimes ignore small charges as, by becoming friendly with the criminals, they hope to obtain information which will lead to the solution of a larger crime. If Harold Christie's story was right, then what chance had they to find the murderers who had left by boat hours before? There are twenty-nine islands in close proximity, six hundred and sixty-one cays, or smaller islands, and more than two thousand 'rocks', mostly of coral, on which people live. Everyone living there has a boat of some size or other and the detectives must have decided it was better for them to concentrate on someone near at hand—someone who could have had a motive.

Melchen and Barker must have tried to impress the Royal Governor with action of some kind, but they must have known from the start that they were up against organized crime. When the trial of de Marigny began, the courtroom and the streets outside were crowded, everyone was in a fever of excitement, and there was widespread sympathy for the suspected man. And everyone remarked about the fact that the Duke and Duchess of Windsor left the island to visit America and stayed away during the whole of the trial.

Both the American detectives are now dead, but it was later proved that one of them, Barker, was involved with the Lansky gang and may have been ordered to cover up the whole affair.

There must be people still living on the island who know the real answer but to the rest this cruel killing on a tropical island still remains . . . a mystery.

HISTORY'S FIRST SPIES

Alastair Scott

Moses looked along the row of tough, bronzed warriors drawn up before him. He smiled grimly. These young men had been chosen, at his command, to undertake a difficult task. A few days earlier he had sent out an order to all the tribes of Israel that he had led out of captivity in Egypt. Acting on divine instructions, he had ordered each of the twelve tribes to send their leading warrior so that he might tell them of his plans.

The tribes had been camping for some time in the desert of Paran and had reached the borders of the country of Canaan. Moses had heard that it was a rich and fertile country, but he had to be sure. These young men would be the ones to scout the land for him.

As he looked along the line of warriors he sighed. He was now nearly eighty years of age and he deeply envied them their youth, their strength and their obvious eagerness for the adventure that lay ahead. He sighed again and then, his voice sounding clear in the thin desert air he said, 'Listen to me carefully. I want you to make your way southward, taking the trail that leads to the mountain ahead. Go carefully. Make sure you are not seen. Your task is to spy out the land beyond, see what kind of country it is, find out something about the people who live there, whether they are strong or weak, few or many.

'I especially want you to find out everything possible about the country; whether it is good or bad; what cities there are and how the people live, whether in tents or in strongholds.'

He paused, looked along the row of keen young men and added, 'Be of good courage and, when you return, bring back something of the fruit of the land so that we may judge what kind of a place it is.'

And so the twelve young men set off on their mission. They were the first recorded spies in history and their task was an important one. The tribes into which the refugees from Egypt had been formed were seeking a place in which to settle down, to grow their own crops and tend their sheep and cattle, to build their own houses, villages and perhaps, in time, even their own cities. The land of Canaan was the first country they had reached. It was one which, if the spies' report was all that they hoped, would offer them a real home.

But the Israelites, fresh from their lives as slaves to the Egyptians, were untried in battle. If the country ahead had strong walled towns, and well-trained and well-armed fighting men, their task would be impossible and they would have to move on and seek refuge elsewhere.

Moses's twelve spies progressed stealthily through the land of Canaan, moving around the great city of Jericho, studying the land, its peoples and its possibilities. Towards the end of their stay they came to the brook of Eshcol, where large vineyards had grapes ripening beneath the summer sun. Remembering Moses's command, they cut down a branch from one of the vines. It was so heavy with lush, purple grapes that they slung it over a staff and two men, in turn, supported each end of the staff on their shoulders.

Forty days of such spying having passed, they made their way back to the Israelite camp, where Moses and his people had been anxiously awaiting their return. As a proof of the richness of the land they showed them the huge bunches of grapes, together with pomegranates and figs they had also gathered as they went. Moses examined the fruit, his old and wizened face showing his pleasure. Then he asked, 'But what of the people who live in the land?'

One of the men replied, 'The Amalekites dwell in the land of the south, and the Hittites and the Jebusites and the Amorites dwell in the mountains, and the Canaanites dwell by the sea and by the coast of Jordan.'

There was a sudden intake of breath at this. Such a group of nations would be far too strong for the band of Israelites. But Caleb, one of the spies, stepped forward and said, boldly, 'Let us go up against it at once and take their land. We are well able to overcome any opposition!'

But all the others who had gone with him—save one—disagreed. 'We are not able to go up and fight these people, for they are stronger than we are!'

Some of the others went on to exaggerate the strength of the country through which they had journeyed, saying, 'The land through which we have searched is a land that would eat up any who tried to come against it. Every man we saw there was of great stature. And we saw giants too, the sons of Anak. By the side of them we seemed like grasshoppers, and about as useless.'

At these ominous words the great mass of people who had gathered to hear the spies' report began to moan and cry. Moreover, some began to grumble about the fact that they had ever been brought out of captivity in Egypt. Many spoke against the Lord, some even suggesting that they find another leader and return to Egypt, beg the Pharaoh's pardon, and return to work again as slaves.

But now another voice was added to that of Caleb. It was that of Joshua, the son of Nun. With Caleb at his side he shouted out to the anxious multitude:

'The land through which we have passed is a very good land. With the blessing of the Lord, he will bring us into this land and give it to us. It is truly a land which flows with milk and honey. Only do not rebel against the Lord, nor fear the people of the land, for they are bread for us, and their defences can be broken down. For the Lord is with us. Do not be afraid of them!'

Joshua went on to explain that with the Lord on their side no one, not even the dreaded giants of Anak, could withstand them. But many of the Israelites shouted at him even as he spoke and, greatly troubled, Moses went apart and prayed for guidance.

As usual his prayers were answered by the Lord, who said to him: 'Tomorrow, turn and go into the wilderness by the way of the Red Sea. And tell this to the children of Israel. As truly as I live, as you have spoken against me, so will I do to you. Your carcases shall fall in the wilderness, every one that has been numbered, from twenty years old and upwards, which have murmured against me.

'None of you will come into the land in which I promised you should live, none except Caleb, the son of Jephunneh and Joshua the son of Nun. Your little ones shall know the land which the rest of you have despised, but as for you—your carcases will fall and lay in the wilderness through which I condemn you to wander for forty years. Then, after forty years, you shall know my promise for I, the Lord have said, I will surely do it unto all this evil congregation, that are gathered together against me! In this wilderness to which I have condemned them, they shall be consumed, and there they shall die.'

Crushed by this terrible decision, Moses went sadly back to his people. As he did so he heard sounds of crying. 'What has happened?' he asked.

'Every one of the men who went to spy out the land of Canaan has died, suddenly, of some kind of plague. Only Caleb and Joshua live, the only two men brave enough to make a good report of the land and who wished us to march into Canaan and take it by force. Shall we not do so now?'

But Moses was forced to repeat what the Lord had bidden him to say; how, for their doubts, they had been ordered to wander in the wilderness for forty years.

Except for two brave men, history's first spies had failed in their duty. And so the long trek began . . .

Forty long years later the Israelites again reached the borders of Canaan. But now they were unified and toughened by their experiences against fierce tribes and marauding beasts. They had even taken on the nation of the Amorites—and beaten them utterly.

Moses, now an old, very old man of six score years, climbed slowly and painfully to the top of a mountain called Pisgah. From this eminence he could see, stretched out before him, the rich and fertile land that had been promised to his people. But he also knew that he would not be privileged to enter the land itself. His successor, as leader of the twelve tribes, was Joshua, now sixty, but still full of the strength and enthusiasm which had made him such a remarkable young man.

After thirty days of mourning had passed for Moses's death, Joshua prayed, knowing that the Lord would give him his orders. He lay quietly, face down, in the special tent reserved for the leader of the tribes. It was very quiet, very still. From outside, the sound of the people of the vast camp were as a faint whisper. Then, at last, came the inner voice he had been awaiting.

'Moses, my servant, is dead. Now therefore arise, go over this river Jordan, thou and all this people, unto the land which I do give to them, even the children of Israel.

'Every place that the sole of your foot shall tread upon, that have I given unto you, as I said to Moses.

'From the wilderness and this Lebanon even unto the great river, the River Euphrates, all the land of the Hittites, and unto the great sea towards the going down of the sun, shall be your coast.

'Have I not commanded thee? Be strong and of a good courage; be not afraid, neither be thou dismayed; for the Lord thy God is with thee whithersoever thou goest.'

Greatly strengthened in mind and spirit, Joshua left the tent and started to give his orders to the Israelites, telling them to prepare for the great adventure that lay ahead. When he had done this he sat quietly and pondered his next move. He realized that the first great stronghold to be attacked would be that of Jericho, but as yet he knew nothing about the city. Remembering his own experience as a spy, some forty years earlier, he sent for two of his most trusted men. They arrived quickly, curiosity plainly written on their tanned young faces. It was obvious that both wondered why they had been sent for in such a fashion. Joshua was soon to tell them.

'I want you two men to cross the Jordan and find out all you can about the stronghold of Jericho. When you are satisfied that you know everything, come back and let me know its strength and, even more important, its weaknesses. For I intend to capture that city, one way or another. And, with the Lord's help, this we will do!'

So the two spies set off on their mission. In time they reached the city of Jericho, and at first stood amazed at its size and strength. Both men had been born in the desert during the forty years of exile and neither had seen such a place before. Its walls stood strong and high, and its single gate could be quickly closed and defended against attack.

They waited until noon, when a large group of farmers and others from outlying districts began to pass through this gateway. They mingled with this crowd of country-folk and soon found themselves inside the city. They walked through the streets, carefully noting everything they saw, but soon realized that the city seemed so strong that it would be almost impossible to overcome.

They strolled along, stopping to look at the piles of fruit and other good things, some of which they had never seen before, until they stopped for a while to have some food themselves. Whilst they were eating in a small tavern, they happened to start talking to a woman of Jericho whose name was Rahab. She saw at once that they were foreigners and asked them when they would be leaving the city, for the gate was always closed at sunset. When they told her they wished to stay in the city for the night but had nowhere to go, she agreed that she would shelter them until morning.

'Why are you doing this?' one of the men asked her.

Before replying, she looked about her to make sure that no one was listening. 'That is something I will tell you later. But first, let us go back to my house, which is built upon the city wall.'

As the three left the tavern, however, someone overheard them talking and, realizing that the men were not of Jericho but might even be of the dreaded Israelites, hurried to the royal court. It was not long before the king was told, 'Behold, there came men in hither tonight who are of the children of Israel. They have doubtless come to spy out the country!'

When the king asked where the men were spending the night, he was told that they had been seen going into Rahab's house. Greatly disturbed by this news, the king sent a number of armed men to the house. The leader knocked loudly on her door and waited impatiently until it was opened. As he saw the woman he said, roughly, 'Bring out the men that are here, for we understand that they have come to spy out all the country and especially this city!'

But Rahab shook her head. 'Two men *have* been here,' she replied, 'but I do not know from whence they came. At dusk, as the gate was being shut, they left in order to leave the city. If you hurry after them at once you will overtake them as they go on their way.'

The leader muttered a curse, gathered his men about him and made

190

at once for the city gate. They passed through then heard it clang shut as they hurried in pursuit of the spies.

But the two men had not left the city; Rahab had concealed them. She had taken them up to the roof of her house, told them to lie down, then covered them with stalks of flax so that they were completely hidden. As soon as she knew that the guard had gone, she returned to the roof and told them what had happened.

'But why do you do this for us, for two strangers?' one asked her.

Her reply was quite unexpected. 'I know by your speech that you are both Israelites. Like so many others living in Jericho, we know that your Lord has promised you all this land and the stories we hear of your army terrifies us all. We have heard how your Lord dried up the waters of the Red Sea so that you might escape the chariots of the Pharaoh of Egypt. We have heard how you fought the two kings of the Amorites on the other side of the Jordan, and how you completely destroyed their armies.

'These, and other such stories, have caused us to tremble in fear. Few of our so-called warriors seem to have courage any more, because of what we have heard of you and your army. Also, many of us now believe that your God is the true God, Lord of heaven above and of the earth beneath. And what can *we* do against such a powerful God?'

She paused, knowing that the two hidden men were carefully following her every word.

'And that is why I have taken you in and hidden you,' she went on. For I have to ask you a favour. Swear to me by that same Lord that because I have shown you a kindness you will also show kindness to me. And not only to me but to my family. Swear to me that when your army breaks into our city—as we all know it will—you will save my father and mother, my brothers and sisters from certain death.'

There was a long silence; then, from the darkness of the night, came the voice of one of the spies. 'Our life for yours if you tell no one that we have been here. And we promise you that when our Lord has given us this land, that we will deal kindly and truly with you and yours.'

Satisfied with this promise, Rahab ran down to her room immediately below, found a stout cord and, after tying one end, cast the other through the window so that it hung down the city wall. She then went back to the roof, feeling her way with care for it was now black mid-

'*Swear to me that when your army breaks into our city,*' *whispered Rahab,* '*you will save my father and mother, my brothers and sisters from death.*'

night, and whispered to the men, 'Get out of the city and make for the mountain. Hide yourselves there, for the men who came here earlier are out searching for you. After three days they will return. Then you may go on your way, back to your own people.'

The piles of flax heaved and shook as both men eased themselves from their hiding place, then followed her down the flight of stairs to her room. As they reached the window one of the men turned to her and said, 'We will be blameless of the oath that you have made us swear. In order that we may keep our word, bind a thread of scarlet on the shutters of this window. Also, tomorrow, go out and bring in your mother and father, your brothers, sisters and others of your father's household and keep them here. If any one of them goes out of the doors of your house, his blood shall be on his head and we cannot be blamed. But if anyone who stays with you in this house is harmed in any way, then his blood will be on our own heads.'

There was silence as the first man clambered through the window and slid quietly to the ground outside the city wall. As his comrade was about to follow he said, ominously, 'Don't forget now. If you tell anyone why we have been here, then we will be quit of the oath you made us swear.'

Her voice came back softly, in the darkness. 'According to your words—so be it,' and a few moments later she heard the second man land on the earth outside. She searched around, found and tied a scarlet line to the window, and went to bed.

Both men hid in the nearby mountain for three days, as Rahab had suggested, and then made their way back to the Israelite camp, where they were received by Joshua. He asked them a number of questions, all of which they answered immediately, proving that they had been keen and efficient spies. He was delighted with their report, saying, 'Truly the Lord has delivered the city and all the land around into our hands, for everyone there has heard of us and seem terrified of our coming.'

It was not long before Jericho was under siege, but the people of the city stared down in amazement as for six days none of their enemies attempted to attack. Instead they merely marched around the city's walls, led by seven priests bearing trumpets of rams' horns. The whole army marched in silence, with only the priests blowing on their horns.

By the third day the people of Jericho were beginning to believe that the Israelites feared to attack such a strong city. By the sixth day they were shouting insults to them as they tramped past underneath.

But on the seventh day everything changed. This time, when the priests blew on their trumpets, every man in the marching army shouted in reply—a vast uprising of sound that seemed to make everything around tremble and shake. The sudden noise obviously affected part of the old city wall where the foundations had become weakened with age. A large part of it suddenly fell inwards with a great crashing of stones and timber and the Israelites, swords and spears in hand, rushed in through the opening that had so dramatically gaped before them.

Yet even at this vital moment, Joshua remembered his two spies and their vow. He looked around and saw them nearby. Beckoning them to his side he said, 'Go at once to the woman's house and bring her out, and all who are with her . . . as you swore to our Lord you would do!'

As the Bible has it, from which both these early spy stories are taken: 'And the young men that were spies went in and brought out Rahab, and her father, and her mother, and her brethren, and all that she had; and they brought out all her kindred and left them without the camp of Israel.

'And they burnt the city with fire, and all that was therein; only the silver, and the gold, and the vessels of brass and of iron they put into the treasury of the house of the Lord.'

YOURS TRULY, JACK THE RIPPER

Robert Bloch

I looked at the stage Englishman. He looked at me.

'Sir Guy Hollis?' I asked.

'Indeed. Have I the pleasure of addressing John Carmody, the psychiatrist?'

I nodded. My eyes swept over the figure of my distinguished visitor. Tall, lean, sandy-haired—with the traditional tufted moustache. And the tweeds. I suspected a monocle concealed in a vest pocket, and wondered if he'd left his umbrella in the outer office.

But more than that, I wondered what the devil had impelled Sir Guy Hollis of the British Embassy to seek out a total stranger here in Chicago.

Sir Guy didn't help matters any as he sat down. He cleared his throat, glanced around nervously, tapped his pipe against the side of the desk. Then he opened his mouth.

'What do you think of London?' he said.

'Why——'

'I'd like to discuss London with you, Mr Carmody.'

I meet all kinds. So I merely smiled, sat back, and gave him his head.

'Have you ever noticed anything strange about that city?' he asked.

'Well, the fog is famous.'

'Yes, the fog. That's important. It usually provides the perfect setting.'

'Setting for what?'

Sir Guy Hollis gave me an enigmatic grin.

'Murder,' he murmured.

'Murder?'

'Yes. Hasn't it struck you that London, of all cities, has a peculiar affinity for those who contemplate homicide?'

They don't talk that way, except in books. Still, it was an interesting thought. London as an ideal spot for a murder!

'As you mentioned,' said Sir Guy, 'there is a natural reason for this. The fog is an ideal background. And then too the British have a peculiar attitude in such matters. You might call it their sporting instinct. They regard murder as sort of a game.'

I sat up straight. Here was a theory.

'Yes, I needn't bore you with homicide statistics. The record is there. Aesthetically, temperamentally, the Englishman is interested in crimes of violence.

'A man commits murder. Then the excitement begins. The game starts. Will the criminal outwit the police? You can read between the lines in their newspaper stories. Everybody is waiting to see who will score.

'British law regards a prisoner as innocent until proved guilty. That's *their* advantage. But first they must catch their prisoner. And London bobbies are not allowed to carry fire-arms. That's a point for the fugitive. You see? All part of the rules of the game.'

I wondered what Sir Guy was driving at. Either a point or a strait-jacket. But I kept my mouth shut and let him continue.

'The logical result of this British attitude towards murder is— Sherlock Holmes,' he said.

'Have you ever noticed how popular the theme of murder is in British fiction and drama?'

I smiled. I was back on familiar ground.

'*Angel Street*,' I suggested.

'*Ladies in Retirement*,' he continued. '*Night Must Fall.*'

'*Payment Deferred*,' I added. '*Laburnum Grove. Kind Lady. Love from a Stranger. Portrait of a Man with Red Hair. Black Limelight.'*

He nodded. 'Think of the motion pictures of Alfred Hitchcock and Emlyn Williams. The actors—Wilfred Lawson and Leslie Banks.'

'Charles Laughton,' I continued for him. 'Edmund Gwenn. Basil Rathbone. Raymond Massey. Sir Cedric Hardwicke.'

'You're quite an expert on this sort of thing yourself,' he told me.

'Not at all.' I smiled. 'I'm a psychiatrist.'

Then I leaned forward. I didn't change my tone of voice. 'All I want to know,' I said sweetly, 'is why you come up to my office and discuss murder melodramas with me.'

It stung him. He sat back and blinked a little.

'That isn't my intention,' he murmured. 'No. Not at all. I was just advancing a theory——'

'Stalling,' I said. 'Stalling. Come on, Sir Guy—spit it out.'

Talking like a gangster is all part of the applied psychiatric technique. At least, it worked for me.

It worked this time.

Sir Guy stopped bleating. His eyes narrowed. When he leaned forward again he meant business.

'Mr Carmody,' he said, 'have you ever heard of—Jack the Ripper?'

'The murderer?' I asked.

'Exactly. The greatest monster of them all. Worse than Spring-heel Jack or Crippen. Jack the Ripper. Red Jack.'

'I've heard of him,' I said.

'Do you know his history?'

I got tough again. 'Listen, Sir Guy,' I muttered. 'I don't think we'll get any place swapping old wives' tales about famous crimes of history.'

Another bull's-eye. He took a deep breath.

'This is no old wives' tale. It's a matter of life or death.'

He was so wrapped up in his obsession he even talked that way. Well—I was willing to listen. We psychiatrists get paid for listening.

'Go ahead,' I told him. 'Let's have the story.'

Sir Guy lit a cigarette and began to talk.

'London, 1888,' he began. 'Late summer and early autumn. That was the time. Out of nowhere came the shadowy figure of Jack the Ripper— a stalking shadow with a knife, prowling through London's East End. Haunting the squalid dives of Whitechapel, Spitalfields. Where he came from no one knew. But he brought death. Death in a knife.

'Six times that knife descended to slash the throats and bodies of London's women. Drabs and alley sluts. August 7 was the date of the first butchery. They found her body lying there with thirty-nine stab wounds. A ghastly murder. On August 31 another victim. The press became interested. The slum inhabitants were more deeply interested still.

'Who was this unknown killer who prowled in their midst and struck at will in the deserted alleyways of night-town? And what was more important—when would he strike again?

'September 8 was the date. Scotland Yard assigned special deputies. Rumours ran rampant. The atrocious nature of the slayings was the subject for shocking speculation.

'The killer used a knife—expertly. He cut throats. He chose victims and settings with a fiendish deliberation. No one saw him or heard him. But watchmen making their grey rounds in the dawn would stumble across the hacked and horrid thing that was the Ripper's handiwork.

'Who was he? What was he? A mad surgeon? A butcher? An insane scientist? A pathological degenerate escaped from an asylum? A de-ranged nobleman? A member of the London police?

'Then the poem appeared in the newspapers. The anonymous poem, designed to put a stop to speculations—but which only aroused public interest to a further frenzy. A mocking little stanza:

I'm not a butcher, I'm not a kid
Nor yet a foreign skipper,
But I'm your own true loving friend,
Yours truly—Jack the Ripper.

'And on September 30, two more throats were slashed open.'

I interrupted Sir Guy for a moment.

'Very interesting,' I commented. I'm afraid a faint hint of sarcasm crept into my voice.

He winced, but didn't falter in his narrative.

'There was silence, then, in London for a time. Silence, and a name-less fear. When would Red Jack strike again? They waited through October. Every figment of fog concealed his phantom presence. Con-cealed it well—for nothing was learned of the Ripper's identity, or his purpose. The drabs of London shivered in the raw wind of early

November. Shivered, and were thankful for the coming of each morning's sun.

'November 9. They found her in her room. She lay there very quietly, limbs neatly arranged. And beside her, with equal neatness, were laid her head and heart. The Ripper had outdone himself in execution.

'Then, panic. But needless panic. For though press, police and populace alike awaited in sick dread, Jack the Ripper did not strike again.

'Months passed. A year. The immediate interest died, but not the memory. They said Jack had skipped to America. That he had committed suicide. They said—and they wrote. They've written ever since. Theories, hypotheses, arguments, treatises. But to this day no one knows who Jack the Ripper was. Or why he killed. Or why he stopped killing.'

Sir Guy was silent. Obviously he expected some comment from me.

'You tell the story well,' I remarked. 'Though with a slight emotional bias.'

'I've got all the documents,' said Sir Guy Hollis. 'I've made a collection of existing data and studied it.'

I stood up. 'Well,' I yawned, in mock fatigue, 'I've enjoyed your little bedtime story a great deal, Sir Guy. It was kind of you to abandon your duties at the British Embassy to drop in on a poor psychiatrist and regale him with your anecdotes.'

Goading him always did the trick.

'I suppose you want to know why I'm interested?' he snapped.

'Yes. That's exactly what I'd like to know. Why are you interested?'

'Because,' said Sir Guy Hollis, 'I am on the trail of Jack the Ripper now. I think he's here—in Chicago!'

I sat down again. This time I did the blinking act.

'Say that again,' I stuttered.

'Jack the Ripper is alive, in Chicago, and I'm out to find him.'

'Wait a minute,' I said. 'Wait—a—minute!'

He wasn't smiling. It wasn't a joke.

'See here,' I said. 'What was the date of these murders?'

'August to November 1888.'

'1888? But if Jack the Ripper was an able-bodied man in 1888, he'd surely be dead today! Why look, man—if he were merely *born* in that year, he'd be fifty-five years old today!'

'Would he?' smiled Sir Guy Hollis. 'Or should I say "Would she?" Because Jack the Ripper may have been a woman. Or any number of things.'

'Sir Guy,' I said. 'You came to the right person when you looked me up. You definitely need the services of a psychiatrist.'

'Perhaps. Tell me, Mr Carmody, do you think I'm crazy?'

I looked at him and shrugged. But I had to give him a truthful answer. 'Frankly—no.'

'Then you might listen to the reasons I believe Jack the Ripper is alive today.'

'I might.'

'I've studied these cases for thirty years. Been over the actual ground. Talked to officials. Talked to friends and acquaintances of the poor drabs who were killed. Visited with men and women in the neighbourhood. Collected an entire library of material touching on Jack the Ripper. Studied all the wild theories or crazy notions.

'I learned a little. Not much, but a little. I won't bore you with my conclusions. But there was another branch of inquiry that yielded more fruitful returns. I have studied unsolved crimes. Murders.

'I could show you clippings from the papers of half the world's great cities. San Francisco. Shanghai. Calcutta. Omsk. Paris. Berlin. Pretoria. Cairo. Milan. Adelaide.

'The trail is there, the pattern. Unsolved crimes. Slashed throats of women. With the peculiar disfigurations and removals. Yes, I've followed a trail of blood. From New York westward across the continent. Then to the Pacific. From there to Africa. During the Great War it was Europe. After that, South America. And since 1930, the United States again. Eighty-seven such murders—and to the trained criminologist, all bear the stigma of the Ripper's handiwork.

'Recently there were the so-called Cleveland torso slayings. Remember? A shocking series. And finally, two recent deaths in Chicago. Within the past six months. One out on South Dearborn, the other somewhere up on Halsted. Same type of crime, same technique. I tell you, there are unmistakable indications in all these affairs—indications of the work of Jack the Ripper!'

I smiled.

'A very tight theory,' I said. 'I'll not question your evidence at all, or the deductions you draw. You're the criminologist, and I'll take your word for it. Just one thing remains to be explained. A minor point, perhaps, but worth mentioning.'

'And what is that?' asked Sir Guy.

'Just how could a man of, let us say, eighty-five years, commit these crimes? For if Jack the Ripper was around thirty in 1888 and lived, he'd be eighty-five today!'

Sir Guy Hollis was silent. I had him there. But——

'*Suppose he didn't get any older?*' whispered Sir Guy.

'What's that?'

'Suppose Jack the Ripper didn't grow old? Suppose he is still a young man today.'

'All right,' I said. 'I'll suppose for a moment. Then I'll stop supposing and call for my nurse to restrain you.'

'I'm serious,' said Sir Guy.

'They all are,' I told him. 'That's the pity of it all, isn't it? They *know* they hear voices and see demons. But we lock them up just the same.'

It was cruel, but it got results. He rose and faced me.

'It's a crazy theory, I grant you,' he said. 'All the theories about the Ripper are crazy. The idea that he was a doctor. Or a maniac. Or a woman. The reasons advanced for such beliefs are flimsy enough. There's nothing to go by. So why should my notion be any worse?'

'Because people grow older,' I reasoned with him. 'Doctors, maniacs and women alike.'

'What about—*sorcerers?*'

'Sorcerers?'

'Necromancers. Wizards. Practisers of black magic?'

'What's the point?'

'I studied,' said Sir Guy. 'I studied everything. After a while I began to study the dates of the murders. The pattern those dates formed. The rhythm. The solar, lunar, stellar rhythm. The sidereal aspect. The astrological significance.'

He *was* crazy. But I still listened.

'Suppose Jack the Ripper didn't murder for murder's sake alone? Suppose he wanted to make—a sacrifice?'

'What kind of a sacrifice?'

201

Sir Guy shrugged. 'It is said that if you offer blood to the dark gods they grant boons. Yes, if a blood offering is made at the proper time—when the moon and the stars are right—and with the proper ceremonies—they grant boons. Boons of youth. Eternal youth.'

'But that's nonsense!'

'No. That's—Jack the Ripper.'

I stood up. 'A most interesting theory,' I told him. 'But Sir Guy—there's just one thing I'm interested in. Why do you come here and tell it to me? I'm not an authority on witchcraft. I'm not a police official or criminologist. I'm a practising psychiatrist. What's the connection?'

Sir Guy smiled.

'You are interested, then?'

'Well, yes. There must be some point.'

'There is. But I wished to be assured of your interest first. Now I can tell you my plan.'

'And just what is that plan?'

Sir Guy gave me a long look. Then he spoke.

'John Carmody,' he said, 'you and I are going to capture Jack the Ripper.'

That's the way it happened. I've given the gist of that first interview in all its intricate and somewhat boring detail because I think it's important. It helps to throw some light on Sir Guy's character and attitude. And in view of what happened after that——

But I'm coming to those matters.

Sir Guy's thought was simple. It wasn't even a thought. Just a hunch.

'You know the people here,' he told me. 'I've inquired. That's why I came to you as the ideal man for my purpose. You number among your acquaintances many writers, painters, poets. The so-called intelligentsia. The Bohemians. The lunatic fringe from the near north side.

'For certain reasons—never mind what they are—my clues lead me to infer that Jack the Ripper is a member of that element. He chooses to pose as an eccentric. I've a feeling that with you to take me around and introduce me to your set, I might hit on the right person.'

'It's all right with me,' I said. 'But just how are you going to look for him? As you say, he might be anybody, anywhere. And you have no idea what he looks like. He might be young or old. Jack the Ripper—

a jack of all trades? Rich man, poor man, beggar man, thief, doctor, lawyer—how will you know?'

'We shall see.' Sir Guy sighed heavily. 'But I must find him. At once.'

'Why the hurry?'

Sir Guy sighed again. 'Because in two days he will kill again.'

'Are you sure?'

'Sure as the stars. I've plotted his chart, you see. All eighty-seven of the murders correspond to certain astrological rhythm patterns. If, as I suspect, he makes a blood sacrifice to renew his youth, he must murder within two days. Notice the pattern of his first crimes in London. August 7. Then August 31. September 8. September 30. November 9. Intervals of twenty-four days, nine days, twenty-two days—he killed two this time—and then forty days. Of course there were crimes in between. There had to be. But they weren't discovered and pinned on him.

'At any rate, I've worked out a pattern for him, based on all my data. And I say that within the next two days he kills. So I must seek him out, somehow, before then.'

'And I'm still asking you what you want me to do.'

'Take me out,' said Sir Guy. 'Introduce me to your friends. Take me to parties.'

'But where do I begin? As far as I know, my artistic friends, despite their eccentricities, are all normal people.'

'So is the Ripper. Perfectly normal. Except on certain nights.' Again that faraway look in Sir Guy's eyes. 'Then he becomes an ageless pathological monster, crouching to kill, on evenings when the stars blaze down in the blazing patterns of death.'

'All right,' I said. 'All right. I'll take you to parties, Sir Guy. I want to go myself, anyway. I need the drinks they'll serve there after listening to your kind of talk.'

We made our plans. And that evening I took him over to Lester Baston's studio.

As we ascended to the penthouse roof in the elevator I took the opportunity to warn Sir Guy.

'Baston's a real screwball,' I cautioned him. 'So are his guests. Be prepared for anything and everything.'

'I am.' Sir Guy Hollis was perfectly serious. He put his hand in his

203

trouser pocket and pulled out a gun.

'What the——' I began.

'If I see him I'll be ready,' Sir Guy said. He didn't smile, either.

'But you can't go running around at a party with a loaded revolver in your pocket, man!'

'Don't worry, I won't behave foolishly.'

I wondered. Sir Guy Hollis was not, to my way of thinking, a normal man.

We stepped out of the elevator and went towards Baston's apartment door.

'By the way,' I murmured, 'just how do you wish to be introduced? Shall I tell them who you are and what you are looking for?'

'I don't care. Perhaps it would be best to be frank.'

'But don't you think that the Ripper—if by some miracle he or she is present—will immediately get the wind up and take cover?'

'I think the shock of the announcement that I am hunting the Ripper would provoke some kind of betraying gesture on his part,' said Sir Guy.

'You'd make a pretty good psychiatrist yourself,' I conceded. 'It's a fine theory. But I warn you, you're going to be in for a lot of ribbing. This is a wild bunch.'

Sir Guy smiled.

'I'm ready,' he announced. 'I have a little plan of my own. Don't be shocked by anything I do,' he warned me.

I nodded and knocked on the door.

Baston opened it and poured out into the hall. He teetered back and forth regarding us very gravely. He squinted at my square-cut Homburg hat and Sir Guy's moustache.

'Aha,' he intoned. 'The Walrus and the Carpenter.'

I introduced Sir Guy.

'Welcome,' said Baston, gesturing us inside with over-elaborate courtesy. He stumbled after us into the garish parlour.

I stared at the crowd that moved restlessly through the fog of cigarette smoke.

It was the shank of the evening for this mob. Every hand held a drink. Every face held a slightly hectic flush. Over in one corner the piano was going full blast.

Sir Guy got a monocle-full right away. He saw LaVerne Gonnister, the poetess, hit Hymie Kralik in the eye. He saw Hymie sit down on the floor and cry until Dick Pool accidentally stepped on his stomach as he walked through to the dining-room for a drink.

He heard Nadia Vilinoff, the commercial artist, tell Johnny Odcutt that she thought his tattooing was in dreadful taste.

His zoological observations might have continued indefinitely if Lester Baston hadn't stepped to the centre of the room and called for silence by dropping a vase on the floor.

'We have distinguished visitors in our midst,' bawled Lester, waving his empty glass in our direction. 'None other than the Walrus and the Carpenter. The Walrus is Sir Guy Hollis, a something-or-other from the British Embassy. The Carpenter, as you all know, is our own John Carmody, the prominent dispenser of libido-liniment.'

He turned and grabbed Sir Guy by the arm, dragging him to the middle of the carpet. For a moment I thought Hollis might object, but a quick wink reassured me. He was prepared for this.

'It is our custom, Sir Guy,' said Baston, loudly, 'to subject our new friends to a little cross-examination. Just a little formality at these very formal gatherings, you understand. Are you prepared to answer questions?'

Sir Guy nodded and grinned.

'Very well,' Baston muttered. 'Friends—I give you this bundle from Britain. Your witness.'

Then the ribbing started. I meant to listen, but at that moment Lydia Dare saw me and dragged me off into the vestibule for one of those Darling-I-waited-for-your-call-all-day routines.

By the time I got rid of her and went back, the impromptu quiz session was in full swing. From the attitude of the crowd, I gathered that Sir Guy was doing all right for himself.

Then Baston himself interjected a question that upset the apple-cart.

'And what, may I ask, brings you to our midst tonight? What is your mission, oh Walrus?'

'I'm looking for Jack the Ripper.'

Nobody laughed.

Perhaps it struck them all the way it did me. I glanced at my neighbours and began to *wonder*.

LaVerne Gonnister. Hymie Kralik. Harmless. Dick Pool. Nadia Vilinoff. Johnny Odcutt and his wife. Barclay Melton. Lydia Dare. All harmless.

But what a forced smile on Dick Pool's face! And that sly, self-conscious smirk that Barclay Melton wore!

Oh, it was absurd, I grant you. But for the first time I saw these people in a new light. I wondered about their lives—their secret lives beyond the scenes of parties.

How many of them were playing a part, concealing something?

Who here would worship Hecate and grant that horrid goddess the dark boon of blood?

Even Lester Baston might be masquerading.

The mood was upon us all, for a moment. I saw questions flicker in the circle of eyes around the room.

Sir Guy stood there, and I could swear he was fully conscious of the situation he'd created, and enjoyed it.

I wondered idly just what was *really* wrong with him. Why he had this odd fixation concerning Jack the Ripper. Maybe he was hiding secrets, too . . .

Baston, as usual, broke the mood. He burlesqued it.

'The Walrus isn't kidding, friends,' he said. He slapped Sir Guy on the back and put his arm around him as he orated. 'Our English cousin is really on the trail of the fabulous Jack the Ripper. You all remember Jack the Ripper, I presume? Quite a cut-up in the old days, as I recall. Really had some ripping good times when he went out on a tear.

'The Walrus has some idea that the Ripper is still alive, probably prowling around Chicago with a boy scout knife. In fact'—Baston paused impressively and shot it out in a rasping stage-whisper—'*in fact, he has reason to believe that Jack the Ripper might even be right here in our midst tonight.*'

There was the expected reaction of giggles and grins. Baston eyed Lydia Dare reprovingly. 'You girls needn't laugh,' he smirked. 'Jack the Ripper might be a woman, too, you know. Sort of a Jill the Ripper.'

'You mean you actually suspect one of us?' shrieked LaVerne Gonnister, simpering up to Sir Guy. 'But that Jack the Ripper person disappeared ages ago, didn't he? In 1888?

'Aha!' interrupted Baston. 'How do you know so much about it, young lady? Sounds suspicious! Watch her, Sir Guy—she may not be as young as she appears. These lady poets have dark pasts.'

The tension was gone, the mood was shattered, and the whole thing was beginning to degenerate into a trivial party joke.

Then Baston caught it.

'Guess what?' he yelled. 'The Walrus has a gun.'

His embracing arm had slipped and encountered the hard outline of the gun in Sir Guy's pocket. He snatched it out before Hollis had the opportunity to protest.

I stared hard at Sir Guy, wondering if this thing had carried far enough. But he flicked a wink my way and I remembered he had told me not to be alarmed.

So I waited as Baston broached a drunken inspiration.

'Let's play fair with our friend the Walrus,' he cried. 'He came all the way from England to our party on this mission. If none of you is willing to confess, I suggest we give him a chance to find out—the hard way.'

'What's up?' asked Johnny Odcutt.

'I'll turn out the lights for one minute. Sir Guy can stand here with his gun. If anyone in this room is the Ripper he can either run for it or take the opportunity to—well, eradicate his pursuer. Fair enough?'

It was even sillier than it sounds, but it caught the popular fancy. Sir Guy's protests went unheard in the ensuing babble. And before I could stride over and put in my two cents' worth, Lester Baston had reached the light switch.

'Don't anybody move,' he announced, with fake solemnity. 'For one minute we will remain in darkness—perhaps at the mercy of a killer. At the end of that time, I'll turn up the lights again and look for bodies. Choose your partners, ladies and gentlemen.'

The lights went out.

Somebody giggled.

I heard footsteps in the darkness. Mutterings.

A hand brushed my face.

The watch on my wrist ticked violently. But even louder, rising above it, I heard another thumping. The beating of my heart.

Absurd. Standing in the dark with a group of tipsy fools. And yet there was real terror lurking here, rustling through the velvet blackness.

Jack the Ripper prowled in darkness like this. And Jack the Ripper

Sir Guy lay sprawled on the floor, the gun still clutched in his hand.

had a knife. Jack the Ripper had a madman's brain and a madman's purpose.

But Jack the Ripper was dead, dead and dust these many years—by every human law.

Only there are no human laws when you feel yourself in the darkness, when the darkness hides and protects and the outer mask slips off your face and you feel something welling up within you, a brooding shapeless purpose that is brother to the blackness.

Sir Guy Hollis shrieked.

There was a grisly thud.

Baston had the lights on.

Everybody screamed.

Sir Guy Hollis lay sprawled on the floor in the centre of the room. The gun was still clutched in his hand.

I glanced at the faces, marvelling at the variety of expressions human beings can assume when confronting horror.

All the faces were present in the circle. Nobody had fled. And yet Sir Guy Hollis lay there . . .

LaVerne Gonnister was wailing and hiding her face.

'All right.'

Sir Guy rolled over and jumped to his feet. He was smiling.

'Just an experiment, eh? If Jack the Ripper *were* among those present, and thought I had been murdered, he would have betrayed himself in some way when the lights went on and he saw me lying there.

'I am convinced of your individual and collective innocence. Just a gentle spoof, my friends.'

Hollis stared at the goggling Baston and the rest of them crowding in behind him.

'Shall we leave, John?' he called to me. 'It's getting late, I think.'

Turning, he headed for the closet. I followed him. Nobody said a word.

It was a pretty dull party after that.

I met Sir Guy the following evening as we agreed, on the corner of 29th Street and South Halsted.

After what had happened the night before, I was prepared for almost anything. But Sir Guy seemed matter-of-fact enough as he stood huddled against a grimy doorway and waited for me to appear.

'Boo!' I said, jumping out suddenly. He smiled. Only the betraying gesture of his left hand indicated that he'd instinctively reached for his gun when I startled him.

'All ready for our wild goose chase?' I asked.

'Yes.' He nodded. 'I'm glad that you agreed to meet me without asking questions,' he told me. 'It shows you trust my judgment.' He took my arm and edged me along the street slowly.

'It's foggy tonight, John,' said Sir Guy. 'Like London.'

I nodded.

'Cold, too, for November.'

I nodded again and half-shivered my agreement.

'Curious,' he mused. 'London fog and November. The place and the time of the Ripper murders.'

I grinned through darkness. 'Let me remind you, Sir Guy, that this isn't London, but Chicago. And it isn't November 1888. It's over fifty years later.

Sir Guy returned my grin, but without mirth. 'I'm not so sure, at that,' he murmured. 'Look about you. These tangled alleys and twisted streets. They're like the East End. Mitre Square. And surely they are as ancient as fifty years, at least.'

'You're in the poor neighbourhood off South Clark Street,' I said, shortly. 'And why you dragged me down here I still don't know.'

'It's a hunch,' Sir Guy admitted. 'Just a hunch on my part, John. I want to wander around down here. There's the same geographical conformation in these streets as in those courts where the Ripper roamed and slew. That's where we'll find him, John. Not in the bright lights of the Bohemian neighbourhood, but down here in the darkness. The darkness where he waits and crouches.'

'Is that why you brought a gun?' I asked. I was unable to keep a trace of sarcastic nervousness from my voice. All of this talk, this incessant obsession with Jack the Ripper, got on my nerves.

'We may need the gun,' said Sir Guy, gravely. 'After all, tonight is the appointed night.'

I sighed. We wandered on through the foggy, deserted streets. Here and there a dim light burned above a doorway. Otherwise, all was darkness and shadow. Deep, gaping alleyways loomed as we proceeded down a slanting side street.

We crawled through that fog, alone and silent, like two tiny maggots floundering within a shroud.

When that thought hit me, I winced. The atmosphere was beginning to get *me*, too. If I didn't watch my step I'd go as loony as Sir Guy.

'Can't you see there's not a soul around these streets?' I said, tugging at his coat impatiently.

'He's bound to come,' said Sir Guy. 'He'll be drawn here. This is what I've been looking for. A *genius loci*. An evil spot that attracts evil. Always, when he slays, it's in the slums.

'You see, that must be one of his weaknesses. He has a fascination for squalor. Besides, the women he needs for sacrifice are more easily found in the dives and stewpots of a great city.'

I smiled. 'Well, let's go into one of the dives or stewpots,' I suggested. 'I'm cold. Need a drink. This fog gets into your bones. You Britishers can stand it, but I like warmth and dry heat.'

We emerged from our side street and stood upon the threshold of an alley.

Through the white clouds of mist ahead, I discerned a dim blue light, a naked bulb dangling from a beer sign above an alley tavern.

'Let's take a chance,' I said. 'I'm beginning to shiver.'

'Lead the way,' said Sir Guy. I led him down the alley passage. We halted before the door of the dive.

'What are you waiting for?' he asked.

'Just looking in,' I told him. 'This is a tough neighbourhood, Sir Guy. Never know what you're liable to run into. And I'd prefer we didn't get into the wrong company.'

'Good idea, John.'

I finished my inspection through the doorway. 'Looks deserted,' I murmured. 'Let's try it.'

We entered a dingy bar. A feeble light flickered above the counter and railing, but failed to penetrate the farther gloom of the back booths.

A gigantic Negro lolled across the bar. He scarcely stirred as we came in, but his eyes flickered open quite suddenly and I knew he noted our presence and was judging us.

'Evening,' I said.

He took his time before replying. Still sizing us up. Then he grinned.

'Evening, gents. What's your pleasure?'

'Gin,' I said. 'Two gins. It's a cold night.'

'That's right, gents.'

He poured. I paid, and took the glasses over to one of the booths. We wasted no time in emptying them. The fiery liquor warmed.

I went over to the bar and got the bottle. Sir Guy and I poured ourselves another drink. The big Negro went back into his doze, with one wary eye half-open against any sudden activity.

The clock over the bar ticked on. The wind was rising outside, tearing the shroud of fog to ragged shreds. Sir Guy and I sat in the warm booth and drank our gin.

He began to talk, and the shadows crept up about us to listen.

He rambled a great deal. He went over everything he'd said in the office when I met him, just as though I hadn't heard it before. The poor devils with obsessions are like that.

I listened very patiently. I poured Sir Guy another drink. And another.

But the liquor only made him more talkative. How he did run on!

211

About ritual killings and prolonging life unnaturally—the whole fantastic tale came out again. And, of course, he maintained his unyielding conviction that the Ripper was abroad tonight.

I suppose I was guilty of goading him.

'Very well,' I said, unable to keep the impatience from my voice. 'Let us say that your theory is correct—even though we must overlook every natural law and swallow a lot of superstition to give it any credence.

'But let us say, for the sake of argument, that you are right. Jack the Ripper was a man who discovered how to prolong his own life through making human sacrifices. He did travel around the world as you believe. He is in Chicago now and he is planning to kill. In other words, let us suppose that everything you claim is gospel truth. So what?'

'What do you mean, "so what"?' said Sir Guy.

'I mean—so what?' I answered. 'If all this is true, it still doesn't prove that by sitting down in a dingy gin-mill on the South Side, Jack the Ripper is going to walk in here and let you kill him, or turn him over to the police. And come to think of it, I don't even know now just what you intend to *do* with him if you ever did find him.'

Sir Guy gulped his gin. 'I'd capture the bloody swine,' he said. 'Capture him and turn him over to the government, together with all the papers and documentary evidence I've collected against him over a period of many years. I've spent a fortune investigating this affair, I tell you, a fortune! His capture will mean the solution of hundreds of unsolved crimes, of that I am convinced.

'I tell you, a mad beast is loose on this world! An ageless, eternal beast, sacrificing to Hecate and the dark gods!'

In vino veritas. Or was all this babbling the result of too much gin? It didn't matter. Sir Guy Hollis had another. I sat there and wondered what to do with him. The man was rapidly working up to a climax of hysterical drunkenness.

'One other point,' I said, more for the sake of conversation than in any hopes of obtaining information. 'You still don't explain how it is that you hope to just blunder into the Ripper.'

'He'll be around,' said Sir Guy. 'I'm psychic. I know.'

Sir Guy wasn't psychic. He was maudlin.

The whole business was beginning to infuriate me. We'd been sitting here an hour, and during all this time I'd been forced to play nursemaid and audience to a babbling idiot. After all, he wasn't a regular patient of mine.

'That's enough,' I said, putting out my hand as Sir Guy reached for the half-emptied bottle again. 'You've had plenty. Now I've got a suggestion to make. Let's call a cab and get out of here. It's getting late and it doesn't look as though your elusive friend is going to put in his appearance. Tomorrow, if I were you, I'd plan to turn all those papers and documents over to the FBI. If you're so convinced of the truth of your wild theory, they are competent to make a very thorough investigation and find your man.

'But let's get out of here anyway,' I said, glancing at my watch. 'It's past midnight.'

He sighed, shrugged, and rose unsteadily. As he started for the door, he tugged the gun free from his pocket.

'Here, give me that!' I whispered. 'You can't walk around the street brandishing that thing.'

I took the gun and slipped it inside my coat. Then I got hold of his right arm and steered him out of the door. The Negro didn't look up as we departed.

We stood shivering in the alleyway. The fog had increased. I couldn't see either end of the alley from where we stood. It was cold. Damp. Dark. Fog or no fog, a little wind was whispering secrets to the shadows at our backs.

The fresh air hit Sir Guy just as I had expected it would. Fog and gin fumes don't mingle very well. He lurched as I guided him slowly through the mist.

Sir Guy, despite his incapacity, still stared apprehensively at the alley, as though he expected to see a figure approaching.

Disgust got the better of me.

'Childish foolishness,' I snorted. 'Jack the Ripper, indeed! I call this carrying a hobby too far.'

'Hobby?' He faced me. Though the fog I could see his distorted face. 'You call this a hobby?'

'Well, what is it?' I grumbled. 'Just why else are you so interested in tracking down this mythical killer?'

My arm held him. But his stare held me.

213

'In London,' he whispered. 'In 1888 . . . one of those women the Ripper
slew . . . was my mother.'

'In London,' he whispered. 'In 1888 . . . one of those women the Ripper slew . . . was my mother.'

'What?'

'My father and I swore to give our lives to find the Ripper. My father was the first to search. He died in Hollywood in 1926—on the trail of the Ripper. They said he was stabbed by an unknown assailant in a brawl. But I know who that assailant was.

'So I've taken up his work, do you see, John? I've carried on. And I will carry on until I do find him and kill him with my own hands.

'He took my mother's life and the lives of hundreds to keep his own hellish being alive. Like a vampire, he battens on blood. Like a ghoul, he is nourished by death. Like a fiend, he stalks the world to kill. He is cunning, devilishly cunning. But I'll never rest until I find him. Never!'

I believed him then. He wouldn't give up. He wasn't just a drunken babbler any more. He was as fanatical, as determined, as relentless as the Ripper himself.

Tomorrow he'd be sober. He'd continue the search. Perhaps he'd turn those papers over the the FBI. Sooner or later, with such persistence —and with his motive—he'd be successful. I'd always known he had a motive.

'Let's go,' I said, steering him down the alley.

'Wait a minute,' said Sir Guy. 'Give me back my gun.' He lurched a little. 'I'd feel better with the gun on me.'

He pressed me into the dark shadows of a little recess.

I tried to shrug him off, but he was insistent.

'Let me carry the gun now, John,' he mumbled.

'All right,' I said.

I reached into my coat, brought my hand out.

'But that's not a gun,' he protested. 'That's a knife.'

'I know.'

I bore down on him swiftly.

'John!' he screamed.

'Never mind the "John",' I whispered, raising the knife. 'Just call me . . . Jack.'

THE KROGERS OF RUISLIP
Betty Grant-Sutherland

On the morning of 12 January 1961, copies of the *Ruislip-Northwood Gazette* were pushed through letter-boxes in and around that area of outer North-West London. Within minutes, subscribers were reading with surprise, amazement and, in some cases, sheer disbelief, that two local residents had been arrested as spies and faced a trial for espionage.

The two concerned were a quiet, friendly couple named Peter Kroger and his wife Helen. They lived in a small, modest bungalow in Ruislip, in a quiet close, and were liked and respected by their neighbours. And now, this apparently very ordinary couple were being charged under the Official Secrets Act which, in wartime, would have been enough, had they been found guilty, to have had them executed.

Also concerned were three other people—Gordon Lonsdale of Regent's Park, London, Henry Houghton of Weymouth, and Ethel Gee of Portland, both of Dorset. Three men and two women, all apparently highly respectable, but all charged as dangerous spies and traitors to the country in which they lived.

The Krogers were arrested in their little bungalow in Cranley Drive, Ruislip, where they had been living for seven years. Their caller on that memorable day was Detective Superintendent George Smith, known to his colleagues as 'Spycatcher Smith', of Scotland Yard's Special Branch. He was accompanied by Chief Inspector Ferguson Smith and other police officers.

Who were the apparently harmless couple they were visiting?

Kroger's real name was Morris Cohen, a man born in New York of Russian parents. He had fought against General Franco's forces in the Spanish Civil War, then returned to New York to work for a Russian company. He met and married a Polish girl named Lona. He later fought in the US Army in the Second World War and, after demobilization, became a teacher. Then, as the Cohens, they made a number of friends in the Jewish community and became deeply involved with the Rosenbergs, active spies for Russia in the United States. When the Rosenbergs were arrested and charged with espionage in 1950 (they were executed three years later) the Cohens decided it was time to move on.

For five years they seemed to vanish, although they spent some time in Australia, using forged Canadian and New Zealand passports. They also had a blank British passport ready for when they needed it. In 1955 they used this passport, which now showed their names as Peter and Helen Kroger. They had no money problems, for they were now acting as Russian agents and were paid by their employers.

Arriving in England, Peter Kroger rented a room opposite the Law Courts in London, setting up as a dealer in old books. He applied for membership of the Antiquarian Booksellers' Association so that he could attend the International Congress of Booksellers in Holland at the end of August 1960. He travelled to Holland with his wife but did not stay with the others attending the conference. Instead he went to Germany for, as he said, a holiday. They even sent postcards of places they visited. Both must have used this visit to establish some important contacts . . .

Within a year of their arrival in England, the Krogers had bought the pleasant bungalow in Ruislip. It was to serve as his business premises as well as a home. Through his book business, he and his wife made regular visits to the continent, and he sent parcels of rare and valuable books all over the world, receiving back many in return. Such books were, of course, ideal hiding places for the microdots used by the spies. The couple must have sent and received hundreds of microdot messages in this fashion.

The Ruislip bungalow was also well equipped for the transfer of messages. Even if someone, accidentally, did pick up a transmission, the duration of the signal was so short it was hardly noticeable. In fact, a keen radio 'ham' did advise the police that a strong signal was coming from somewhere in the area. But no action was taken. In any case, the messages were always in code, so they would not have meant anything to the casual listener.

The Krogers' sophisticated transmitting equipment was, literally, unearthed when the police began a search that almost took the bungalow apart. Many of the houses in that part of Ruislip are built on sloping ground and many with apertures under the floors. A detective found a trap-door to the foundations and, going down, found a pile of rubble. Beneath that was a hole containing five packages in polythene bags, a brown paper bag, a linen bag and a green plastic tray. And in the middle of all this was a grey metal box, the size of an attaché-case. Within this case was a radio transmitter, powerful enough to send messages direct to Moscow.

The Krogers also had a telescopic ladder fitted to connect to the loft of the bungalow. They told inquisitive visitors that they needed the loft for the storage of books. But the police found that it also contained a long and highly effective aerial, fitted expertly among the wooden beams, together with skilfully prepared hiding places for foreign currency and other articles that would, finally, help to convict them.

A large quantity of fascinating equipment also came to light during the intensive police search. Two photographers moved in to take flash-light pictures of each room while the Special Branch men began to make an inventory of all the things they thought should be examined, once the photographers had finished their work. One of these was an ordinary looking table-lighter, part of which was a wooden ball. One of the men flicked it and found it worked. Then, very carefully, he pulled the metal part away from the wood to reveal a metal container for the lighter mechanism. This was also removed and beneath was a cavity nearly five inches across. This contained signal plans covering transmission times and frequencies for eight months of that year, one of them with headings in Russian and pads to put messages into code.

There were many locks on this small, suburban home—one on every window and every door. Even the tiny pantry had a patent locking device. Obviously they did not want anyone to enter the bungalow—and with good reason.

After Chief Inspector Smith had found the vital box containing the radio transmitter, he had another, equally incriminating find. This was a bag which contained a false torch battery, lenses which could be used to make microdots, a camera and other photographic material. There were also 6,000 American dollars in 20-dollar bills and also a keying device which would enable long messages to be sent in a very short time.

Meanwhile, up in the loft, Sergeant Rowland Ellis had already uncovered the aerial. He then carefully rolled back the insulating material above the rafters and found yet another brown paper parcel. This one contained 2,563 American dollars together with a quantity of travellers' cheques, all signed by Kroger.

Downstairs, following the discovery of the table-lighter, the rest of the Special Branch men were having a field day. In the bedroom they found a blue box inside which was a microscope and five glass slides with, nearby, a 35 mm film magazine wrapped in a blue bathing suit. In the same place was fifty feet of electric flex with a bulb at one end and a plug at the other. This appeared to be an innocent article, one found in many homes, but later its use was found to be more sinister.

Beside the bed was a crowded bookcase and every book was searched page by page, and then the bindings. From, of all books, the Bible, came a very significant piece of evidence. This was a white-coated piece of cellophane which, to the eyes of an expert, was immediately seen as a makeshift form of light-sensitive paper used by the Russian espionage service for their microdot photographs.

A whisky flask on a bedside table was found to contain three compartments, only one of which was used for the fluid. The others contained black powder used with the cellophane to make microdots. A torch found in the drawer of the same table would not work. Where the batteries should have been was more incriminating evidence. This tied up with the other torch found in the loft.

The searchers were not surprised to find that the bathroom could be quickly blacked out to form a darkroom, but were amused to find that a tin of a popular brand of talcum powder had a middle compartment

The transmitter was to be the most definite piece of evidence.

which held the powder, while the rest were places for microdot readers. The soiled linen basket in one corner was also searched. It was found to contain £200 in five-pound notes.

They then returned to the apparently harmless long flex with the plug and bulb. It was soon realized that it was used to light up the basement when messages were being sent and received. That settled, the transmitter was brought up to be packed, like the rest of the evidence, into wooden tea-chests and then taken to the police station to be examined by experts. It was said that so much was found that there was a constant stream of cars in and out of the usually quiet close.

The transmitter was of particular interest to the experts. Indeed, it was to be the most definite piece of evidence against the Krogers. The set bore no maker's name and was not of any design made in England. It had a single earpiece and no loudspeaker. Also, the mains plug with which it was fitted was of a type unknown in Britain. It worked on a high-frequency band with a 150-watt output.

As the men from the Special Branch, and later their experts, worked on all this material, it became obvious what Kroger had been doing. His bookselling business gave him the perfect cover, with customers all over the world. He used to take boxes of chocolates to the girls in the Ruislip Post Office, he became so well known to them. Often the addresses on his packages were just post-boxes—pick-up places for people who either did not wish their real addresses to be known or who were constantly on the move. The packages reached their final destination in Moscow in various ways and the code messages from Ruislip would tell the Russians where the package might be recovered.

It became obvious that the modest Ruislip bungalow was the headquarters for a ring of spies in Britain, and that the large sum of money found there was for the use of anyone who needed immediate payment or who had to leave the country in a hurry.

So, until 'Spycatcher Smith' got on to their trail, the Krogers were 'all set'. He first had his suspicions when a man he was sure was a spy—Gordon Lonsdale—was seen leaving 45 Cranley Drive. That put the Krogers under immediate suspicion and when later, Lonsdale and his two accomplices, Harold Houghton and Ethel Gee, were arrested, the hunt was on.

A search of Lonsdale's flat in London's West End revealed a tin of photographic fixing salt and a receipt which showed that it had been bought by a Mr Kroger of Cranley Drive, Ruislip.

At 7.15 on Saturday, 7 January 1961, 'Spycatcher Smith' formed a cordon around the bungalow and, accompanied by Ferguson Smith, walked to the front door. The two officials were allowed in by Kroger and then Detective Superintendent George Smith turned to Mrs Kroger and said, 'I would like you to tell me the name of the gentleman who stays with you each weekend, particularly the first Saturday in every month. He arrives about 7.15.'

When neither she nor her husband mentioned the name of Lonsdale, Smith said they would have to go with him. Mrs Kroger went to get her coat from her bedroom and picked up her handbag. She then asked, 'May I stoke the boiler before we go out?'

The inspector gave her permission but, noticing her handbag, went to take it from her. She resisted and it took the combined efforts of the inspector and a policewoman to wrest it from her. Inside the handbag was a letter with seven pages written in Russian. Obviously Mrs Kroger had hoped to have thrown it into the boiler to destroy such damning evidence. Also some microdots were found, together with a typed sheet of cipher.

The Krogers were taken to Hayes Police Station, charged, then put in separate rooms. They were later asked to give their finger-prints, but both refused. Two days after their arrest the police applied for an order to be made for them to be finger-printed. Both still objected, Mrs Kroger in particular, claiming that they were not criminals. A few minutes later their prints were taken.

The Criminal Records Office at Scotland Yard has records of finger-prints taken from records from all over the world. Within minutes the experts had found matching prints that came from a file marked 'espionage suspects' and bore the symbol of the American Federal Bureau of Investigation. The prints belonged to a Morris and Lona Cohen.

On 31 March 1961, the five people accused of spying were taken from their separate prisons to stand trial at the Old Bailey before Lord Parker, the Chief Justice of England.

The five accused were led into a packed court, for the press comments

had attracted a tremendous amount of interest. First came Peter and
Helen Kroger, carrying bundles of newspapers and also scribbling
paper; then their friend Gordon Lonsdale, big, dark and Russian-born;
then Harold Houghton and Ethel Gee, two Admiralty civil servants
who were said to have obtained vital information through their work
in the Portland office . . .

After the all-man jury had been sworn in, the trial was begun by Sir
Reginald Manningham Buller, the Attorney-General. He stated that
the prosecution had to satisfy the jury that each of the five persons in
the dock had been party to a plot and to a conspiracy. He then produced
the letter found in Mrs Kroger's handbag. It was written in Russian and
addressed to Lonsdale's wife, who was living at her home in Russia.
After reading translated parts of it to the court, Sir Reginald suggested
that if the letter was a reply by Lonsdale to the microdots—also in
Russian and found in the same handbag—then it might be thought that
Lonsdale was a Russian.

He was on his feet for more than three hours, telling the court of what
had been found at Ruislip: 'Here was the hub of a spy ring and also,
possibly, in view of the money found there, the *bank* of a spy ring!'

He then went on to describe documents found in the homes of the
other three suspects. He said, 'The answers to all the subjects raised in
those documents would give a complete picture of our current anti-
submarine effort, information that would be of the highest value to a
probable enemy.'

The hushed courtroom heard how various MI5 agents had followed
and watched these people for so long. One, a woman agent known as
'Miss K', looking like a secretary in a smart blue coat, told of her part.
She had been watching the Krogers and their bungalow for months.
When asked from where she had watched them she replied, 'I was in a
house on the corner.'

It then became clear that some of the Krogers' neighbours had been
asked to keep watch. They had little idea of what might be going on.
One who did not was a Mrs Swann, living in a flat nearby. She had
acquired a new car but found that the space allotted to her was frequently taken by a large American Studebaker. She assumed it belonged to an American who was visiting his girlfriend, and when this
was proved wrong, she kept a look-out for the owner of the car. She

223

actually saw him one evening coming from the alley that led to the Krogers' bungalow. She did not know it, of course, but it was actually Gordon Lonsdale. She said that she was going to speak to him about his use of her parking space, but something stopped her. Later she said, 'If I'd known he was Russian I should probably have fainted on the spot.'

So Gordon Lonsdale, unaware that he had created so much interest, continued to park his car there, and it was there again the weekend before all the arrests were made.

Houghton and Miss Gee were the first to be put into the witness-box. After their examination by the prosecutor, no one was in any doubt that both, for gain, had been guilty of selling their country's secrets.

The next session began with the examination of Lonsdale. He went into the witness-box and tried hard to save the Krogers. He said that all the articles found in their home had been taken there by him and that in their absence he had made a hiding place in which to store his transmitter. It was obvious that he hoped, by accepting all the blame, that they would be released. But his testimony was ruthlessly destroyed by the prosecutor.

When placed in the dock, Kroger proved to be flamboyant and theatrical. He claimed he was a very respectable bookseller and one who had worked years to build up his image. He objected, he said, to being called to court to give an account of himself as if he was a common criminal. Helen Kroger gave the impression of being the typical suburban, tidy housewife whose main aim in life was to make a nice home for her husband. When her Canadian friend came (she meant Lonsdale) he helped with getting in the coal and also made himself very useful in the kitchen. She claimed that she knew nothing about spying at all.

Eight days after it began, the trial ended. It did not take the jury long to bring in a verdict of guilty.

Superintendent Smith then went into the witness-box and told the court of the past history of the prisoners and especially of the Krogers, who had so narrowly escaped being convicted of spying in their own country. There it was known that they had been connected with the Rosenbergs, who had been executed in the electric chair.

He was followed by the Attorney-General, who gave details of the money possessed by the convicted five. He stated that of them all, Ethel Gee, the humble civil servant earning less than £11 a week, was the wealthiest. In cash and securities she possessed nearly £5,000.

There was a hush as Lord Parker made his summing up of the case. 'You have been found guilty of the offences charged on, if I may say so, the fairest possible evidence. You must each of you know full well the gravity of your offence and for peace time this must be one of the most disgraceful cases to come before this court.'

He described Lonsdale as the mastermind, organizing the activities of the group, and sentenced him to prison for twenty-five years. Although he knew he also must receive a heavy sentence, Peter Kroger turned white when he heard the sentence of twenty years pronounced on him. It was obvious that the judge did not believe Helen Kroger's story of the 'little housewife': she received the same term of imprisonment—twenty years.

Harold Houghton and Ethel Gee now stood alone in the dock. Lord Parker turned to the former. 'In many ways your conduct is the worst —to betray the secrets of your own country—and selling secret information about Her Majesty's Navy. I commit you for fifteen years.'

All eyes in the court then turned to the last of the five, Ethel Gee. The judge made it clear that he could not make any difference between her and Houghton then said, 'Having heard you, and watched you, I am inclined to think that yours is the strongest character of the two and that you acted for greed.' He then passed a similar sentence of fifteen years on Miss Gee.

The spies had hardly left the court, however, when they were ordered to return. The Attorney-General asked for costs—to cover the fees of the lawyers who had been assisting them in their defence. The Krogers were ordered to pay £1,000 between them, the others £1,000 each.

Winding up this significant spy trial, the judge said, 'At the end, security depends, and must depend, on the honesty of the people in positions of trust. If a person suddenly becomes dishonest, no security measures can prevent it, and detection becomes a matter of urgency.'

In October 1969 the Krogers were exchanged for a young English lecturer named Gerald Brook. He was not a spy but had been arrested in Russia with anti-Communist leaflets in his luggage. The Krogers were flown to Poland and Brook was allowed to return to Britain.

EILEEN, A QUIET ENGLISH MISS

Joseph Hutton

One of the most sensational of women spies was Eileen Jenkins. She was a quiet, unassuming spinster who emigrated from England to Canada and opened a small shop in Ottawa.

Eileen was so typically English that many of her Canadian friends and customers frequently joked about her Oxford-type behaviour. But she was liked and many a customer came to her little shop merely because of its 'so-English atmosphere'.

But Eileen was not English. Her true name was Tanya Markovna Radyonska. She was born in 1924 in Murmansk as the daughter of an OGPU (Russia's secret police) major. She had the 'right' background and so her party organizer considered her suitable for secret service work. At the age of twenty-one she passed all her qualifying exams and became 'Eileen Jenkins' when she arrived at Gaczyna. Her registration number was B-480822/039-G.

In May 1958, Eileen was smuggled into England and for nine days acclimatized herself to conditions in the United Kingdom. She spent most of the time in Carlisle.

She came to London, found lodgings in the King's Cross area and pretended to be seeking work as a shop assistant. But although she tried her utmost to find suitable employment, she returned each day to her lodgings without success.

This was all preparation for her future plans. She was under orders from Moscow to stay in London without engaging in espionage, therefore creating a plausible reason for wishing to emigrate to Canada.

On numerous occasions she told her landlady and other lodgers that she was fed up being out of work while her savings dwindled. When she mentioned she was thinking of emigrating to Canada some encouraged her, but her landlady maintained that life was sweeter in England.

Eileen had been supplied by the third division of the Foreign Directorate in Moscow with Canadian 'relatives' and 'friends'. But Moscow warned her not to attract suspicion by forcing issues. So Eileen drifted along without a job, still pretending to toy with the idea of emigrating to Canada. But she did not waste these months in London. She learned to be more English than most English-born people. She made friends with office and shop girls who invited her to their houses. These invitations were rarely repeated because Eileen proved herself a bore and spoiled many a party. Her hosts had no reason to suspect her behaviour was brilliant acting. By nature she was a gay person, but her specialized work prevented her from developing close friendships.

Eileen Jenkins finally forsook her 'country of birth' and sailed for Canada, where she arrived in March 1959.

She had no need to acclimatize herself to this new country. She was an immigrant. It was to be expected that she would be unaccustomed to the Canadian way of life. However, Moscow ordered her to await further orders before engaging in espionage. So she stayed six weeks in Montreal, where she took a job as a saleswoman in a bakery. When she was ordered to Ottawa, the manageress tried to persuade her efficient saleswoman to stay, but Eileen invented an aunt in Ottawa who had fallen ill and who needed her at her side.

Eileen rented an expensive apartment in Ottawa, where she spread the story of an aunt who had recently died and left her a comfortable nest-egg.

During her first week in Ottawa, she recruited her first collaborator.

She met him casually in a snack bar and soon discovered he was interested in meeting someone from England. She decided to use him, and in a microdot message to Moscow reported: 'I have found a nineteen-year-old junior clerk who works in a well-known firm. I have told him it is inconvenient for me to receive personal letters from Europe at my home. He agrees they can be sent to his address.'

The youngster had no suspicions and from then onwards microdot messages from Moscow were sent to Eileen through her new 'post-box'.

Eileen was a good friend to the boy and frequently gave him presents. But she never recruited him for spy duties. In his employment he had no opportunity of gaining any secret information, and he was far too naive for go-between duties. Eileen preferred to use him as a 'post-box' without his knowing that he was an important link in an espionage network.

Within four months of arriving in Ottawa, Eileen had successfully established herself as a master spy. Her greatest asset was her role as a typical Englishwoman in her middle thirties.

She devoted herself to charity work and was always eager to help anyone in need. Yet behind the scenes she not only operated an espionage set-up, but maintained a terror group which kidnapped and murdered.

She ordered the execution of an electronics engineer who was born in Germany and worked in a Canadian armaments factory. She had tackled him as a potential informer and threatened him. If he did not provide her with information his relatives, who still lived in Communist East Germany, would be 'dealt with' for his lack of cooperation. The German foolishly retorted that he would tell the authorities of her threats, so Eileen arranged for him to be drugged and executed by her terror squad. His death was made to look like suicide.

Eileen also kidnapped and transported to Russia a Slovak immigrant working as a draughtsman in an aircraft design office. He too resisted her threats and tried to inform the authorities. He never managed to contact the police. While walking along the street, he was overtaken by a car, pulled inside and driven to an isolated country house. When transport was arranged, he was injected and, while unconscious, smuggled aboard a ship sailing to Russia.

By August 1959, Eileen had organized so many kidnappings and killings of 'elements who constituted a danger to the group' that Moscow became worried. Too-frequent deaths and disappearances could arouse suspicion. A control agent was sent to observe Eileen's activities and report on her.

Eileen was too well Gaczyna-trained to disobey Moscow's orders to go easy with her strong-arm tactics. But she continued to use blackmail and threats of violence in her recruitment of informers. Moscow did not interfere. She was transmitting more valuable information than any other resident network operator.

Until July 1959 Eileen worked as a saleslady in a lingerie shop. But as her espionage network grew, her time-consuming job became a handicap. She decided to acquire a business of her own, and with the help of a business transfer agent soon found a shop in the same line of business. She was careful, however, not to use her 'cover' business as a meeting point for go-betweens, informers and sub-agents.

That Christmas, Eileen's life took a strange twist. An attractive man came to her shop seeking a suitable present for his mother. He liked Eileen and dated her. For the first time in her career as a master spy, Eileen allowed herself to become emotionally involved with another human being. But in January 1960 she discovered that her lover was a police official. She reported this to Moscow and received orders to continue her friendship and try to learn how much the Canadian authorities knew about Soviet espionage. Soviet Secret Service Headquarters recommended she should accept the police official's offer of marriage.

Eileen drained useful information from her lover, and from him heard about Igor Guzenko, a cipher clerk at the Soviet Embassy in Charlotte Street, Ottawa, who had decided to defect to the Canadians.

When Igor Guzenko finally decided to ask for political asylum in Canada, he was fully prepared for his break with the Soviets. He had listed a large number of documents which exposed a dozen Soviet diplomats in Canada who were engaged in most undiplomatic activities. However, it was essential that the highly confidential Embassy files, to which he had access, should not betray him if they should be spot-checked by a control agent. Therefore he left the documents in their files with their edges turned down so he could locate them swiftly when he needed them.

In the early hours of the evening of 5 September, Guzenko decided his D-day had come. He left the Embassy and went straight to the editorial offices of a newspaper, bearing sufficient documentary evidence in his pockets to put a dozen diplomat spies behind bars. But the editor believed the documents the cipher clerk presented to be forgeries. Editors are constantly being offered news stories backed by false evidence for which they are expected to make fabulous payments. Guzenko was shown the door.

Guzenko panicked. He had burnt his bridges and Soviet agents in Ottawa might already be searching for him. In desperation he went to various Canadian government offices and told numerous officials he wished to defect to the West. To his consternation, nobody would take him seriously. He was believed to be a 'nut' and his increasingly frantic insistence and agitation strengthened this belief.

But Guzenko was unwittingly aided by the Soviet Embassy. Alarmed by the inexplicable absence of the cipher clerk, the chief security officer took emergency precautions. The door of Guzenko's apartment was broken down by unidentified raiders and his belongings were ransacked. The Canadian police were called to the scene, made a search for Guzenko and took him into protective custody. At last the defector could tell his story, show the documents he had stolen and be heard out without scepticism.

The Canadian authorities rejected the subsequent demand from the Soviet Embassy to surrender Guzenko on a 'capital charge', and granted him political asylum. Later it was admitted that Western counter-intelligence might well have remained in ignorance that the Soviet Embassy in Ottawa was the mainspring of an espionage network had Guzenko not defected.

When Eileen was told this story she scoffed at her lover. She performed a perfect piece of acting when she refused to believe the Canadian counter-intelligence had to depend on information from a Soviet defector to unmask Russian spies. But her lover did not rise to the bait. Eileen had to report to Moscow that her fiancé 'either does not know or is too careful' to divulge Western counter-intelligence methods.

Eileen carried on her unique espionage activities until Moscow Secret Service Headquarters decided to change her country of operation. She received orders to leave Canada, the third division supplied her with 'genuine' letters from England saying her uncle was seriously ill, and her story was so plausible that her fiancé suspected nothing. He urged Eileen to leave without delay.

In which English-speaking country Tanya Markovna Radyonska has assumed a new identity is, as yet, unknown.

THE FATAL SIX CABLES

Kenneth Allen

It was a warm evening in June and the London season was in full swing. At her first large reception of the season, Lady Tryon was receiving in her elegant residence in Eaton Square, where a continual flow of shining carriages and broughams brought her guests to the door. Within the house, ladies in magnificent gowns and glittering jewels chatted with their escorts in sober black or the red, blue and gold of military and naval uniforms. There was naturally a preponderance of the latter for their hostess was the wife of Sir George Tryon, Commander-in-Chief Mediterranean.

During the evening, several of the two hundred guests made a point of expressing their pleasure at seeing her husband again, adding how pleased she must be to have him with her on such an occasion. At first Lady Tryon was amused, gently hinting that there was obviously some mistake as her husband was at sea with the fleet, but as others made the same remark she became slightly incensed, especially when several guests were quite adamant that he had greeted them on arrival.

The next morning, however, her vexation turned to incredulity and then to horror as first her brother-in-law and son, then a long procession of other relatives and close friends arrived at her home to sympathize with her in her tragic bereavement. For during the late afternoon of the previous day her husband, in company with hundreds of his officers and men, had lost his life in one of the strangest disasters in naval history.

During the morning of 22 June 1893, the Mediterranean fleet steamed majestically out of Beruit and, when clear of the land, altered course for Tripoli, some sixty miles along the coast. The grimly beautiful line of warships reflected the power and might of the world's leading maritime nation. There were eight battleships, three large cruisers and two light cruisers steaming in an immaculate single line abreast formation. 'Navy grey' had not yet come into use and the black hulls, white upperworks and bright yellow funnels of the ships sparkled in the morning sunshine. It was a wonderful day, made all the more enjoyable by the fact that it was a Thursday, the afternoon of which was, by long established custom, the time for 'make-and-mend'. Only the duty watches above and below were active; otherwise the thousands of officers and men, made drowsy by midday dinner and by the hot sun, did not bother with making *or* mending . . . they slept.

Vice-Admiral Tryon, however, rarely slept and seemed quite unaffected by the torpor into which most of the fleet had sunk. He was determined to think up an evolution prior to anchoring at Tripoli that would have everyone throughout his fleet fully awake. Deep in thought, he strolled back and forth on his stern-walk, only occasionally glancing at the following ships. He was tall and magnificently bearded, the epitome of what the Victorians expected an admiral to be.

His career had been one long record of distinction, from the days when he had served with the Naval Brigade before Sebastopol until two years previously, when he had taken command of the Mediterranean station. During that time he had established a great reputation as a tactician and disciplinarian and his officers were very much in awe of the man. He had one personal regret—that he should have come to such high command at a time of universal peace, a period which afforded him no opportunities to prove himself during actual combat.

The ship he commanded, the *Victoria*, was one of the finest warships afloat. She was built at Elswick, Newcastle-on-Tyne by Armstrong, Mitchell and Co. and was launched in 1887. At this time she and her sister ship, the *Sans Pareil*, were the fastest armour-clads afloat in the

British Navy, and her launching in Queen Victoria's Golden Jubilee year caused her name to be changed from the original *Renown* to one more flattering to her majesty. She was 340 feet from ram to stern, her breadth seventy feet and her indicated horse-power of 14,000 was able to thrust her 10,470 tons through the water at nearly seventeen knots. A single turret forward housed two big guns—16.25 weapons, each 110 tons—the largest in the world. Her auxiliary armament consisted of twelve six-inch five-ton guns, twelve six-pounder rapid-firing guns, nine three-pounders, six Nordenfeldt guns and eight torpedo tubes.

The Mediterranean fleet was in itself superior in ships, tonnage and metal to the entire fleet of any other country, and Tryon regarded it very much as his personal command, continually putting it through a series of complex manoeuvres which were frequently baffling to all but himself. When he had brought such an exercise to its usual successful conclusion he would summon his captains to the flagship and discuss what had happened. By question and answer he would ascertain how much—or how little—the others had grasped of what had occurred. Many of his officers were reluctant to contribute much to these post-mortems, for they knew that if they said anything amiss they would come in for a verbal lashing of irony and sarcasm.

Tryon had never been known to make a tactical mistake and it was because of this tremendous reputation that, at his order, the whole fleet was to set itself to perform an obvious impossibility.

With a grunt of satisfaction at the sight of his ships steaming in immaculate formation, he returned to his cabin and summoned his flag-captain, the Hon. Maurice Bourke, and his staff-commander, Thomas Hawkins-Smith. When they had joined him he began to outline a manoeuvre which would bring the fleet to anchor in a brilliant if highly unorthodox manner. The ships would change their formation from single line abreast to two divisions; steaming six cables apart and then, by turning through an angle of 180 degrees inwards towards each other, would be steaming on the opposite course.

It immediately occurred to Hawkins-Smith that the distance of six cables—1200 yards—would bring the ships dangerously close together. Indeed, as the turning circle of the *Victoria* was three cables and that of her parallel ship, the *Camperdown*, was about the same, it was obvious that if these ships turned towards each other at the distance Tryon had stipulated a collision must inevitably result. After a pause he said, 'It will require at least *eight* cables for that, sir.'

The admiral hesitated for a brief moment then replied, 'Yes, it shall be eight cables.'

The staff-commander then left the cabin to go on deck whilst Tryon sent for his flag-lieutenant, Lord Gillford, giving him the order that the signal should be made to 'form columns of divisions in line ahead, disposed abeam to port, columns to be *six cables* apart.'

So that there would be no mistake, he pencilled the figure '6' on a piece of paper and passed it to Lord Gillford. This signal was passed to the yeoman, but Hawkins-Smith, reading the figure '6' in the hoist which was being made ready, anxiously asked the flag-lieutenant whether he had not made a mistake. The other replied that the signal was as ordered by the admiral and produced the piece of paper bearing that figure.

But Hawkins-Smith was not satisfied and ordered Lord Gillford to go below to Tryon's cabin and confirm the distance with him. In some trepidation, Gillford did so and was relieved when Bourke, who was still with the admiral, added, 'You did say that it was to be *more* than six cables, sir.'

At this, Tryon's heavy brows drew together in a frown. To have his orders questioned in this manner was, to him, unthinkable. 'Leave it at *six* cables!' he barked, and the flag-lieutenant was glad to escape from the cabin and report back to Hawkins-Smith that the admiral had confirmed the distance.

Just before 14.30 the warships changed their formation to form two divisions of line ahead, an evolution which they had done many times before and which was, in any case, a comparatively simple operation. The fleet was now sailing as:

Second Division		First Division
Camperdown	6 cables	*Victoria*
Edinburgh	or	*Nile*
Sans Pareil	1200 yards	*Dreadnought*
Edgar		*Inflexible*
Amphion		*Phaeton*
		Collingwood

235

When this had been done, Tryon left his customary position on the after-bridge and joined Bourke, Hawkins-Smith, Lieutenant Collins, the officer-of-the-watch, Midshipman Lanyon and the yeoman of signals on a platform above the fore-bridge and conning tower—an unusual station for him to occupy during an exercise.

The signal was then made from the *Victoria*:

'Second division alter course in succession 16 points to starboard, preserving the order of the fleet

and

First division alter course 16 points to port, preserving the order of the fleet'

Over on the *Camperdown*, Flag-Lieutenant Bradshaw read the signal and reported it to Rear-Admiral Markham, the second-in-command, who immediately remarked, 'It is impossible; it is an impracticable manoeuvre!' and ordered him to keep the signal, which was being repeated, flying 'at the dip' and not hauled to the top—an indication that it was not understood. He then walked forward and, meeting Captain Johnstone of the *Camperdown*, who had also been puzzled by the signal, reassured him by saying, 'It's all right; don't do anything. I have not answered the signal.'

He walked aft again and ordered his flag-lieutenant to semaphore to the *Victoria* for more explicit instructions. Before this could be done, however, Tryon had a signal made asking bluntly what *Camperdown* was waiting for and also ordered that ship's pennants to be hoisted as a public rebuke that she was holding up the manoeuvre. Hardly had the message been received than Markham ordered his repeat hoist, which had been flying 'at the dip' all this time, to be hoisted to the yard-arm as a signal that the admiral's order had been understood.

An interpretation of the order had struck Markham. It was that instead of inverting the lines together, making a collision inevitable, Tryon proposed to ease his own helm and circle *outside* the port division, leaving it on his port hand, in which case the *Camperdown* had nothing to do but turn inwards sixteen points to starboard, as ordered.

With the inevitability of a Greek tragedy, the great ships began to turn, the *Victoria* to port, the *Camperdown* to starboard. The sea was smooth, its surface ruffled by a slight breeze. Those on board the *Cam-*

perdown watched the *Victoria* anxiously, every moment expecting to see that her helm signal had changed. But the other came straight on and, at a combined speed of some eighteen knots, the two ponderous battleships began to draw rapidly together.

Tryon was looking aft, watching the five other ships in his division as they turned in concert with his own. Bourke, who as captain was responsible for the safety of his ship, walked across to him and said, 'We had better do something, we shall be very close to the *Camperdown*,' but received no answer.

A few moments later he spoke again, more urgently this time. 'May I go astern full speed with the port screw?'

He again received no reply, for the admiral seemed too preoccupied with the following ships. Again he asked and this time Tryon turned and, for the first time, saw the vast bulk of the *Camperdown* moving inexorably down upon his own flagship. 'Yes, go astern' he replied, urgently.

The port telegraph was at once put to full speed astern and almost immediately the starboard telegraph also. The *Camperdown* had already reversed her engines but it was too late—nothing could now prevent a collision. Frantic orders were bawled out—'Close all water-tight doors!' and 'Out collision mats!' Tryon and his staff watched with horror as the two huge ships drew steadily closer, their great screws churning the water into a cauldron of white as they tried, hopelessly, to stop the forward motion of both ships. At the moment before the impact Tryon cupped his hands and futilely called out to Markham in the other ship, 'Go astern! Go astern!'

Three and a half minutes after the ships had begun their turn the *Camperdown*'s great ram struck the *Victoria* on her starboard bow, some twenty feet before the turret, penetrating almost to the other's centre line. The ram accurately performed the task for which it had been made, shearing through the thick armour plating, tearing into the stores and coal bunkers and smashing into the petty officers' mess, where some of the men were still rising from the table. Although there was a tremendous sound of clanging, ripping metal, the impact was not felt as a giant blow, but as a prolonged jarring sensation that was not sufficient to throw a man off his feet.

For a moment both ships hung together, the *Camperdown*'s ram

The Camperdown's great ram struck the Victoria on her starboard bow, some twenty feet before the turret, penetrating almost to the centre line.

238

buried deep inside the other's bows; then, with a hideous grinding of tortured steel, she backed away, her great engines at last exerting their reverse thrust. As she pulled free, a flood of water began to pour through a large triangular rent and Bourke immediately ran from the bridge to go below to make sure that all the doors were closed and also to ascertain the extent of the damage. He went in the starboard-flats and called out, inquiring whether everything was tight. A voice answered 'Yes'. He then heard the order passed down for everyone to go on deck. Making his way to the starboard engine-room he found the engines still being worked and was told that all water-tight doors were closed and that there was no water in the engine-room. Satisfied that the ship was only flooded at the bows, he made his way back to the deck.

Tryon, meanwhile, had asked the staff-commander his opinion of the damage and was told that the *Victoria* would be able to keep afloat long enough for her to be beached, as she had been struck so far forward. Hawkins-Smith then added, 'Shall we steer in for the land?'

Tryon agreed that this should be done then, in a lower voice, said to Gillford, who stood at his side, 'It is my fault, entirely my fault.'

Lord Gillford walked to the rail and saw that several of the other ships were beginning to lower their boats and were obviously showing more anxiety than those in the flagship. At this Tryon became angry. 'Make a signal to annul sending boats,' he said.

This action by the other warships, well-intentioned as it undoubtedly was, seemed to imply a lack of confidence in his ship. With the damage only at the bows, and with all water-tight doors closed, there was, he felt sure, no likelihood that his ship would sink. Below him, on the forecastle, a party of men were trying to draw the huge and unwieldy collision mat over the side to prevent the inrush of water through the ugly twelve-foot gash, but they were unable to work quickly enough. The calm sea began to well over the forecastle, to ripple along the deck. It covered the men's feet, then their ankles and finally swirled about their knees.

Realizing that their struggles to get the mat over the hole were useless, they retreated, followed by the water which began to pour down the apertures in the deck—hatches, gun ports and ventilators, adding to the tremendous weight of water that was still pouring in through the gaping hole at the rate of hundreds of tons a minute, pulling the ship's bows deeper and deeper into the water.

The men were now falling in on the deck and, as Captain Bourke said later, 'There was absolutely no panic, no shouting, no rushing aimlessly about. Everything was prepared, and the men were all in their positions for hoisting out the boats or performing any duty they may have been ordered to carry out.'

The *Victoria* was now listing considerably and the sea was swirling past the six-inch guns, down into the main passage and into the magazine. She was now at such an angle that it seemed incredible to those watching from the other ships that she could still remain afloat. On her decks perfect discipline was retained. The men were drawn up four deep, with their backs to the ship's side. A minute or so before the end the order was given, 'Right about turn!' to bring them with their faces to the bulwarks. The voice of the chaplain, the Reverend Samuel Morris, was heard saying, 'Steady men, steady.'

It was about ten minutes after the collision that Tryon turned to the staff-commander and said, coolly, 'I think she is going.'

'Yes, sir, I think she is,' the other replied equally calmly.

Tryon turned to give the order for a signal to be made for rescue boats to be sent and as he did so he saw Midshipman Lanyon, Bourke's aide, standing close by and he said kindly, 'Don't stop there, youngster, go to a boat.'

Those were his last words. As he spoke the *Victoria* turned over and sank.

It was at this very last moment that the order was given for the men to jump and they rushed to the side and flung themselves overboard. As the ship turned turtle, however, many were thrown backwards and head-first down the side they had been descending feet-first a moment before. But no one had given any orders to the men still below in the boiler- and engine-rooms and they remained at their posts when the ship disappeared. The great screws were still revolving and the engines continued to throb as the ship plunged down to the sea-bed some four hundred and fifty feet below.

Not a single one of the engine-room staff was saved.

Even though the ship herself had gone, she remained as a terrible menace, for a great mass of wreckage—boats, timber, derricks, and so on—came hurtling up from below to kill and maim many of the men struggling desperately in the water. An even greater danger was a tremendous wave that sucked down scores of men, especially the poor swimmers, many of whom, in their terror, dragged down some of the good swimmers with them.

A letter home from a midshipman who witnessed the tragedy was later published in *The Times* and said:

'Now comes the part which I hope never to witness again. At the time of the collision I was down below dozing when someone said, "Wake up, old chap; the *Victoria*'s rammed." I hardly believed it, but on rushing up on deck I saw the *Victoria* slowly steaming ahead, with her bows gradually sinking below the water. We could see from our poop the whole thing. The *Victoria*'s men worked beautifully. Never, I should think, was such perfect discipline ever seen in such a trying time. We could see them evidently trying to get the collision mat over the tremendous rent.

'To our great surprise they made the signal, "Negative send boats". However, we carried on, getting all our boats ready, although we presumed their water-tight doors were closed and they were probably all right. They then made the signal "Open", and began to slowly steam ahead and run ashore. No sooner had she begun to do this than her bows commenced sinking very rapidly. She then heeled over to such an extent that the port screw was above the water. Then, and not till then, we could see all the men jumping overboard. She continued heeling over, and it was simply agonizing to watch the wretched men struggling out of the ports over the ship's bottom in masses. All this of course happened in less time than it takes to write. You could see the poor men who, in their hurry to jump over, jumped on to the screw, being cut to pieces as it revolved. She keeled right over, the water rushing in through her funnels. A great explosion of steam arose; she turned right over, and you could see all the men eagerly endeavouring to crawl over her bottom, when with a plunge she went down bows first.

'We could see her stern rise right out of the water and plunge down, the screws still revolving. It was simply a dreadful sight. We could not realize it. Personally, I was away in my boat, pulling as hard as we could to the scene of the disaster. We were a good way

241

off, and by the time I got there, being the first of our boats, all the people had been saved by the boats of the ships which were nearer.

'After pulling up and down for two hours we reorganized the fleet, leaving two ships on the scene of the disaster; and, making for Tripoli, anchored for the night. However, dropping the *Victoria* for a minute, we must turn to the *Camperdown*. She appeared to be in a very bad way. Her bow was sinking gradually, and I must say at the time I thought it quite on the cards that she might be lost also, but thanks to the indomitable way in which the crew worked they managed to check the inrush by means of the collision mats and water-tight doors.

'All last night, however, they were working hard to keep her afloat. You can imagine our feelings—the flagship sunk with nearly all hands, the other flagship anchored in a sinking condition. We have a lot of the survivors of the *Victoria* on board, but their accounts vary greatly. Some say the water-tight doors were closed, but immediately the ship went ahead they must have burst open. Anyhow, what is quite certain is that the admiral did not realize the gravity of his situation, or else they would have abandoned the ship at once, instead of trying to save her.

'The discipline was splendid. Not until the order was given did a single man jump overboard. The last thing that was seen was the admiral refusing to save himself, whilst his coxswain was entreating him to go. Another instance of pluck was exhibited by the boatswain of signals, who was making a general semaphore until the water washed him away. Unfortunately the poor chap was drowned. Many of the survivors are in a dreadful state of mental prostration.

'Most people say that Admiral Marham should have refused to obey the signal, but I think that Admiral Tryon infused so much awe in most of the captains of the fleet that few would have disobeyed him. However, he stuck to his ship to the last, and went down with her.'

At about ten o'clock on Friday morning, 23 June, a whisper spread around London that one of the finest ships of our Mediterranean squadron had gone down with terrible loss of life. The Admiralty had received the news soon after nine o'clock; by ten it was known in all the service clubs. But it is a remarkable fact that rumours of the loss of a battleship were current in London five or six hours earlier—long before the official news was received.

Where these rumours came from no one could tell, although inquiries began as early as six o'clock. The first known telegram came from Her Majesty's Consul at Tripoli, followed, at about eleven o'clock, by another from Rear-Admiral Markham, which read:

'Regret to report whilst manoeuvring this afternoon off Tripoli *Victoria* and *Camperdown* collided. *Victoria* sank in fifteen minutes after in eighty fathoms, bottom upwards. The *Camperdown*'s ram struck the *Victoria* before the turret-starboard. The following officers were drowned: Commander-in-Chief; Clerk Allen; Lieutenant Munro; Chaplain Morris; Chief-Engineer Foreman; Engineer Harding; Assistant-Engineer Deadman; Assistant-Engineer Hatherley; Assistant-Engineer Seaton; Gunner Howell; Boatswain Barnard; Carpenter Beal; Midshipman Inglis; Midshipman Grieve; Midshipman Fawkes; Midshipman Lanyon; Midshipman Henley; Midshipman Gambier; Midshipman Scarlett; Naval-Cadet Stooks; Assistant-Clerk Savage; Fleet-Paymaster Rickord. 255 saved. Will report their names by telegraph. Injury to *Camperdown* not yet fully ascertained, but so serious as to necessitate docking.

'Await instructions. (signed) MARKHAM'

Some four hundred seamen had also perished in the disaster. Their relatives and those of the '255 saved' had to wait in an agony of fear and distress until the lists were finally published.

Hawkins-Smith was later to write, with reference to Admiral Tryon: 'He was perfectly calm and collected to the last. He went down and was seen by no one again . . . He died as he had lived, a brave man.'

And, one is tempted to add, a very stubborn and foolish one.

OPERATION CICERO

Geoffrey Palmer

The nondescript little man in his cheap brown suit faced the Nazi security officer, Ludwig Moyzisch, across the desk in a luxurious office of the German Embassy in Ankara, the capital of Turkey. The date was October 1943. The Second World War was raging, and Turkey, still a neutral country, was under pressure from both the British and the German authorities to give up her neutrality and enter the war. The Germans needed allies to restore their flagging fortunes, the British needed support for their forthcoming invasion of German-occupied Europe. Below its apparently peaceful surface, Ankara was seething. Every embassy had its secret agents, and rumours and counter-rumours were flying around like bats in the night.

Moyzisch listened to the stranger's story and could hardly believe his ears. When the man had finished the officer took a deep breath, and a thousand questions tumbled haphazardly into his mind. He tried to get them in order. 'Your name again?' he rapped out.

'Elyesa Bazna,' the man replied flatly. 'I was born in Albania, but my parents came to Turkey when I was a small child. I can speak Turkish, French, German and Greek.'

'Not English?'

'I can read and understand it, but I do not speak it very well.'

Moyzisch stroked his chin. 'You have told me a most amazing story. You say you are employed by the British Embassy as personal valet to the Ambassador. Surely your background and credentials were thoroughly checked?'

Bazna gave a thin smile. 'Not thoroughly enough,' he said. 'When I applied for the post I was already chauffeur to the First Secretary at the Embassy, and he had no reason to think that I was anything but a good Turk anxious to earn an honest living. The British can be very foolish.'

'Not all the time, unfortunately,' Moyzisch murmured. Then he added, sharply, 'And why do you want to spy for Germany?'

Bazna's cold eyes blazed suddenly. 'I hate the British. They shot my father.'

'Shot him? How?'

'Many years ago my father was a beater for a shooting party of English sportsmen on holiday in Turkey, and one of them shot him. Accidentally, no doubt, but my father died in agony, and my mother was left to bring up a large family. I swore revenge at the time, and now I have the opportunity.'

'You are certainly in a position that would be very useful to us,' Moyzisch admitted. 'We are desperate to know what Turkey's intentions are. But what exactly can you do? We already have two of our people working in the Embassy kitchens. They provide us with some useful gossip, but nothing of real importance.'

Bazna lowered his voice, and Moyzisch had to lean forward to catch the dry words. 'It will be easier than you think. All the telegrams, despatches and memoranda that the Embassy receives every day are of course closely guarded, but the Ambassador prefers to do his work at home, and every evening he takes home the papers that need his personal attention. He keeps them in a locked case in his bedroom.'

'But if the case is locked . . .' began Moyzisch.

'Sir Hughe usually carries the keys in his dressing-gown pocket,' Bazna went on in the same soft and unhurried tone, 'and normally I would not have access to them. But last week he left them on his bedside table when he went to his office, and before he had discovered his loss I had taken an impression in wax. I had duplicates made, and now I can read any secret documents at almost any time I like—when Sir Hughe is out at an evening function, when I am pressing his clothes or cleaning his shoes, or when he has taken a sleeping tablet, which he does most evenings.'

Moyzisch said bluntly, 'But you are not an educated man. Even if you can read the papers, can you understand them? Can you memorize them?'

'There is no need for understanding or memory,' Bazna replied shortly. 'I have an excellent Leica camera. I photograph them and return them to the case. The Ambassador, a most charming man, by the way, has no idea what is going on. I have access to every document of importance that comes into the British Embassy—and leaves it. I already have more than fifty photographs of top secret telegrams relating to many aspects of the war, not only those dealing with Turkey.'

Moyzisch drew in his breath sharply. 'And you are willing to sell them to us?'

'Yes, at a price.'

'And that is?'

'Twenty thousand pounds in British five-pound notes for each roll of film.'

The officer made a gesture of dissent. 'Preposterous! Out of the question! I do not wish to hear any more. You have overplayed your hand.'

Bazna shrugged his shoulders, turned and started to walk towards the door. 'As you will. If you are not interested, there are others who certainly will be. The Soviet Embassy will be only too willing to pay my price. They and the British may be allies, but they are uneasy ones, and each has agents trying to find out the secrets of the other.' He reached the door and put his hand on the knob.

'Wait! Perhaps I was too hasty.' Moyzisch had lost a little of his arrogance. 'If we decided to pay you this money for your services only my superiors in Berlin could authorize it. First I would have to tell Ambassador von Papen and he would have to obtain instructions from Foreign Minister von Ribbentrop. It will take time.'

Bazna allowed himself a small smirk of triumph. 'I will wait four days. Today is Tuesday. The Soviet Ambassador will be returning to Ankara at the weekend . . .'

'Very well. I will see you again on Saturday night. Come to the

Embassy garden at ten o'clock. The side gate will be open. Just inside the gate there is a toolshed. I shall be there. Bring some film with you, and if everything is as you say, there will be money for you.'

'Twenty thousand pounds,' Bazna repeated. 'But I shall only require fifteen thousand pounds for every roll of film after the first. I am not a greedy man. I will see you on Saturday.'

It took von Ribbentrop three days to answer the German Ambassador's urgent signal. His reply was not enthusiastic. The Foreign Minister had decided that the valet was a small-time crook, but in the unlikely event of his story being true he authorized the money to be spent and said that a courier would arrive with it within a few hours. 'Take all precautions,' his signal demanded, 'and do not squander the money unnecessarily.'

To Moyzisch's surprise Bazna arrived at the toolshed at the appointed time and produced two rolls of film. Then he held out his hand. 'Now I will have the money,' he said quietly.

'Not so fast.' Moyzisch took a bundle from his pocket. 'Here it is, but before I hand it over we must have proof that you have not brought us pictures of the Taj Mahal by moonlight! There is a darkroom in the Embassy cellar and I have a photographer ready to develop the film. Come, follow me. You will agree that all precautions must be taken.'

The valet followed him, his face betraying neither anxiety nor foreboding. In the cellar the photographer began work quickly, and soon he was able to show Moyzisch the first damp print. The officer took it out of the cellar and examined it in the light. The subject was unmistakable, a document from the British Foreign Service addressed to the British Ambassador in Ankara, and it contained information about the number of RAF personnel who were already in neutral Turkey . . .

Moyzisch could not trust himself to speak. He shakily handed the bundle of notes to Bazna. 'T-twenty thousand p-pounds,' he stuttered.

Bazna expressed no emotion. He casually put the money into his pocket. 'I'll see you again tomorrow night,' he muttered, and slipped out into the night.

So began Operation Cicero, a name devised by Ambassador von Papen. As far as the Germans were concerned Bazna the valet had no existence; there was only Cicero the spy. Twice a week Cicero secretly entered the garden of the German Embassy, handed over to Moyzisch the film he had taken the night before, and left as secretly with his fifteen thousand pounds. There was too much risk involved in depositing the money in a bank, so he hid it under the floor of an unoccupied room in the British Embassy.

The contents of the documents which the Germans were receiving so regularly made sensational reading. Reports of secret meetings, troop movements, details of highly confidential British and American plans, even the names of all the British secret agents in Turkey—all passed into the hands of the German Ambassador. They were cabled to Berlin in code, and the developed pictures were sent later by diplomatic bag. No one at the Embassy had any reason to suspect the poker-faced valet with duplicate keys in his pocket, who assured his employer, each evening, that his official uniform and decorations would be all ready for him the next morning!

In Berlin there was intense interest in the information that was coming in so regularly and in such quantities. Inquiries as to its source almost overwhelmed the German Ambassador and his security officer. Who was Cicero, apart from being a humble valet? How did he get the documents? Were they satisfied that they were not being double-crossed? Surely the whole thing was too good to be true? It was as though Winston Churchill himself were solemnly handing over all his secrets to Hitler!

Von Ribbentrop was the leader of those who thought that Cicero was a double agent, and that the information was being deliberately planted by the British in order to mislead the Germans. 'I just do not believe in this Cicero,' he declared, 'and I shall take no notice of the information he is providing. It is too correct, too accurate. The British would not be so stupid as to give him the opportunity of getting hold of it. It is a clumsy British trick. The photographed documents are cunning forgeries . . .'

Moyzisch was summoned to Berlin to appear before von Ribbentrop, but the two men disliked each other, having had other disagreements in the past, and the atmosphere at their meeting was frigid. Moyzisch could not convince his superior that Cicero was a genuine spy. He was not allowed to return to Ankara for two weeks, during which time Cicero had obtained details of an important meeting between President Roosevelt of America, Prime Minister Churchill and Generalissimo

Chiang Kai-shek of China, and later of another meeting between Roosevelt, Churchill and Stalin.

Moyzisch sighed when the films were printed and he saw what they contained. 'The war is going badly for us. All this stupendous news could help to turn the tide—if it were not for that idiot Foreign Minister of ours. Will *nothing* convince him?'

All through November Cicero was hard at work with his Leica, and by the beginning of December his meetings with Moyzisch took place almost every night. For security reasons they had stopped meeting in the garden toolshed. Now the Nazi officer picked up Cicero in a different spot in the Ankara streets in a civilian car, and the spy would slip into the back and hide in the shadows. When Moyzisch was sure that they were not being followed he would stop in some quiet place and hand over the fifteen thousand pounds which had come from Berlin, in return for the roll of film.

The routine did not continue without incident, however. One evening Moyzisch was driving around looking for a convenient spot for the exchange to take place when he became aware that he was being followed. In his mirror he could make out a long black car, typically American. He did not panic, but methodically tried to shake off the pursuer, trying all the obvious tricks. He dawdled, he accelerated, he dodged round corners and doubled back on his tracks; but every time he looked in the mirror the car was on his tail.

Cicero was crouching on the floor at the back, a gun in his hand. He did not speak, but there was menace in his usually blank face, and the gun, pointing towards the back window, did not waver. When the black car had to pull up sharply to allow an elderly couple to cross the road Moyzisch was able to accelerate ahead and disappear round a corner and into the night. At last he thought it safe to pull up and Cicero prepared to get out.

'Did you see his face?' Moyzisch asked.

'Someone I've never seen before,' Cicero replied, 'but I would recognize him if I ever saw him again.'

'Who do you think it was?'

Cicero did not seem to be particularly interested. 'The Americans—the British—the Russians—perhaps even the Germans—who knows? Anyway, it is you he was after, not me, so why should I worry?' He lifted his hand briefly in farewell and walked off without a backward glance.

At the end of December Cicero handed over the film of a document that revealed that Turkey was beginning to yield to pressure from the Allies to join their cause. In anticipation of this the British were smuggling into the country a large number of soldiers, sailors and airmen and dressing them in civilian clothes. This was grave from the German standpoint, for their military situation was getting steadily worse.

Von Papen, the Ambassador, decided that it would be futile to approach von Ribbentrop, who was still denying the importance of Cicero's work, and took it upon himself to arrange a meeting with the Turkish Foreign Minister at which he complained that Turkey was allowing her neutrality to be breached. As evidence he produced a photograph of what he claimed were British soldiers in Turkish dress. In doing so he made the first mistake that was to lead to a breakup of Operation Cicero. Cicero's luck was about to desert him . . .

The Turkish minister dismissed von Papen's criticism. 'I do not know from what source you have received your information,' he said, 'but I

Moyzisch tried all the tricks to shake off his pursuer, but ever

can assure you that it is very much exaggerated. There may be some extra tourists in Ankara, but as for British forces in civilian clothes . . . somebody has been having a nightmare, my dear sir.' As soon as von Papen had left, however, he sent for Sir Hughe Knatchbull-Hugessen and told him what he had just heard.

Sir Hughe's alarm was considerable. So too was his concern as to how the photographs had been obtained. He must inform London of the position immediately.

In a few hours the German Ambassador was reading a copy of the despatch Sir Hughe had sent, and the worried lines on his forehead grew deeper when he realized how rash he had been.

The Foreign Office in London sent orders for a complete check of the security arrangements at the Embassy. Staff were questioned closely, and new precautions were taken, with warning devices attached to the safes and the locks on doors and windows doubled. Unfortunately, no one suspected that the locked despatch case on Sir Hughe's bedside table was being tampered with. The activities that went on in the Embassy were, of course, duly reported, and Cicero was instructed to be even

ne he looked in the mirror the American car was on his tail.

more careful when taking his photographs.

The next outstanding event of which the Germans had prior knowledge, thanks to Cicero, was a plan to bomb Sofia, the capital of Bul-
garia and one of the key places in the Balkans held by the Germans.
It was to be a massive attack, arranged by the British, Americans and
Russians, to be carried out on 14 January 1944. The information was
signalled to Berlin in the usual way, and the German High Command
was intrigued, though not unduly worried. There was much argument
over the best course to adopt, and finally it was decided to do nothing.
If the raid took place, those who believed in Cicero would be vindi-
cated; if it did not, then Cicero would be discredited for good. No
warning was given to Sofia.

The raid did take place, and four thousand Bulgarian men, women
and children were killed. Von Ribbentrop was forced to admit that he
had been wrong, but he was stubborn to the last. 'This time Operation
Cicero was successful,' he said, 'but it was probably done to put us off
the scent. I am still not convinced that Cicero is working for us alone.'

In Ankara there was a fresh development to the story—one which
turned out to be another factor in the eventual breakdown of Operation
Cicero. Moyzisch was given a new assistant secretary, a beautiful blonde
girl called Cornelia Knapp. She was the daughter of a German diplomat
but spoke English and French perfectly because she had lived for some
years in America and in France. Her main work was to translate foreign
newspapers, and she was not told of the importance of Cicero in the
affairs of the Embassy. Only Moyzisch and von Papen in Ankara were
in on the secret. Neither of them realized that Fraulein Knapp would
play a key role in the next chapter of the Cicero story.

In the first few weeks of 1944, with British documents still appearing
regularly in German hands, Moyzisch noticed that the code name
'Operation Overlord' was appearing in despatch after despatch and he
informed his superiors in Berlin of the mysterious words. They showed
little concern, and Moyzisch decided to try to solve the mystery himself. After studying a whole series of documents the truth struck him
like a thunderbolt. Operation Overlord meant that the second front
was going to be launched in the near future, that the Allies were about
to smash their way into Europe and invade all the countries that the
Germans were occupying.

In great excitement he sent a signal to Berlin. 'This time von Ribbentrop *must* be impressed,' he thought. But he was mistaken. The reply was, 'Possible, but not very likely.'

In the German Embassy the new secretary was causing concern. She seemed to be very nervous, indeed often hysterical, and she was extremely inefficient, her work full of mistakes. Furthermore, she asked too many questions. Cicero met her and felt an instinctive distrust of her, though he could not explain why. The girl was a good German, her father an important member of the diplomatic service. There was nothing he could put his finger on. Yet still he wondered. She had no access to secret papers so he tried to put her strange behaviour out of his mind and concentrate on his real job.

But it was not long before his disquiet returned. In the lounge of the Ankara Palace Hotel, where he had been sent to deliver a message to Sir Hughe, who was at a diplomatic function, he saw Fraulein Knapp. She was not alone. The young man talking to her earnestly was the driver of the black car which had chased Moyzisch and himself through the alleys of Ankara!

For a moment panic gripped him, but he pulled himself together, thinking furiously. The man was obviously a British or American agent, and the girl must be his assistant. They must be on his track. Time was getting short. Perhaps he should get out of Turkey while the going was still good. Yet it would mean the end of his work, his supply of money, and even worse, the end of his secret power. He returned home in a state of nerves that was entirely foreign to him, and for the next few days his camera remained unused.

Then Cornelia Knapp disappeared. She had asked for a week's leave to spend Easter with her family in Bucharest, and Moyzisch had agreed to her request promptly, glad of a respite from her eccentric behaviour and inefficient translating. But when the week was up the girl did not return. Nor was she the only deserter from the German diplomatic service at that time. There was the smell of defeat in the air, rumours that the Allies would soon be crushing the might of Germany. 'Escape' was a word that was being heard more and more frequently.

Moyzisch sent for Cicero, and both men knew that they were meeting for the last time. 'The war is coming to an end,' Moyzisch told the spy bluntly, 'and we shall not be the winners. Fraulein Knapp was a spy

—we now have proof. She was passing information to the Americans all the time she was here. There is to be an inquiry into her disappearance and I have been ordered to go to Berlin to account for my part in it. It is now a case of every man for himself.'

But Cicero was not interested in Moyzisch's fate. 'Did Fraulein Knapp know anything about me?' he demanded.

Moyzisch opened a drawer and took out a sheet of paper. 'This came this morning,' he said, 'and the envelope had an Ankara postmark.'

Cicero took the letter and read its typed contents aloud. ' "Everything is known about Cicero in the British Embassy." There are two typing errors in one sentence,' he commented dryly. 'Only Fraulein Knapp could have written it. So everything is known about Cicero—except who he is . . .'

There was a heavy silence. Then Cicero let the letter drop on to the desk. 'Operation Cicero has come to an end,' he said. 'I must go and make plans for the future. Farewell, Moyzisch.'

Cicero returned to the Ambassador's house and immediately gave in his notice. The next day he left, with the three hundred thousand pounds he had earned as a spy. He had spent seven months in the business, and during that time had wrested with ease from the British more secrets than any other spy in Germany's history. If only the information had been acted on by the Germans the effect on Allied fortunes would have been disastrous. The second front would not have taken place when it did, and the war might have dragged on for years. It was only von Ribbentrop's obstinacy, and the jealousies and quarrels in the German High Command, that caused Cicero's work to come to nothing.

The last ironic twist to the Cicero story happened when the ex-spy took his enormous bundle of five-pound notes to his bank and was told that they were all forgeries! They had not been printed at the Royal Mint in London, but in Berlin. The Germans had forged millions of British currency notes in order to upset the economy by spreading them, not only over Britain, but through all the neutral countries of Europe. No wonder the large amounts that Cicero had demanded had presented no problem to the Germans. Cicero's plans to live in luxury for the rest of his life melted into thin air. He ended up as he began—a poor, unimportant and friendless man who would always have to work for his living.

THE STRANGE CASE OF DR JEKYLL AND MR HYDE

Robert Louis Stevenson

For something like ten years Edinburgh-born Robert Louis Stevenson was known to but a comparative few as a contributor to several magazines and one who had published a book of short stories. Then, in 1885, when living in Bournemouth, he had a vivid dream, a dream of a man who discovered a drug which could turn him from a respectable doctor by day to a hideous, evil dwarf at night. The resulting story made him famous; and later books—such as Treasure Island, Kidnapped *and* The Black Arrow—*made 'R.L.S.' into one of Britain's best-loved authors.*

In the month of October 1880, London was startled by a crime of singular ferocity, and rendered all the more notable by the high position of the victim. A maid-servant living alone in a house not far from the river had gone upstairs to bed about eleven. She was looking from her window when she saw two men talking in the street below. One was a tall, gentlemanly person with white hair; the other she recognized as a certain Mr Hyde who had once visited her master and for whom she had conceived a dislike. He had in his hand a heavy cane and was carrying it (as the maid described) like a madman. As she watched, the old gentleman took a step back, with the air of one very much surprised and a trifle hurt; and at that Mr Hyde broke out of all bounds, and clubbed him to the earth.

The next moment, with ape-like fury, he was trampling his victim under foot, and hailing down a storm of blows, under which the bones were audibly shattered and the body jumped upon the roadway. At the horror of these sights and sounds the maid fainted.

It was two o'clock when she came to herself and called for the police. The murderer was gone long ago, but there lay his victim in the middle

255

of the lane, incredibly mangled. The stick with which the deed had been done, although it was of some rare and very tough and heavy wood, had broken under the stress of the cruelty and one splintered half had rolled into the neighbouring gutter. A purse and a gold watch were found upon the victim; but no cards or papers, except a sealed envelope which bore the name of Mr Utterson.

Mr Utterson, a lawyer, was taken to the body and identified the victim as Sir Danvers Carew. The police officer briefly narrated what the maid had seen, and showed the broken stick. Mr Utterson had already been surprised when the officer had mentioned that the maid had recognized the assailant as a Mr Hyde, but when the stick was laid before him he identified it for one that he had himself presented many years before to his friend, Dr Henry Jekyll.

'Is this Mr Hyde a person of small stature?' he inquired.

'Particularly small and particularly wicked-looking, is what the maid calls him,' said the officer.

As it happened, Mr Utterson knew the address of Hyde, for his client, Dr Jekyll, had made out a will in his favour, a will which Mr Utterson had helped draw up. He went to Hyde's address, a small house in a dingy street, but there was no sign of the man they sought. The two rooms which Hyde had occupied were well, almost elegantly furnished, but showed signs of having recently been ransacked. Clothes lay about the floor, drawers stood open, and in the hearth lay a pile of grey ashes, as though many papers had been burnt. The officer was highly delighted when, behind the door, the other half of the stick was found.

'You may depend upon it, sir. I have him in my hand,' he said, confidently.

Later that day, Mr Utterson found his way to Dr Jekyll's door, where he was at once admitted by Poole, the doctor's principal servant. He was shown into the doctor's laboratory—a place he had never visited before—and found Dr Jekyll seated by the fireplace, looking deadly sick. When Mr Utterson challenged him, he confessed that he had heard the terrible news of Sir Danvers' death and did not seem too surprised when his friend mentioned the name of Hyde, the man for whom the lawyer had altered the doctor's will. Yet he was obviously very upset. He pleaded with his friend, saying, 'I swear to God I will never set eyes on him again. I bind my honour to you that I am done with him in this world. It is all at an end,' and with that the lawyer had to be satisfied.

Time ran on. Thousands of pounds were offered in reward, for the death of Sir Danvers was resented as a public injury. But Mr Hyde had disappeared out of the ken of the police as though he had never existed. Although much of his past was unearthed, it seemed that from the time he had left the house in Soho on the morning of the murder he was simply blotted out. Gradually, as time drew on, Mr Utterson began to recover from his alarm and to grow more at quiet with himself. It was obvious that the mysterious Hyde had been an evil influence upon his friend the doctor for whom now, it seemed, a new life had begun. He renewed relations with his friends, became once more their familiar guest and entertainer, and while he had always been known for charity, he was now no less distinguished for religion. He was busy, he was much in the open air, he did good. His face seemed to open and brighten, as if with an inward consciousness of service, and for more than two months the doctor was at peace.

Yet by early January of the following year, all this was changed. The doctor's door was shut against Mr Utterson and his other old friend, also a doctor, Dr Lanyon. Soon afterwards Dr Lanyon took to his bed and in something less than a fortnight he was dead. He had left a letter on which, beneath his name, was written 'PRIVATE: for the hands of J. G. Utterson ALONE, and in the case of his predecease *to be destroyed unread.*'

The letter quoted at length another letter that the recently deceased had had from Dr Jekyll. It was, in fact, a cry for help. In it the doctor had said, 'I want you to postpone all other engagements for tonight— ay, even if you were summoned to the bedside of an emperor,' and begged him to drive straight to his house. There Poole, Dr Jekyll's butler, would be waiting for him together with a locksmith.

'The door of my laboratory is then to be forced,' the letter went on, 'and you are to go in alone, to open the glazed press on the left hand, breaking the lock if it be shut, and to draw out, *with all its contents as they stand*, the fourth drawer from the top or (which is the same thing) the third from the bottom. This drawer I beg of you to carry back with you to Cavendish Square exactly as it stands.

'That is the first part of the service: now for the second. At midnight, then, I have to ask you to be alone in your consulting room, to admit with your own hand into the house a man who will present himself in my name, and to place in his hands the drawer that you will have brought with you from my laboratory . . .'

Although almost convinced that his colleague was insane, Lanyon did as he was bid and, with the drawer intact as ordered, waited in his consulting room in Cavendish Square. Whilst he waited he examined the contents of the drawer, which seemed to contain various chemicals including a phial half full of a blood-red liquor.

Promptly at midnight, there came a gentle knocking on his door and he admitted the small man whom he found crouching against the pillars of the portico. When he led him into the light Dr Lanyon was able to examine him more closely. As the main letter said, 'This person was dressed in a fashion that would have made an ordinary person laughable. His clothes, that is to say, although they were of rich and sober fabric, were enormously too large for him in every measurement —the trousers hanging on his legs and rolled up to keep them from the ground, the waist of the coat below his haunches, and the collar sprawling wide upon his shoulders. Strange to relate, this ludicrous accoutrement was far from moving me to laughter. Rather, as there was something abnormal and misbegotten in the very essence of the creature that now faced me, this fresh disparity seemed but to fit in with and to reinforce it, so that to my interest in the man's nature and character there was added a curiosity as to his origin, his life, his fortune and status in the world.

'These observations, though they have taken so great a space to be set down in, were yet the work of a few seconds. My visitor was, indeed, on fire with sombre excitement.

' "Have you got it?" he cried. "Have you got it?" and so lively was his impatience that he even laid his hand upon my arm and sought to shake me.'

Dr Lanyon tried to curb the other's impatience and then said, 'There it is, sir,' and pointed to the drawer where it lay on the floor behind a table. The other sprang upon it then, turning, asked, 'Have you a graduated glass?'

Lanyon gave him what he asked and watched as the other measured

He reeled, staggered, clutched at the table and held on, staring with injected
eyes, gasping with open mouth ...

out a few minims of the red tincture and added one of the powders. The mixture, which was at first of a reddish hue, began to brighten in colour, to effervesce audibly, and to throw off small fumes of vapour. Suddenly the compound changed to a deep purple, which faded again more slowly to a watery green. Lanyon's visitor, who had watched these changes with a keen eye, smiled, set down the glass upon the table, and then turned and looked upon the doctor with an air of scrutiny.

He offered him a choice. Either to be allowed to take the glass and go from the house without further talk, or, if the greed of curiosity had taken command of him, watch what would happen next.

'Sir,' said Dr Lanyon, 'you speak enigmas, and you will perhaps not wonder that I hear you with no very strong impression of belief. But I have gone too far in the way of inexplicable services to pause before I see the end.'

'It is well,' replied the visitor, 'Lanyon, you remember your vows. What follows is under the seal of our profession. And now, you who have so long been bound to the most narrow and material views, you who have denied the virtue of transcendental medicine, you who have derided your superiors—behold!'

He put the glass to his lips, and drank at one gulp. A cry followed. He reeled, staggered, clutched at the table and held on, staring with injected eyes, gasping with open mouth and as Lanyon watched there came a change. The other seemed to swell, his face became suddenly black, and the features seemed to melt and alter. The next moment Lanyon had sprung to his feet and leaped back against the wall, his arm raised to shield him from that prodigy, his mind submerged in terror.

'O God!' he screamed, and 'O God!' again and again. For there, before his eyes, pale and shaken and half fainting, and groping before him with his hands like a man restored from death—there stood Henry Jekyll!

The letter went on, 'What he told me in the next hour I cannot bring my mind to set on paper. I saw what I saw, I heard what I heard, and my soul sickened at it. And yet now, when that sight has faded from my eyes I ask myself if I believe it, and I cannot answer.'

The letter ended with, 'The creature who crept into my house that night was, on Jekyll's own confession, known by the name of Hyde and hunted for in every corner of the land as the murderer of Carew.'

How had this sad state of affairs come about? How was it that the highly respected Dr Jekyll had, by some strange means, also become the loathsome murderer known as Mr Hyde? The reasons for this were in his full statement, read when the whole sad business was finally at an end.

'I was born to a large fortune,' the statement began, 'endowed besides with excellent parts, inclined by nature to industry, fond of the respect of the wise and good among my fellow men and this, as might have been supposed, with every guarantee of an honourable and distinguished future. And indeed, the worst of my faults was a certain impatient gaiety of disposition, such as has made the happiness of many, but such as I found hard to reconcile with my imperious desire to carry my head high, and wear a more than commonly grave countenance before the public. Hence it came about that I concealed my pleasures; and that when I reached years of reflection, and began to look around me, and take stock of my progress and position in the world, I stood already committed to a profound duplicity of life.'

What he was saying was that to the world he was a staid, hardworking doctor; but he had a bad, almost evil side to his character, that no one else knew about. He had already concluded that almost everyone has such a dual personality—goodness mixed with occasional feelings of wickedness—but in his own personality he felt that this dividing line was more marked than usual. From this he had the thought—what would happen if he could actually separate these two opposite emotions? Could he, as a doctor and a chemist, actually do this?

The more he thought about the idea, the more absorbed he became. As he said in his statement: 'I hesitated long before I put this theory to the test of practice. I knew well that I risked death; for any drug that so potently controlled and shook the very fortress of identity might, by the least scruple of an overdose, utterly blot out that immaterial tabernacle which I looked to it to change. But the temptation of a discovery so singular and profound at last overcame the suggestions of alarm. I had long since prepared my tincture; I purchased from a firm of wholesale chemists a large quantity of particular salt which I knew, from my experiments, to be the last ingredient required; and, late one accursed night, I compounded the elements, watched them boil and smoke together in the glass, and when the boiling had subsided, with a strong glow of courage, drank of the potion.

261

'The most racking pains succeeded; a grinding in the bones, deadly nausea, and a horror of the spirit that cannot be exceeded at the hour of birth or death. Then these agonies began swiftly to subside, and I came to myself as if out of a great sickness. There was something strange in my sensations, something indescribably new and, from its very novelty, incredibly sweet. I felt younger, lighter, happier in body. I knew myself at the first breath of this new life to be more wicked, tenfold more wicked, sold a slave to my original evil, and the thought, at that moment, braced and delighted me like wine. I stretched out my hands, exulting in the freshness of these sensations and, in the act, I was suddenly aware that I had lost in stature.

'And hence, as I think, it came about that Edward Hyde was so much smaller, slighter, and younger than Henry Jekyll. Even as good shone upon the countenance of the one, evil was written broadly and plainly on the face of the other.'

He looked at himself in a mirror, noting the many differences between his two beings and then drank again, once more suffered the pangs of dissolution, and once more saw himself as Henry Jekyll.

Later he took and furnished the house in Soho to which Hyde was tracked by the police. He also announced to his servants that a Mr Hyde (whom he described) was to have full liberty and power about his own house. He then drew up a will so that if anything befel him in the person of Dr Jekyll, he could become Edward Hyde without loss.

He then began his strange, double life. No matter what he did outside the walls of his home he knew that he did not even exist! Let him but escape into his laboratory door, give him but a second to mix and swallow the draught that he always had standing ready, then, whatever he had done, Edward Hyde would pass away like a stain of breath upon a mirror. And there, in his stead, quietly at home, trimming the midnight lamp in his study, a man who could afford to laugh at suspicion . . . would be Henry Jekyll!

But this was to end. Some two months before the murder of Sir Danvers he had been out on one of his adventures and had returned late. When he woke the next day he had an odd sensation. He looked about him. The room was as usual, nothing had changed. Yet something was wrong. Then he looked down on his hand. The hand of Henry Jekyll was large, firm, white and comely. The hand he saw was lean, corded, knuckly, of a dusky pallor and thickly shaded with a swart growth of hair.

He knew at once what had happened. He had gone to bed Dr Jekyll, he had awakened Edward Hyde. He managed to pass through the house—to the surprise of the servants—disappeared into his laboratory, and ten minutes later, Dr Jekyll was sitting down, with a darkened brow, to make a feint of breakfasting.

This was the beginning. He decided—for he was forced to make the choice—to let Hyde go forever and remain as the familiar, friendly doctor. For two months he led a life of severity and the pleasure of the company of his friends. Then he began to be tortured with longings and, as if he was Hyde struggling after freedom, once again compounded and swallowed the transforming draught.

It was on this night that he met and murdered the kindly, aged Sir Danvers. With a transport of glee, he mauled the unresisting body, tasting delight from every blow and it was not until weariness had begun to succeed that he was suddenly, in the top fit of his delirium, struck through the heart by a cold chill of terror. Seeing his life forfeit,

He mauled the unresisting body, tasting delight from every blow.

he fled from the scene, running to his little house in Soho, still gloating on his crime, yet still listening for the sound behind him of the steps of the avenger. He drank the draught, even pledging the dead man. Then the next moment, Henry Jekyll, with streaming tears of remorse, had fallen on his knees and lifted his clasped hands to God.

He realized that, never again, would the terrible Hyde be allowed to roam the streets, maiming and killing. He locked the door and ground the key under his heel. Enough was enough!

But it was not to be. One fine January day he sat quietly in Regent's Park, at peace with the world. And then he was filled with a horrid nausea, and the most deadly shuddering. He looked down. His clothes hung formlessly on his shrunken limbs, the hand that lay on his knee was corded and hairy. A moment before he had been wealthy, beloved, the cloth being laid for him in the dining-room in his home. Now he was the common quarry of mankind, a known murderer.

He took a cab to a hotel he knew and wrote two important letters— one to Lanyon and one to his butler, Poole—then sent them out with directions they should be registered. He paced the room, desperately. Now it was no longer the fear of the gallows, it was the horror of being Hyde that racked him. He slept for a while then made his way back to his laboratory. This time it took a double dose to recall him to himself and six hours later, as he sat looking sadly into the fire, the pangs returned and the drug had to be retaken.

From that day it seemed that only by a great effort as of gymnastics, and only under the immediate stimulation of the drug, that he could continue to wear the countenance of Jekyll. If he slept, or even dozed for a moment in his chair, it was always as Hyde that he awoke. His very existence had become intolerable. It was then that he sat down to write his full statement, ending with: 'I am now finishing this statement under the influence of the last of the old powders. This then, is the last time, short of a miracle, that Henry Jekyll can think his own thoughts or see his own face (now how sadly altered) in the glass.

'Will Hyde die upon the scaffold? Or will he find the courage to release himself at the last moment? God knows; I am careless; this is my true hour of death, and what is to follow concerns another than myself. Here, then, as I lay down the pen, and proceed to seal up my confession, I bring the life of that unhappy Henry Jekyll to an end.'

Mr Utterson was sitting by his fireside when he was surprised to receive a visit from Poole. He soon learned from Dr Jekyll's butler that he suspected something was very wrong with the doctor. Would he come at once? Mr Utterson did not hesitate and the two men set out for the doctor's home. Reaching it, the butler led him through the house until they reached the door of the laboratory. He knocked upon it and announced that Mr Utterson had called to see him. A voice answered from within, 'Tell him I cannot see anyone.'

'Sir,' Poole asked, looking Mr Utterson in the eyes, 'was that the voice of my master?'

'It seems very changed,' replied the lawyer, very pale, but giving look for look.

'Changed? Well, yes, I think so. Have I been twenty years in this man's house, to be deceived about his voice? No, sir. Master's been made away with. He was made away with about eight days ago, when we heard him cry out upon the name of God. And *who's* in there instead of him, and *why* it stays there, is a thing that cries to heaven.'

The two men discussed the problem for some time, the butler insisting that, in his view, murder had been done by the person who had answered him through the door. He went further. He insisted that the *thing* inside the laboratory was the man he knew as Mr Hyde. He asked if the other had ever seen him.

'Yes,' said the lawyer, 'I once spoke with him.'

'Then you must know, sir, as well as the rest of us, that there was something queer about that gentleman—something that gave a man a turn—I don't rightly know how to say it, sir, beyond this; that you felt it in your marrow—kind of cold and thin.'

'I own I felt something of what you describe,' said Mr Utterson.

By now the lawyer's mind was made up. He called another male servant to help and told him that he and Poole were going to force their way into the laboratory.

'If all is well,' he said, 'my shoulders are broad enough to bear the blame. Meanwhile, lest anything should really be amiss, or any criminal seek to escape by the back, you and the boy must go round the corner with a pair of good sticks, and take your post at the laboratory door. We give you ten minutes to get to your stations.'

The ten minutes came to an end at last. 'Jekyll!' cried Utterson. with

265

a loud voice. 'I demand to see you!' He paused a moment but there came no reply. 'I give you fair warning, our suspicions are aroused and I must and shall see you. If not by fair means, then by foul. If not of your consent, then by brute force!'

'Utterson,' said the voice, 'for God's sake, have mercy!'

'Ah, that's not Jekyll's voice—it's Hyde's!' cried Utterson. 'Down with the door, Poole!'

The other swung an axe he had taken from another room and the door leaped against the lock and hinges. A dismal screech, as of mere animal terror, rang from the other side. Up went the axe again and again, and it was not until the fifth blow that the lock burst in sunder and the wreck of the door fell inwards. The besiegers, appalled by their own riot and the stillness that had followed, stood back a little and peered in. There lay the room before their eyes in the quiet lamplight, a good fire glowing and chattering on the hearth, the kettle singing its thin strain, a drawer or two open, papers neatly set forth on the business table, and nearer the fire, the things laid out for tea. The quietest room, one would have said, and, but for the glazed presses full of chemicals, the most commonplace that night in London.

Right in the midst there lay the body of a man sorely contorted and still twitching. They drew near on tiptoe, turned it on its back, and beheld the face of Edward Hyde. He was dressed in clothes far too large for him, clothes of the doctor's bigness; the cords of his face still moved with a semblance of life, but life was quite gone; and by the crushed phial in the hand and the strong smell of kernels that hung upon the air, Utterson knew that we was looking on the body of a self-destroyer.

'We have come too late,' he said sternly, 'whether to save or punish. Hyde is gone to his account; and it only remains for us to find the body of your master.'

The two men searched the house but with no success. Finally, turning to the business table, they saw a large envelope bearing, in the doctor's hand, the name of Mr Utterson. The lawyer unsealed it and several enclosures fell to the floor. The first was a will, made out as before, but in place of the name of Edward Hyde the lawyer, with indescribable amazement, read the name of Gabriel John Utterson. He opened the next enclosure and read:

'My dear Utterson. When this shall fall into your hands, I shall have disappeared, under what circumstances I have not the penetration to foresee; but my instincts and all the circumstances of my nameless situation tell me that the end is sure and must be early. Go then, and first read the narrative which Lanyon warned me he was to place in your hands; and if you care to hear more, turn to the confession of

Your unworthy and unhappy friend, Henry Jekyll.'

'There was a third enclosure?' asked Utterson.

'Here, sir,' said Poole, and gave into his hands a considerable packet sealed in several places.

The lawyer put it in his pocket. 'I would say nothing of this paper. If your master is fled or is dead, we may at least save his credit. It is now ten. I must go home and read these documents in quiet; but I shall be back before midnight, when we shall send for the police.'

And Utterson returned home to read, with growing amazement, Dr Jekyll's full statement together with an account of the change witnessed by Dr Lanyon. When he had finished, he arose with a sigh. The mystery of Dr Jekyll and Mr Hyde had been explained—at last!

THE DEATH OF EDITH CAVELL

H. R. Berndorff

The fate of Edith Cavell was that of a noble-hearted woman who died for her country. There is no doubt whatever that her transactions during the war inflicted appreciable damage on the German Army. When her activities against the German Army were discovered she was tried by court-martial and shot. Her last words to the clergyman who attended her were: 'But this I would say, standing as I do in view of God and eternity; I realize that patriotism is not enough. I must have no hatred or bitterness towards anyone.'

The fate of this woman, whose life was ended by the bullets of a firing-party, stirred the whole world. Here is her story, impartially related.

Edith Cavell died in her fiftieth year. She was a British subject, and a trained nurse. When the war broke out she was '*Directrice de l'École Belge d'infirmières diplomées, Rue de la Culture, Bruxelles*'; in other words, the principal of a training-school for nurses.

When, after the first great battles of the war, the hospitals of Brussels and the neighbourhood of the capital began to fill with the Belgian wounded, Edith established a private hospital for Belgian soldiers.

In a few days Brussels was full to overflowing with Allied wounded. This was still the state of affairs when the German Army occupied the capital. Not only in Brussels, but all over Belgium, so far as it was in German occupation, the Belgian wounded, whom their own units, in their hasty retreat, had been unable to remove, were being cared for in hospitals and private houses. When these men had recovered from their wounds there would be a small army of them in the rear of the enemy troops. The measures taken by the German High Command in respect of this state of affairs were simple and practical. Every inhabitant of the occupied area was ordered to report whether he was harbouring enemy wounded; and all directors of public or private hospitals had to make similar reports. During the first days of the German occupation these wounded were collected by the German military authorities, and, according to their condition, were removed to hospitals in the interior of Germany, or to internment camps.

For the French and Belgian armies it was for two reasons of great importance to frustrate these measures as far as possible. The Dutch frontier was near at hand, and during the early days of the war many Belgians and Frenchmen who had for whatever reason remained in the rear of the German troops had escaped over this frontier. The measures taken by the German authorities were at once reported to the enemy intelligence services, and counter-measures were devised.

These counter-measures were taken for two reasons. In the first place, it was of course desirable that the French and Belgian wounded soldiers should return to their units, as soon as they were fit for active service, as many of the wounded were officers and men of the regular armies—that is, they were trained and experienced soldiers. And the men who were wounded in the fighting of the first few days were, of course, among the best of the enemy soldiers. The second consideration was even more important. Every soldier who rejoined the ranks from the rear of the hostile army was a valuable source of information. A trained soldier would be able to give information as to the military situation of the enemy, and if it were possible to question a large number of such men, who had escaped from a great number of different localities, and to compare and supplement the data thus obtained, it should be possible to obtain information of the greatest importance.

The French Intelligence Service accordingly proceeded to create an

269

organization whose purpose was to assist in the escape of such French and Belgian soldiers. Its agents, who slipped across the Dutch frontier, came to an understanding with the civil population of Belgium; above all, they found a ready hearing amongst the Belgian nobility, and the Prince de Croy and the Princesse de Croy were among those Belgians who sought to save their country in this and in many other ways. An organization was created, under the leadership of a few men and women, some of whose names were never discovered, which was so purposeful and efficient in its methods that it had soon spread all over Belgium.

During the early days of the German invasion the smuggling of men over the Dutch frontier attained enormous dimensions. There had always been a great deal of smuggling over this frontier; there were footpaths and waterways known only to the initiated, who had their own methods of evading the frontier guards, and these routes were now utilized. No goods were smuggled now, but native guides, followed by whole troops of French and Belgian soldiers, made their way into Holland, and thence to the Allied armies. The crossing of the frontier, which was only a matter of evading the guards in the darkness, or in foggy weather, was, at all events in the early part of the war, the easiest part of the whole undertaking. In case of need, if the fugitives were numerous enough, and if they were confronted by the frontier pickets, they drew their revolvers and forced a passage. The work of organizing these secret convoys was much more difficult. To begin with, the wounded soldier had to be taken out of the hands of the German military authorities.

It was here that Edith Cavell was able to help. There were many patients in her hospital, and she had in her care a very large number of wounded soldiers who were lying in private houses. Under these circumstances it was inevitable that Edith Cavell should be approached at the very outset by the Belgian Intelligence Service. She was entreated to assist all wounded soldiers in her hospital, or in her care outside the hospital, to cross the Dutch frontier.

England, of course, had already entered the war. Edith Cavell was an Englishwoman, and she maintained, during the whole of her trial, that her principal motive had been the following: her Belgian friends had assured her that all those soldiers in Belgium who had remained un-

270

known to the German authorities after a certain date would be shot on apprehension. Of her own accord she had taken a first step on her perilous path. In order to save the soldiers in her care from becoming prisoners of war she procured civilian clothing for them and destroyed their uniforms. Having done this, she needed only to obtain forged civilian passports for them, and she was able to declare that they were Belgian civilians, who could be identified as harmless citizens. She distributed the wounded in the houses of her numerous acquaintances and wrote, for greater security, forged medical certificates, transforming wounded soldiers into sick civilians. That was the first step; but in order to procure civilian passports, and arrange for the crossing of the frontier, Edith Cavell had to work in close cooperation with the organization already mentioned.

After the war we were given a full description of this organization by a very reliable witness of its operations. The counsel who defended Edith Cavell before the court martial, an advocate of the Brussels Bar, Sadi Kirschen, described it, in the *Echo de Paris* of 14 February 1919, in the following terms:

'An organization was created. The soldiers from the northern departments of France applied to Prince Reginald de Croy, at his château of Belligny; he gave them money and a false passport; he was seconded by his sister, Princess Marie Elizabeth de Croy, and they were further assisted by Mademoiselle Louise Thuliez, a young Frenchwoman from Lille, who went by the name of Mademoiselle Martin.'

The writer proceeds to enumerate the towns in which this organization had its representatives, and to name the local leaders.

It was this organization that assisted Edith Cavell. It supplied her with the Prince de Croy's false passports, which she distributed to her patients. This organization, whose activity was indefatigable, supplied also the forged medical certificates, in which a leg-wound became appendicitis, and a head-wound erysipelas. The German authorities could not possibly have every sick man in the whole of the occupied area of Belgium examined in order to determine the nature of his malady, so that the medical certificate was only a measure of precaution.

Edith Cavell was like a mother to her disguised patients. She nursed them with fanatical devotion until the agent of the organization made his appearance, in order to collect the now convalescent soldiers for the march across the frontier.

The crossing of the frontier was organized as follows. In the first place, groups of five or six men were formed, and to each a guide was allotted. This guide was perfectly acquainted with the country on either side of the frontier. Each man was given a false pass, in the name of some local Belgian authority, to the effect that he was an inhabitant of some village on the Dutch frontier. He was further provided with a document, signed by a municipal officer, from which it appeared that he was a craftsman of some kind, who was now returning home, either because his work was finished, or because the war had made it impossible to continue it. To complete these documents the fugitive was also given a skilfully forged order, signed by one of the German military authorities, to the effect that the artisan was to return immediately to his own home.

The falsifications of these last documents were constantly improved. In order that no doubt should be entertained as to their genuine character, the holders of such documents were required to return home within a definite time, or the railway journey which they were to make was prescribed. Sometimes the order required the holder to report himself, on his way home, at other military posts, and to see that the day and hour of reporting himself was noted on the document.

In this way many wounded officers and men in the care of Edith Cavell found their way across the Dutch frontier and rejoined the combatant troops. Presently the day arrived when Miss Cavell had sent the last of her convalescent soldiers back to the army, and she subsequently served the organization in other ways.

At the beginning of the war many enemy soldiers were lurking behind the German front. They formed themselves into companies; they were still armed, and had no intention of surrendering to the German troops. These companies hid in the forests and hilly districts; they lived on game and such food as the countryfolk brought them by night. The number of these fugitives in the rear of the army was considerable. In some places the leaders of these companies contrived to hold out as late as June 1915. As a matter of course, they inflicted such damage as they could on the enemy.

The author still remembers with a slight shudder an incident in which he himself was concerned. It was in 1915, and he was resting with his company in the district lying between the Argonne and the small French town of Dun. With a comrade he was walking through the moonlit night; a long way from the rest billets, or from any German troops, and a long way behind the front, in the neighbourhood of the village of Montigny. There had been some talk of shooting a wild boar that night. A narrow path wound into the forest, so steep that neither of us had breath to spare for speech. The path led us to the edge of a meadow, which lay at a lower level; suddenly we turned a corner into a forest ride, and stood still, in sudden alarm. About a hundred yards distant, in marching order, rifle on shoulder, a body of French soldiers were approaching us over the soft woodland soil. There seemed to be about a hundred of them, and their officers were marching at the head of the column.

As we caught sight of the French, and the French caught sight of us, both parties stood still for some moments. The French may have supposed that a whole company was marching up behind us. But since this was not the case, the two of us closed the incident by taking one leap into the wood, scrambling down a few slopes, still under cover of the wood, rushing back to our billets, and giving the alarm. It was not until a month later that a whole battalion, which was still holding out in this hilly district, was rounded up and taken prisoner.

The soldiers whom the organization now began to send to Edith Cavell may perhaps have come from such formations. It was her business to harbour these men in Brussels until they could be sent over the frontier.

Just as the organization was beginning, on an extensive scale, to withdraw these unwounded soldiers from Belgium, the German authorities got wind of its existence. It was a series of accidents that led to its discovery. The fact that strange men were often seen in Miss Cavell's house was the first circumstance to arouse suspicion. The police and the counter-espionage agents began to observe the house, and their suspicions were confirmed by their observations. The authorities did not move at once; they continued to watch the house, hoping to catch the individual accomplices in the act. As a matter of fact, this was not particularly difficult; the transactions of the organization were becoming

273

more and more obvious, less and less cautious, and it needed no great ingenuity to break the net and expose its methods.

In the spring of 1915, when the organization had been nine months at work, the counter-espionage service intervened. Edith Cavell and a large number of the members of the organization were arrested. All the accused, including Edith Cavell, confessed to their activities, so that the whole matter was handed over to the military court. The court proceeded to indict the prisoners 'in respect of the case of Phillippe Baucq and others,' since the Belgian, Phillippe Baucq, was regarded as the chief offender.

When the trial opened Edith Cavell sat in the midst of a numerous group of prisoners, all of whom were charged with military conspiracy. The prosecution was represented by Kriegsgerichtsrat Stöber; the court consisted of German officers; and the counsel for the defence were the Brussels advocates, Sadi Kirschen and Thomas Braun. After the indictment had been read Edith Cavell was called, and her interrogation began. This interrogation, which was recorded by her advocate, and subsequently published in the *Echo de Paris*, began as follows:

'Edith Cavell declared that she was forty-nine years of age, and a British subject.

JUDGE: Between November 1914 and July 1915 you harboured French and English soldiers, among them a colonel, all being in civilian clothing. You have assisted Belgians, Frenchmen and Englishmen to return to military service at the front. You have supported them and have given them money.

EDITH CAVELL: I have.

JUDGE: With whom were you associated in carrying out these transactions?

CAVELL: With Monsieur Capian, Mademoiselle Martin, and Messieurs Derveau and Libiez.

JUDGE: Who was the head, the creator of the organization?

CAVELL: There was no head.

JUDGE: Was not the Prince de Croy the head of it?

CAVELL: No, the Prince de Croy confined himself to sending us men whom he had helped with money.

JUDGE: Why have you committed the actions of which you are accused?

The officer's command had not died away before the bullets had killed her.

To this Edith Cavell answered at some length, stating that she had believed that all the men whom she had helped to cross the frontier were in danger of their lives. This was her whole defence, her whole justification.'

Edith Cavell, like the majority of the accused, was sentenced to death. Since it was evident that she had never at any time acted from avaricious or otherwise morally reprehensible motives, the opinion was immediately expressed in Germany, even by officers of high rank, that the sentence of death should be commuted to one of imprisonment. By military law the supreme instance of the military court was the general commanding the army. He confirmed the verdict. The Governor-General of Belgium, the Freiherr von Bissing, did not countersign the death warrant of the English nurse. It is positively known today that the political department of the German Government General, of which the Freiherr von Bissing was the head, did everything humanly possible to avert the execution of the death sentence.

The Freiherr von Bissing, a man whose noble and chivalrous character has always been recognized even by the enemy, did his utmost, but his efforts were unavailing. Edith Cavell was shot. The statement which was current in the whole of the enemy press, during and after the war, and was later revived in an English film, to the effect that the execution was carried out in a horrible manner, is absolutely false. Edith Cavell was bound to a post; and the officer's word of command had not died away before the bullets of the German soldiers had killed her on the spot.

How seriously detrimental to the success of the German troops the activities of Nurse Cavell must have been is shown by a very conclusive document. Lord Bryce has published his war speeches and articles in volume form. The book was reviewed by Robert Arch in *Justice* (30 January 1919). What the reviewer says of the fate of Edith Cavell is all the more significant in that his review is, on the whole, animated by a spirit which is anything but friendly to Germany:

'Lord Bryce, and others also, would have done well to refrain from exploiting such incidents as the execution of Miss Cavell. What Miss Cavell did was unquestionably deserving of capital punishment in accordance with the laws of war. The privilege of sex in such matters was recognized neither by our allies nor by our enemies, and it is time that we recognized this, and admitted that Miss Cavell heroically ventured her life and died for her country, but that she was no more and no less "murdered" than thousands of men who fell in honourable fight on the field of battle.'

GUNPOWDER, TREASON AND PLOT

Avis Murton Carter

Remember, remember, the Fifth of November,
Gunpowder, treason and plot!
I see no reason, why gunpowder treason
Should ever be forgot.

These famous lines usually accompany 'Guy Fawkes Day', a time when bonfires crackle and flare all over England, when fireworks explode in bangs or in breathtaking colours, when rockets soar heavenwards to erupt in showers of beauty. These are lines that have been sung in England to celebrate something that nearly happened more than three and a half centuries ago.

Yet what do they mean? And who was this Guy Fawkes whose effigy is trundled through the streets on a barrow or which, perched on top of a bonfire, is finally consumed by the leaping flames?

It all recalls a great conspiracy against King James I of England, a conspiracy in which, curiously, Guy Fawkes—or Guido, as his friends called him—the only name that seems to be remembered today, played a comparatively small if vital part.

Queen Elizabeth I, who had reigned over England for 45 years, had died in 1603 and James, son of Mary, Queen of Scots, became James I of England and James VI of Scotland. The latter title he had already held for his whole life, some 36 years. His right to the throne was undisputed, for his mother was a descendant of Henry VII of England, whose daughter had married James IV of Scotland in 1502.

He was soon to prove a very unpopular king. Much of the opposition to his rule came from the Catholics because James, like Elizabeth before him, was a Protestant. Many of his nobles, however, still clung to the religion that was practised throughout England before Henry VIII broke all ties with Rome and the Pope and made himself head of the English church instead.

Naturally there was most discontent among the Catholics, and it was not long before a leader came forward. He was Robert Catesby, an English nobleman possessing great estates in Warwickshire. He had been in trouble when he had joined the uprising against Elizabeth led by the Earl of Essex and only escaped beheading—the fate of the earl— by paying a huge fine. It was entirely due to him that the new conspiracy—the gunpowder plot—came into being.

A devout Catholic, his mind was filled with plans by which he could rid his country of both Protestant king and a parliament which oppressed his fellow-Catholics at the same time. After he was sure what he wanted to do, he called on his friend, Robert Winter.

'I have given this matter a great deal of thought,' he said to Winter. 'There is only one way in which we can despatch this king and his parliament to the devil. We shall blow them all up with gunpowder!'

The suggestion struck his friend with horror. 'You surely are not serious, Robert. This is not only criminal, it is inhuman. To kill men in this, well, this cowardly fashion is against all the laws of decent people. No, you cannot do it. I, for one, will have nothing whatever to do with it!'

But Catesby persisted. 'Just think for a moment. Think of the long, pitiless and many cruelties that have been inflicted on us Catholics.'

He then went on to list some of their friends who had been executed by the axe or the rope, had been allowed to starve to death in tiny, damp cells, or who had been reduced from men of property and honour to become little more than beggars. And all because of this king and his parliament.

'Apart from us,' he went on, 'what hope do we have? We can expect no help from Spain. No. We must fight force with force. And my plan, at one fell swoop, will begin our great and divine fight for freedom.'

Winter was moved by his friend's arguments, but not entirely convinced. 'I will tell you what I will do, my dear friend. I will travel to the Netherlands where the Spanish ambassador, Signor Velasco, has arrived to conclude a treaty between England and Spain. I will see this Velasco and insist that he inserts a clause in this treaty that will protect all Catholics in this country from this continual persecution.'

But Winter's journey was in vain. Velasco promised to use his influence, but secretly he knew he could not risk the treaty by inserting such a clause. Furious at the way he had been treated, Winter travelled to Ostend to sail for England. By one of fate's curious chances, he met there an old comrade with whom he had fought during the wars in the Netherlands. He was Guy Fawkes, son of a well-to-do lawyer, a man of great courage and of much military experience. Winter saw at once how useful he would be to Catesby and himself and decided that he should join them. But as yet he was not prepared to let him into the full secret.

Meanwhile, Catesby had been busy gaining other supporters. One was Thomas Percy, a nobleman of the great Northumberland family; the other was John Wright, Percy's brother-in-law and reputed to be the finest swordsman in England. Both were zealous Catholics, and both immediately agreed to help Catesby with his plot.

Thus the number of conspirators had become five, and a few days later they all met at Catesby's lodgings. He did not immediately tell them the details of his plot but after several days, as it was later confessed, they 'met at a house in the fields beyond St Clement's Inn, where they did confer and agree upon the plot, and there took a solemn oath and vows by all their force and power to execute the same, and of secrecy not to reveal it to any of their fellows but of such as should be thought fit persons to enter into that action.'

This oath was taken on 1 May 1604, but the conspirators decided to wait in case any good *did* come out of the negotiations between England and Spain. When the treaty was concluded on 18 August, however, there was nothing in it that would protect the Catholics in England. King James then ordered his judges and magistrates to enforce the laws against Catholics with the utmost rigour.

This was what the conspirators had been half-expecting. Now they were determined to go ahead with Catesby's plan.

They hired a house in Lambeth, on the south bank of the Thames, where they began to lay in a store of gunpowder—ready to take it, in barrels, across the river to another house that Percy had hired in Westminster, close to Parliament House. They finally moved into this house on 11 December and began to prepare for the big occasion.

Fawkes became one of their group, but assumed the name of Johnson and pretended to be the servant of Percy. While the others worked in the basement of the house they had rented, attempting to tunnel a way through to an area beneath the Houses of Parliament, he pretended to be a gardener, keeping watch overhead. During the day his colleagues laboured at their tunnelling, and at night they would bring up the earth and dump it on the garden; there Fawkes would spread it about to avoid suspicion.

After two weeks of this work, however, they learned that parliament had been prorogued—or ended for a time—from 7 February until 3 October. It was therefore agreed to suspend the work until after Christmas and for each man to retire to his home until January. But already, during the first two weeks of tunnelling, some of them had begun to doubt the lawfulness of their attempt. Surely, some argued, the innocent might well perish with the guilty? Would that be right?

Catesby, who had been newly commissioned in a regiment of cavalry, decided to consult a priest. 'What if I am ordered to make attacks against an enemy in which the innocent might fall with the guilty?' he asked. 'What would happen if I found women and children amongst the armed soldiers facing me during a charge?'

'That cannot be helped, my son,' replied the priest. 'Otherwise an aggressor could always defeat the object of the charge by placing innocent persons amongst the guilty ones in his ranks.'

Catesby explained this reasoning to the others, and they agreed to continue with his plan. On 30 January they resumed the operation. It was very hard work, for the wall through which they had to hack their way was nearly ten feet thick and composed of huge stones. But there were more helpers now, because four more had joined the conspiracy. They were the brothers of Wright and Winter and John Grant of Norbrook in Warwickshire, who was Winters' brother-in-law. Catesby had also admitted Thomas Bates, his servant, whose physical strength was of great help in the tunnelling; all the other conspirators working below ground were of the nobility and not used to such hard labour.

As they fought their way on, inch by painful inch, they were suddenly alarmed. A loud noise was heard coming from overhead. They knew that parliament was not in session so they sent Fawkes to find out the cause. He discovered that a coal merchant was going out of business and was selling off his stock. The sound they had heard was that of coal being wheeled out of his cellar, which was immediately above their own. Overjoyed at this news, the conspirators sent Fawkes to lease this cellar in the name of Percy, his pretended master.

In a very short time they removed thirty-six barrels of gunpowder from the storehouse in Lambeth, carrying it at night across the river and stacking it in their new cellar. With the new cellar immediately beneath the Houses of Parliament, everything was soon ready.

They separated until September, a few days before parliament was due to reassemble. During this time Fawkes was sent over to Flanders to obtain the support of several officers in the cavalry regiment of which Catesby was captain. Many of the officers in this regiment were Catholics, and Fawkes told them that there was a plot afoot in England whereby all Catholics were to be exterminated. The only way they and their families could survive, he told them, was by the sword. Little came of this excursion, however, except that it was brought to the notice of the King's Secretary Cecil, Earl of Shaftesbury, who had his spies everywhere.

But in England Catesby continued his efforts. He had obtained a fresh accomplice, named Robert Keyes, a noble who had been stripped of his property and had a grudge against the throne in consequence. When Fawkes returned from Flanders in September the plotters were ready to proceed but, once again, parliament was prorogued—this time until 5 November. By now some of the conspirators were beginning to wonder whether their plan had become known, and Thomas Winter went to the House of Lords to watch the faces of the members whilst the notice of prorogation was read out. He returned satisfied; members walked about and chatted casually, obviously unaware that they did so on top of a volcano—thirty-six barrels of gunpowder, each containing a hundred pounds.

Yet these delays were to prove fatal. By now the conspirators had used nearly all their money and fresh recruits had to be obtained.

Catesby was forced to divulge the scheme to three more nobles—Sir Everard Digby, Ambrose Rookwood and Sir Francis Tresham of Rushton. All were Catholics, all had some grudge against the king and parliament. Tresham, though the wealthiest, was also a possible source of danger, for he was known to be selfish and imprudent. Indeed, some of the plotters were furious when they learned that Catesby had allowed him to join their enterprise. But it had been done.

As the vital day approached the final plans were made. They consisted of far more than just blowing up parliament. The young Prince Charles (later Charles I) was to be seized and taken into captivity. Digby, Tresham and others were to hasten to Combe Abbey and secure the person of the young Princess Elizabeth. With the two young princes—Charles had an elder brother Henry, who was to accompany the king to parliament—out of the way, the princess would be declared queen. A protector was to be appointed to rule the country during the minority of the sovereign, who would be brought up as a Catholic.

All this, of course, would take place once Guy Fawkes had fired the gunpowder and sent king and parliament sky-high. The barrels had been piled in the form of a pyramid and covered with wood and faggots. Fawkes would light the powder with a slow-burning fuse which would allow him fifteen minutes to escape. A ship was lying in the river nearby to take him to Flanders, where he was to call on all Catholic powers for aid.

But as the time drew near, Tresham had second thoughts. One of the members due to be present was his brother-in-law, Lord Monteagle, and he wished to warn him to keep away. He sent him a letter by messenger. Monteagle, who was at dinner when it arrived, seeing that it had neither date nor signature, handed it to one of his gentlemen friends to read out. Written in the casual spelling of the time, it began:

'My lord out of the love i beare to some of youere frends i have a caer of youer preseruacion therfor i would advyse yowe as yowe tender youer lyf to devys some excuse to shift of youer attendance at this parleament for god and man hath concurred to punishe the wickednes of this time and think not slightlye of this advertisement butretyre youre self into toure contri wheare you may expect the event in safti for thowghe theare be no apparance of anni stir yet i says they shall receive a terrible blow this parleament . . .'

It was Lord Monteagle, as some say, who was actually a spy in Cecil's employ, who was to reveal the whole plot. He had originally been a Catholic, but when Protestant James became king, he changed his religion. None of the conspirators apparently knew this fact.

Despite the lateness of the hour, Monteagle hurried from his home to lay the letter before Cecil and some of the other ministers. After much deliberation, Cecil decided that nothing should be done at the moment, the king being out of London. Catesby soon learned of this incident of the letter and sent Fawkes to the cellar beneath Parliament House to make sure everything was in order. Fawkes reported back that nothing had been touched, and agreed to visit the cellar every day until 5 November.

But not one of the conspirators had realized Cecil's cunning. He was waiting to pounce—hoping to grab all the conspirators at once rather than just a few.

King James returned to London on 31 October and was shown the letter. He discussed the matter for several hours with his ministers. They finally decided that on the night before the opening of parliament the cellars below the buildings should be thoroughly searched.

It was a miserable night, with fog rolling up from the shrouded Thames, when a small group of armed men crept stealthily into the cellars. As they turned the corner into one room they saw before them the figure of a masked man. It was Guy Fawkes, checking that everything was in order for the morrow. The leader of the group, Sir Thomas Knyvett, stepped forward, sword in hand. 'I arrest you in the name of the king!'

Fawkes tried to wrench out his own sword but he was seized by several of the armed men. Three slow matches were discovered in his pocket and a dark lantern found placed behind the door. Kicking and struggling, he was dragged before Cecil; when he refused to speak, he was taken to the Tower of London. As he sat in his damp, stone cell next to the torture chamber, he was heard to say 'Oh, would I had been quicker. Would I had set fire to the powder. Death would have been sweet had some of my enemies gone with me.'

The terrible torture of the rack followed, but no matter what pain was inflicted on him, Fawkes refused to reveal the name of his fellow conspirators. It was only when he learned that they had given them-

As the guards turned the corner into one room they saw before them the figure of a masked man. It was Guy Fawkes . . .

selves away by staging an armed revolt that he finally agreed to his inquisitors' demands.

The rising was ill-fated from the start. Catesby was sheltering with some of his fellow conspirators when the house was surrounded by a troop of the king's men. The house was set on fire and he rushed into the courtyard ready to die with his sword in his hand. He, the two Wrights and Percy were mortally wounded, Rookwood was wounded and burned, and Winter had his arm broken.

The others were soon taken; the conspiracy was over.

The trial that followed naturally aroused great public interest, Fawkes and seven others being sentenced to death. He was taken from the Tower on 31 January 1606 and conveyed to the gibbet in Old Palace Yard, Westminster, to be hanged opposite the very building he had hoped to destroy.

And the memory of this attempt still lingers on in bonfires and fireworks every 5 November.

There is more. Early on the morning of the day on which parliament assembles, a body of the Yeomen of the Guard gather in the House of Lords and then, lamps in hand and halberds at the ready, they search the vaults beneath the Houses of Parliament. They then return to make their report after which they are rewarded with a meal of bread, cheese and beer.

A THING ON
THE GROUND

Ivan T. Sanderson

Dr Hynek, during his nearly twenty years as consultant to the US Air Force on UFOs, once propounded a dictum in a radio broadcast that is of great importance to our inquiry. When asked what evidence he, as a scientist, needed to evaluate reports of these aerial phenomena, he replied with a list of most carefully considered requirements. One of these was that he would like a minimum of four witnesses in each case. Reviewing the cases I have recorded, I would point out that, while the bolide I saw off the coast of Nicaragua did not occur in curcumstances that met these standards, the matter of 'green lights' in the Caribbean generally did so, since tens of thousands of people witnessed them, and up to hundreds together at one time. The second case also does not fulfil this requirement since only Michael Freedman and I saw it at that time, as far as I have been able to ascertain.

The third case, however, did meet the test, and rather more than well for with us we had one top-notch technician and an amateur astrono-mer, while the fifth witness arrived in the middle of events and was able to confirm all that the other four of us had been seeing. At the time of writing my report on the fourth case, I was under the impression that only my wife and I had made the observation. However, I later learned from my newspaperman friend that the Stroudsburg police had received several phone calls asking why the 'sun keeps on flashing in and out' at precisely that time. Later still, I further learned that two New Jersey state police officers on road patrol had observed the object from directly below in the Delaware Water Gap itself. Thus, I think we may say that at least this standard was met in this case. The same may, I believe, be said for my next case.

Before presenting this to you, however, I would like to quote Dr Hynek again. Another important observation that he made on the same broadcast was to the effect that, as of now, we have nothing to go on in this business but reports; but that, once an honest report is made, it itself becomes a fact.

Now, it is the duty of both reporters and scientists to investigate facts. However, a scientist does not have the time to investigate fancies, though he is at liberty to do so—and many of the greatest scientists have done so, often with surprising results. Nevertheless, it is often very hard to draw the line precisely between fact and fancy. Reports of the sort of which we are speaking are of this nature, especially when they are made by persons who appear to be sane, sensible, and even technically and scientifically educated. As Dr Hynek suggested, once such persons report they have seen something, the report of itself becomes a fact and is thus, in his opinion, worthy of both consideration and examination. If, moreover, such a report is confirmed by at least four witnesses, and meets certain other requirements, it should be most thoroughly investigated.

As a reporter, specializing in the fields of the natural sciences and trained in scientific methodology, I endeavour to approach the investigation of facts along scientific lines. During thirty-five years of scientific reporting, I have run into some extraordinary things that seemed to defy logic, and which certainly flew in the face of our present beliefs, both general and scientific. But it clearly is the duty of a reporter to investigate any fact, however preposterous it may at first appear. It was in this frame of reference that I investigated the following extraordinary event.

This incident had broken in the national press in 1952 with rather startling clarity and emphasis. For some reason which I have never fathomed, the press reported it in a serious and straightforward manner, though it was, on the face of it, much more fantastic than even the average silly-season story. The gist of it was that a 'monster, with glowing red eyes' had been encountered by a number of citizens in a place called Flatwoods, in Braxton County, West Virginia. I had ignored the story, but a few days later a leading national magazine and next the North American Newspaper Alliance, with whom I have been associated for twenty years, phoned me about it. I must say that I was quite surprised. In short order, my then assistant, Eddie Schoenenberger and I were on our way to Flatwoods. And this is our story.

My assistant and I left on the evening of 18 September 1952, at 8.30 p.m. and, after driving all night, arrived at Sutton, the centre of Braxton County, late next morning.

After leaving our baggage at a motel, we proceeded to the place in Flatwoods, some five miles north-east, where the alleged monster had been seen. There we immediately encountered five of the people who had seen the thing—all boys aged between nine and fourteen years. We talked with them and walked over the ground until sundown.

Returning to the motel in Sutton, we contacted a group of expert cave explorers in Charleston—members of the National Speleological Society and personal friends of ours—and appealed to them for help. Two, who happen to be chemists, kindly responded and drove the eighty miles to Sutton immediately, arriving shortly after midnight.

Next morning, the 20th, we went back to Flatwoods accompanied by Mr J. Holt Byrne (publisher of *The Braxton Central*) and, with five younger members of his reportorial staff, went over the ground in great detail, covering several acres in as thorough a manner as possible. We again interviewed and cross-questioned the boys—individually, in pairs, and as a group.

In the afternoon we motored to Gassaway, on the Elk River some ten miles to the south-west, and interviewed a Mr Anderson Hughes on the advice of the sheriff of Sutton. Mr Hughes pointed out to us roughly the spot on a wooded mountain above Sugar Creek where a Mr Woodrow Eagle had said he sighted the crash of a flaming object, which he thought was a burning plane. We obtained the loan of the only boat on that stretch of the river and spent four hours searching the forested slopes on the other side, and some other hills beyond them.

At sundown we proceeded down the road along the river toward Charleston and stopped first at Duck Creek, where we tried to locate Woodrow Eagle. Finally, a roadhouse owner who knew him personally located him at the house of a relative in Gassaway, and we spoke to him on the phone. It was too late to meet him in person, and he had nothing to add to his story (which we had already heard from Mr Hughes), so we continued on to Frametown.

Here we located the residence of a Mr J. C. Dean who contributes a small social column about the activities of this town to *The Braxton Democrat*—the other newspaper in Sutton. He had reported on the previous day that still another aerial object had crashed or landed on a nearby farm. Mr Dean received us most courteously and informed us that this example had landed on an overgrown and isolated field at the top of a hill known as James' Knoll or Knob but that, although seen by the two young James boys, it had not been investigated because it had been regarded as a fireball.

Since it was by then nearly midnight, we continued on to Charleston where we spent the night. The next day we met other members of the National Speleological Society. One of them—Mrs Alice Williams— informed us that she had witnessed the disintegration of still another fiery object in the air at a height of not more than a few hundred feet, to the west of Charleston on the evening of 12 September. This was also witnessed by a couple named Mr and Mrs Clarence McClane, who affirmed that when the object disintegrated 'a lot of ashes fell to the ground.'

We left Charleston at 4.30 p.m. that afternoon and drove to Washington, D.C., arriving in the early morning of the 22nd, and then returned to New York later that day.

The Initial Reports

These are the newspaper reports that led us to our investigation in the first place. They must be paraphrased since they are too long for complete quotation. They contain much essential information and will serve to fix the names and locale of the participants and of the incidents. There were four of these preliminary reports.

Report No. 1. This was a local Baltimore account, later picked up by the wire services but not extensively used. It related the passage of a 'fireball' over that city at 7.00 p.m. on the evening of Friday 12 September. It so happens that my assistant and I were driving into Baltimore that evening, and we met two people who had seen a slow-moving reddish object pass over from east to west. This was later described and 'explained' by a Mr P. M. Reese of the Maryland Academy of Sciences staff, as a 'fireball meteor'. He concluded—incorrectly, we believe—that it was 'travelling at a height of from sixty to seventy miles' and was about the 'size of your fist'. He further stated that it 'was burned out'. However, a similar, if not the same, object was seen over both Frederick and Hagerstown. Also, something comparable was reported about the same time from Kingsport, Tennessee, and from Wheeling and Parkersburg, in West Virginia.

Report No. 2. This was wire service material that was widely printed and commented upon. Its central theme was that a twelve-foot, man-shaped, green monster with bulging red eyes and 'clawy' hands had been seen on a hilltop near the small village of Flatwoods, five miles from the seat of Braxton County, West Virginia.

It stated that: (a) People were attracted to the hill by a 'meteor' that had passed over it about 7.15 p.m.

(b) This appeared to have landed and 'pulsed' with light.

(c) A group of seven people shone *a flashlight on it* and saw the 'monster'.

(d) A sheriff and others went to investigate the next morning, when there were still signs of 'a dreadful, sickening, hot, stuffy odour'.

(e) The first reporter on the scene, a Mr A. Lee Stewart, son of the owner of *The Braxton Democrat* of Sutton, emphatically did not think the people who witnessed all this were lying. However, he ends his report with, 'Of course, at twilight you can see a lot of things. They could have seen an owl sitting up there in a tree, and put a body under it.'

The significance of these accounts is that, although reporting something that apparently occurred, they were considerably inaccurate, as subsequent investigations on the spot have shown.

Report No. 3. This appeared in *The Braxton Democrat*, Mr Stewart's own paper, but does not carry his or any other by-line. This report more or less ignores the meteor-like object that passed over the village of Flatwoods and was observed by the youngsters who were playing football. These were Ronald Shaver, Theodore Neal and Neal Nunley. However, it states that since they thought it had landed on the hilltop they set off to investigate and, passing some houses, were joined by Mrs Kathleen May, her two sons, Edward and Theodore May, and seventeen-year-old Eugene Lemon. As they approached the place where they thought it had landed, they noticed a 'foggy mist' and a 'peculiar nauseating odour that had a tendency to burn their nostrils and throats.' At this point Eugene Lemon 'suddenly sighted a pair of eyes, shining through the fog'. He turned his flash on it, and they all saw 'a huge man-like creature. It was in the shape of a man with an oversized head of a fiery orange colour.'

They figured it was 'at least ten or twelve feet tall, and its eyes protruded and seemed to throw off beams of light.' They described the body as of a dark green colour and said the creature had small, claw-like hands that extended in front of it. Lemon seems to have fainted at this juncture, but then they all ran. Mrs May called the sheriff and road patrol, who were not available. Mr Stewart, however, 'went at once to the place and talked with each member of the party, receiving the same story from each one.' According to the published report also, he returned at seven o'clock the next morning and found 'two wide skid marks about ten or twelve feet apart and each about ten yards long, and trampled grass at each end. The odour still persisted on the grass when you got close to the ground, and there were grease marks on some spots.' These observations require careful analysis in view of the actual first-hand reports the boys gave us, and the matter of the smell and the grease.

Report No. 4. This comes from the rival paper in Sutton, *The Braxton Central*, which is owned, published, and edited by J. Holt Byrne. This story differs considerably from that of *The Braxton Democrat*. For instance, the *Central*'s account of this affair starts off by admitting that it was written 'almost a full week after the appearance on the hilltop'. However, it adds a great deal of new information, changes the spelling of the names of some of the participants and adds another. Its main thesis was that the people definitely did see something and that it could only be one of three things: (1) a man from another planet; (2) vapour from a falling meteorite that took the form of a man; (3) an omen of disaster.

It then refers to a 'meteor' that was visible that night over parts of Pennsylvania, Maryland, and West Virginia. It adds that this passed over Flatwoods at 7.15, and that one of the boys said that a flying saucer had landed and they were going to look at it. Mrs May joined them and they made a 'three-quarter mile trip up the hill' (Mr Stewart said three hundred yards). The actual distance was a mile and a bit from the football field, and eight hundred and fifty yards from Mrs May's house. The actual description obtained from Mrs May is very illuminating, and we quote:

'There suddenly appeared two lights resembling flashlights which seemed to be about a foot apart. One of the boys turned his flashlight on the lights and there stood a huge man about ten feet in height and four feet wide. It had a bright red face, bright green clothing, and a head which resembled the ace of spades, and its clothing from the waist down hung in great folds. It appeared to be moving towards us as if it were floating through the air.'

The report, written by Mr Byrne, adds that Sheriff Carr and his deputy Mr Burnell Long, were away investigating another landing of what a man named Woodrow Eagle described as 'a small Cub airplane' that he saw crash into a hillside beyond Gassaway while afire.

Analysis of the Reports

From the above reports two things are fairly clear. First, that something very unusual and normally inexplicable appears to have been seen by seven (and perhaps eight) people at Flatwoods, in Braxton County, West Virginia, about 7.15 p.m. on the evening of 12 September. Second, the details of what they saw and even of who saw the phenomenon have been confused. There are, however, a number of both important and worthwhile points that stand out. These may be summarized as follows:

(1) There were unexplained objects in the sky over Maryland and West Virginia, and possibly Pennsylvania, that night about sundown, which was at seven o'clock.

(2) Something that gave light landed at Flatwoods and another at Sugar Creek about 7.15 that evening.

(3) Seven or eight people inspected the former, at least five of them juveniles (this is very important).

(4) Somebody—Woodrow Eagle—saw something crash in flames on a wooded hillside at Sugar Creek, and was sufficiently convinced that it was a construction to call the sheriff, who investigated.

Beyond this nobody should be prepared to go on the evidence presented by these reports. Nevertheless, these four points are sufficiently strong, when taken in combination, to prompt any seasoned investigator to pay the location a visit. This we did, and what we encountered tells an almost entirely different and extremely peculiar story.

The 'Something' at Flatwoods

What we encountered when we got to Braxton County, West Virginia, was something quite other than that which we had expected. Everybody had seen the 'meteor' and heard about the 'monster' at Flatwoods. Most people appeared to take both reports at their face value. There were many who scoffed, but they usually concluded their remarks with the strange observation that 'I saw that meteor'. We interviewed and spoke to hundreds, and their stories were frankly amazing. We could not record them all and could not reproduce them had we done so, but their substance is as follows:

The Boys' Story. This is a composite of the stories given us by Neal Nunley, Edward and Theodore May, Ronald Shaver, Theodore Neal and Thomas Hyer.

Several of the boys were playing a game on the Flatwoods football field. At about 7.15 p.m. something glowing bright red, as large as a small outhouse, roundish and travelling at a slow speed, *came round the corner* of a hill (meteors don't go round corners), crossed the valley from north-west to south-east, and then paused in mid-air before dropping abruptly behind the crest of the hill. The boys watched this strange performance, and Neal Nunley (who was extraordinarily intelligent and well-informed) suggested that it might be a meteorite, any fallen parts of which, he said, he had been told in school should be collected for the State Geological Department. He therefore suggested they go to look. At this moment they were amazed to see a very bright orange light flare up behind the ridge of the hill and then fade away again to a dull, cherry-red glow. As they started forward up the route, they saw this light repeatedly and regularly flashing bright and dim with the same colours.

They had to run up the main road toward Sutton, cross the railway tracks, and climb a rough hill road to the corner where there are three houses, one occupied by the May family. As they reached this point (which takes ten full minutes), Mrs May came out on the porch and asked them where they were going, and Neal Nunley states that Ronald Shaver said, 'A flying saucer has landed on the hill and we're going to look at it.' He must have sounded convincing because Mrs May, who works as a beautician in Sutton, decided to accompany them along with her two sons, and asked them to wait while she had a visiting neighbour—Eugene Lemon—get a flashlight.

The party then set out up the grass pathway which leads along the crest of the ridge. Somewhere along this route little Tommy Hyer joined them.

The path leads along a fence to a five-bar gate closed by a stout chain and a heavy wire, marking the Bailey Fisher property. As good country folk, they unwired the gate, passed through, and then rewired it behind them, despite the fact that something was now clearly visible lying on the steep inner slope of the hill about fifty yards from the ridge crest, and pulsing with eerie light. They proceeded up the path, which makes four bends, and finally—Eugene Lemon and Neal Nunley in the lead—rounded the last bend through an abandoned gateway. The order of procession after Lemon and Nunley was Mrs May and one of her sons (Eddie), then Ronald Shaver and Teddie May, with Teddie Neal alongside, and trailing somewhere not far behind was Tommy Hyer. Eugene Lemon had taken his large dog with him, and this, running ahead, had first set up a terrible racket as it turned the last bend in the path. Then they met it streaking homeward, giving tongue. At the same time they noticed an unnatural mist that had spread all over the ground around the area. As they entered this mist, an atrocious, sickly, 'warm' smell like that of hot, greased metal—but overpowering—had assailed them. Their eyes began to water and their noses smarted.

As they rounded the last bend, Mrs May called out to Eugene Lemon that she saw a pair of eyes in an oak tree to the left ahead, saying there was either a possum or a racoon in the tree. She asked Neal Nunley, who said that he was carrying the torch, to flash it in that direction. When he did so, its light disclosed what one and all affirm—despite any published reports to the contrary—answers to the following des-

It was the size of an enormous man down to the waist . . . with a 'head'
shaped like the ace of spades.

cription. Each person added individual details, but the group was never in conflict.

The entity's top was level with a branch of the tree, and it seemed to end about some six feet below. It was about the size of an enormous man down to the waist. It did *not* have any arms or anything else sticking out of it, but it had a distinct 'head'. This was shaped like an 'ace of spades' (they all repeated this). However, this 'head' had a large circular window in it through which they could see (a) 'darkness' and (b) two 'things like eyes, which stayed fixed and shone straight out'. When further questioned about the latter, the witnesses agreed that these were two objects behind a translucent panel, that emitted light, pale blue in colour, in the form of direct, fixed beams of about the dimensions of a standard three-cell flashlight. These, they all said, were focused way above their heads and to the south, and only moved with the entity as it began to glide around. This it finally did, first towards them and then in the direction of an object which was still lying pulsing in the tall grass nearby.

There was no disagreement about the 'object', but a great deal of debate among the boys. All stated that it was there, plainly visible from the time they rounded the corner at the May house, and that it continued to pulse from a dull cherry glow to a vivid orange emanation that first caused them to spot the 'eyes' in the tree. But they disagreed violently on their interpretation of this object. All said it was about the size of an outhouse behind the May residence (which proved to be over twenty feet across), and that it was also shaped like the ace of spades with the point reaching skyward. They also agreed that it was black. Pressed on this point, Ronald Shaver came up with the remark (unprompted) that it was 'obviously black, really, but as it was hot, it was getting red like a hot poker.' Leading from this, we asked if it *was* hot, as they had been within fifty feet of it. Their amazing reply, after much debate among themselves, was that it had *not* been so, though the whole general area seemed to be unnaturally warm and certainly hotter than the rest of the hillside. This puzzled them more than it did us. (Later, and at *our* suggestion, they agreed that it seemed more like a neon sign.)

When he saw the entity, Lemon 'passed out'. There was general confusion, but some of the boys hauled him to his feet and then, as the thing advanced toward them with a gliding motion as if afloat in mid-air, they all ran. To us, a significant statement made by the boys was that 'Mrs May cleared that there gate in one. Don't know how she did it, but she did.' We don't know either: its top bar reached my chin and I stand exactly six feet. Ronald Shaver is unable to say whether he jumped or climbed it, or went under, through, or around it!

There is only one thing that may be added. The party fled to the May house and administered restoratives to Mr Lemon. They also called other adults who rather reluctantly, it seems, formed a posse and, carrying guns, went up the hill. As Neal Nunley told me, they were back in twenty-five minutes stating they had searched the place and found nothing. He pointed out that it later had taken us—about a dozen of us—three hours to search the field, and in broad daylight!

The sheriff did arrive that evening, about two hours later. But according to the boys, he scoffed at the whole story and refused even to go up the hill. Three hours later two reporters arrived. (One must have been Mr Stewart.) They did go up the hill, but saw nothing, though they noted the same powerful, metallic stench.

Subsequent Investigation. The following day many persons visited the area. They found a fifteen-foot circular area in the tall grass of the field at the point where the object was said to have landed and lain. Here the grass was completely flattened and the ground depressed, and still was when we arrived a week later.

Otherwise, there was no substantial material evidence. Mr Stewart stated that he had found two 'skid marks'. But we could not find these when we arrived, nor could any of the boys point them out to us.

Everybody drew our attention to a strange smell in the grass. I still cannot place it, but it is a fairly common odour in organic chemistry laboratories and is almost surely derived from a kind of grass that abounds in the area. We found this grass growing all over the county and it always smelt the same, though not perhaps quite as strongly.

Everyone also pointed out an 'oily substance still on the grass'. There may have been such, but all we could find was a natural sticky exudate produced by the same grass, known locally as 'tar-grass'. This leaves a dark, sticky substance on the hands.

The boys, however, showed us one other thing that seemed to puzzle them. They showed us an area on the crest of the ridge where a patch or strip of vegetation seemed suddenly to have turned brown

297

while the rest of the foliage had not. This was immediately above where the object had landed. What is more, some of the leaves of a vine which we picked there seemed to have been burned all around the edge, rather than to have died from the stem out as others had done nearby. However, this might well have been evidence of a fungoid disease.

The most significant fact of all, however, was the path of the object as it fell. It could not have been a meteorite or anything else following a trajectory from free fall. Had it been, it would have hit at another point and either stayed there or rolled on down the slope. It must, therefore, have stopped in mid-air and deliberately landed vertically.

The Sugar Creek Incident

The facts of this event, which must have occurred at almost the same, if not identical, time but some ten miles to the south-west of Flatwoods, are quite different.

Woodrow Eagle's Story. Mr Eagle, who lives at a place named Duck Creek, five miles from Gassaway, was driving to Sutton. At a point some three miles south-west of Gassaway, he saw a flaming object, which he thought from his army experience to be a small Piper Cub plane, shoot out over a saddle to his left, cross the main road, the river, and the rail line beyond, and crash into the wooded side of a steep hill immediately to the south.

So struck was he with this 'accident' that he turned his car about and drove back to the nearest house, that of Anderson Hughes. He, however, did not have a telephone, so Mr Eagle drove back another two miles to a gasoline station, and there phoned the sheriff in Sutton.

Then he retraced his steps and went on to Gassaway, where he was to meet his sister. Picking her up with her husband, he drove them back to the place where the incident had occurred. By then it was dark, and he saw lights moving about on the hill beyond the river. As there was no boat available, they went on their way, believing that the sheriff had started to investigate.

It later turned out that the sheriff had not crossed the river, and that the lights were probably carried by fox hunters, who just happened by. In fact the matter was never investigated by anybody until we arrived.

Subsequent Investigation. We made the best attempt possible to investigate the hill at Sugar Creek, but the terrain was difficult. The first cliff rose about eight hundred feet almost perpendicularly. There was a mile-long saddle above, and two five hundred foot hills beyond.

On the comparatively open saddle above the cliff, we found three shallow holes. Beyond each of these, there were wedge-shaped spatters of a strange white substance in small, curled cylinders. This, at first, looked to use like dried snake or turtle eggshell, but we collected some and had it subjected to X-ray and general chemical analysis. It proved to have three layers, the outer smooth, the inner rough, the central, columnar in structure as far as could be ascertained. It contained arago-nite, and the whole was porous, which would seem to agree with the description of a reptile eggshell. However, one piece that we soaked and softened measured six and a half inches when unrolled, and this seems excessive for any North American reptilian eggshell.

Friends from Charleston, under the direction of Earl Walter, went back a week later and searched some more but found only a large tree that had fallen down, bringing other vegetation with it. This they thought might have created a large dust cloud, since the ground was dry.

A man who lived in a house across the river from the point where the object struck was extremely sceptical of the whole affair. But he then calmly stated that he had seen the 'meteor'. Another man, an exceed-ingly solid-looking farmer, told us that he and others had been puzzled by smoke that had hung about the face of the hill in question on the evening of 12 September, and he remarked that there had been 'a strong smell of the woods burning'. Further, he also stated that his brother, who lived on a farm above the road, had that night seen the flaming object come around a low hill opposite him, *horizontally* and below its crest, making a neat turn, and then go into the valley where Mr Eagle said he saw it crash. He described it as like a 'flaming bucket with a tail'.

Other Sightings

The other reports would be of little more consequence than the usual 'flying saucer sightings' were it not for the remarkable pattern that they display:

(1) a bright globular object was seen passing fairly slowly through the sky at low altitude and at the same time as the others, slightly to the east of the settlement known as Heaters, five miles north of Flatwoods.

This was allegedly seen by several people along a line to the south-east and to a point about due east of Sutton.

(2) An exactly similar object was said to have passed over Sutton Airport at the same time.

(3) Again a similar object was reported to have landed on James' Knoll or Knob, about three miles south-east of the small community of Frametown, in a pasture at the top of a hill surrounded by woods.

(4) Still another slow-moving, low-flying, glowing object was seen west of Charleston by Alice Williams, travelling in the same direction but disintegrating in the air with a rain of ashes.

There is no need to discuss this further. A glance at a map ought to be sufficient to demonstrate at least one highly significant fact: all of the objects were travelling in the same direction and apparently at the same speed and at exactly the same time. Five of them were just five miles away from their colleagues on either side. The Charleston specimen was just seven times this distance to the west of the Frametown example.

Is this, then, evidence of some natural force or of integrated intelligent manoeuvring? And manoeuvring it was, for at least two of them (the Flatwoods and Sugar Creek specimens) were described as *having rounded hills below their crests.*

Conclusions

In view of the initial reports and our own first-hand investigations, and more especially as a result of plotting the incidents on a map, we are of the opinion that a flight of intelligently controlled objects flew over West Virginia on the evening of 12 September 1952, and further, that one of them landed or crashed, a second and third crashed, and a fourth blew up in the air. If we are to be logical about this affair we would say that a flight of aerial machines, manoeuvring in formation, initially came in over the Eastern seaboard from the Atlantic at about seven o'clock, passed over Baltimore travelling north-west, then veered around and headed back over central West Virginia fifteen minutes later, from the north-west to south-east. Something went wrong and they began to go out of control.

The one that reached Flatwoods *landed*, rather than crashed, and its 'pilot' or 'occupant' managed to get out before it disintegrated. He or 'it' did so in a space-suit or the equivalent of our deep-sea diving bells,

300

regulated to counteract gravity by adjustment to the density of air at ground level. It then moved to the highest point available, either to scout out the land or to look for its colleagues. It was caught in the act by the seven human beings, but, being 'fixed' in a pressurized suit, when it 'saw' that it had been observed, it headed back to its 'ship'. However, either it, its suit, or both were already disintegrating for one of several reasons—either too great local heat, too great cold, or through contact with hostile chemical structures (silicones with hydro-carbons, for instance).

This would explain a number of, if not all, the oddities of the case. If this object at Flatwoods was at a different temperature than the sur-face of our earth when it landed, after heating up by friction while passing through our atmosphere, it might have warmed up too rapidly and thus started to glow. As it began to melt, it gave rise to the gaseous form of whatever it may have been constructed—as dry ice does. This caused the mist and the stench. It rapidly dissolved altogether, which ex-plains its disappearance before the first posse arrived at the hill crest. Its intelligent entity could not cope with our environment except in a diving suit, which was itself disintegrating.

The other constructions that crashed at Sugar Creek and at James' Knoll in Frametown similarly vapourized. That near Charleston burned up in mid-air, possibly due to carbonaceous material in the lower atmosphere.

If this is not the explanation, then sombody has to explain two things, namely: (a) what did the people see at Flatwoods? and (b) what happened to it?

DARK RENDEZVOUS

John Agee

The dark-haired man's eyes seemed to glitter in the candlelight, almost as though he was laughing. But he wasn't.

He was dead, and the neat, riny, red-rimmed hole in the centre of his forehead testified to this fact.

He lay slumped across the rickety table, his head at an angle, one side against the dark surface, so that his eyes were gazing directly across the room. His left arm was flung over the table-top in front of him; his right arm dangled to the floor, a revolver lying on the stone flags just out of reach of the nerveless fingers.

The dead eyes stared up at Meissen, and Meissen stared back, frowning, his hands deep in the pockets of his long coat. There was a sardonic expression on the man's face, as though he was enjoying a private joke. Perhaps, thought Meissen, he was.

Still . . . it was a mess. Meissen wasn't sure what to do. This man's death had changed things drastically. There was no knowing how von Kessering would react to the news . . . what steps he would take. But one thing was for sure—unless this was handled very carefully the whole plan, built up painstakingly over three years, would be destroyed.

Meissen felt that he was on the edge of an abyss . . . that he was staring disaster straight in the face. Literally, as well as metaphorically. He leaned forward over the table and stretched out a hand, gently closing the dead man's eyes.

As he did so, he heard the clack of the gate outside the cottage. For two seconds he stood stock-still, then, turning to one side, he blew out the candle.

Instantly, the room was plunged into darkness. Meissen stooped and gathered up the dead man's revolver from under the table, then reached for his own attaché-case, which he'd left beside the table. He straightened as he heard footsteps crunching up the path, and moved silently across the dusty floor towards the window.

Presently, the man—whoever he was—must turn the corner of the cottage and come into view. Luckily, this window did not look out directly on to the front path, and Meissen hoped that the newcomer had glimpsed the light of the candle through the trees and was simply coming to investigate. If that was the case, now the candle was out the man might think he'd just made a mistake.

Meissen happened to know—because he'd made it his business to know—that this old cottage had been empty for six months or more. That was why he'd pointed it out to von Kessering in the first place as being the ideal spot for the first rendezvous.

Von Kessering was a stickler for caution. He had to be. One slip, and he might find himself, early one foggy morning, standing against a stone wall in the Tower of London with a blindfold over his eyes and half a dozen rifles trained on his heart.

So, although the third and final rendezvous, this hot late-summer night, was amongst the rolling dunes two miles away, and the second was the bar of the inn half a mile down the road, this first rendezvous was the most important in terms of safety. Whoever entered it would know at a glance whether it was dangerous to continue on to the second rendezvous.

Meissen's plan had been simplicity itself. Anyone not in on it would never suspect that the table and chair in this otherwise bare room (the only sticks of furniture that still remained in the empty cottage) constituted a message . . . or a warning.

If the chair was standing upright beside the table, it was safe to continue on to the inn. If, on the other hand, the chair was lying on the floor, there was danger, and each member of the group had instructions to return to the safe house in London with all speed.

Von Kessering's group had come down from London singly, in a pre-arranged order. Meissen had been last to arrive. He had moved silently through the overgrown garden at the rear, crept along the passage and opened the door—to find himself in a candlelit room, staring straight at Hammell's sardonic face. It had been quite a shock.

Meissen was thinking about all this when the sound of the footsteps outside ceased. A bulky figure blotted out the stars. Meissen flattened himself against the wall, Hammell's revolver gripped in his right hand, hardly daring to breathe.

He could now see the man quite plainly: a fat and red-cheeked farmer, dressed in thick tweeds, a perplexed expression on his face as he peered through the broken panes.

The man grunted, and then turned away. Meissen heard him muttering 'Could've sworn I saw . . .' before he trudged round the corner of the building and his footsteps faded.

Meissen smiled. He knew well enough what the man had thought he'd seen: light, shining through the trees.

But he hadn't been sure. And now that he'd found there was no light coming from this seemingly deserted cottage, he'd gone away . . . satisfied that he'd made a mistake.

Meissen felt that things couldn't have panned out better. He opened his coat and stuck Hammell's revolver down inside his shirt, then glanced around the room once more.

The light from the moon outside only reached a few feet beyond the window; the rest of the room was in darkness. But he could just see Hammell's body sprawled across the table in the centre, a deeper shade of black than the rest, with a whitish blob for the face.

For a moment, it seemed to Meissen that those lids opened and the dead eyes came to life, staring across at him intently. He shivered.

But it was only a trick of the light—or the darkness. He turned and, still gripping his attaché-case, stealthily opened the window, hitching a leg across the sill. Hammell was dead and there was an end to it. It was a real spanner in the works, but doubtless he could overcome it and set the machinery of this colossal scheme back into smooth motion.

He made his way across the front of the house, parallel with the path. The gate had been left open by the inquisitive farmer, but Meissen didn't bother going out that way. Instead, he pushed his way through the tangled hedge, jumped a ditch, landed on the road—and stood stock-still for the second time in five minutes.

Two hundred yards ahead, where the road curved round and vanished under overhanging trees, stood the figure of the farmer, holding a bicycle by its handlebars and staring back suspiciously along the moonlit way.

Meissen set his case down on the road, fumbled in an inside pocket and brought out a battered pipe and some matches. He lit up, his hands shaking, and began to walk slowly along the road towards the stocky, tweed-suited figure.

Then, as he tossed the spent match aside and puffed smoke, the farmer suddenly turned, mounted his bicycle and rode off round the corner into the deeper shadows of the trees.

Meissen let out a gusty sigh of relief and mopped his brow. First Hammell and now this. Things were getting a bit too hectic.

The moon, so clear before, was now beginning to be threatened by ragged clouds piling up from the west and sailing across the sky like tattered galleons after a battle. Meissen heard the faint mutter of thunder. The heat of the summer night was approaching furnace level.

Meissen cursed under his breath. This was going to disorganize things . . . and might even destroy von Kessering's plans altogether.

On the other hand, perhaps a storm might be the perfect cover for the arrival of the submarine—the submarine that was to disgorge twenty of the most brilliant agents of the German Secret Service onto the shores of Britain, ready to start their deadly work of espionage, sabotage and the destruction of the British way of life.

Ready for the war that must be only hours away.

Meissen smiled wolfishly. Von Kessering's plan must not fail. Whatever happened—despite the death of Hammell, and the interference of that fool of a farmer—it must succeed.

Meissen set off down the road, heading for the second rendezvous.

The inn lay to one side of a crossroads, its frontage looking out over the dunes towards the dark sea a quarter of a mile away.

Ragged moonlight shone fitfully down on its chimneys and gables and creaking sign. In the old days, it had been a haven for smugglers running brandy and lace in from France and Germany. Now only farmers, and the villagers from the hamlet a mile inland, ever drank there.

And spies, thought Meissen grimly, as he strode towards its lighted windows.

He pushed open the front door and instantly coughed at the heavy smoke-laden atmosphere that was so thick it was almost substantial. Heads turned from the bar—jovial, bovine faces regarding him without curiosity—and then the drinkers turned back to the serious business of the evening. A stranger was nothing to get worked up about in this part of Suffolk.

Meissen spotted von Kessering almost immediately. A big man with a beard, he was roaring with laughter at something the landlord was saying to him. Meissen turned his head. He saw Gossler playing darts with a group of locals, and grinning with delight as he threw three double-tops in succession. Heine was sitting next to an old woman in the fireside inglenook and beaming with goodwill as he bought the old crone another gin.

Meissen wondered, as he threaded his way through the packed room, how long the smiles of his colleagues would stay on their faces when they heard the news about Hammell.

He also wondered how these country yokels would react if they discovered that among their number was a group of highly dangerous German spies.

Von Kessering saw him first.

'Good Lord! If it isn't old Alf Blake!' the big man said, dragging Meissen to the bar. 'Bit of luck, old boy! What'll you have? You doing the coast for your firm, too?'

Meissen nodded amiably. Each of them could move about the country unhindered as commercial travellers. It was the perfect cover for their sinister activities.

He plumped his case on the bar and said 'Pint of old-and-mild'; then, as the landlord turned away, he muttered 'Trouble!' out of the corner of his mouth.

Von Kessering's expression did not change.

He was a true professional. He had lived in England for more than ten years, digging himself deeper and deeper into the fabric of society with each passing year. He was head of a spy-ring whose tentacles reached into every part of English life, and yet he looked more English than the landlord of the pub, who was even now pushing forward a foaming tankard across the bar . . . more English than the yokel standing next to him . . . more English than the red-faced man in the tweed suit who was——

Meissen looked away quickly, appalled. What cursed luck! The farmer had been coming here!

He had to act fast. There must be no more slip-ups. The man had recognized him and was clearly suspicious; he was obviously thinking that maybe he hadn't been mistaken after all; that maybe there had been a light in that empty cottage; that maybe this man in the long coat, who had suddenly appeared on the road outside the cottage and now shown up here at the inn, was up to no good. Any moment now he'd start asking awkward questions, and that didn't suit Meissen's book at all. He had to be silenced.

Meissen picked up his case again and caught the man's eye. He smiled, waved in a friendly fashion, and pushed his way through the crowd.

The man stared at him, frowning. Luckily, he was near one of the side doors. Meissen flung an arm round his shoulders.

'Something I've got to see you about, old man!'

The farmer gaped at him.

'Now look here . . .'

Meissen propelled him towards the door, and through it, babbling the first thing that came into his head. Outside, it was hotter than ever, and the moon was completely obscured. The man in the tweed suit said 'What's this all about?' angrily, and Meissen, his right hand inside his coat, thrust the attaché-case at him with his left.

'Hold this. Quickly.'

The man took it automatically.

'What . . .?'

That was the last thing he said. Meissen withdrew his right hand, which now held his revolver. He pushed the man round, and clubbed him hard behind his left ear with the barrel. The farmer gave a grunt and crumpled to the ground.

Light suddenly spilled out on to the small inn-yard, and Meissen turned, his revolver levelled at the door. Von Kessering stood in the doorway.

With a quick movement, the big man slammed the door shut and strode forward.

'What the devil's going on?'

Meissen stuffed his revolver into his coat pocket and dragged the tweed-suited man into the deeper shadows to one side of the yard.

'Hammell's dead,' he said. 'Shot through the head, in the cottage. This fool spotted me outside in the road, and I was afraid he was going to start asking questions. We must move fast, Herr von Kessering!'

The big man's eyes narrowed to slits. 'Hammell's death only goes to prove what I have suspected for some time, Meissen. We have a traitor in our midst—someone who has been systematically betraying us to the British for months!'

The four men trudged across the sand dunes. It was very still, and hot, and close. Each of them was sweating profusely. No breeze came in from the sea.

The night was full of sounds: the crash of surf on their left; the mutter and grumble of thunder overhead; their own harsh, laboured breathing as they scrambled up and over the wind-sculpted heaps of soft sand.

'There!' said Meissen, suddenly pointing.

Ahead was a narrow beach, just visible in the darkness. There were low cliffs on the opposite side, but here the dunes ran right down to the sand.

'Well done, Meissen,' said von Kessering. He turned to Gossler. 'It looks as though we shall have to use Plan Two after all . . .'

Meissen frowned. He had never heard of it. 'Plan Two . . .?'

Von Kessering shook his head. 'Merely a precautionary measure, my friend.'

They jumped down on to the beach, and the bearded man took out his watch. Lightning flickered, revealing the sea stretching out before them. Von Kessering opened the bag he'd been carrying and took out a lamp.

'It is nearly time. But before I signal, we must clear up this matter of the traitor. War is nearly upon us—a war in which we will utterly smash England and her allies. But we all know that battles are not only fought by armies on the ground and ships on the high seas. Our fight is, if anything, more important . . . more significant . . . than the thunderous clash of mighty armies. We are a secret army. Our weapons are sabotage and assassination behind the lines—anything that can be used to sap the civilian morale of our enemy!'

'And for three years we have been sowing the seed,' added Meissen, nodding. 'Now we can reap the harvest.'

'Precisely, my dear Meissen. But there is a tare among the wheat. I who used to scoff at the British Secret Service must now admit to the fact that they are perhaps more cunning than I suspected. That there is a traitor among us is not open to question. The question is—who is this cur? For months, our agents in the field have been disappearing. Our supposedly safe houses have been raided. We are on the brink of disaster, and before our top men can be landed from the submarine that is, even now, waiting out there, this swine must be rooted out. Fortunately,' he paused, and glanced round at the three men who were gazing at him intently, 'fortunately, I not only know who this man is, but have taken steps to curtail his activities . . . permanently.'

Meissen's eyes flicked round at the other two. Who did von Kessering have in mind?

The bearded man nodded suddenly. 'Yes, Gossler. Now!'

Gossler's right hand came out of his pocket, and Meissen saw the glitter of steel. He tensed, then gasped—as Gossler turned and, in one swift movement, thrust the knife at Heine.

Heine gave a choking cry, his hands grasping at the knife in his chest. He fell to the sand and lay on one side, a crumpled figure in the gloom.

'So perish all traitors,' muttered Gossler. 'The swine can keep my knife, Herr von Kessering. It's good German steel will be defiled by his blood!'

'Heine?' said Meissen. 'It . . . it seems incredible.'

Von Kessering's face was bleak. 'I have been watching him for some time now, my friend. He was the last to join our little group, but there is no doubt that he has been in the pay of the British for years.'

Gossler laughed hoarsely. 'We have just saved his paymasters much money!'

Von Kessering turned towards the sea. He held the lamp up and began

Heine gave a choking cry, his hands grasping at the knife in his chest.

to signal. The two men behind him watched as the seconds ticked by, and the night remained dark. Then, suddenly, far out to sea, they saw a flicker of light.

'Good!' said von Kessering, putting down the lamp. 'They are on their way. The journey will have to be done in relays, since the submarine will only have two dinghies and there are twenty men to land. But as soon as the operation is over, Meissen, we can start heading across country towards the covered truck that you have left in the spot we agreed.'

'To be perfectly honest,' said Meissen, 'no.'

His revolver was in his hand. It was pointing at von Kessering and Gossler. The bearded man's face was impassive. 'No?' he said softly.

Meissen shook his head.

'No truck where we agreed. But plenty of trucks on the road just over the dunes from here. All ready and waiting . . . for you and Gossler, and twenty of your countrymen.'

Von Kessering nodded slowly. He did not seem surprised.

'So you were the tare in the wheat, Meissen,' he said.

'Mason, actually,' said the man with the revolver. 'A good name, though: Meissen. I chose it because it was so close to my own that I didn't have to think twice about answering to it.'

In contrast to von Kessering's impassive features, Gossler's face was dark with rage. 'Traitorous scum!' he cried.

'Hardly. Simply doing my job, which was to infiltrate your group and destroy it. We could see there was going to be a war years ago. We were prepared. The capture of twenty top men will be the British Secret Service's greatest coup.' A brief smile flickered across his face. 'I'll admit that when I entered the cottage an hour ago, I wasn't prepared to find Hammell waiting for me, with a gun in his hand. He tried to shoot me, but I was faster. I thought the game was up, but then figured that perhaps it was only Hammell who was suspicious of me.

'I decided to go ahead with my original plan. That farmer had me worried. I had to out him to stop him blabbing in the crowded bar. The whole object of the exercise has been to capture the agents from the submarine, and I didn't want anything to foul that up. The poor chap will have a headache when he wakes up, but doubtless he'll agree it was worth it when we tell him why I had to hit him. But now your

311

agents are on their way I can relax slightly. This whole area is ringed by our men; you're caught like rats in a trap. One revolver shot is my signal, and after that, von Kessering, it's the Tower for you, and a short eight o'clock walk in the morning.' He frowned. 'You were wrong about Heine, though. He wasn't the rotten apple in the barrel.'

'Correct, Englander,' said Heine's voice behind him.

Mason half-swung round and glimpsed the flash of steel. Then he went over sideways as the hurled knife slammed between his ribs.

'His gun!' hissed von Kessering, panic rising in his voice. 'He mustn't fire it!'

But Gossler was already springing forward. He jabbed down with the side of his hand at Mason's wrist, and the gun fell to the sand. As Mason collapsed, gasping, Gossler scooped it up.

The British agent lay hunched sideways in the sand. Everything was going round and round: the mocking faces of the three Germans looking down at him; the sky; even the soft surface he was lying on felt like a swiftly-moving carousel.

'Too bad, Mason,' said von Kessering. 'You see, I win in the end. Although you joined us three years ago with excellent credentials, I knew you had to be the spy when things began to go wrong. Hammell, Heine and Gossler were hand-picked by me, and you weren't. I set Hammell on to you, but when you appeared at the inn, I realized something had gone wrong. Fortunately, I had a contingency plan—Plan Two, remember? Heine is a good play-actor, isn't he? And now I can signal the dinghies that the operation has been aborted for the moment, and we three will fade away—leaving you to die, and your colleagues to await a signal that will never come.'

Mason had never known such pain before. It washed through him in fierce stabbing waves. Things were beginning to get blurred . . . hazy. He made a last effort . . . his fingers scrabbling at his chest. Blood ran down from the corners of his mouth as he mumbled half-deliriously.

'What's he saying?' snapped von Kessering, leaning over.

'Wrong . . .' The dying man gave a croaking laugh. 'Can signal . . . Hammell's . . . gun . . .'

Von Kessering stiffened. 'No!' he gasped.

But Mason was already clawing at the weapon he'd jammed down his shirt. The big weapon bucked and roared once, its heavy calibre bullet punching von Kessering backwards. An instant later, the small beach was awash with light as brilliant sodium flares soared high, ripping the hot darkness of the night apart.

The man in the colonel's uniform sucked thoughtfully at his pipe.

'A good show, sir,' he said.

His companion, a meek-looking man in civilian clothes, nodded. He was polishing a pair of glasses with a handkerchief.

'I'm thankful we got the sub,' he said. 'Good of them to surrender it intact.'

'Didn't have much choice when our gunboat came round the headland. Pity about Mason, though. He did a damn fine job.'

The civilian looked down at the huddled figure at their feet. 'Yes,' he concurred. 'A great pity.'

A captain hurried up, waving a piece of paper. The colonel glanced at it, his lips pulled back behind the stem of his pipe in a mirthless smile.

'It's come, sir,' he said. 'We've got a busy time in front of us.'

The civilian nodded again. 'We're ahead now,' he said. 'Mason gave us a breathing-space. There'll be other Germans . . . other spies. We must make sure we stay ahead.' He pulled a silver Hunter watch from the fob pocket of his waistcoat, looked at it, and sighed.

It was 11.50 p.m. on the night of 3 August 1914.

The terrible conflict that was to become known as the Great War had been in progress for precisely forty-five minutes. Though he never knew it, and though the fact never went down in the record-books . . . the man called Mason was its first casualty.

THE HOODOO SHIP

K. Alan Macdonald

The first British steamship, the *Charlotte Dundas*, first puffed its way along the still waters of the Forth and Clyde Canal. It was a moment of great excitement in that year of 1802 for, spurred on by shouts and cheers from the people on the bank, the tiny vessel gallantly pulled two barges, each laden with seventy tons of cargo. Although there was a strong head-wind, the *Charlotte Dundas* covered nearly twenty miles in six hours! History had been made.

Yet, curiously, no one in Britain was prepared to support the inventor, William Symington, when he wished to build similar vessels or another British inventor, Henry Bell, who also wished to build steamships. It was left to an American inventor and engineer, Robert Fulton of Pennsylvania, to come to Britain and carefully examine the *Charlotte Dundas*. He was excited with what he saw and, on returning home, built the *Clermont*. This was a twin-paddle, steam-driven ferry boat which in 1807 began to carry passengers on the river between New York and Albany. Thus the *Clermont*, thanks to the lack of interest among British shipbuilders, was destined to become the world's first commercial steamship.

News of the success of the *Clermont* reached Britain and at last the British shipbuilding industry awoke to the possibilities of ships driven by steam. The first passenger-carrying steamer was Bell's *Comet*, which began to ply between Glasgow and Helensburgh.

Steamship companies sprung up and bigger and better steamships were built. The first ship to cross the Atlantic using steam was an American vessel, the *Savannah*, sailing from the port of the same name on 24 May 1819 and anchoring off Liverpool just under a month later. Much of the time, however, she relied on her sails. The first ship to complete the east to west Atlantic crossing relying almost entirely on her engines was the Liverpool-built *Royal William*, sailing on 5 July 1838 from Liverpool for New York.

The Americans led in the field of steam-driven ships until one of Britain's—and the world's—greatest engineers, Isambard Kingdom Brunel, decided to do something about it. He had already designed a successful transatlantic liner called the *Great Western*, and now felt it was time to build a ship that would astonish the world.

His creation was the *Great Eastern*, a ship which has been said to be 'born out of her time'.

Brunel intended her to be a super-ship in every way. She would be at least *five* times larger than anything afloat and would use new methods of building which, in many ways, are similar to those used today, well over a century later.

She was built on the Thames, at Millwall, and took four years to build. Work went on normally except for one strange incident. One morning in 1856 a woman came to the dock gates and asked why her husband, a master shipwright, had not come home as usual the night before. The chief engineer was sent for and a search was made among the men. The man was nowhere to be found and his anxious wife had to return home, hoping against hope that, somehow and sometime, he would return.

The work went on and, by November 1857, the great ship was ready for launching. She made a fine sight as she lay on two huge cradles, ready to slide sideways down into the Thames. Her gross tonnage was nearly 19,000; she was 680 feet long and 80 feet across; she had five funnels and six masts. On either side were two huge paddle-wheels each 56 feet in diameter, and at the stern was a 24-foot screw—one

The cheering slowly died away, giving place to an awe-struck silence.

which her designer claimed would develop at least 5,000 horse power.

She was truly a giant in every respect.

The great day arrived and she was ready to slip into the river. To make sure that both cradles moved at the same speed, a great ram was built behind each. Strong hawsers also ran from the ship to the opposite bank, where two steam engines were waiting to haul on them and keep the ship moving smoothly. Enormous crowds flocked to Millwall; everywhere there were gay flags and bunting; toppers and fashionable bonnets mingled with cloth caps and shawls. The whole occasion had a carnival air. Many famous people, including Brunel, were seated on a raised platform ready to watch the largest ship the world had ever seen take to the water.

A bottle of champagne dashed against her side, the chairman's young daughter named her the *Great Eastern*, and amid a great cheer her massive bulk began to move. Then the cheering slowly died away, giving place to an awe-struck silence as, halfway down the slips, the monstrous ship stuck fast. One cradle had moved faster than the other and the ship lay motionless, her stern nearer the water than the bows.

The crowd waited patiently until high water, when the two steam engines on the other bank began to chug. Still the ship stuck fast. Then one of the hawsers broke. As darkness fell, the disappointed crowds slowly dispersed. Many felt that the incident was an unhappy omen of things to come. One man was overheard saying, 'It's flying in the face of nature building a ship that size. Mark my words, no good will come of it. She's a *hoodoo ship*!'

All kinds of methods were used to try and free the *Great Eastern*, but without success. Then, quite suddenly, after three months stuck on the launching ways, she quietly floated off. It was the last day of January 1858. But all this time the word hoodoo had been frequently heard. There was obviously some mystery surrounding the huge vessel. But what was it? That was something no one could answer.

Those three months delay had cost £120,000. By then she had bankrupted her owners and Brunel had died from a stroke brought on by worry.

Over a year later the *Great Eastern* was still lying in the Thames, waiting for someone to buy her. Finally the Great Ship Company bought her for £160,000—a quarter of what she had cost to build. She moved from the Thames down to the Solent, where she made her trial voyage in September 1859. Once again she proved herself a hoodoo ship. An explosion in one of her two engine-rooms killed six firemen. It was not until June of the following year that she made her maiden voyage. By then her reputation had become so bad, even before she sailed, that few were brave enough to make the crossing. She had accommodation for four thousand passengers—but only forty brave souls were willing to risk travelling on her to America.

Even as she entered the Atlantic her troubles began. A huge sea tore away one of her paddle-wheels, her rudder-stock went adrift and as night fell she lay wallowing helplessly in heavy seas. During that night some of the crew broke into the ship's store and stole a large number of bottles of spirits. This so alarmed the captain that he armed the male passengers and divided them into deck patrols, while the female passengers huddled together all night and sang hymns!

The next day the captain forced a now-sober crew to work hard at the necessary repairs. These were done, and with a burst of speed that surprised everyone—nearly fifteen knots—the *Great Eastern* reached

317

New York on June 28. The crowds waiting to greet her were so astonished at her vast size that 143,764 people paid fifty cents each to be shown round her. She was, after all, the largest ship in the world.

Ill-luck still seemed to pursue her, however. When she reached Southampton on her return voyage, her captain died.

She was to make several Atlantic crossings, but each proved financially disastrous. Then, when it seemed as if she would end her days as a floating 'white elephant', fortune briefly smiled on her. She was taken over to be used as a cable-laying ship. Indeed, she was the only ship large enough to carry the 2,500 miles of cable needed to span the Atlantic.

She steamed from the Medway in Kent on 24 June 1865 with 4,600 tons of cable and 7,000 tons of coal on board, to arrive in a cove off Valentia Harbour, Ireland. The shore-end of the cable was brought ashore and the Secretary for Ireland made his official speech: 'We are about to lay down at the very bottom of the mighty Atlantic, which beats against your shore with everlasting pulsations, this silver-toned zone to join the United Kingdom to America . . .'

Despite his fine words, the first attempt was a failure. The mysterious hoodoo that surrounded the *Great Eastern* persisted. Cables broke, the sea became rough, fog slowed down the work. The whole effort was something of a disaster and it looked as if, once again, the unfortunate ship's career was ended. Then, in March 1866, a new company, Anglo-American Telegraph, was formed, and they promised to raise the old cable and lay a new one. Although there were several near-accidents, this venture was a success. After two weeks the *Great Eastern* steamed into the harbour of Heart's Content, Newfoundland, and a day later the shore-end was landed. Finally, by 8 September, the great vessel steamed back into Heart's Content and two cables snaked across the Atlantic to join Ireland with Canada.

In all the *Great Eastern* was to lay five transatlantic cables. In 1870 she rounded the Cape of Good Hope with 4,000 miles of cable and a tremendous tonnage of coal, a total deadweight of nearly 16,000 tons— which was little short of her own tonnage.

After successfully laying the Bombay-Aden cable link to Europe there was no more work for her and she was laid up for eleven years. During that time, Brunel's masterpiece was reduced to being a floating

318

amusement park, with all kinds of entertainments on board and with huge and gaudy advertising slogans painted along her sides.

They say that ships have a heart. What indignities she, the world's largest and most advanced ship, must have suffered if that is true.

The *Great Eastern* was finally towed away to be broken up in 1888. Her great iron hull proved tremendously strong, and it took the ship-breakers three years to demolish it. Towards the end workmen made a gruesome discovery. When the double bottom was ripped open they found a human skeleton. By its side, rusted after thirty years of neglect, lay a kit of tools. It was the master shipwright whose widow had inquired after him all those years before and whose disappearance no one could understand. He must have been sealed by accident in his living tomb by his workmates, and his cries gone unheard.

Was he the 'Jonah', the reason for the great ship's series of strange misfortunes?

THE 'AMERICAN COLONEL'
Edwin T. Woodhall

My association with the American Secret Service began in April 1917.

It was at the Gare des Voyageurs, Le Havre. The American Intelligence Department at that time was new to France and its system of counter-espionage. In consequence, the British Intelligence deputed selected men to work with, advise, and aid the Americans until they had entrenched themselves and commenced active operations.

They soon mastered the intricacies of counter-espionage in their thorough, practical, business-like way. I have the highest regard for American methods in espionage. I liked their clean-cut method of elimination. They always appeared so cool, so skilful and so careful.

As master in the game of human intrigue, where it is check and counter-check, I suppose the greatest detective or secret service man in the world is the Frenchman. His temperament, if he has the trained mind of the investigator, lends itself to such things. He is highly imaginative.

The American is perhaps inclined to be a little too confident. The Englishman—not confident enough. However, as allies, they all worked well together, as I found in my multifarious duties.

To return to my story.

The 'Five o'clock Rapide' train was waiting in Le Havre Junction, ready to take the boat passengers from England, via Paris, to different parts of Europe and other countries.

American activity prevailed on all sides. There were American civilians, officers and soldiers to be seen everywhere, many of them on short leave to Paris and other places. By the new American Army order only those of the fighting forces in uniform were allowed to travel on the railway provided they possessed the railway military movement order. Non-military American citizens, of course, carried passports.

The crush through the barrier at my control on this particular day, 28 April 1917, was very heavy. My French and Belgian colleagues had a busy time grappling with the scores of passports thrust into their hands by anxious and clamouring passengers loudly protesting at delay and eager to obtain seats.

I noticed one of the French detectives take an American passport from a tall, upright soldier dressed in the uniform of a colonel in the United States Infantry.

Actually, it was not his place to interrogate British and American subjects when an English or American Intelligence Police agent was present. But we often did things of this description for each other if the pressure of people was very heavy. Everything had to be done in a rush. I always considered this to be one of the great defects in our passport control. Important people did not like to be kept waiting, but I made an iron rule I would keep *anybody* waiting if I had the slightest doubt as to their credentials.

Somehow, that American officer passing through my control on a passport, instead of a military movement order, seemed out of order. It was not consistent with their own orders that had been laid down. There was an American Intelligence agent present, so I was at a loss as to what to do.

Fortunately, one of the English Intelligence Police. came to my assistance, Sergeant Robert Hadfield, an alert and shrewd member of our department; asking him to take over my control, I went in search of the American officer.

A long train, packed with civilians, and military and naval officers of all ranks and grades, with porters pushing and struggling along the narrow corridors in every direction, is no easy matter to search. I only had seven minutes to find my man. However, there he was with other officers in the dining-car, seated for tea. I had three minutes left. The position was very awkward. I was in civilian clothes addressing American officers in uniform. But I had to take the chance.

'Gentlemen,' I said, 'I am sorry to trouble you. I am a sergeant of the British Intelligence Police. I am responsible to the American Army Intelligence for the bona-fides of all their rank and file passing through the civilian barrier control of this station. Will you all be so kind as to produce your movement orders?'

They might have been offensive, these American officers, but, with good grace, permits were produced.

Two minutes left. My suspect American, however, was playing for time; he said his movement order was in his valise. This only tended to increase my suspicion.

'Sorry, sir, but I *must* see it.' He demurred. I ran to the nearest door.

The *chef de gare*, with watch in hand, was on the point of signalling to the chief train conductor to start the train. My French colleague came running up. 'Keep the express waiting, I have a "suspect",' I shouted from the door.

Meantime the other American officers, seeing my predicament, came to my rescue. They brought the 'suspect' into the corridor. He had only an American civilian passport. At once I ordered him off the train, snatching at his automatic revolver holster and whipping out the gun. The photograph on the passport had been tampered with. I could see it was a forgery.

He left in my company—and the train roared away to Paris.

Now here was an awkward position. In the presence of many people, I, an English non-commissioned officer in civilian clothes, had hauled off the train a colonel of the United States Army.

Yet my long experience of handling passports had made me almost an expert. I instinctively knew that the owner and the passport were not identical.

Suddenly there was a commotion on the platform. Hurrying towards me were two French detectives of the Paris Sûreté, a French officer and some soldiers. I recognized the officer as one of the camp commandants of the German officers' prison compound. 'Good work, Woodhall,' they shouted as they saw my capture.

The 'American colonel' was a prisoner of war, a very daring and brave type of Prussian Cavalry Guard officer, who had resided in England before the war.

He had only escaped at three o'clock that same afternoon. His method was a clever one. A stolen American uniform and his knowledge of English nearly won the day. But his accomplice or accomplices forgot one important detail: his travelling papers. It was just as easy to forge a movement order as to forge a stolen civilian passport. In fact, much easier. His high rank would have enabled him to pass easily.

What his intentions were is hard to say. He might have been making for Germany via Geneva, in Switzerland. On the other hand, he might have been going to make a tour of the American lines and general dispositions. If so, his mission would have been indeed dangerous to the Allied cause. Equally, he might have set his mind on some act of sabotage, such as the blowing up of one of the French munition factories, or the placing of a time-bomb in a train packed with thousands of English, American or French troops; in fact, many motives may be attributed to his escape. However, his capture brought to light a most ingenious plot at the German officers' prison compound, and three weeks later I was privileged to aid the French Intelligence in breaking up the whole plot.

During the war, King George V made several trips to France to visit headquarters, hospitals and the battlefields.

Needless to say these journeys were a source of very great anxiety to the General Staff and all concerned with the King's safety. Every precaution was taken to guard his majesty. A selected detective, generally from the ranks of the Intelligence Police, was always attached to him as a personal guard. As bad luck would have it, during these visits there were nearly always some unpleasant incident, and I remember one occasion when a plot to assassinate his majesty was defeated in the nick of time by the sagacity and intelligence displayed by a private in a Scottish regiment.

On that occasion the King was staying at a château which was used sometimes as a temporary headquarters by Sir Douglas Haig. At the time of the King's visit the British Commander-in-Chief was established on his famous train in a siding only a short distance from the château, and here his majesty dined and lunched frequently.

It was arranged for the King to visit certain hospitals and to review certain divisions of troops newly arrived in France. On the day before the big review, word came to the Inter-Allied Secret Service that there was obviously a serious leakage of information. The enemy were getting most accurate intelligence as to the movements of troops in the vicinity of the place where the King intended to hold his review.

Special efforts were made to trace the leakage, and at the request of my Chief of Intelligence, I went down to the suspected district and made a few independent inquiries. After careful work I learned of an old Flemish woman who seemed to be living far more comfortably than the present hard circumstances warranted to one in the battle zones. I detailed one of my best men to watch her. After nightfall he saw her leave her cottage and make her way along a shell-torn path to a ruined château. She entered and he followed. He had two assistants at hand, and, as soon as the old woman came out of the building, he arrested her. Accompanied by one man, he made his way up the stairs leading to a shell-broken turret.

Partly demolished by long-range gunfire, the steps were unsafe, and great care had to be exercised lest he fell through a hole in the side. He neared the top. Twice he heard the hoot of an owl, but paid no attention. He could see the stars above him. He was perhaps seven feet from the top when a vicious crack, a flash and the heat of flame instinctively made him duck. He saw a pair of legs and grabbed at them. *Crash!* His assailant fell down the stairs. A groan. My man struck a match. He saw lying beneath him a young, thick-set man, unconscious and bleeding freely from a wound on the side of the head. Calling his comrade by name several times, he received no answer. Striking another match, he saw by the light another body—it was his comrade. He was dead—shot through the heart.

The unconscious man was searched and an identity disc of a German infantry regiment round his neck revealed him as a spy in disguise. A search of the top tower soon revealed the presence of a wireless signalling apparatus, and on his person were found details of the King's movements for the next three days.

The spy was shot following a court-martial.

That is why the King's tour was suddenly changed.

A THIRD MAN?

Alan Stuart

In 1951 the newspapers were full of an exciting story. Two Britons, both of whom had held important positions, had suddenly disappeared and then turned up in Russia. Soon everyone was talking about them. Without doubt, these two men were espionage agents and had done their spying on behalf of the Soviet Union. Their names were Guy Burgess and Donald Maclean.

Their escape immediately started a hunt. What information had they taken with them? How had they escaped? Who had helped them? It seemed obvious that a third person, at least, must have been involved. But who was he? Who was this mysterious 'third man'? Three government departments did their best to find out. They were the Security Department of the Foreign Office, MI5, and the Secret Intelligence Service, known as the SIS. After a great deal of investigation their search narrowed down to one man. He was a member of the SIS and his name was Kim Philby. Men from all three departments began to delve into his past. Although nothing definite was uncovered, he was forced to leave his position, but with many parting gifts and regret on both sides.

Yet the talk of the 'third man' still went on. Finally, four years later, a Member of Parliament, Marcus Lipton, rose in the House of Commons and defiantly named Philby as the mysterious third agent. The Prime Minister of the time, Sir Anthony Eden, promised to look into the matter. In November 1955, the answer was given by Mr Harold Macmillan, the Foreign Secretary. He looked round the eager House of Commons and, in slow and deliberate tones, said: 'It is now known that Mr Philby had Communist associates during and after his university days. In view of the circumstances, he was asked in July 1951 to resign from the Foreign Service. Since that date his case has been the subject of close investigation. No evidence has been found to show that he was responsible for warning Burgess or Maclean. While in government service he carried out his duties ably and conscientiously. I have no reason to conclude that Mr Philby has at any time betrayed the interests of this country, or to identify him with the so-called "third man", if indeed there was one.'

He sat down. The House, with the exception, of course, of Colonel Lipton, seemed satisfied, and went on to other business. But little did the members know. That same Philby, whom Mr Macmillan had declared to be so innocent, had been betraying his country for more than twenty years! His activities, in fact, made him one of the most unusual and most dangerous spies of this or any other century!

He was born in India on New Year's Day, 1912, the son of Harry St John Philby, an officer in the Indian Civil Service. He was christened Harold Adrian Russell Philby, but was nicknamed 'Kim' after the little Indian boy in Kipling's famous *Jungle Book*. He was to be known as 'Kim' for the rest of his life.

He had his first taste of espionage when quite small, for during the First World War his father was working in the intelligence department of the British forces in Mesopotamia. There were times when St John Kilby, as his father preferred to be called, left his desk and went off, disguised as an Arab beggar, helping to find the whereabouts of two much-wanted German spies. St John Philby then went to Arabia, where he fell in love with the Arabian customs; he learned to speak Arabic as well as the natives of that country, and became a Muslim.

The young Kim greatly admired his father's exploits and hoped, one day, to be like him. When he was thirteen, he went to Westminster

School in the shelter of the great Abbey. He was not a very spectacular pupil, just one of many, slightly scruffy in the top hat and tails that all the scholars had to wear. After school he went up to Trinity College, Cambridge to read history, for it was hoped that he would become a civil servant.

A little under average size, thick-set and usually very casually dressed, he looked much younger than his years. At university he became friendly with a fellow student at Trinity, a rather spoiled son of a rich family, named Guy Burgess. Both lads were keen on politics and were Socialists. When the Labour Government was defeated at the 1931 elections, they swore they would work hard to see that their party was returned at the next election. Indeed, to this end, Philby became treasurer of the Cambridge University Socialist Society. He was an ardent speaker and often began his speeches with a telling phrase. 'My friends, the heart of England does not beat in stately homes and castles. It beats in the factories and on the farms.'

Even as he accepted this position in university life, his politics were changing somewhat. Within the Socialist group a new party was forming—that of Communists. Philby was not at first an active member of the tiny 'cell' of Marxists which had been formed, while his well-to-do friend Burgess joined the party. By 1933, however, when Philby left university, he was a fully converted Communist.

Almost immediately he decided to go to Vienna. There he stayed with a Polish family and the daughter of the house, Litzi, took a great liking to the handsome young Englishman and started to show him events and sights that a tourist would never have seen normally.

In 1933, Austria was still suffering terribly from the effects of the Great War—a war she was responsible for starting by declaring war on Serbia. After the defeated Austrians signed the armistice in 1918 the once-great Habsburg Empire began to split up into its natural elements, with Poland, Czechoslovakia, Rumania and Hungary, for example, becoming totally independent. Finally all that was left was the small territory known as German Austria, where a republic was formed. It was a difficult time for all Austrians, especially for those trying to maintain a huge imperial city like Vienna in a tiny state without an outlet to the sea.

Although by 1933 the war had been over for fifteen years, the still

327

fresh-from-college Philby saw sights he was never to forget. Almost every day there were clashes between demonstrators and the authorities, often ending with mounted policemen charging the people gathered in the streets with sabres drawn. Indeed, there were street battles and wounded everywhere, or so it seemed, and Litzi made sure that he saw it all. The air was full of talk—almost every type of party politics being argued and fought over.

After a while the Allies, fearing that such fighting and starvation would turn the whole country towards Russia and Communism, began to send in food and money. But even this did little to stop the trouble for Seipel, Austria's Chancellor, who had organized this relief, swore that his country would not be at peace until his country's Socialists were crushed. So the fighting continued, with the Socialists on one side and the Conservatives and the Monarchists on the other.

Litzi had become a keen Communist and kept taking Philby to all her party meetings and to visit people who had been injured in the street fighting. Like so many converts, Philby became more intense than those who had been members for years. He had intended to stay in Vienna for a brief while but, finding himself involved, he stayed on, full of enthusiasm for his newly discovered cause.

Early in 1924 Austria's new Chancellor, a very small man named Dr Dolfuss, began what was outright civil war, the Government versus the Socialists. In the midst of the fighting that followed, Philby was very useful to his new friends, for the police could not believe that such an English gentleman would have anything to do with the Communists, or anyone like them. But Litzi had already become known as a leading Communist and the police were searching for her to arrest and possibly execute her. Philby did the only thing he could to save her. In February 1934 he married her. Now, as the wife of an Englishman, and with a British passport, she was safe.

The fighting ended in May with the collapse of the Socialist resistance, and Philby returned to England with his bride of three months. He was determined on two things—to keep quiet about the fact he was a Communist and to try and get a job with British Intelligence. This was in obedience to his new masters—the Russians—who were determined, after a 'trial period', to make him one of their agents in England.

His first job was on a Liberal monthly magazine called the *Review of*

Reviews, on which he worked in a minor role as sub-editor. Soon, everyone who met him believed him to be an anti-Communist, but whether a Liberal or a middle-of-the-road Socialist they could not decide. Yet, secretly, he was meeting his Communist controller and was ordered, on every occasion when they met, to wait and do nothing. He soon found he had time on his hands and joined the Anglo-German Fellowship, a society of which his university friend, Guy Burgess, was also a member. The Fellowship published a pro-Hitler magazine which Philby was asked to edit. This he did gladly, for it gave him an opportunity to visit Berlin and visit the German propaganda ministry.

He was, in fact, losing some of his Communist ideals and leaning towards Hitler and Fascism. But this suddenly came to an end when civil war broke out in Spain in July 1936. He followed the fighting very closely and then, managing to obtain a press pass, went to Spain himself in February 1937. Although the opposing side contained many Communists and men of the International Brigade, of whom he secretly approved, he chose to join the army led by General Franco. Within five months he had become the official correspondent of *The Times*.

He now began to see a lot of action, following the Nationalist Army as it fought towards Republican-held northern Spain. On one occasion he went with a group of other journalists to watch an attack launched by Franco against Republican troops besieging the town of Teruel. The cars carrying the journalists stopped near the town for the passengers to warm themselves by a fire. Suddenly, without warning, a shell dropped in the middle of them. Some of the journalists were killed instantly, one of whom was actually sitting by Philby's side in their car. Philby had cuts on his wrist and forehead but was otherwise unharmed. He later filed a dispatch to *The Times*, telling of the incident and added, 'Your correspondent, who was in the same car, escaped with light wounds and has recovered.'

All the while Philby was with Franco he hated the Fascist leader and everything he stood for, and it must have been a telling moment for him when he was summoned to meet the General—who pinned the Red Cross of Military Merit on his chest.

Altogether, Philby was to stay in Spain for two and a half years—and hated every minute of it. Yet all the time he was learning, for he knew that some of the other journalists were also acting as Intelligence agents for their various countries and he was interested to see how they operated. By July 1939, however, he was back in London. A new phase of his life was about to begin.

In less than two months, the Second World War began, but in the early months there was little fighting. This period became known as the 'Phoney War'. He went to France as war correspondent of *The Times*, but there was little news to send home. Then, suddenly, everything seemed to happen at once. The German *blitzkrieg* began and the Allied armies were forced to retreat. Philby was among the thousands who had to evacuate France and he returned to London. He soon divorced Litzi on orders from his controller, for it would not have done for him to have a wife who was a well-known Communist.

Now the years of patient waiting paid off at last. Soon after his return he was recruited by the British Secret Service as an agent, and was attached to Section D of the Secret Intelligence Service (SIS). Here he found himself under his old college friend, Guy Burgess, who had been a secret agent since the beginning of the war. Indeed, it may well have been Burgess who got him his long-awaited posting. He went back to 'school' to learn undercover work. One of the things he quickly learned was that there existed a rivalry, almost a hatred, between the two British Intelligence services, his own SIS (sometimes known as MI6) and MI5. He learned to use this antagonism to his advantage later on. Basically, MI5 looked after espionage and counter-espionage on British territory, and SIS on all foreign territory. This, however, led to a certain amount of overlapping and consequent argument between the two sectors.

In 1941 Philby was transferred to Section V of SIS. Here he had a very responsible post, being in charge of all British Intelligence in Spain and Portugal. His promotion was rapid because he had the right background and experience. He had been to Westminster, an old and Trinity, Cambridge, one of Britain's leading colleges; he belonged to respected public school; he had obtained a degree in economics at good clubs and had had experience of warfare, having been wounded and decorated in the process. Strangely, no one bothered to check his former Communist activities or that, just before the war, he had edited a pro-Hitler magazine.

On 7 December 1941, the United States entered the war after the bombing of Pearl Harbour and many Intelligence agents, members of

America's Office of Strategic Services (OSS) came to Britain to liaise with her Secret Service. Their coming gave Philby further promotion. Whilst still retaining responsibility for Spain and Portugal, he was now also in charge of all British espionage work in North Africa and Italy. No one in the SIS even remotely suspected that everything of importance was going back to Russia through his contact in Britain.

In 1944 came the ultimate irony. A new section known as Section IX was formed. It was to operate against Communism and the Soviet Union, despite the fact that the Russians had been allies of Britain since the German invasion of their country in June 1941. And who was put in charge of this new section? Kim Philby!

Soon he had a hundred people working under him and nearly everything that was discussed and then decided on went straight back to the Soviet Union.

In May 1945 the German forces surrendered and Berlin was captured by the Russians. Now only Japan was left to face the entire might of the Allied forces. The Soviet espionage service, at that moment in time, must have felt very pleased. One of their agents, Philby, was at the head of the anti-Soviet section of the SIS, channelling back every piece of worthwhile information; Guy Burgess, another Soviet agent, was at the Foreign Office and mixing with Cabinet Ministers and others, sending back anything of interest they might carelessly let drop; a third, Donald Maclean, who had also been at Cambridge with the others, was in Washington working on the Anglo-American atomic energy programme. Three key men in key situations.

Yet suddenly there came danger. A Russian named Konstantin Volkov walked into the British Consulate in Turkey and offered to hand over a list of all the important spies working for the Soviet Union as well as many other details. When asked how he knew these facts he told the surprised diplomat who interviewed him that he was a member of the Soviet Intelligence Service, the NKVD. For £27,500 he would hand over the list—and then disappear. He mentioned that, on his list, were three men in responsible positions. Two, he claimed, were in the Foreign Office, a third was in charge of a counter-espionage department in London. Obviously the latter was Philby; the other two may well have been Burgess and Maclean.

The British Ambassador was told and replied that everything would

331

have to be done through London. The renegade spy agreed to this but put a time limit of twenty-one days on his offer. Days passed and then, on the very last day, an official arrived from London. It was Philby! He casually gave some kind of explanation why there had been a delay, and waited for the return of Volkov. But the man was never seen again —although a figure, covered in bandages, was later carried out to a Russian aircraft which had most unexpectedly touched down at Istanbul airport. Obviously, Philby had tipped off some of the Russian agents in Turkey and they had arranged the rest. Nevertheless, it must have been a worrying time for him until he knew that Volkov was safely out of the country—and his 'list' with him.

In the following year, 1946, Philby was appointed First Secretary with the British Embassy in Turkey. Actually, he was in charge of the SIS department in that country, a useful posting from which to send reports to his Soviet masters.

His work in Turkey, the British authorities considered, had earned him further promotion and in 1949 he was given a 'plum' job. This was the position of First Secretary at the British Embassy in Washington.

Here he actually worked as the senior British Secret Service agent working closely with the American Central Intelligence Agency (CIA) and the Federal Bureau of Investigation (FBI). They let him in on many of their secrets which he, in turn, passed on to Russia.

The following year his old friend, Guy Burgess, arrived as Second Secretary, and Philby invited him to stay at his own home. They must often have laughed at the way they fooled the top men of the British Intelligence Service.

Yet that same service was already becoming suspicious of leaks about atomic energy. Finally they traced them back to the man who had been at the Embassy before Philby . . . Donald Maclean. That man had served on the Combined Policy Committee on Atomic Energy and had learned every piece of information that had been discussed in secret.

The British Ambassador also became suspicious of Burgess—or at least did not like his somewhat drunken, madcap behaviour—and had him sent back to England. On his return Burgess immediately made contact with Maclean and, realizing that it would only be a question of time before their work was revealed, both men secretly left England

A figure was later carried out to a mysterious Russian aircraft.

on 25 May 1951. Travelling via the Baltic Sea, they arrived in Russia.

Their disappearance, of course, made a tremendous stir in Whitehall, at the SIS, MI5 and at the Foreign Office. Investigators went to work even harder and they soon noticed that one name kept appearing . . . that of Kim Philby. The reason for this was actually due to the fact that, whilst in Washington, he had been indiscreet enough to allow the frequently drunken Burgess the use of his house. Then, when Burgess, as well as Maclean, disappeared as they did, the suspicion became stronger.

Philby was summoned to London, leaving a furious CIA and FBI behind him. Many of their men were calling him the 'Russian man in Washington'. After a few days he was examined by a board and then asked to resign from the Diplomatic Service.

It was soon after this that Colonel Lipton asked about 'the third man' and received Macmillan's reply. The following year Philby left England to live in Beirut as a correspondent for two British papers. By then MI5 had a new head, Dick White, a man who had suspected Philby of being an enemy agent for some time. His own service, together with the SIS, began even closer investigations. For some time they made no progress; but then came the breakthrough. George Blake, who had also been spying for Russia, had been arrested and the news soon reached Philby in Beirut. He quickly realized that the man who had given Blake away could also betray him. There was no time to lose.

Even as SIS agents were on their way to arrest him, Philby disappeared from Beirut during the night of 23 January 1963. Not long afterwards the Soviet Union announced to the world that Kim Philby had sought, and been granted, political asylum in Moscow.

The 'third man' had at last been exposed.

THE ALIBI
Anonymous

I wholly disbelieve in spirit-rapping, table-turning, and all supernatural eccentricities of that nature. I refuse credence to the best authenticated ghost story.

I can sleep in the gloomiest haunted room in the gloomiest haunted house without the slightest fear of a nocturnal visit from the other world.

But, although I scoff at white ladies and bleeding nuns, there is a species of supernatural occurrence in which I am, I confess, an unwilling and hesitating believer.

The circumstances I am about to relate are of this nature, and were told me by an intimate friend of mine, as having lately occurred to a relation of his own.

I give the story as he gave it to me, namely, in the words as nearly as possible of the principal actor in it.

Two years ago, towards the end of the London season, weary of the noise and bustle that for the last three months had been ceaselessly going on around me, I determined upon seeking a few days' rest and quiet in the country. The next evening saw me comfortably installed in a pretty farmhouse about two miles from a cathedral town. The little cottage in which I had taken up my quarters belonged to an old servant of my father's, and had long been a favourite resort of mine when wishing for quiet and fresh air.

The evening of the second day after my arrival was unusually close and sultry, even for the time of year. Weary with the heat, and somewhat sated with the two days' experience I had enjoyed of a quiet country life, I went up to my bedroom about half-past ten, with the intention of taking refuge from the *ennui* which was growing on me in a good long night's sleep. Finding, however, the heat an insuperable obstacle to closing my eyes, I got up, put on my dressing-gown, and, lighting a cigar, sat down at the open window, and dreamily gazed out on the garden in front of the cottage.

Before me several low, flat meadows stretched down to the river, which separated us from the town. In the distance the massive towers of the cathedral appeared in strong and bright relief against the sky. The whole landscape, indeed, was bathed in a flood of light from the clear summer moon.

I was gradually getting sleepy, and beginning to think of turning in, when I heard a soft, clear voice, proceeding apparently from some one just beneath my window, saying: 'George, George, be quick! You are wanted in the town.'

I immediately looked from the window, and although the moon still shone most brilliantly, somewhat to my surprise I could see no one. Thinking, however, that it was some friend of my landlord's who was begging him to come into the town upon business, I turned from the window, and, getting into bed, in a few minutes was fast asleep.

I must have slept about three hours, when I awoke with a sudden start, and with a shivering 'goose-skin' feeling all over me. Fancying that this was caused by the morning air from the open window, I was getting out of bed to close it, when I heard the same voice proceeding from the very window itself. 'George, be quick! You are wanted in the town.'

These words produced an indescribable effect upon me. I trembled from head to foot, and, with a curious creeping about the roots of the hair, stood and listened. Hearing nothing more, I walked quickly to the window, and looked out. As before, nothing was to be seen. I stood in the shade of the curtain for some minutes, watching for the speaker to show himself, and then, laughing at my own nervousness, closed the window and returned to bed.

The grey morning light was now gradually overspreading the heavens, and daylight is antagonistic to all those fears which under cover of the darkness will steal at times over the boldest. In spite of this, I could not shake off the uncomfortable feeling produced by that voice. Vainly I tried to close my eyes. Eyes remained obstinately open; ears sensitively alive to the smallest sound.

Some half-hour had elapsed, when again I felt the same chill stealing over me. With the perspiration standing on my forehead, I started up in bed, and listened with all my might. An instant of dead silence, and the mysterious voice followed: 'George, be quick! You *must* go into the town.'

The voice was in the room—nay, more, by my very bedside. The miserable fear that came over me I cannot attempt to describe. I felt that the words were addressed to me, and by no human mouth.

Hearing nothing more, I slowly got out of bed, and by every means in my power convinced myself that I was wide awake and not dreaming. Looking at myself in the glass on the dressing-table, I was at first shocked, and then, in spite of myself, somewhat amused by the pallid hue and scared expression of my countenance.

I grinned a ghastly grin at myself, whistled a bit of a polka, and got into bed again.

I had a horrible sort of notion that some one was looking at me, and that it would never do to let them see that I was the least uneasy.

I soon found out, however, that bed, in the circumstances, was a mistake, and I determined to get up and calm my nerves in the fresh morning air.

I dressed hurriedly, with many a look over my shoulder, keeping as much as possible to one corner of the room, where nobody could get behind me. The grass in front of my window was glistening with the heavy morning dew, on which no foot could press without leaving a visible trace.

I searched the whole garden thoroughly, but no sign could I see of any person having been there.

Pondering over the events of the night, which, in spite of broad day-light and common sense, persisted in assuming a somewhat super-natural aspect, I wandered across the meadows towards the river by a footpath which led to the ferry. As I drew near to the boatman's cottage I saw him standing at his door, looking up the path by which I was approaching. As soon as he saw me, he turned and walked down to his boat, where he waited my arrival. 'You are early on foot, my friend, this morning,' said I, as I joined him.

'Early, sir,' answered he, in a somewhat grumbling tone. 'Yes, it is early sir, and I have been waiting here for you this two hours or more.'

'Waiting for me, my friend—how so?'

'Yes, sir, I have; for they seemed so very anxious that you should not be kept waiting; they have been down from the farm twice this blessed night telling me that you would want to cross the ferry very early this morning.'

I answered the man not a word, and, getting into his boat, was quickly put across the water. As I walked rapidly up towards the town, I endeavoured to persuade myself that somebody was attempting to play a silly hoax upon me. At last, stopping at a gate through which I had to pass, I determined upon proceeding no further. As I turned to retrace my steps, suddenly the same shivering sensation passed over me—I can only describe it as a cold damp blast of air meeting me in the face, and then, stealing round and behind me, enveloping me in its icy folds.

I distinctly heard the words, 'George, George,' uttered in my very ear, in a somewhat plaintive and entreating tone.

I shuddered with a craven fear, and, turning hastily round, hurried on towards the town.

A few minutes' walking brought me into the market-place. It was evidently market day, for, in spite of the early hour, there was already a considerable bustle going on. Shops were being opened, and the country people were exposing their butter, poultry, and eggs for sale, and for about two hours I wandered among the busy and constantly increasing crowd, listening to every scrap of conversation that reached my ear, and vainly endeavouring to connect them with the strange summons that had roused me from my bed, and led me to the town.

I could hear nothing that interested me in any way, and, feeling tired and hungry, I decided on breakfasting at the hotel, which overlooked the market-place, and then taking myself back to the cottage, in spite of the mysterious voice.

The cheerful and noisy bustle of the market had indeed partly dissipated the morbid turn which my fancies had taken.

After I had breakfasted I lit my cigar, and strolled into the bar, where I talked for ten minutes with the landlord without elucidating anything of greater moment than that it was his (the landlord's) opinion that things were bad—very; that Squire Thornbury was going to give a great ball on the occasion of his daughter's approaching marriage; and that Mr Weston's ox was certain to carry off the prize at the next agricultural meeting.

I bade him good morning, and turned my steps homeward. I was checked on my way down the High Street by a considerable crowd, and upon inquiring what was the matter, was informed that the assizes were being held and that an 'interesting murder case' was going on. My curiosity was roused, I turned into the court-house, and, meeting an acquaintance who fortunately happened to be a man in authority, was introduced into the court, and accommodated with a seat.

The prisoner at the bar, who was accused of robbing and murdering a poor country girl, was a man of low, slight stature, with a coarse, brutal cast of features, rendered peculiarly striking by their strangely sinister expression.

As his small bright eyes wandered furtively round the court they met mine, and for an instant rested upon me. I shrank involuntarily from his gaze, as I would from that of some loathsome reptile, and kept my eyes steadily averted from him till the end of the trial, which had been nearly concluded the previous evening. The evidence, as summed up by the judge, was principally circumstantial, though apparently overwhelming in its nature. In spite of his counsel's really excellent defence, the jury unhesitatingly found him 'guilty'.

The judge, before passing sentence, asked the prisoner, as usual, if he had anything further to urge why sentence of death should not be passed upon him.

The unfortunate prisoner, in an eager, excited manner, emphatically denied his guilt—declared that he was an honest, hard-working, travelling glazier, that he was at Bristol, many miles from the scene of

The unfortunate prisoner emphatically denied his guilt.

the murder on the day of its commission, and that he knew no more about it than a babe unborn. When asked why he had not brought forward this line of defence during the trial, he declared that he had wished it, but that the gentleman who had conducted his defence had refused to do so.

His counsel, in a few words of explanation, stated that, although he had every reason to believe the story told by the prisoner, he had been forced to confine his endeavours in his behalf to breaking down the circumstantial evidence for the prosecution—that most minute and searching inquiries had been made at Bristol, but that from the short time the prisoner had passed in that town (some three or four hours), and from the lengthened period which had elapsed since the murder, he had been unable to find witnesses who could satisfactorily have proved an alibi, and had therefore been forced to rely upon the weakness of the evidence produced by the prosecution. Sentence of death was passed upon the prisoner, who was removed from the bar loudly and persistently declaring his innocence.

I left the court painfully impressed with the conviction that he was

340

innocent. The passionate earnestness with which he had pleaded his own cause, the fearless, haughty expression that crossed his ill-omened features, when, finding his assertions entirely valueless, he exclaimed with an imprecation, 'Well, then, do your worst, but I am *innocent*! I never saw the poor girl in my life, much less murdered her,' caused the whole court, at least the unprofessional part of it, to feel that there was some doubt about the case, and that circumstantial evidence, however strong, should rarely be permitted to carry a verdict of 'guilty'. I am sure that the fervent though unsupported assertions made by the prisoner affected the jury far more than the florid defence made for him by his counsel.

The painful scene that I had just witnessed entirely put the events of the morning out of my head, and I walked home with my thoughts fully occupied with the trial.

The earnest protestations of the unfortunate man rang in my ears, and his face, distorted with anxiety and passion, rose ever before me.

I passed the afternoon writing answers to several business letters, which had found me out in my retreat, and soon after dinner retired to my room, weary with want of sleep the previous night and with the excitement of the day.

It had been my habit for many years to make every night short notes of the events of the day, and this evening, as usual, I sat down to write my journal. I had hardly opened the book when, to my horror, the deadly chill that I had experienced in the morning again crept round me.

I listened eagerly for the voice that had hitherto followed, but this time in vain; not a sound could I hear but the ticking of my watch upon the table, and, I fear I must add, the beating of my own coward heart.

I got up and walked about, endeavouring to shake off my fears. The cold shadow, however, followed me about, impeding, as it seemed, my very respiration. I hesitated for a moment at the door, longing to call up the servant upon some pretext, but, checking myself, I turned to the table, and resolutely sitting down, again opened my journal.

As I turned over the leaves of the book, the word Bristol caught my eye. One glance at the page, and in an instant the following circumstances flashed across my memory.

I had been in Bristol on that very day—the day on which this dreadful murder had been committed!

On my way to a friend's house I had missed at Bristol the train I had expected to catch, and having a couple of hours to spare, wandered into the town, and entering the first hotel I came to, called for some luncheon. The annoyance I felt at having some hours to wait was aggravated by the noise a workman was making in replacing a pane of glass in one of the coffee-room windows. I spoke to him once or twice, and finding my remonstrances of no avail, walked to the window and, with the assistance of the waiter, forced the man to discontinue his work.

In an instant I recalled the features of the workman. It was the very man I had seen in the felons' dock that morning. There was no doubt about it. That hideous face as it peered through the broken pane had fixed itself indelibly in my memory, and now identified itself beyond the possibility of doubt with the sinister countenace that had impressed me so painfully in the morning.

I have little more to add. I immediately hurried back to the town and laid these facts before the judge. On communicating with the landlady of the hotel at Bristol, she was able to prove the payment of a small sum on that day to a travelling glazier. She came to the town, and from among a crowd of felonsunhesitatingly picked out the convicted man as the person to whom she had paid the money.

The poor fellow, being a stranger at Bristol and having only passed two or three hours there, was utterly unable to remember at what houses he had been employed. I myself had forgotten the fact of my having ever been in that town.

A week later the man was at liberty. Some matter-of-fact people may endeavour to divest these circumstances of their, to me, mysterious nature by ascribing them to a disordered imagination and the fortuitous recognition of a prisoner condemned to die.

Nothing will ever efface from my mind the conviction that providence in this case chose to work out its ends by extraordinary and supernatural means.

Here ended his story. I give it you without addition or embellishment as he told it to me. It is second-hand, I confess, but hitherto I have never been fortunate enough to hear a story with anything supernatural in it that was not open to the same objection.

HITLER'S SPIES

Bernard Newman

The German spies of the First World War were incompetent. So, with few exceptions, were those of the Second. Few of them could even speak English! Many of them were collected from Dutch and Belgian jails and offered their freedom if they would undertake to act as spies. Naturally, many of them volunteered and then gave themselves up when reaching England. The training of the rest was so meagre that they had little chance against MI5 and the Special Branch. But, as in 1914 so in 1939, the number of German spies in action was only a small fraction of that claimed by rumour or imagination—or by authors.

All suspected spies were promptly rounded up at the beginning of the war. Others, whether of enemy origin or British Fascists, were brought before special tribunals. Again, rumour exaggerated their number. Denunciations poured in; a man need only have a German name and he would be hustled before the tribunal. Of the 73,253 people examined, 569 were interned. A further 6,782 were restricted in the places where they could live. At the outbreak of war I had an Austrian housekeeper, a refugee from Hitler, but as I happened to live within a few miles of an important headquarters, she was ordered to move fifty miles away. It was hard, but such things are part of the fortunes of war.

A spy, a criminal or a policeman will all admit that there is one thing they need—luck. That seldom came the German way. Consider some of the earliest cases. Karl Richter parachuted to earth near St Albans: he was a Sudeten German who spoke English. As instructed, he made for a nearby wood, hid his parachute, radio and other equipment, and began to walk along the road.

Then he met a lorry, and the driver had lost his way. He pulled up, and asked for directions. And Richter could not tell him—he did not know where he was himself.

'But where have you come from?' the driver asked. Surely the mumbling man knew that. But no: he did not want to talk.

At the next crossroads the driver met a policeman with a bicycle. He got his directions and mentioned casually the man who didn't know where he was. The policeman, his curiosity roused, rode along and found Richter. 'Where are you from? Where are you going?' he asked. But the man did not know.

He collapsed under expert examination and was hanged as a spy; but he had only been at large for twelve hours, and never did any spying.

Josef Jacobs was a German soldier, a specialist in meteorology. He had been sent to establish a weather-reporting station. But he made a bad landing and broke his ankle. So all he could do was to crawl to the roadside and give himself up.

The policeman who arrested him stared at him in surprise. He was wearing a grey suit, a brown bowler and spats! Beside him was a five-valve radio set. He had forged identity and ration cards, five hundred pounds in one-pound notes and a German sausage. This proved to be the standard outfit for a German spy.

Being a soldier, he was shot, not hanged like the rest. Again, he never did any spying.

Even less lucky was a man who parachuted with his radio strapped to his chest. As he hit the ground, his nose struck the radio and began to bleed profusely. The first man he met was a kindly clergyman, who insisted on rendering first aid. But his patient spoke English so badly that the clergyman's suspicions were aroused.

Yet surely the outstanding example of ill-luck took place before the war. The French police sent to Scotland Yard a description and photograph of a man 'wanted', among other things, for espionage. A detective read the account, walked into Whitehall and almost bumped into the very man!

In September 1940 the spy target area transferred to Scotland. Two men and a woman flew in a German seaplane from Norway and landed in a dinghy on the Banffshire coast. One of the men and the woman went to a local railway station, Port Gordon. The station-master looked at them keenly; their legs were wet—on a dry morning!—and they did not even know where they were! He called in the village policeman, who noticed peculiarities in their identity cards.

Their stories were confused and contradictory, but they admitted that another man had accompanied them. He had made his way to Edinburgh and left his luggage in the cloakroom. There the police awaited him.

The baggage of both men included some hundreds of pounds in notes, a radio and—of course—a German sausage. They also had cardboard discs which could be used to make up the sliding-alphabet cipher as used by Julius Caesar. The two men scarcely troubled to defend themselves, and the jury was out only a few minutes.

Earl Jowitt, who prosecuted them, ends the chapter in his book, *Some Were Spies*: 'It only remains to add that it was decided to take no proceedings against the woman, Madame Erikson. I have no doubt that she was detained here during the war, and it may be that she was able to be of some use to our authorities.'

She was!

Before the war an Italian countess lived in London. She appeared to be anti-British and pro-Mussolini, so it was not difficult for the Germans to enlist her services. She was elderly, and needed an assistant, and a 'niece' was found for her—actually the mistress of one of the Abwehr leaders. The 'niece' was flown from Norway with the two men; she used the name of Madame Erikson.

She was a Dane, and had no love for the Nazis. It was easy to 'turn her round'. She was indeed 'able to be of some use to our authorities'.

And the Italian countess? She had been a *British* agent, long before the Nazis approached her.

Most of the German spies sent to Britain during the war were captured before they could do any spying.

One refugee arrived with a very convincing story. Oswald Job had been born in England and lived in France. He had been interned by the Germans, but escaped to Spain and thence to England. Such details as could be checked were found to be accurate.

Then he wrote to his friends in the internment camp, and the device he was using was obvious. Between the lines of his letter were messages in chemical—invisible—ink. 'His cover story was just too perfect,' said one of our spy-catchers.

Another man talked too much. Alphonse Tammermann was an exhibitionist and frequented the Belgian Club, telling his story to anyone who would listen. But one day a man in his audience recognized him; he had last seen him as a Gestapo agent in Brussels.

One autumn day in 1940 a ploughman in the Home Counties found a German parachute, and the Special Branch collected it. This did not necessarily mean that a spy had landed, however, for the Germans occasionally dropped parachutes merely to persuade people that spies were everywhere.

A few days later Dr Jan Willam Ter Brank, a Dutch refugee, arrived in Cambridge. He was writing a book on the medicinal properties of plants growing in the Dutch Empire, he explained, and he wanted to use the university libraries. He spent most of his time there but occasionally visited London. There he was a keen sightseer, hanging about Downing Street and the Cabinet offices in Storey's Gate. Apparently he was especially anxious to see Churchill. In this he was by no means unique.

Then he made a slip. A letter was addressed to him at 7 Oxford Street, Cambridge. There was an Oxford Road, but no Oxford Street, so Brank's lodging was searched while he was in London. It was never known how he realized that he was under suspicion, but the following day his body was found in an air-raid shelter, shot through the head. Papers revealed that he was not an ordinary spy. He had been sent by the Nazis to assassinate Churchill!

Another Dutchman, Johannes Marinus Dronkers, seemed overjoyed to get to England. When his boat had been sighted by a British patrol ship he had danced with delight and sung hymns at the top of his voice.

But his cover story had flaws, and again his cipher was ancient: pin-pricks under letters in a Dutch-English dictionary. That was enough to send him to the scaffold.

In all, fifteen German spies were executed during the war. Of the fifteen, four were British traitors.

George Johnson Armstrong was a known petty criminal, devoid of moral scruples. When not in prison, he was a sailor. In Lisbon he contacted some German agents and offered them information about British shipping. To his surprise, they turned him down—they thought he must be a British agent infiltrating the German service!

When his ship was in New York, he tried again, at the German consulate. This time he was accepted. He was of no great intelligence, otherwise he would have realized that British agents would be watching a German consulate.

Duncan Scott-Ford was a young man of good family. He also went to sea, and when in a pub in Lisbon he found himself talking to another sailor. Scott-Ford mentioned that he was hard up. The other man suggested that he supply lists of ships and cargoes—he could easily pick up details by listening to gossip in sailors' clubs. Scott-Ford knew precisely what he was doing; it seemed to be an easy way of making money. Once he had fallen, he could be blackmailed into further service.

But a young seaman in a south English port got suspicious: Scott-Ford was asking too many questions. The young fellow told the warden of a seamen's hotel, and soon the local representative of the Special Branch—there is a section in every police force—had taken charge. Scott-Ford broke down almost at once: maybe his crime lay heavy on his conscience.

Yet to the chiefs of MI5 the most interesting case was that of Mrs Dorothy Pamela O'Grady of the Isle of Wight. A woman spy is a novelty, and after the war journalists let themselves go. Authors too; almost all those who wrote about women spies included a chapter on Mrs O'Grady. We can summarize her story, *as then told*—one account appeared in a popular magazine as recently as 1962.

Mrs O'Grady, the authors explain, was a German who acquired British nationality by marrying an Englishman, a favourite device of

347

German women agents. She was recruited as a spy by the lover of Dr Hermann Goertz and acquired a boarding house at Sandown. Most of her guests were Germans.

She was a good amateur artist and tramped the countryside with her sketching pad; she seemed to be showing a special interest in the new radar stations. After the war began, she made frequent journeys to Portsmouth, Southampton and London, where she visited an address already under suspicion.

At last 'Sweet Rosie O'Grady', as MI5 called her, was arrested. Hidden in the springs of easy chairs at her home were sketches of military installations and plans of naval dockyards. She had even cut the cables connecting the Isle of Wight with the mainland—which might have led to disaster in the event of a German invasion.

She faced her trial calmly. 'I do not think that I was the only man in that court-room to feel ungrudging admiration for the tall, eloquent woman who conducted herself with great skill and courage and who put up such a desperate fight for life,' one writer declared.

He must have been singularly unobservant. He was evidently not present at her trial and describes her as 'tall and eloquent'. She was short, dumpy, and said not a word.

In fact, there is scarcely a vestige of truth in this and many other accounts, which differ only in their dramatic embellishments. She was released five years after the war ended, but did *not* go back to Germany. She had in fact never been abroad. She returned to the Isle of Wight, where I found her and heard her own story.

She was no German: she was born near Clapham Common. She married a fireman of Irish stock; he was recalled from retirement during the blitz, and rendered yeoman service. I went through the visitors' book of her boarding house in Sandown—not a German name was among the entries. I made notes of our conversation, and she gave me the 'confession' she had written while in jail.

'All my life, since I was a child, I have loved to make up stories. I used to love to shock people and pretend I was ever so bad. I remember at school writing on bits of paper that I had killed my mother. I hoped that I would be hanged. I was very fond of my mother—who had died a year earlier.

When my husband was posted to London, I had only Rob—my

black retriever—as my companion. He loved to swim in the sea, but the beach at Sandown was closed. So I used to take Rob further along the cliffs, where we could evade the soldiers and get down to the beach.

One day I was near Whitecliff Bay. There was a public path down the cliff—no barbed wire, no notice. So we went down. After Rob had his swim, I sat down. Two soldiers came along, and said that I was in a prohibited place, right under their secret guns. I was scared—I don't like bangs.

Then a soldier noticed a little swastika flag under my lapel. I had a map of Europe at home, and used to stick in flags to show the battle line. One of the flags got caught in my hair, so I pinned it on my lapel. They must have thought that I was a spy. They said I must go with them to their headquarters.

It was a very hot day, and I did not want to walk so far. Then I did a silly thing, I admit. I had often taken out a cup of tea or a cigarette to a sentry near my home. So now I offered them a ten-shilling note, and said, 'I'm sorry to have bothered you. Buy some cigarettes with this.'

They took me to their officer, and told him that they had found me in a prohibited place, and that I had tried to bribe them to let me go.

The officer was very nice, and he did let me go. But later a young policeman came round, and asked my views on Hitler. I was flattered, and told him a lot of nonsense. I said that Hitler was a great man. Why shouldn't he take Poland? Hadn't we taken other countries in our time? I said that the war was a lot of nonsense.

The policeman was very serious, and took it all down.

I was quite excited. They seemed to think that I was a spy! I thought what fun it would be to *pretend* to be a spy. I tried to do things a spy would do. I drew little sketch maps, and dropped them where soldiers would find them.

Then all of a sudden I got a summons, ordering me to appear on a charge of being in a prohibited place, and attempting to bribe the guards.

I thought, 'Why should I go to court? I've done nothing wrong. To hell with them.' So I packed a bag and went to Totland Bay.

It was all very thrilling. I guessed that there would be a warrant out for my arrest, and the police would be searching for me. So I left swastikas in my room, and the woman gave me away.

The police questioned me for hours. I admitted everything, and added more. They wanted to know how I got my information to Germany, and I told them that a man landed in a rubber dinghy from a submarine. I had read that in a book.

They said I had better have a solicitor, so my husband engaged one. He was a nice old silly. He said, 'Oh, we'll soon have you out of this.' I thought, 'Oh, will you!' So I tried to make him believe that I *was* a spy.

You understand what I was doing? It had all become a huge joke. You write stories—I was *living* one. In my imagination I *was* a spy. I had always been a nobody: now I was somebody, with people taking notice of me.

My solicitor had said that if I were a spy I might be condemned to death. I was delighted. But I intended to tell my counsel. My idea was that I would tell the whole truth when I got into the witness-box.

'*I admitted everything, and added more.*'

My solicitor believed that I had already told him the truth, and that in the witness-box I should tell a pack of lies.

So when my counsel came—I only saw him for two minutes. He said that he would not be a party to perjury—he would not act for me unless I agreed *not* to go into the witness-box. So I signed a paper.

The head of MI5 came to see me. He wanted to know who my contact was, and how I met him. He did not seem to believe my story about the man from the submarine.

Then came my trial, at Winchester. I had looked forward to it as a tremendous thrill. I didn't hear very much of what was being said in court. In fact, I was very surprised when I learned later that I had been charged with cutting telephone wires, and had confessed to it. I would not have cut any wires, of course.

As my counsel wouldn't let me go into the witness-box I had no chance to tell the truth.

The excitement of being tried for my life was intense. The supreme moment came when an official stood behind the judge and put on his black cap for him. The man didn't put it on straight. It went over one of the judge's eyes and looked so funny that I was giggling inside and had a job not to laugh.

But it had been so thrilling. I was now living in a real-life drama.

I found it disappointing that I was going to be hanged instead of shot. I thought spies were always shot. But I had always wanted to see what happened when they hanged somebody.

My next disappointment was to learn that they would put a hood over my head before they took me to the scaffold. I said, 'What is the good of being hanged if I can't see what's happening?'

Mrs O'Grady was not hanged, of course; she is still alive, in fact—still living in the Isle of Wight. The Court of Criminal Appeal quashed her sentence. It was held that the learned judge had misdirected the jury in laying undue stress on the charge of 'communicating information to the enemy', when there was not a scrap of evidence to this effect. Instead, she was sentenced to fourteen years' imprisonment on the other charges.

Mrs O'Grady had lived comfortably at home and did not like prison. She wrote down the full story to send to her husband—it is on my desk as I write. Another prisoner about to be released tried to smuggle it out, but it was discovered.

Now the secret was out. The whole thing was a 'joke'. Mrs O'Grady appealed for a pardon, but she was not released until early in 1950. Her story was probably true, it was admitted, but it was stressed that by her folly she had forced an expensive realignment of the defences of the Isle of Wight.

As Mrs O'Grady was *not* a spy, why should her story be included in a history of espionage? There are some lessons to be learned from it.

First, it is a fascinating psychological study. It is far from unique: consider the people who falsely confess to a murder. Second, it shows that MI5 are fair. They are anxious to catch spies and punish them, but they want to be certain of their prey. It was the head of MI5 who pointed out the absurdity of the man-from-the-submarine yarn, and the absence of any evidence about communication with the enemy. He was a stern man who used to watch the executions of his prey, but he was greatly relieved when Mrs O'Grady was not hanged. And the evidence against her was flimsy indeed.

Lawyers will draw a lesson from the failure to put a prisoner in the witness-box. Army security officers will probably find much to learn from this absurd incident. And even writers and editors can find something to note. Mrs O'Grady was released in 1950, and this was not kept secret. The *Sunday Express* bought and published her own story. At the same time I published it in a magazine and in a book, *Epics of Espionage*, which appeared in half a dozen countries. Yet still the original story of Mrs O'Grady, as told at her trial, absurd as it is, is trotted out from time to time.

The only person who has nothing to learn from this extraordinary case is the spy.

During the war I met a young officer who greeted me almost effusively, though I did not know him. He pointed to his Military Cross ribbon.

'Really I owe this to you,' he said.

'Sorry. I'm not with you.'

'Do you remember coming to lecture to a group of us—Intelligence types—a year ago at Canterbury?'

'Yes.'

'Among other things, you talked about interrogating prisoners. And I remembered one thing you said: "Always interrogate a German as soon as you catch him, when he is scared and apprehensive. If you leave him for an hour or two, he will recover his nerve. He is usually courageous, and once he has got over the fright of his capture you are not likely to move him. So get at him quickly!'

The young man went on to tell his story. He was attached to the Marines, and his task was to snatch a German prisoner from the Channel coast. He would take a fast motor-boat, by night, to within a couple of miles of the shore. Two powerful men, stripped and blackened, would swim to the beach. Then a German sentry, bored with his task, would suddenly find himself seized and hustled to the water's edge. Within minutes he would be in the boat, heading for England.

At one time, the officer explained, he used to guard his prisoner until he reached his home port. By that time, he now realized, the man had recovered enough to control himself. So a different method was now adopted.

The prisoner sat in the little cabin, the officer facing him—a revolver at the ready. By the door stood two grinning and blackened men holding knives.

'Now, you understand the position,' the officer began—he had, of course, been chosen as German-speaking. 'You know what I want to know. So you will talk.'

'No.'

'You will. You have disappeared from your post. For all your headquarters know, you have deserted. No one knows that you are in this boat. No one knows that you may never arrive in England. Why should we have to feed you for the rest of the war? Much easier to knock you out and throw you overboard. There are lots of crabs about here—big fat crabs. Have you ever seen a body after the crabs have been at it?'

And so on. I am not quite sure why men should be particular about what happens to their bodies after death, but they are. His method was not pretty, but it worked quite often—so often that they gave him the Military Cross.

THE HAUNTING OF
U-BOAT 65
Michael & Mollie Hardwick

Ghosts are one thing. Accidents are another. When a ship has a reputation for both she is liable to be shunned by men who might otherwise have signed on with her. But in time of war a seaman has no choice. Whether he likes it or not he must leave his superstitions behind, even though he fears he may be sailing in a doomed vessel. Such was the case with the crew of the U-boat UB 65.

She was one of the light submarines launched by the Germans in 1916 to patrol the heavily protected Belgian coastline, thick with mines and nets. The earliest versions of these frail little craft had a surface speed of only six and a half knots, and carried only two torpedoes. They plodded up and down Belgian waters, dodging British patrols, weaving in and out of sandbanks, edging up to terrorize fishing fleets or sink the occasional Allied ship. They pierced the Dover barrage and defied the famous Dover patrol. Little, but game, were the UBs.

UB 65 was new in 1916. Her surface speed was an improvement on that of her elder sisters—thirteen knots. She carried a crew of thirty-four, including three officers. The trouble that was to make her the jinx of the German Navy began while she was still building. A steel girder was being slowly, steadily lowered into place. There was a jerk, a shout of warning, and the massive thing slid sideways and fell with a mighty crash. The noise of its fall and the splintering of wood were mingled with fearful screams. It had fallen on two workmen.

Slowly, with difficulty, their horrified mates raised the heavy mass as far as they could. But it was jammed, and the tackle had broken— they could not lift it clear of the two victims. One, it was obvious, was beyond help, a broken, bloody pulp. The other, trapped by the legs, screamed for an hour as they fought to free him. Soon after they got him out he died.

In the Dark Ages a blood sacrifice was made to bring good fortune to a new building. It seemed that UB 65 had taken her toll of blood, and would now be satisfied. But she had only begun.

Work was resumed, and for some weeks went on without mishap. Then came a second fatal accident. The UB 65 was almost ready for launching when three workmen, putting the finishing touches to equipment in the engine-room, were heard coughing and calling for help. When help came, the engine-room door was found to be jammed. Inside was a haze of noxious fumes, and on the floor were three corpses. An inquiry produced no satisfactory reason for the escape of the fumes and the submarine was declared seaworthy.

'*Deutschland, Deutschland über alles!*' The Fatherland had a new weapon to hurl against the enemy. The UB 65 slid out for her trials. The day was calm, the omens propitious. She had scarcely got into the open sea before a sharp squall blew up. The sea rose, swamped her decks, and swept one of her ratings overboard. A boat was hastily lowered, but no trace of him was to be seen. Victim number six had died by drowning.

Then UB 65 was put through the diving trials in which a submarine must prove itself. A certain gloom prevailed amongst the crew. It was justified. Sure enough, when the U-boat was submerged a leak developed in one of her tanks with the result that submarine and crew were trapped underwater for twelve hours. Once again death-bringing fumes filled her, perhaps due to sea-water in the batteries—it was never proved. When she finally surfaced and the officers and crew were released they were half-stupefied, sick, choking—but alive, *Gott sei dank*. For once the jinx had only been joking.

The next time was no joke. The submarine's private fiend had dealt out death by crushing, by asphyxiation and drowning. Now it experimented with explosives—and most successfully. The UB 65 made an uneventful maiden patrol, returned to base and started taking in torpedoes. Without warning, or reason, a warhead exploded. A fearful detonation, screams, chaos, followed, and five dead men lay huddled and twisted on the submarine's deck. Others were badly hurt. The fateful submarine, itself considerably damaged, went out of action for repairs during which any workmen in possession of good-luck charms undoubtedly wore them. A cemetery at Wilhelmshaven, the chief German naval station, received the bodies of the dead, including that of the second officer, a man of striking appearance.

Once more fighting fit, UB 65 was manned and prepared to sail. It was evening, and her captain and his officers were discussing plans in the wardroom while the crew settled in. Suddenly, the door burst open and a white-faced rating stood before them, panting and trembling. The captain's head jerked up, his beard bristling with affront.

'What's the meaning of this, Schmidt? Don't you know better than to enter the wardroom without knocking?'

'I beg pardon, Herr Oberleutnant, but the second officer . . . I—I've just seen him!" gasped out Schmidt.

The captain's lip curled sarcastically. "Not unlikely, Schmidt, as you're looking at him now!" The new second officer, who was indeed sitting at the captain's side, looked in surprise at the seaman.

'No, sir,' stammered the man. 'I mean the late second officer—the one who died in the explosion!'

The captain banged the table. 'You're drunk, man—get out! You'll be in trouble for this!'

But the bluejacket stood his ground. He *had* seen the dead man, he repeated—strolling up the gang-plank. And somebody else had seen him, a man called Petersen. They would both swear to it, and they were stone cold sober.

The captain sighed.

'All right. Bring Petersen here, and let him tell his own fairy-tale.'

'He won't come, Herr Oberleutnant. He's up on deck, behind the conning-tower. Shaking like a leaf, he is.'

'Come along, gentlemen—we'd better investigate for ourselves.'

said the captain, and led the way on deck. There, indeed, was Petersen, huddled in a corner, in a worse state of fear than his shipmate. Patient questioning produced the information that he had seen the ghost of the dead officer come up the gang-plank, stroll along to the bows, and stand there, arms folded, looking calmly out to sea. Petersen had rushed in panic to the corner where he was now crouching. When he dared to peer out again the phantom had gone.

The captain was a reasonable man. He knew the symptoms of drunkenness, and neither of these men had them. They had obviously seen something—but what? The captain had never believed in ghosts; he did not intend to start now. In his opinion, someone was either playing a grisly joke or deliberately trying to undermine the crew's morale. He investigated every possibility, questioned everyone who might have had access to UB 65, checked on the activities of other members of the crew. But no evidence of trickery came to light and he was obliged to let the matter rest. If a fake ghost had been produced with malicious intent, the faker must have been thoroughly satisfied, for the experience of the two sailors had infected the crew with panic. Petersen could not face the prospect of sailing on a death-boat. Two days before she was due to sail he vanished, risking the chance of a deserter's punishment.

Two years had passed since UB 65's keel had been laid. In the latter part of 1917 the U-boat menace had slowly been overcome by the Allies. Until the summer of that year the terror under the sea had been destroying British shipping at an alarming rate. In May 1917, out of every four vessels that left British shores one had not returned. In April, U-boats had sunk 840,000 tons of British and Allied merchant shipping. But by the autumn the picture was changing. The Ministry of Shipping had boosted production; the convoy system was working. Germany would have to think hard and quickly if she were to win the war at sea and would need to throw every vessel she had into the fight. So UB 65, which in less needful times might have been written off, was kept in service.

On New Year's Day, 1918, she cruised from Heligoland to Zeebrugge where she spent ten days. To the immense relief of the crew, nothing untoward happened. They felt that their luck might have changed with the calendar. Then orders came to sail into the Channel, in search of merchant vessels and fishing fleets.

The evening of 21 January was wild as UB 65 ran on the surface. A gale was rising, the sea threatened to wash over the conning-tower. It was a night to be down in the stuffy warmth of your cramped quarters if you were not absolutely obliged to be outside, like the starboard look-out, keeping his lonely watch. But suddenly, to his amazement, he saw that he was not alone. Below him, on the narrow, plunging deck, bathed in recurrent showers of spray, was the figure of an officer.

Cupping his hands, the look-out shouted a warning. 'Don't stay there, sir—you'll be washed overboard!'

The officer looked up—with the face of the dead man who had appeared to Petersen and his mate. It was a frightened look-out who stammered out his tale to the captain as he came up through the hatch. Looking from the coning-tower, the captain was just in time to see a figure. By the time he had blinked and looked again it had gone.

We are not told what eventually happened to the deserter Petersen, or to the other sailor who had first seen the apparition. But to the captain the sight he saw on 21 January was a death-warning. A few weeks

To his amazement, he saw that he was not alone. Below him

later, while UB 65 was moored in a bomb-proof pen in a canal dock at Bruges, he went ashore to pass the evening at the local casino.

The air-raid sirens sounded as he walked through the streets: British planes were approaching. The captain's place was with his ship. He turned to go back—and a shell fragment severed his head from his body.

After this dreadful happening an official inquiry into the submarine's troubles was held. The investigating officer in charge of it did not transfer the crew wholesale to another vessel as they asked, but some neat paper-work resulted in most of them being drafted, one after another, to less alarming environments. The German Navy could not afford to have even one boat manned by demoralized men.

While the jinxed U-boat lay at Bruges it was someone's bright idea to have a pastor come aboard and hold a service of exorcism, bidding any devils who might be aboard to leave the ship, in the name of God. Nothing more tactless could have been planned. The new crew had heard unpleasant rumours from their predecessors and at this confirmation that there *were* devils sailing with them they became infected with fear. Ghost stories flew about until the captain issued an order that any-

on the narrow, plunging deck, was the figure of an officer.

one who claimed to see even a vestige of a phantom would be heavily punished.

A first-hand account exists of the events of the next few months. A petty officer who served on UB 65 from beginning to end of her career wrote frankly of his experiences and beliefs.

'UB 65 was never a happy ship,' he wrote, 'though we were always fortunate in our officers. There was something in the atmosphere on board which made one uneasy. Perhaps, knowing her evil history, we imagined things, but I am convinced myself that she was haunted. One night at sea I saw an officer standing on deck. He was not one of us. I caught only a glimpse of him, but a shipmate who was nearer swore that he recognized our former second officer walk through the ship. He always went into the forward torpedo-room, but never came out again. Several of the bluejackets saw the ghost quite often, but others were unable to see it, even when it was pointed out to them standing only a few feet away.

'Our last captain but one would never admit the existence of anything supernatural, but once or twice, when coming on deck, I observed him to be very agitated, and was told by the men that the ghost had been walking on the foredeck. When the captain's attention was drawn to it he pretended to see nothing and scolded the watch for being a pack of nervous fools. But afterwards I heard from a mess steward at the officers' casino that our captain openly declared his ship to be haunted.'

During May, went on the story-teller, the U-boat was cruising up and down the Channel and off Spain. It was a terrible trip. After two days at sea a torpedo gunner named Eberhard went screaming mad and had to be tied hand and foot and given morphia to quieten him. The treatment seemed to take effect and he was released and sent on deck for air in the company of another of the crew. No sooner did he reach the deck than he again went beserk. Pushing away the man at his side he leapt over the rail and went down like a stone. His body was never recovered.

Off Ushant, when high seas were raging, the chief engineer slipped and broke a leg. The submarine was hopefully chasing a British tramp steamer, firing with her deck gun, when waves towered over the gun-crew and washed one of them, Richard Meyer, overboard. He, too, was never seen again.

Now the submarine began to avoid encounters with British or Allied boats that would otherwise have seemed her natural prey—for each one might be the instrument of the final fate that her entire crew were sure was in store for her. 'The men were so depressed that they went about like sleep-walkers, performing their duties automatically and starting at every unusual sound.' They were not reassured to find themselves approaching the dreaded Straits of Dover, where three U-boats—UB 55, UB 33 and UB 79—had just been blown up.

Their fears were justified. They were shot at on the surface, depth-charged when submerged and Coxswain Lohmann received injuries from which he died. A battered UB 65 limped away to Zeebrugge, almost sorry to have escaped. 'Most of us felt that it was merely prolonging the agony.'

At this point the story-teller, to his own immense relief, was attacked by such severe rheumatism that he was sent to hospital. He was visited there by another officer, Wernicke. The UB 65 was due to sail next day, and Wernicke felt that it would be her last voyage—and his. He brought his messmate most of his personal belongings, to be sent on to his wife when the news everybody expected came.

It broke on 31 July. UB 65 was posted as missing. Her end was as mysterious as everything else that had happened to her.

On 10 July an American submarine off Cape Clear, on the west coast of Ireland, sighted a U-boat. Through the periscope her number could be made out—it was UB 65. Hasty orders were given for attack.

But just before the American torpedoes were fired, something happened that made it unnecessary. With a fearful detonation, UB 65 blew up.

The reason was never known. Possibly one of her own torpedoes exploded in its tube, or another U-boat attacked her by mistake and made off without being sighted by the American. But there were no remains on which to hold an inquest.

The mystery of UB 65, surely one of the strangest in naval history, was investigated thoroughly after the war by a psychologist, Professor Hecht, who published a pamphlet on the subject. In 1932 Hector C. Bywater, the English naval historian, followed this up with an investigation of his own, carefully checking all the evidence and testimonies. Neither Professor Hecht nor he was able to draw any firm conclusions.

As a scientist, Dr Hecht did not care for the supernatural explanation, but he could not suggest a watertight rational one. Today, so far away in time from the events, it would be even more difficult to do so. The ghost stories are convincing and well attested. But nothing is easier than to see a ghost if you expect to see one, and sailors, particularly the isolated, hemmed-in men on a submarine, are the most superstitious of folk. Given one convincing faked 'appearance', the spectre seen walking up the gang-plank, it was pretty certain that other apparent manifestations would follow, in the dark, in the mist, amidst flying spray.

Several who had sailed in UB 65 felt that there was malicious human agency behind the 'accidents'. Were they the work of a British secret agent? It is hard to see how some of them were contrived, and others, like the washing overboard of the gunner, and the beheading of the captain, were obvious coincidences. But the whole thing has a very strong smell of sabotage. Another possibility is that the 'ghost' and various disasters were the work of some *Till Eulenspiegel* with a grudge, or a taste for killing. If the last accident of all was a planned one, the saboteur must have blown himself up with his victims. He might have saved himself the trouble, for within four months the war was over, and 138 U-boats were meekly brought as captives into Harwich.

THE NIGHT OF 6 SEPTEMBER

John Baker White

The evening of 6 September 1945 was fine and warm in Ottawa. At about 7 p.m. Sergeant Main of the Royal Canadian Air Force was sitting with his family on the balcony of his flat, Number 5 at 511 Somerset Street. The balcony was separated by a low rail from that of Flat 4, which the sergeant knew was occupied by a Mr Gouzenko, his wife and small boy. They were friendly neighbours, but the sergeant and his wife knew little about them except that Mr Gouzenko's name was Igor and that he worked at the Soviet Embassy. They had occupied the flat since June 1943.

Round about 7.30 p.m. Gouzenko came out on to the balcony and asked Sergeant Main if he could speak to him. He was obviously very worried and apparently frightened. His request was a curious one. He asked the Air Force man 'if anything should happen to him and his wife' whether his wife would look after their little boy Andrei.

Let Sergeant Main continue the story in his own words. 'I figured maybe we should go inside, so we went into our apartment and while in there he said he figured that the Russians were going to try to kill him and his wife, and that he wanted to be sure that somebody would look after his little boy if anything should happen to him. So after a bit of a conference my wife and I decided we would look after him, because we didn't want to see him stuck with nobody to look after him should anything happen to them.'

What caused Gouzenko to take this action? After a busy day and a night, the full story of which will be told later, he had got back to his flat about an hour earlier. He had not been home long when he noticed two men standing on the opposite side of the street and keeping it under observation. A few minutes later there was a sharp knock on his front door and a voice called him by name. He did not reply or open the door, hoping the caller would think the flat was empty, but at that moment his son Andrei ran across the polished floor of the living-room. The caller heard the tap-tap of his feet, and again called out Gouzenko's name. He recognized the voice as that of Under-Lieutenant Lavrentiev, one of the drivers for the Soviet Military Attaché, Colonel Zabotin. There was another peremptory knock on the door. To Igor Gouzenko it was the knock of death, certain death for himself, probable death for his wife Svetliana. He knew the Canadian next door and liked him. He decided to seek his help.

After Main had heard Gouzenko's story they both went out on to the balcony again. They both saw a man walking along behind the flats, apparently looking for a back way in. Shaken with fear, the Russian begged his companion not only to give shelter to his boy, but to his wife and himself as well. This the Canadian agreed to do. By good fortune a friend of theirs, Mrs Elliot, the tenant of Flat 6 on the same floor, called on them, and heard the story. Although alone in her apartment, she agreed to take the whole Gouzenko family for the night. The Air Force man, on his own initiative, set off on his bicycle to get help.

He made contact with the police and two constables, Walsh and McCulloch, in a radio patrol car, were sent to the flat. They interviewed Gouzenko in Flat 6. He told them that he was a member of the Soviet Embassy staff and had information of value to the Canadian Government. He also told them that he was being followed, that he was in fear of his life, and wanted protection. The police officers agreed to keep the building under observation. The light in the bathroom of the flat was turned on. The turning off of the light was to be the signal for help. Nothing more happened until about 11.30 p.m., when Sergeant Main heard footsteps and voices in the passageway outside his flat. Then he heard a knock at the door of Gouzenko's flat. Thinking it was the police returning, he opened his door. Four men were standing in the passage. They asked him whether he knew where the Russian was; he replied that he did not. The men continued to knock at the door, but not getting any answer they went downstairs as if to leave the building. Instead of doing so they crept back and, after knocking once more, broke open the door of Gouzenko's flat and entered. The Canadian, hearing what was going on, summoned the police.

There followed a scene that must be almost unprecedented in diplomatic history. Constables Walsh and McCulloch entered the flat and found the four men busy ransacking it. One of them was found inside a clothes cupboard. He proved to be Vitali Pavlov, the Second Secretary and Consul of the Soviet Embassy. Though the police officers did not know it at the time he was also head of the NKVD—the Soviet Secret Political Police (Commissariat for Internal Affairs)—in Canada. Inside another cupboard, busy ransacking it, was another man, dressed in Red Army uniform—Lieutenant Colonel Rogov, the Soviet Assistant Military Attaché (Air). The other two men were shown by their identity papers to be Lieutenant Angelov, a member of the staff of the Military Attaché, and Alexandre Farafontov, one of the Embassy cipher clerks.

When Pavloc had extricated himself from the cupboard he endeavoured to reply to Constable Walsh's question as to what they were doing. He said that they were Russians, that they were looking for papers belonging to the Soviet Embassy, that the owner of the apartment was in Toronto and that they had his permission to enter his flat to get what they wanted. The hard-headed policeman commented that it was funny that if they had permission they had broken the lock to get in. He picked up the keeper of the lock off the floor, remarking: 'This does not look as if it had been done with a key. You must have used a bit of pressure to get in and from the marks on the door you didn't put them there with your fingers.' Pavlov, who did most of the talking for his companions, replied: 'We had lost the key but there was something in here that we had to get.' He added, quite inaccurately, that the premises were Soviet property and they could do as they pleased. He then became truculent and ordered the police officers to leave the flat. Rogov chimed in, saying that he and his companions had been insulted. The policemen were quite unmoved by his novel interpretation of diplomatic privilege. They refused to leave until their Inspector arrived and asked the men to produce their identification cards. This they did.

When the Inspector arrived he asked the four Russians to remain while he went outside to make some inquiries, but during his absence they left, the police making no attempt to stop them. They noticed that as he went out Pavlov took a key out of his pocket and locked the ordinary lock of the flat door—the Yale lock, of course, being out of commission. During the night some unknown person visited the flat but left after a few minutes. Gouzenko, his wife and child spent the night in Flat 6 under police guard.

On 8 September 1945 the Canadian Department of External Affairs received from the Soviet Embassy a note, dated 7 September, which would not have convinced a child of ten. It read as follows:

'The Embassy of the USSR in Canada presents its compliments and has the honour to inform the Department of External Affairs of the following:

'A colleague of the Embassy, Igor Sergeievitch Gouzenko, living at 511 Somerset St., failed to report for work at the proper time on 6 September.

In connection with this and for the purpose of clarifying the reasons for the failure of I. Gouzenko's reporting for work, Consul V. G. Pavlov and two other colleagues of the Embassy visited the apartment of I. Gouzenko at 11.30 on 6 September.

When Mr. Pavlov knocked at the door of Gouzenko's apartment no one answered. After this the apartment was opened by the above-mentioned colleagues of the Embassy with Gouzenko's duplicate key, when it was discovered that neither Gouzenko, nor his wife, Svetliana Borisovna Gouzenko, nor their son Andrei, were in the apartment.

It was later established that I. Gouzenko robbed some money belonging to the Embassy and had hidden himself together with his family.

At the time when Consul Pavlov and the two other colleagues of the Embassy were in Gouzenko's apartment, i.e. about 11.30

p.m., Constable Walsh of the Ottawa City Police appeared together with another policeman and tried in a rude manner to detain the diplomatic colleagues of the Embassy, in spite of explanations given by Consul Pavlov and the showing of diplomatic cards.

As a result of the protest expressed by Mr Pavlov, Walsh called Inspector of the City Police Macdonald, who appeared at the Gouzenko apartment in fifteen minutes, and also in a rude manner demanded that Consul V. G. Pavlov and the other diplomatic colleagues of the Embassy go with him to the Police Station, refusing to recognize the diplomatic card shown by Consul Pavlov.

Upon the refusal of Mr V. G. Pavlov to go to the Police Station, Mr Macdonald went away, leaving a policeman in the Gouzenko apartment with the colleagues of the Embassy, for the alleged purpose of finding out who it was who had notified the police of the forced entry into the Gouzenko apartment.

Consul V. G. Pavlov and the other two colleagues of the Embassy, after waiting for Mr Macdonald to return for fifteen minutes, left, having locked the Gouzenko apartment.

The Embassy of the USSR asks the Department of External Affairs to take urgent measures to seek and arrest I. Gouzenko and to hand him over for deportation as a capital criminal, who has stolen money belonging to the Embassy.

In addition the Embassy brings to the attention of the Department of External Affairs the rude treatment accorded to the diplomatic colleagues of the Embassy by Constable Walsh and Inspector of the City Police Macdonald, and expresses its confidence that the Department will investigate this incident and will make those guilty answerable for their actions.

The Embassy asks the Department that it should be informed of action taken in relation to the above.

Ottawa, 7 September, 1945.'

In a further note dated 14 September, 'The Embassy, upon instructions from the Government of the USSR, repeats its request to the Government of Canada to apprehend Gouzenko and his wife, and without trial, to hand them over to the Embassy for deportation to the Soviet Union'.

367

By this date the Canadian Government were in no mood to pay attention to requests of this nature. On the morning of 7 September Gouzenko had been taken to the offices of the Royal Canadian Mounted Police, where he told his story and turned over his documents. He asked that, as he feared for his safety and that of his wife and child, he should be kept in protective custody. By the evening of 7 September the Canadian authorities realized that they had in their hands the fullest possible evidence of the existence of a large espionage network serving the Soviet Government and seeking not only general military information but in particular the closely guarded secrets of the atomic research that was being carried on in the Dominion. Gouzenko had disclosed the largest and most dangerous spy-plot ever known in the Dominion in peace or war.

THE SEA'S GREATEST MYSTERY

K. Alan Macdonald

'Deck there! Sailing ship on the port bow! Looks like a brigantine, sir.'

The high-pitched call of the look-out overhead caused both Captain Morehouse and his mate, Oliver Deveau, to stare out over the smoothly heaving sea. At first they could see nothing. Then, as the distance between the two vessels grew less, the shape of the stranger became steadily clearer. Suddenly Captain Morehouse slammed his right fist into the palm of his left. 'I know her!' he cried. 'She's the *Mary Celeste*, Cap'n Ben Briggs's command.'

He turned to his mate. 'Briggs and I are old friends. It will be nice to close her and exchange greetings. You may remember she left New York just before us.'

Time went by, each minute bringing the two ships closer together. After a while Morehouse called to one of his men. 'Hey, you there. Run up our signal!'

Within a few moments the identifying flags of the brig, *Dei Gratia*, were fluttering from her mainmast. All eyes were now turned on the smaller vessel, the brigantine, that they were steadily overhauling. Morehouse, who had been studying her carefully, exclaimed, 'That's

'There's no one at the wheel and no one on deck,' said Captain Morehouse.
'I don't like it. I don't like it at all!'

THE SEA'S GREATEST MYSTERY

funny. Deuced funny. D'ye see that, Mister Mate. She's yawing all over the place, luffing up one minute then falling off several points the next. That's not like Cap'n Briggs. He's a first-class seaman and always runs a taut ship. To look at her you'd think they were all drunk on board!'

He sent a seaman down to his cabin for his telescope and carefully focused it on the other vessel. He stared for a long time, removed the glass for a moment, replaced it to his eye and then lowered it once more. 'D'ye know. There's no one at the wheel. And there's no one on deck, either. I don't like it. I don't like it at all. Something's wrong aboard her I'll wager. Helmsman, steer direct for that brigantine!'

As the distance continued to close with every passing second it became even plainer that something was very wrong with the *Mary Celeste*. She was a wooden ship, less than 100 feet long, with a 25 feet beam and a draught of 11 feet. Being a brigantine she had two masts—square-rigged on the foremast, fore-and-aft only on the main—and had a registered tonnage of 282. She was small by some standards, but was well-built and very seaworthy. She was 11 years old, having been built in 1861.

This, the day of the crucial sighting, was 5 December 1872.

During their stay in New York, Morehouse had visited her several times to chat to his friend, Captain Briggs. From him he learned that in addition to the crew of seven men Mrs Briggs and her two-year-old daughter were also sailing, making ten souls on board in all. When she sailed on 7 November her cargo was mainly barrels of commercial alcohol, to be unloaded in Genoa.

Morehouse, by now, was extremely anxious. 'Hoist the "urgent" signal!' he shouted to the seaman standing by the halliards. The flags fluttered upwards, but there came no answering signal. Soon the ships were close enough for Morehouse to bellow across the expanse of sparkling water, 'Mary Celeste. Mary Celeste ahoy! Is anyone there? Answer me. Ahoy, there!'

But the other ship quietly drifted along, her decks deserted.

Morehouse took a turn up and down his deck and then, his mind made up, began to shout out his orders. 'Starboard watch! Aloft and shorten sail! Port watch! Lower the cutter!'

The *Dei Gratia* began to lose way and within minutes the cutter was being rowed across to the vessel that was behaving so mysteriously. At its helm was the first mate with two seamen straining at the oars. The boat was soon rubbing against the *Mary Celeste*'s side, and leaving one man to fend her off, Deveau clambered aboard with the other seaman. Reaching the deck he looked around then, pushing back his cap, scratched his head in bewilderment. Everything seemed in perfect order: ropes were neatly coiled down, and nothing was out of place. But there was not a soul to be seen!

He paused only a moment. Walking to the taffrail he called down to the man tending the boat, 'Go back and fetch the cap'n!'

When Morehouse joined him on the brigantine's deck, both officers made their way aft. They were very ill at ease, for both felt they might suddenly come across some terrible sight. Murdered bodies, perhaps, or something equally blood-chilling. But there was nothing. Everything was in its place, a fact that became even more apparent when both men entered the main cabin. On the table, for example, stood Mrs Briggs's sewing machine. Beside it was a reel of cotton and a small oil-can, objects which would have quickly dropped to the deck had the ship given a violent roll. On the other side of the table were the remains of a meal. They looked further, their curiosity equalled by their amazement. On the table was a half-finished letter, Briggs's watch, and other personal items.

Nearby, the bunks had been carefully made up, one pillow still showing the impression of a small child's head. Briggs's money was on a locker by one bunk, on another some trinkets, obviously those of his wife, which included a valuable gold locket. Morehouse and Deveau continued to search, muttering to themselves as they did so.

Back in the main cabin they found the ship's log, but her papers, which included her muster-lists, bills of loading, and so on, were missing. There was also no sign of a sextant or a chronometer. They did, however, make one sinister discovery—a cutlass showing what seemed like traces of dried blood on its blade. And that was all.

'Well I'll be darned!' said Morehouse. 'There seems to be nothing wrong here at all. What do you make of it, Mister Mate?' But Deveau was forced so say that he, too, was just as mystified.

'Then let's look for'ard,' said Morehouse, and the two men went on with their search. In the forecastle, as before, everything was as usual.

Seamen's clothes were hanging on lines to dry, personal effects such as razors, tobacco and pipes were lying about as if waiting for their owners to walk in and pick them up. The seamen's chests were neatly arranged along either bulkhead; each was full, nothing seemed out of place. There was certainly no signs of a hurried, desperate exit.

The two officers went lower, into the hatches, to look at the cargo. Everything was neatly stowed, all was in order. They sounded the well. It was dry. There was certainly no problem there.

Back on deck they discussed the situation in shaking voices. 'I—I don't understand it at all,' Morehouse said. 'There's nothing wrong below and, look aloft, sails and rigging are in perfect trim.'

'There's plenty of food and water on board, too, sir,' the mate added.

'There is indeed. So what's this all about? Suppose—just suppose—they had to abandon ship in a hurry. Surely they would have taken some food and water with them, and their money and pipes, at least.'

'Yes, sir. It's a queer mystery, all right.'

Morehouse had already noticed that the *Mary Celeste*'s only boat was missing from the davits at the ship's stern. Now only its falls were left dangling to suggest that the captain and the rest had, probably, made their escape in that manner. Then the mate called his attention to something more sinister. 'Here, sir,' he called. 'Look at this!'

Morehouse joined him and stared down at one of the ship's wooden rails. There, plain to see, was a gash which might well have been made by an axe or a cutlass. As Morehouse stared at it, rubbing his chin in thought, the latter called to him again.

'And at this, sir!'

Following his pointing finger, the captain saw several dark spots on the deck which, like the stains on the cutlass, could have been blood.

They continued their search but found only one other unusual thing: a cover which normally closed one of the hatches was lying near it, upside-down.

There was nothing else.

Both men, thoroughly bemused now, stood and stared around. There was no doubt about it. No one was on board, so the *Mary Celeste* had to be regarded as a derelict. She was now Morehouse's responsibility as the finder. He thought about this for some time and then, his mind made up, turned to his mate.

'Deveau, you will take command of this ship. I will return to our own and send back two hands to be your crew. Sail her to Gibraltar and I will try and keep company with you in case anything else goes wrong.

And so it turned out. A week later the *Dei Gratia* sighted the gaunt outline of the vast rock rising from the sea and docked during the evening of 12 December, while the *Mary Celeste* slid into a berth nearby a few hours later.

Morehouse went ashore and at once reported the strange story to the harbour authorities. It was obviously one without parallel, and the authorities worked quickly. Mr Solly Flood, the Admiralty Proctor for Gibraltar, had the ship 'arrested' and a further search from stem to stern was undertaken. The findings—or rather lack of them—were the same. Meanwhile Morehouse, quite properly, put in a claim for salvage, his mate and crew swearing to the truth of his statements.

On 2 January 1873 the principal shareholder, J. H. Winchester, received an official letter from Gibraltar which stated:

'The American brig, *Mary Celeste* of New York, was brought into this port by the British barque *Dei Gratia*. *Mary Celeste* picked up on high seas on 5 December, abandoned. Brig in perfect condition but was taken possession of by Admiralty Court as a derelict. Fate of crew unknown.'

Meanwhile Solly Flood continued to be very busy. He had the ship thoroughly scrutinized in detail, even sending down a diver to examine her hull, and had a team of men working under the local surveyor of shipping. He did this because he had not been satisfied with the earlier reports, explaining that, 'the account which they gave of the soundness and good condition of the derelict was so extraordinary that I found it necessary to apply for a survey.' He was sure that something was wrong; why should a ship in perfect condition be discovered sailing along with not a soul on board?

Finally he went to the dockside personally and made his own thorough inspection, attended by an imposing group consisting of four naval captains, a marshal of the Vice-Admiralty Court and a colonel of the Royal Engineers. Nothing fresh came to light. If anything the mystery grew even deeper.

It was about this time that the theories began. Some were possible, some were downright stupid. Flood's own theory was far-fetched, to say the least. He wrote: 'My own theory, or guess, is that the crew got at the alcohol, and in the fury of drunkenness murdered the master, whose name was Briggs, his wife and child, and the chief mate; that they then damaged the bows of the vessel, with the view of giving it the appearance of having struck on rocks, or suffered a collision—and that they did, sometime between 25 November and 5 December, escape on board some vessel bound for some North or South American port or the West Indies.'

He did not bother to explain why the seamen, after doing this terrible deed, should calmly leave behind their cash, pipes and tobacco and also the cash belonging to the captain. Nevertheless, his report was taken seriously and customs officers were ordered to keep a sharp look-out for any mutineers or for any ship which might report having picked up any mutineers as Flood suggested. Nothing ever came to light.

Meanwhile Mr Winchester was sailing from New York to find out what was happening to his ship. He, too, had a theory. The ship's cargo had been one of crude alcohol. Perhaps this had generated a gas which finally exploded and blew off the hatch cover reported by Captain Morehouse? Scared that another such explosion might blow the ship apart, everyone had rushed for the one boat—which was missing—and perhaps stood by, hoping to regain the ship if nothing else happened. Then, and also perhaps, a wind had sprung up and borne the *Mary Celeste* away from the men rowing frantically in the boat.

One theory put forward was that the ship had been attacked by a giant sea-monster, perhaps an enormous cuttle-fish. The crew had tried to fend it off with an axe—cutting into the rail as they did so. This would also have given a reason for the blood stains on the deck. But this theory was exposed when marine biologists swore that no such monster could have attacked the ship and then eaten the ten missing persons *and* the boat in which they were trying to escape. Also, when properly examined, the 'blood stains' on deck were proved to be simply . . . wine!

This was reported by the US Consul on Gibraltar, who was particularly interested as the *Mary Celeste* was of American registration. His report read: 'Result of analysis adverse to blood existing on sword and

375

woodwork belonging to the brig *Mary Celeste*.'

Two weeks later another report issued from the same office stated: 'Principal owner of brig *Mary Celeste* arrived from New York to claim brig from Admiralty Court. Nothing heard of missing crew. Chronometer and ship's papers not to be found on board the brig.'

On 25 March 1873, the Vice-Admiralty Court at Gibraltar awarded one-fifth of the value of the derelict to the *Dei Gratia*. It amounted to £1,700, a fair sum in those days.

Weeks passed and the ill-fated brigantine remained at the dockside in Gibraltar. For a while it seemed as if her fate,·after all, might have been solved. Some fishermen off the north-western coast of the Spanish peninsula discovered two rafts. They had been roped together and bore six dead bodies. One of the rafts even had a stumpy mast from which flew a tattered American flag. On reflection, however, it became obvious that this sad discovery had nothing to do with the *Mary Celeste*. Why should experienced seamen leave a perfectly good ship to set off in two hastily-made rafts? Also, none of the brigantine's woodwork was missing, so what had the rafts been made from? Other factors also served to rule out this solution to what by now had become a much-discussed mystery.

At first it was impossible to collect a crew for the brigantine. Seamen are very superstitious people and they argued that what had happened once—whatever it was—could happen again. At last, however, enough seamen were found to sail her to Genoa, where her original cargo of crude alcohol was unloaded.

She then sailed back to America, where she changed hands many times. Her story had gone ahead of her and, as a 'hoodoo ship', it was still difficult to obtain crews. Her last voyage began at the end of 1884, from Boston to Haiti, with a cargo consisting mainly of barrels of molasses. She never reached her destination, for she ran on to Roshell's Reef off the coast of Haiti. She did not founder, however, and when investigators went on board they found that the barrels of 'molasses' were actually filled with sea-water! Her captain and owner were arrested on a charge of barratry—deliberately wrecking a ship to obtain the insurance.

Yet this ending of the *Mary Celeste* was by no means the end of the affair. Her influence seemed to linger on. Her captain and mate both died before the case could come to court, the shipper responsible for the barrels of sea-water committed suicide, and every firm that had been involved in the fraud went bankrupt.

There was even more. The ship that had sighted her soon after she ran on to the reef and rescued her crew, went down on her very next voyage.

That, then, should have been the last of the *Mary Celeste*. But the theories still continued. One was written by the then young and still unknown Conan Doyle, who had *his* account published in a popular magazine of the time. He called the brigantine the '*Marie*' *Celeste*, an error that has since occurred in the works of many stories and 'explanations'. The denial of Conan Doyle's theory by Solly Flood gave the young writer much valuable publicity.

Other theories included an attack by pirates from a ship wanting more hands; the ship sailing into a lethal gas-cloud, which had the effect of driving everyone mad and causing them to jump overboard; one of the crew had, indeed, drunk some of the alcohol, gone mad and killed everyone on board. He then escaped in the ship's boat.

A confession, supposed to have been made by a Captain Briggs, curiously the same as that of the *Mary Celeste*'s captain, was that his ship had sighted a derelict. On going on board he found a chest containing a fortune in gold and silver. He kept some of it and handed the rest to his crew as a means of bribing their silence. They then took the derelict's boats, scuttled her, and made for Cadiz. This could have been a plausible theory except for one thing. The real Captain Briggs owned a third of the *Mary Celeste* and his share was worth more than the money claimed to have been found in the derelict's chest.

The *Mary Celeste* was discovered, a floating ghost-ship, in 1872. Today, more than a century later, it still remains a mystery. But the theories continue . . .

THE SPY IN THE BARREL
Robert Louis Stevenson

*Here is a chapter from one of the finest books ever written for the younger reader—*Treasure Island, *by Robert Louis Stevenson. It is taken from the journal of young Jim Hawkins whose mother keeps the Admiral Benbow inn. By a strange series of happenings, he gains possession of a map which shows the location of treasure buried by the famous pirate, Captain Flint. Jim, with his friends Squire Trelawney and Doctor Livesey, set off in search of it. But the crew of their ship, the* Hispaniola, *has for the most part been gathered together by a rascal named Long John Silver. Although Captain Smollett has doubts about his crew's loyalty, nothing is certain until, by accident, Jim becomes a spy, overhearing a plot hatched by Long John Silver. But let young Jim tell the tale . . .*

Just after sundown, when all my work was over, and I was on my way to my berth, it occurred to me that I should like an apple. I went on deck. The watch was all forward, looking out for the island. The man at the helm was watching the luff of the sail, and whistling away gently to himself; and that was the only sound excepting the swish of the sea against the bows and around the sides of the ship.

I got bodily into the apple barrel, and found there was scarce an apple left; but sitting down there in the dark, what with the sound of the waters and the rocking movement of the ship, I had either fallen asleep, or was on the point of doing so, when a heavy man sat down with rather a crash close by. The barrel shook as he leaned his shoulders against it, and I was just about to jump up when the man began to speak. It was Silver's voice, and, before I had heard a dozen words, I would not have shown myself for all the world, but lay there, trembling and listening, in the extreme of fear and curiosity; for from these dozen words I understood that the lives of the honest men aboard depended upon me.

'It was Silver's voice, and I would not have shown myself for all the world.'

'No, not I,' said Silver. 'Flint was cap'n; I was quartermaster, along of my timber leg. The same broadside I lost my leg, old Pew lost his deadlights. It was a master surgeon, him that ampytated me—out of college and all—Latin by the bucket, and what not; but he was hanged like a dog, and sundried like the rest, at Corso Castle. That was Roberts' men, that was, and comed of changing names to their ships—*Royal Fortune* and so on. Now, what a ship was christened, so let her stay, I says. So it was with the *Cassandra*, as brought us all safe home from Malabar, after England took the *Viceroy of the Indies*; so it was with the old *Walrus*, Flint's old ship, as I've seen a-muck with the red blood and fit to sink with gold.'

'Ah!' cried another voice, that of the youngest hand on board, and evidently full of admiration, 'he was the flower of the flock, was Flint!'

'Davis was a man, too, by all accounts,' said Silver. 'I never sailed along of him; first with England, then with Flint, that's my story; and now here on my own account, in a manner of speaking. I laid by nine hundred safe, from England, and two thousand after Flint. That ain't bad for a man before the mast—all safe in bank. 'Tain't earning now, it's saving does it, you may lay to that. Where's all England's men now? I dunno. Where's Flint's? Why, most of 'em aboard here, and glad to get the duff—been begging before that, some of 'em. Old Pew, as had lost his sight, and might have thought shame, spends twelve hundred pound in a year, like a lord in parliament. Where is he now? Well, he's dead now and under hatches; but for two year before that, shiver my timbers! the man was starving. He begged, and he stole, and he cut throats, and starved at that, by the powers!'

'Well, it ain't much use, after all,' said the young seaman.

''Tain't much use for fools, you may lay to it—that, nor nothing,' cried Silver. 'But now, you look here: you're young, you are, but you're as smart as paint. I see that when I set my eyes on you, and I'll talk to you like a man.'

You may imagine how I felt when I heard this abominable old rogue addressing another in the very same words of flattery as he had used to myself. I think, if I had been able, that I would have killed him through the barrel. Meantime, he ran on, little supposing he was overheard.

'Here it is about gentlemen of fortune. They lives rough, and they risk swinging, but they eat and drink like fighting-cocks, and when a cruise is done, why it's hundreds of pounds instead of hundreds of farthings in their pockets. Now, the most goes for rum and a good fling, and to sea again in their shirts. But that's not the course I lay. I puts it all away, some here, some there, and none too much anywhere, by reason of suspicion. I'm fifty, mark you; once back from this cruise, I set up as a gentleman in earnest. Time enough, too, says you. Ah, but I've lived easy in the meantime; never denied myself o' nothing heart desires, and slep' soft and ate dainty all my days, but when at sea. And how did I begin? Before the mast, like you!'

'Well,' said the other, 'but all the other money's gone now, ain't it? You daren't show face in Bristol after this.'

'Why, where might you suppose it was?' asked Silver, derisively.

'At Bristol, in banks and places,' answered his companion.

'It were,' said the cook, 'it were when we weighed anchor. But my old missus has it all by now. And the "Spy-glass" is sold, lease and good-will and rigging; and the old girl's off to meet me. I would tell you where, for I trust you; but it 'ud make jealousy among the mates.'

'And can you trust your missus?' asked the other.

'Gentlemen of fortune,' returned the cook, 'usually trust little among themselves, and right they are, you may lay to it. But I have a way with me, I have. When a mate brings a slip on his cable—one as knows me, I mean—it won't be in the same world with old John. There was some that was feared of Pew, and some that was feared of Flint; and Flint his own self was feared of me. Feared he was, and proud. They was the roughest crew afloat, was Flint's; the devil himself would have been feared to go to sea with them. Well, now, I tell you, I'm not a boasting man, and you seen yourself how easy I keep company; but when I was quartermaster, *lambs* wasn't the word for Flint's old buccaneers. Ah, you may be sure of yourself in old John's ship.'

'Well, I tell you now,' replied the lad, 'I didn't half a quarter like the job till I had this talk with you, John; but there's my hand on it now.'

'And a brave lad you were, and smart, too,' answered Silver, shaking hands so heartily that all the barrel shook, 'and a finer figurehead for a gentleman of fortune I never clapped my eyes on.'

By this time I had begun to understand the meaning of their terms. By a 'gentleman of fortune' they plainly meant neither more nor less than a common pirate, and the little scene that I had overheard was the last act in the corruption of one of the honest hands—perhaps of the last one left aboard. But on this point I was soon to be relieved, for on Silver giving a little whistle, a third man strolled up and sat down by the party.

'Dick's square,' said Silver.

'Oh, I know'd Dick was square,' returned the voice of the coxswain, Israel Hands. 'He's no fool, is Dick.' And he turned his quid and spat. 'But look here,' he went on, 'here's what I want to know, Barbecue: how long are we a-going to stand off and on like a blessed bum-boat? I've had a'most enough o' Cap'n Smollett; he's hazed me long enough, by thunder! I want to go into that cabin, I do. I want their pickles and wines, and that.'

'Israel,' said Silver, 'your head ain't much account, nor ever was. But you're able to hear, I reckon; leastways, your ears is big enough. Now, here's what I say: you'll berth forward, and you'll live hard, and you'll speak soft, and you'll keep sober, till I give the word; and you may lay to that, my son.'

'Well, I don't say no, do I?' growled the coxswain. 'What I say is, when? That's what I say.'

'When! by the powers!' cried Silver. 'Well, now, if you want to know, I'll tell you when. The last moment I can manage; and that's when. Here's a first-rate seaman, Cap'n Smollett, sails the blessed ship for us. Here's this squire and doctor with a map and such—I don't know where it is, do I? No more do you, says you. Well, then, I mean this squire and doctor shall find the stuff, and help us to get it aboard, by the powers. Then we'll see. If I was sure of you all, sons of double Dutchmen, I'd have Cap'n Smollett navigate us halfway back again before I struck.'

'Why, we're all seamen aboard here, I should think,' said Dick.

'We're all foc's'le hands, you mean,' snapped Silver. 'We can steer a course, but who's to set one? That's what all you gentlemen split on, first and last. If I had my way, I'd have Cap'n Smollett work us back into the trades at least; then we'd have no blessed miscalculations and a spoonful of water a day. But I know the sort you are. I'll finish with 'em at the island, as soon's the blunt's on board, and a pity it is. But you're never happy till you're drunk. Split my sides, I've a sick heart to sail with the likes of you!'

'Easy all, Long John,' cried Israel. 'Who's a-crossin' of you?'

'Why, how many tall ships, think ye, now, have I seen laid aboard? And how many brisk lads drying in the sun at Execution Dock?' cried Silver, 'and all for this same hurry and hurry and hurry. You hear me? I seen a thing or two at sea, I have. If you would on'y lay your course, and a p'int to windward, you would ride in carriages, you would. But not you! I know you. You'll have your mouthful of rum tomorrow, and go hang.'

'Everybody know'd you was a kind of a chapling, John; but there's others as could hand and steer as well as you,' said Israel. 'They liked a bit o' fun, they did. They wasn't so high and dry, nohow, but took their fling, like jolly companions every one.'

'So?' says Silver. 'Well, and where are they now? Pew was that sort, and he died a beggar-man. Flint was, and he died of rum at Savannah. Ah, they was a sweet crew, they was! On'y, where are they?'

'But,' asked Dick, 'when we do lay 'em athwart, what are we to do with 'em, anyhow?'

'There's the man for me!' cried the cook, admiringly. 'That's what I call business. Well, what would you think? Put 'em ashore like maroons? That would have been England's way. Or cut 'em down like that much pork? That would have been Flint's or Billy Bones's.'

'Billy was the man for that,' said Israel. '"Dead men don't bite," says he. Well, he's dead now hisself; he knows the long and short on it now; and if ever a rough hand come to port, it was Billy.'

'Right you are,' said Silver, 'rough and ready. But mark you here: I'm an easy man—I'm quite the gentleman, says you; but this time it's serious. Dooty is dooty, mates. I give my vote—death. When I'm in parliament, and riding in my coach, I don't want none of these sea-lawyers in the cabin a-coming home, unlooked for, like the devil at prayers. Wait is what I say; but when the time comes, why let her rip!'

'John,' cries the coxswain, 'you're a man!'

'You'll say so, Israel, when you see,' said Silver. 'Only one thing I claim—I claim Trelawney. I'll wing his calf's head off his body with these hands. Dick!' he added, breaking off, 'you just jump up, like a sweet lad, and get me an apple, to wet my pipe like.'

You may fancy the terror I was in! I should have leaped out and run for it, if I had found the strength; but my limbs and heart alike misgave me. I heard Dick begin to rise, and then someone seemingly stopped him, and the voice of Hands exclaimed:

'Oh, stow that! Don't you get sucking of that bilge, John. Let's have a go of the rum.'

'Dick,' said Silver, 'I trust you. I've a gauge on the keg, mind. There's the key; you fill a pannikin and bring it up.'

Terrified as I was, I could not help thinking to myself that this must have been how Mr Arrow got the strong waters that destroyed him.

Dick was gone but a little while, and during his absence Israel spoke straight on in the cook's ear. It was but a word or two that I could catch, and yet I gathered some important news; for, besides other scraps that tended to the same purpose, this whole clause was audible: 'Not another man of them'll jine.'' Hence there were still faithful men on board.

When Dick returned, one after another of the trio took the pannikin and drank—one 'to luck'; another with a 'here's to old Flint'; and Silver himself saying, in a kind of song, 'Here's to ourselves, and hold your luff, plenty of prizes and plenty of duff.'

Just then a sort of brightness fell upon me in the barrel, and, looking up, I found the moon had risen, and was silvering the mizzen-top and shining white on the luff of the foresail; and almost at the same time the voice of the look-out shouted, 'Land ho!'

The sighting of 'Treasure Island' is but the beginning of a series of fantastic adventures. Long John Silver and his men stage a mutiny but, thanks to what Jim Hawkins overheard in the apple barrel, he and his friends are ready. In the end, Flint's treasure is found, but its finding costs the lives of seventeen men from the *Hispaniola*. Indeed, only five men of those who had sailed return with her. Jim and his friends share the treasure and, as Stevenson says in this wonderful book, 'used it wisely or foolishly, according to our nature.'

THE BERMUDA TRIANGLE

David S. Allen

On 16 September 1492, three tiny ships were sailing westwards . . . and into history. They were the *Santa Maria*, *Nina* and *Pinta*, three ships flying the flag of Spain, whose commander, Christopher Columbus, was destined to discover a new world. Since 6 September, when they had left the island of Gomera, the vessels had ventured out on to a strange, forbidding wilderness of sea. This was the unexplored Atlantic, an ocean that the Arabs of the time called the 'Green Sea of Darkness'.

As they sailed, most of the men began to fear for their lives and urged their leader to turn back. But Columbus would have none of such talk. He knew (or thought he knew) where he was going and expected to make a landfall very shortly. Yet on this day, the 16th, even he became a little uneasy. The ships were crossing 33° west longitude when he saw the first signs of sargassum, the gulfweed. His historian was to note that they saw 'many bunches of very green weed, which had a short time (as it seemed) been torn from land; whereby all judged that they were near some island, but not the mainland according to the Admiral.'

The ships were, in fact, beginning the plunge into the Sargasso Sea, a large area of the Western Ocean, extending roughly from the latitude of Florida halfway across the Atlantic towards Africa. Three days later the sea, on every side, seemed like a huge green meadow, or a maritime desert, caused by the vast expanse of the strange, floating weed. The men now became frightened, fearing that their small ships would be held by the masses of weed, that they would never be able to struggle free, and that they would eventually all die of hunger or thirst.

Actually there was no fear of this, for gulfweed is rarely more than half an inch thick and easily parted by a ship's bows. But the men were not to know this and, even when clear water was reached, they still muttered amongst themselves about 'what might have been'. From this first venture into the Sargasso Sea came the many stories of ships that had been trapped and forced to become derelict while the unfortunate men of the crew died one by one.

Yet in many cases these stories were true. Derelict ships, some surprisingly seaworthy and apparently in excellent condition, were occasionally found drifting in this area. As the years passed, so the mystery of the Sargasso Sea and the surrounding ocean grew even more bewildering. As each derelict was discovered, so the fear of the area grew until it was being called such names as the 'ship's graveyard' and the 'sea of lost ships'. Then it slowly became apparent that strange events were occurring outside the region of the Sargasso Sea and a number of modern writers, intrigued by the continual mysterious happenings, defined a new and larger area.

In his book, *This Baffling World* (1968), John Godwin considers that the extent of the whole area—what he called the 'Hoodoo Sea'—is a 'rough square whose limits stretch between Bermuda and the Virginia coast' with its southern boundary 'formed by the islands of Cuba, Hispañola and Puerto Rico'. Another author, Vincent Gaddis, in an article in the *Argosy* magazine, stated that the mysterious area was more triangular in shape, lying within 'a line from Florida to Bermuda, another from Bermuda to Puerto Rico, and a third line back to Florida through the Bahamas.'

In this same article the author was the first to refer to the whole area as the 'Bermuda Triangle', a name that has slowly come into general use since about 1966.

Charles Berlitz, recognized as the great authority on the Bermuda Triangle—his book of the same name having become an international best-seller—states that it extends 'from Bermuda in the north to southern Florida, and then east to a point through the Bahamas past Puerto Rico to about 40° west longitude and then back again to Bermuda.'

Within this restless sinister triangle have occurred some of the sea's weirdest unsolved mysteries and, as we shall see, of the air also. In this anthology, K. Alan Macdonald has told the exciting story of the *Mary Celeste*, calling it 'The Sea's Greatest Mystery'. That is surely true, yet other incidents that have happened within the Bermuda Triangle are equally puzzling. In many ways, the story concerning the American sailing ship *Ellen Austin* is even more of a mystery.

In 1881 she was making her way through the—as yet—unnamed Bermuda Triangle when her look-out sighted a small schooner. From the way she was sailing it was obvious that she was a derelict and the *Ellen Austin*'s captain, sensing salvage money for taking her into port, sent a boat's crew to board her. Like the *Mary Celeste*, which had been sighted in similar circumstances nine years earlier, she was entirely 'ship-shape and Bristol fashion'. Everything was in its place, everything was as it should be—except that there was no one on board!

The two vessels sailed in company for a time then a sudden gale forced them apart and, for a while, out of sight of each other. A day later, when the schooner was sighted again, she seemed to be sailing in the same haphazard manner as when they had first seen her, as if no hand was on the helm. Understandably puzzled by this behaviour, the captain of the *Ellen Austin* sent another boat's crew across to board her. The men were soon back, stammering out their amazing story. Once again they had found the schooner completely deserted. Where were their comrades? What had forced them to leave such a well-found vessel?

Their captain, still with salvage money on his mind, asked for volunteers to go back to the other vessel and take over, keeping her close to his own for the rest of the voyage. But sailors are very superstitious men and all refused to go. Finally, by promises of a big share of the reward, a few volunteers came forward. They rowed across to the schooner, trimmed her sails and for a while both vessels kept within sight of each other. Then another sudden storm arose, they were parted once more and neither the schooner nor her new crew were ever seen again.

The list of ships that have been found as derelicts or which have disappeared without trace within the Bermuda Triangle is frighteningly long. During the early years of the nineteenth century, for example, a number of warships of the United States Navy set off to sail through the area and vanished. One of them, *USS Pickering*, disappeared in 1800 on her way to the West Indies with a crew of 90 on board.

An even greater disaster came in 1824, when *USS Wasp* disappeared with a crew of 140 men.

The worst of such disappearances, however, happened to a British warship, *HMS Atalanta*. She had an unusually large complement, some 290 men, because she carried a number of cadets who had joined her for a training cruise. She had completed a successful voyage and, during January 1880, left Bermuda and set course for England. Crowds lined the Bermuda quay to wave her good-bye, for the cadets had become very popular with many families ashore; and that was the last that any living soul ever saw of them. The warship vanished completely from the surface of the sea. When she was obviously overdue, the Royal Navy mounted a big search, six warships being ordered to cover the same route that it was presumed the missing *Atalanta* had taken. The search lasted until May. Nothing was ever found.

All these strange disappearances are but a few of many similar disasters which have never been explained. There had been no reports of storms in the area, and thorough investigations found no signs of wreckage or the usual flotsam—floating spars, an upturned boat, an empty barrel or two. Just . . . nothing.

So what was happening, with frightening regularity, in this triangle of death? All the ships that were found as derelicts or which simply vanished, were strong, well-built and with experienced captains and crews. Indeed, one captain whose yacht disappeared in strange circumstances was one of the finest the world has known. He was Joshua Slocum, the first man to sail single-handed around the world. In his small thirty-seven-foot, nine-ton sloop *Spray*, he set sail from Boston, Massachusetts on 24 April 1895, crossed the North Atlantic to the Azores and Gibraltar and then across the South Atlantic to Brazil and Uruguay. He next passed through the Strait of Magellan, round Cape Horn, and into the Pacific. He touched at Australia, crossed the Indian Ocean to South Africa and then, by way of the Leeward and Windward Islands, reached Newport, Rhode Island, USA, on 27 June 1898.

Quite alone he had completed a voyage of 46,000 miles. It had taken him three years, two months and two days. Yet this most experienced of seamen was fated to be but one of the many who, somewhere in the fateful triangle, completely disappeared. In 1909, and alone as usual, he sailed the *Spray* out of New York harbour. Later, sailing south from Miami, he sighted a schooner. The men on board this schooner warned him of possible bad weather ahead. He waved his hand in thanks . . . and was never seen again.

And so the list of unsolved mysteries grew steadily longer. Slocum's little sloop was the first of an increasing number of medium-sized and smaller yachts that were to follow him into obscurity, especially when ocean-yachting, as a sport or for pleasure, became very popular. One such yacht, the 46-foot *Revonoc*, actually disappeared within sight of land. One would have expected wreckage to have been washed up on the shore, but none was ever found.

This happened in December 1967, and by then the Bermuda Triangle had apparently become even more deadly. It was no longer satisfied with ships, sailing or steaming on her usually calm surface. It now sought fresh prey—and seemed ready to pluck it from the sky.

On 5 December 1945, a training flight of five American aircraft took off from Fort Lauderdale, Florida. It consisted of TBM Grumman Avenger torpedo-bombers, carrying five officer-pilots and nine crew members. All were experienced airmen. It seemed a normal routine flight. Then, with frightening suddenness, radio contact between Fort Lauderdale and the aircraft stopped, although the ground operators could hear the planes speaking to each other. What they said was difficult to follow because of heavy static, but one thing became clear— every compass in every plane had 'gone crazy' and no one in the flight had any idea where they were.

Realizing that the aircraft were in serious trouble, the authorities sent a number of rescue aircraft out to investigate. One of them was a twin-engined Martin Mariner flying-boat with a crew of thirteen. Radio contact was kept up with it for a while then this, too, abruptly stopped. The last message stated that the flying-boat was running into very strong winds. Then nothing more.

On that day, six aircraft, carrying a total of twenty-seven men, had completely disappeared!

A vast search was begun for the missing planes. In addition to coast-guard vessels, destroyers and submarines, yachts and boats, more than 300 US service aircraft took part, together with hundreds of private planes. It has been estimated that nearly 400,000 square miles of land and sea were minutely searched. The result—no wreckage, no life-rafts, no oil slicks . . . nothing!

A board of inquiry was set up but no one could offer any explanation for this amazing incident—one that was to be the first of many. Now, side by side with large ships—for even large freighters such as the *Anita*, a 20,000-ton freighter which disappeared during March 1973, are still vanishing—aircraft are taking the same route to oblivion. These include two sister aeroplanes, *Star Tiger* and *Star Ariel*, both four-engined Tudor passenger planes, and a powerful Super Constellation which disappeared in October 1954.

In most cases the luckless plane would radio that all was well and then . . . silence!

A great many 'solutions' have, of course, been put forward. Sudden underwater or, in the case of aircraft, aerial disturbances; giant sea monsters (in the case of the ships); even attacks by creatures from another planet, using the frequently reported unidentified flying objects.

But so far there has been no really acceptable explanation for the continuing loss of life caused by the disappearance of ships, yachts and planes within that frightening area . . . the area that has now become known as the Bermuda Triangle.

THE CAMPDEN WONDER
Noel Lloyd

In 1660, the year Charles II acceded to the throne, the strange events known as *The Campden Wonder* took place. It is a mystery that has never been solved, but which has excited the imagination of many people. Some think that the story is pure fiction, but most investigators are convinced that it did take place. There have been many attempts to play the detective, but it is a difficult task when it all happened more than three hundred years ago.

The first account was written by a magistrate named Sir Thomas Overbury, himself concerned in the events, in a letter to his father-in-law published in 1676. In the letter he told of a man called William Harrison, steward to Lady Juliana, Viscountess Campden, of Chipping Campden in Gloucestershire. He was sent to the nearby village of Charringworth to collect rents from some of his mistress's tenants, a task he had to undertake every three months. Harrison had been in the service of the Campden family for fifty years, and was a highly respected old man.

On this occasion, when he had not returned, many hours after he was expected, his wife grew alarmed and sent their servant, John Perry, to search for him. But Perry did not return that night either, and early the next morning Harrison's son Edward set off to try to find his father and their servant.

On the road to the village of Ebrington, Edward saw Perry in the distance and hurried towards him. 'Have you found my father?' he asked.

The servant, a large, dull-faced man, gave him a furtine look. 'I have been searching all night,' he mumbled, 'but I have seen no sign of him.'

'Then we will go back to Ebrington and make further inquiries,' Edward said. 'It is very worrying. What can have happened to him?'

Perry said nothing but turned round and followed the young man to the village. There they learned that William Harrison had called at the house of a friend on his return from Charringworth, but had only stayed a short time. There had been nothing strange about his manner; indeed, he had been cheerful at the thought of getting back home to a good meal. Puzzled and worried, Edward and Perry returned home.

On the way they met an old woman whom Edward knew slightly, and he asked her if she had seen his father anywhere. 'No, sir,' she answered, 'but I found these in a clump of gorse bushes by the side of the road,' and she produced a blood-stained hat-band and a comb.

Edward examined them with a growing fear. 'They belong to my father,' he declared. 'Take us to where you found them.'

They searched the area round the gorse bushes thoroughly, but there was no sign of a body, and no other clues came to light. 'It looks as though my father has been murdered and robbed of the money he was carrying,' Edward said in agitated tones. 'I must organize a search of the whole neighbourhood.'

But though a large number of men, women and children combed the area between Ebrington and Charringworth, not a trace of the missing steward could be found.

Chipping Campden seethed with rumours, and numerous theories about the possible murder were bandied about. It was not long before suspicion settled on John Perry, due to the unsatisfactory account of his movements he had given. Mrs Harrison at last went to the magistrate—Sir Thomas Overbury—and accused Perry of murdering her husband and disposing of the body. Perry was arrested.

When he was asked to account for his behaviour, his story was confused. 'When my mistress sent me out to look for the master,' he said, 'it was dark, and I was afraid to go too far. I met a friend named William Reed and told him of my fears. He suggested that I should go on horseback and returned with me to the Harrison's house, where I intended to saddle the mare. He left me at the gate, but before I went in I saw another acquaintance, Harry Pearce, and we had a long talk. I then decided that it was too late to continue the search that night, and went into one of the outhouses, where I slept for an hour or two.

Soon after midnight, however, I set out again, not wishing to arouse the mistress's wrath if she knew I had disobeyed her, but before I reached Charringworth a mist came up and I lost my way. I spent the rest of the night under a hedge. I reached Charringworth at daybreak and called on two of the men who owed rent to Lady Juliana. They told me that Mr Harrison had visited them the previous day but they had no idea where had had gone afterwards. On my way home I met Master Edward; and that is all I know . . .'

The story was confirmed by Reed, Pearce and the two tenants at Charringworth, but there were aspects about it that the magistrate felt were not quite satisfactory, and Perry was kept in custody in the town gaol, where a lawyer questioned him closely, going over all the details again and again. 'The truth—I want the truth', the lawyer constantly insisted.

Under the relentless cross-examination Perry began to change his story, and offered other explanations of his conduct and guesses as to what had happened to William Harrison. 'A tinker killed him,' he said. 'Or if it wasn't a tinker it was one of Lady Juliana's servants who had quarrelled with him.' The lawyer looked dubious. 'You'll find his body hidden in a rick of beans just outside Campden,' Perry went on desperately.

The rick was searched but nothing was found. 'Perry is lying. He must know something but refuses to tell,' the lawyer said. 'At least, there is enough evidence to warrant bringing him to trial.'

John Perry stood before Sir Thomas Overbury again. He was in a sorry condition—nervous, twitching, his words an indistinct mumble. 'Sir, I did not murder William Harrison,' he said, 'though I know that he was done to death.'

'Then you must know by whom,' said the magistrate. 'If you do not wish to be hanged, you had better tell me the name of the murderer.'

'It was—it was—my m-mother, Joan Perry!'

'Your mother?' Sir Thomas sat bolt upright, his jaw dropping.

'It's true,' said Perry, 'and she was helped by my brother Richard. They have been trying to persuade me to rob and kill my master ever since I entered his service. They got me to tell them when he went off to collect the rents, and that night we all laid in wait for him as he returned from Charringworth. When he had almost reached the spot where we were hiding I decided that I had done my part and wanted nothing to do with what was to come next, so I left them. But I was curious to know whether they were serious in their intent, and I crept back to the place. My brother was holding Mr Harrison down. I implored him not to kill the old man, but he only laughed and put his hands round his throat.

When his body had gone limp, Richard took a bag of money from his pocket and threw it to my mother. We carried the body to the mill-pond nearby, weighted it with stones, and threw it in. I myself put the hat-band and comb near the road so that people should think he was killed by a footpad or passing tinker. That is the truth, sir,' Perry finished, raising his voice. 'I was concerned in my master's death, but I did not kill him. My mother and my brother planned it all.'

This amazing confession led immediately to the arrest of Joan and Richard Perry, and in September all three were committed for trial at the Gloucester Assizes. Before the trial started the millpond was searched, and every other place where a body could have been hidden, but William Harrison's whereabouts remained a mystery.

At the trial John Perry changed his story again and claimed that he knew nothing about his master's disappearance. 'I must have been mad when I made my confession,' he said. But the jury returned a verdict of guilty, and the three Perry's were taken to be hanged on Broadway Hill, near Chipping Campden, an event which was attended by people from all over the district.

Joan Perry, who had long been thought to be a witch, was hanged first. She had said nothing during her imprisonment and trial, but her black eyes had burned with sullen contempt. Richard burst into tears and begged the crowd to believe that he and his mother were innocent. 'Brother John,' he cried, 'tell the truth and ease your conscience. Tell them that we had nothing to do with it. Tell them!'

Perry gave a gurgling gasp as the rope tightened round his neck.

But John Perry shook his head, watching calmly as his brother was executed. Then it was his turn. He looked on the gloating upturned faces of the crowd. 'I solemnly swear,' he said in ringing tones, quite unlike his usual mumble, 'that I know nothing about this whole matter, and I do not know what has become of William Harrison. I am now to die but, mark my words, some day you will learn the truth . . .' He gave a gurgling gasp as the rope tightened round his neck. There was a hiss of excitement from the crowd and a flock of startled birds wheeled around the three swinging figures.

That, apparently, was the end of the affair, though it was an unsatisfactory end, with many questions left unanswered, and in retrospect few people thought that justice had been done. The feeling was that John Perry, under the influence of his witch mother, had become crazy and had confessed to the crime without realizing the full consequences of his action. It was clear that he had possessed some knowledge of what had happened to William Harrison but his mind had been so clouded that he had not been able to give a precise account.

Two years went by—the gossip had died down and the whole matter almost forgotten—when the startling news burst on the village that William Harrison had returned from the dead! In the dusk of an autumn evening he opened the door of his house and presented himself, foot-sore and bedraggled, to his wife and son. Mrs Harrison shrieked and fainted and Edward, white as a ghost, staggered and almost fell.

When they had partially recovered, William Harrison told them his incredible story. 'On the day I went to Charringworth to collect the rents,' he explained, 'I was returning by a short cut along a path through the gorse bushes when a man on horseback appeared in front of me. I stepped to one side but he tried to ride me down, then drew his sword and made a lunge at me. I only had my stick but I fought back as well as I could. But when a second man appeared out of the half-light and stabbed me in the thigh, and then a third man came into view, I realized that I was done for. I was knocked down and bound up. They took all the rent money from me, then carried me to a lonely cottage in the middle of a forest miles away from Campden, where an old woman, deaf and nearly blind, bathed my wound and nursed me back to health.

'For two weeks I stayed in the cottage, unable to escape, until one day the three men reappeared, put me on a horse, my hands tied behind me, and carried me off to Deal, in Kent, and put me aboard a ship. I do not know where the ship was bound for because, after sailing for some weeks, it was captured by two Turkish warships and everybody was taken prisoner. When we reached the Turkish coast I was sold as a slave to an old doctor who lived in Smyrna. He had lived in England for a time and I was able to talk to him. Because of that, and because I am an old man, I was not unkindly treated, though the work was hard and tiring. After a year the doctor died suddenly, and in the confusion that followed I was able to slip away, with a silver chalice that the doctor had given me. I sold it and had enough money to reach Lisbon, in Portugal. On the way I had many adventures, which I will tell you about later.

'Eventually my money ran out, and I wondered if I was ever going to get back to England. But luckily I met an Englishman who took pity on me and paid my passage back home. The ship berthed in London Docks, and I have walked to Campden. Three days it has taken me, and I am very weary. But I am home again, having thought, two years ago, that I would never see you both again . . .'

There was a stunned silence. Mrs Harrison was gazing at her husband as though she could not believe it was really him. A thousand questions sprang to Edward's lips, but he found he could not get a single one out. As the three people sat staring at one another there was a thunderous noise outside, of raised voices, thumping on the door and tapping at the windows. The village people, one of whom had seen the old man trudging along the High Street, had come to see for themselves the miracle of the 'murdered' man's return. Chipping Campden had known nothing so sensational within living memory.

Sir Thomas Overbury tells us that Mrs Harrison, for some unexplained reason, committed suicide a year after her husband's return, but William Harrison lived to be over eighty, still sticking staunchly to his story.

The two great and unanswered questions about *The Campden Wonder* are: why did John Perry confess to a crime that he did not commit, and was William Harrison's story true? If not, where had he been for two years? As far as John Perry is concerned, he was known to be a strange man with a twisted mind. He may have believed that his mother, reputed to be a witch, had put a spell on him, and that only by causing her death by hanging would he be released. His own death on the gallows was unimportant. What was important to him was to be cleared of witch-possession. Even though he protested his innocence at the end, he met death almost unconcernedly.

William Harrison, however, presents a bigger problem. It seems unbelievable that a man of seventy could have gone through all that he claimed and survive. His adventures read like something out of *The Arabian Nights*, and it has been suggested that Sir Thomas Overbury, who had travelled all over Europe in his younger days, invented that part of the story in order to make it more exciting. But the fact that the steward was missing for two years is not in doubt.

Those were troubled times. Up to and after the restoration of the monarchy in 1660 many people were engaged on mysterious missions. Could William Harrison have been a spy? The sober, respectable family man was the sort of person who could travel around on his mistress's business without arousing suspicion. Or, perhaps, because of what he knew about Lady Juliana's activities, it was necessary for him to be kidnapped and hidden during all the military and political upheavals of the time. A simpler explanation is that he was indeed attacked and robbed by thieves, and as a result of his injuries he lost his memory, created in his mind a story made up of fragments of adventure stories he had heard as a child, and had spent the two years wandering about the country, begging for food, sleeping in outhouses and under hedges, until his mind cleared enough for him to find his way home.

No amount of guessing, however, will bring the real truth to light, and it is not likely, after three hundred years, that any further evidence will be found. The whole affair will remain unsolved, a frustrating and fascinating mystery.

Acknowledgements

The editors would like to thank the following authors, publishers and literary agents for their kind permission to include the following copyright material in this book:

Hughes Massie Ltd. and Dodd, Mead & Co. Inc. for THE VEILED LADY from *Poirot Investigates* by Agatha Christie.

George Weidenfeld & Nicolson Ltd. for THE GERMAN WHO SUCCEEDED by John Bulloch from *MI5*.

John Farquharson Ltd., executors of the Late Colonel Oreste Pinto, for THE THIRTEENTH MAN from *The Spycatcher Omnibus*.

Dobson Books Ltd. and Doubleday & Co. Inc. for THE YOUNG SABOTEURS OF THE CHURCHILL CLUB by Samuel Epstein and Beryl Williams from *The Real Book of Spies No. 11*.

Scott, Meredith Literary Agency and Robert Bloch for YOURS TRULY, JACK THE RIPPER from *Weird Tales*.

W. H. Allen & Co. Ltd. for EILEEN—A QUIET ENGLISH MISS from *Women Spies* by Joseph Hutton.

Macdonald and Jane's Publishers Ltd. for THE DEATH OF EDITH CAVELL from *Espionage* by H. R. Berndorff, translated by Bernard Miall.

Neville Spearman Ltd. for A THING ON THE GROUND from *Uninvited Visitors* by Ivan T. Sanderson.

Edwin T. Woodhall, author of THE 'AMERICAN COLONEL' AND HOW HE SAVED THE LIFE OF THE KING OF ENGLAND from *Spies of The Great War*.

Robert Hale and the author for HITLER'S SPIES from *Spy and Counter-Spy* by Bernard Newman.

The Falcon Press for THE NIGHT OF 6 SEPTEMBER from *The Soviet Spy System* by John Baker White.

and to John Agee, David S. Allen, Elizabeth Bennett, Avis Murton Carter, Elizabeth Grant-Sutherland, Michael and Mollie Hardwick, Noel Lloyd, K. Alan Macdonald, Geoffrey Palmer, Alastair Scott, Alan Stuart and John Baker White for the use of copyright or their own original submissions to this anthology.

Every effort has been made to clear all copyrights and the publishers trust that their apologies will be accepted for any errors or omissions.